# Kant's *Critique of Pure Reason*

**Critical Essays on the Classics**

General Editor: Steven M. Cahn

The volumes in this new series offer insightful and accessible essays that shed light on the classics of philosophy. Each of the distinguished editors has selected outstanding work in recent scholarship to provide today's readers with a deepened understanding of the most timely issues raised in these important texts.

Descartes's *Meditations*: Critical Essays
*edited by Vere Chappell*

Kant's Groundwork on the Metaphysics of Morals: Critical Essays
*edited by Paul Guyer*

Mill's *On Liberty*: Critical Essays
*edited by Gerald Dworkin*

Mill's *Utilitarianism*: Critical Essays
*edited by David Lyons*

Plato's *Republic*: Critical Essays
*edited by Richard Kraut*

Kant's *Critique of Pure Reason*: Critical Essays
*edited by Patricia Kitcher*

Forthcoming in the series:

The Empiricists: Critical Essays
*edited by Margaret Atherton*

The Rationalists: Critical Essays
*edited by Derk Pereboom*

The Social Contract Theorists: Critical Essays
*edited by Christopher Morris*

Aristotle's *Ethics*: Critical Essays
*edited by Nancy Sherman*

# Kant's *Critique of Pure Reason*

## *Critical Essays*

Edited by
Patricia Kitcher

ROWMAN & LITTLEFIELD PUBLISHERS, INC.
*Lanham • Boulder • New York • Oxford*

ROWMAN & LITTLEFIELD PUBLISHERS, INC.

Published in the United States of America
by Rowman & Littlefield Publishers, Inc.
4720 Boston Way, Lanham, Maryland 20706

12 Hid's Copse Road
Cumnor Hill, Oxford OX2 9JJ, England

British Library Cataloguing in Publication Information Available

**Library of Congress Cataloging-in-Publication Data**

Kant's Critique of pure reason : critical essays / edited by Patricia
    Kitcher.
        p.    cm.—(Critical essays on the classics)
    Includes bibliographical references and index.
    ISBN 0-8476-8916-6 (alk. paper)—ISBN 0-8476-8917-4 (pbk. :
alk. paper)
        1. Kant, Immanuel, 1724-1804. Kritik der reinen Vernunft.
I. Kitcher, Patricia.   II. Series.
B2779.K365   1998
121—dc21                                                        98-24541
                                                                    CIP

Printed in the United States of America

♾ ™ The paper used in this publication meets the minimum requirements of
American National Standard for Information Sciences—Permanence of Paper
for Printed Library Materials, ANSI Z39.49–1984.

# Contents

Introduction                                                                vii

Acknowledgments                                                             xix

1  Kant's *A Priori* Framework                                                1
   *Philip Kitcher*

2  Was Kant a Nativist?                                                      21
   *Lorne Falkenstein*

3  Infinity and Kant's Conception of the "Possibility of
   Experience"                                                              45
   *Charles Parsons*

4  Kant's Cognitive Self                                                     59
   *Patricia Kitcher*

5  Kant's Transcendental Deduction as a Regressive
   Argument                                                                 85
   *Karl Ameriks*

6  Did the Sage of Königsberg Have No Dreams?                              103
   *Lewis White Beck*

7  Kant's Second Analogy: Objects, Events and Causal Laws                  117
   *Paul Guyer*

8  The Metaphysics of Transcendental Idealism [partial],
   from *The Bounds of Sense*                                              145
   *P. F. Strawson*

9  An Introduction to the Problem, and Transcendental
   Realism and Transcendental Idealism, from *Kant's
   Transcendental Idealism*                                                181
   *Henry Allison*

**10**  Projecting the Order of Nature                          219
       *Philip Kitcher*

**11**  Kant's Compatibilism                                   239
       *Allen W. Wood*

**12**  Kant's Critique of the Three Theistic Proofs [partial],
       from *Kant's Rational Theology*                         265
       *Allen W. Wood*

       Annotated Bibliography                                  283

       Index                                                   291

       About the Authors                                       299

# Introduction

*Patricia Kitcher*

In the preface to the first edition of the *Critique of Pure Reason*, Kant describes his era as the "age of criticism" (A xi note).[1] His popular essay, "What is Enlightenment?" examines the relation between enlightenment and the critical attitude. Kant regards the lack of enlightenment as a serious moral failing. For those old enough to think for themselves, slavish acceptance of official and popular opinion indicates a lack of courage and resolution. By contrast, the enlightenment appropriate to intellectually responsible adults depends not on unusual gifts of intelligence or insight but simply on examining accepted truths for oneself. Kant summarizes the critical, enlightened attitude in a simple motto: Think for yourself (Ak. VIII: 35).[2]

Given the conflicts of his century, Kant stressed the importance of a critical attitude in matters of religion. He notes, however, that this emphasis merely reflects that of contemporary rulers, who have no interest in enforcing their views of the arts and sciences. In fact, responsible adults should submit all the cultural influences that shape their lives to critical reflection—including, art, science, politics, ethics, education, and religion (Ak. VIII: 41). The alternative is blind acceptance, followed by a growing lack of conviction about the soundness of society's guiding institutions (A xi note).

Rather than passively allowing their minds to be shaped by prevailing intellectual and social forces, enlightened citizens must use their own understanding and reason to take the measure of those forces. But what about human understanding and reason themselves? If intellectual integrity requires a critical attitude, and if the assessment of cultural institutions rests on our cognitive faculties, then surely those must also be subject to searching criticism. The essential purpose of the *Critique of Pure Reason* is to take the measure of our own capacity for knowledge. Although it ranges over many other topics, the central project of the *Critique* is to answer two questions: (i) what can we know and how can we know it? (ii) what can't we know and why can't we know these things?

Kant's *magnum opus* is a landmark of Western thought because of the revolutionary nature of its answers to both questions. In the latter half of the book, the "Dialectic of Pure Reason," Kant argues that answers to what had been regarded as the most important questions of metaphysics—the existence of God and the free will and immortality of the human soul—are beyond the capacities of human understanding. The positive first half maintains that knowledge depends on the active contributions of our higher cognitive faculties to the data provided by our senses—but that knowledge is nonetheless objective, because those contributions can be defended as necessary for the possibility of any cognition whatsoever.

Unfortunately, the *Critique of Pure Reason* is as difficult to read as it is central to understanding the subsequent history of Western ideas. The principal cause of Kant's infamous obscurity is the abstractness of his topic. Neither science nor ordinary language provides a vocabulary adequate for discussing the preconditions of science and understanding. Like other philosophers, Kant had to invent a special set of terms, which he introduced in the course of presenting his theories. The first essay in the collection, "Kant's *A Priori* Framework" takes on the difficult, but essential task of clarifying some of the *Critique's* most important and interrelated terms: "*a priori*," as that expression occurs in the phrases "*a priori* knowledge," "*a priori* concept," and "synthetic *a priori* proposition"; "analytic" and "synthetic"; "necessity" and "the possibility of experience."

Kant's introductory presentation of the concept of the "*a priori*" links these technical terms: "*a priori* knowledge" is said to be universal, necessary, and obtainable independently of any experience (B 3, B 2). The "Introduction" also presents the key contrast between "analytic" and "synthetic" propositions that enables Kant to frame his quest in a distinctive way: how is synthetic *a priori* knowledge possible? That is, how is it possible for us to have knowledge of claims, such as "all events have causes," which are universal and necessary, even though their truth is not a matter of the definition of our terms, and cannot be established by sensory evidence?

Philip Kitcher develops his analyses of these key terms by considering a familiar paradox of the "Introduction." Kant proclaims that all cognition begins with experience (A 1, B 1); one page later in the second edition, he characterizes "*a priori*" knowledge as "absolutely independent of experience"! Kitcher makes the obvious assumption that Kant must mean that *a priori* knowledge is independent of any particular experience—not all experience whatsoever. He reasons that subjects could not possibly know a proposition unless they understand its terms. Hence, he concludes that Kant's point must be that an *a priori* claim or proposition must be able to be known to be true whatever experiences a subject has, just so long as those experiences are sufficient for understanding the terms it contains.

Kitcher's account of *a priori* knowledge depends on two further, plausible assumptions. First, knowing is a process—subjects come to know things by undergoing some sort of cognitive process or other. Second, when Kant describes *a priori* claims as "necessary," he employs an epistemological and relativized rather than metaphysical and absolute sense of "necessity." That is, to say that a claim such as "all events are caused" is "necessary" is to say that it is true in any possible circumstances where creatures with our sense organs and cognitive faculties could have any knowledge at all. (No claim is made about how the world must be apart from our ways of knowing.) Putting these claims together, Kitcher's position is that what Kant means by characterizing a proposition as "synthetic *a priori*" is that although it is not known through definitions, it can be known to be true in any possible circumstances in which we could engage in cognition and have learned the terms it contains, and that such knowledge is possible only if some process is available to us—in any circumstances like those just described—which warrants the claim. Much subsequent philosophy has debated whether this or that proposition is *a priori*, often without providing any explication of the notion of "*a priority*" in question. Although the exact nature of the processes that produce *a priori* "warrants" for particular claims is somewhat vague, as Kitcher observes, Kant offers a reasonably clear account of how *a priori* knowledge is possible.

One aspect of Kant's notion of *apriority* that Kitcher does not explore is the link to innate mental structures. At B 1, Kant connects *a priori* cognition with the possibility that cognition is a composite, consisting of both what is provided by sensory experience and "what our own cognitive power supplies from itself." In the nineteenth century, Kant was considered a "nativist" who maintained in particular that the ideas or representations of space and time were inborn. Kant himself regarded his theories as combining the best of the previous "nativist" and "empiricist" philosophies. In "Was Kant a Nativist?" Lorne Falkenstein tries to answer this question for the important cases of the representations of space and time. Like Kitcher, he addresses an apparent inconsistency in Kant's most explicit pronouncements: as noted, the "Introduction" claims that cognition begins with experience, but the "Transcendental Aesthetic concludes that the "representation . . . of space . . . must be met in us *a priori*, that is, before all perception of objects . . ." (B 41). Falkenstein resolves this textual conflict through the plausible hypothesis that what Kant takes to be "in us" before any perceptions are not spatial and temporal representations, but the spatial and temporal "forms of intuition" that determine the manner in which sensory data are received. That is, prior to sensory experience, there are no representations of spatial or temporal arrays, but prior to sensory experience, the faculty of sense perception has a particular constitution that determines the ways in which it will receive sensory data. So, for example, our senses are so constituted that they take in data sequentially, much the way in which a computer keyboard inputs data one piece after another, regardless of any particular content. Hence, our form of intuition is temporal.

Besides offering a plausible defense of Kant's claim that his position combines empiricism and nativism, Falkenstein is concerned to combat a popular reading of "forms of intuition." According to this view, the forms of intuition should be understood as cognitive processes that produce temporal and spatial representations out of given sensory data. Falkentstein argues that this reading seriously undercuts one of Kant's central distinctions, between the receptivity of sensory intuition and the spontaneity of the understanding (A 51/B 75). He takes Kant at his word that, although the forms of intuition influence the nature of our cognitions, they do not combine (or "synthesize" in Kant's technical terminology, see below, p. 29) sensory data into further representations. Unlike the concepts of the understanding, spatial and temporal intuitions are given, not constructed.

In addition to his distinctive position on the representations of space and time, the "Transcendental Aesthetic" also presents Kant's views on what he unexpectedly takes to be a related topic—the nature of mathematics. Like many other major philosophers, including Descartes and Leibniz, Kant was also a mathematician. Throughout his long teaching career, first in mathematics, and then in philosophy, he was troubled by a deep and unexplained coincidence: if mathematics is nothing more than an arbitrary collection of symbols and rules invented by mathematicians, then why is it so useful in describing the nature of physical reality? Or, turning Galileo's slogan into a question: why *should* the book of nature be written in the language of mathematics? Kant's answer, which is criticized by Charles Parsons in "Infinity and Kant's Conception of the 'Possibility of Experience,' " is that every natural object we perceive will be characterizable in Euclidean terms, because Euclidean geometry is the form of human sensory intuition. Borrowing Falkenstein's (and Kant's) terminology, Euclidean geometry applies to the world we perceive, because the manner in which we receive data imbues objects with Euclidean properties.

Parsons raises a question that goes to the heart of Kant's theory: how do we know that the form of human spatial (or "outer") intuition is Euclidean? Kant discusses mathematics both in the "Transcendental Aesthetic," where he introduces his theory, and in the "Antinomy[3] of Pure Reason," where he tries to use that theory to resolve some then outstanding mathematical paradoxes. Parsons focuses on a property from the "Second Antinomy," which concerns the infinite divisibility of spatial objects. According to Euclidean geometry—and many other mathematical systems—any line in space is infinitely divisible. It can be divided into ever smaller parts, with no part being the smallest. If Kant's account of the applicability of mathematics to nature were correct, then the human perceptual system would be such that any spatial expanses it intuits must have the property of infinite divisibility. But how could we tell? If I look at a computer monitor, I can then look at half of it, and half of that half, and so on, but quite quickly I will be unable to discern further smaller parts. So Parsons argues that Kant's solution to the mathematization of nature founders on our inability to determine the properties of the human perceptual system merely by considering our perceptions. If he is right, then Kant did not and could not establish one of the central conclusions of the "Transcendental Aesthetic," that the propositions of Euclidean geometry are universally and necessarily true in the world of our perceptions (B 41).

The "Transcendental Analytic" introduces a second, central cognitive faculty for Kant, the spontaneous faculty of understanding. The understanding serves cognition, not by taking in sensory data, but by "synthesizing" them, that is "by adding the contents of various representations together and grasping them in one cognition" (A 77/B 103).

Eventually Kant will try to defend his well-known claim that there are twelve synthetic *a priori* concepts—the famous "categories of the understanding"—by arguing that these representations arise from the operations of various syntheses that are necessary for the possibility of any cognition whatsoever. But for that argument to be successful, he must defend his use of the idea of "synthesis." As Kant presents it, synthesis is a "real" connection among mental states or representations, because the resulting representation in which various information is combined would not exist, and would not have the content it does, but for the existence of the states out of which it is synthesized. Such a defense is necessary because Kant's important predecessor, David Hume, had denied the existence of any such connections among mental states. Because he could not countenance relations of real connection or existential dependence among mental states, Hume offered the startling thesis that there is no such thing as a continuing mind or person through time. Rather, what we call a mind is just a disconnected collection—a heap—of different perceptions.

In "Kant's Cognitive Self," I argue that Kant deliberately set out to refute Hume's notorious denial of personal identity, both because of its intrinsic interest, and because his argument for the categories depends on the possibility of real connections among mental states. Throughout the "Deduction of the Categories of the Understanding," Kant refers again and again to a "necessary" or "synthetic" "unity" of "apperception," to the fact that it must be possible for different mental states or representations to be connected to one another (e.g., A 116, A 117 note, B 132, B 133–35). As I read this section, Kant's principle of the "transcendental unity of apperception" is not a first premise, in the manner of Descartes's *Cogito*, but the conclusion of an anti-Humean argument to the effect that a real, synthetic connection among mental states is a necessary condition for the possibility of any kinds of cognition, including those Hume readily acknowledged. Only with that conclusion established can he argue that particular categories are necessary, because they arise in the course of syntheses that are necessary to cognition. Although Kant argued that an analysis of the necessary conditions for cognition can reveal certain abstract properties of cognitive subjects, he also warned his readers not to expect too much. In the "Paralogisms of Pure Reason" section of the "Dialectic," he explains in detail why such analyses can offer no insight about the immortality of the soul.

In "Kant's Transcendental Deduction as a Regressive Argument,"

Karl Ameriks raises a question that must be asked about any important philosophical thesis: what is the nature of the argument for the categories? Although students sometimes believe that philosophy must be presuppositionless, Ameriks makes the sensible point that without some assumptions, it is impossible to argue for any interesting conclusion. In Ameriks's view, the "transcendental deduction" of the categories—the argument that is to establish the legitimacy of the categories by demonstrating that they are indispensable to all cognition (A 93–94/ B 125–36)—can only be "regressive." That is, it must start with premises about the kinds of cognition we enjoy and "regress," or work backwards, to the necessary conditions that make such cognition possible. The concern with regressive arguments is that they may beg important questions. Since some of Kant's predecessors doubted the possibility of certain kinds of cognition, he cannot simply help himself to the assumption that we do, in fact, enjoy the disputed forms of cognition. As Ameriks notes, Kant must get around this formidable obstacle by being careful never to assume more elaborate kinds of cognition than his opponents will grant.

The central category for Kant is "causation," and his defense of the necessity of using a causal concept in the second Analogy is often considered the centerpiece of the *Critique*. Hundreds of articles have been written appraising the many aspects of Kant's discussions. One reason for this section's enduring fascination is that it offers a direct clash between two of the most important figures in Western philosophy— Hume and Kant—on a question of great philosophical importance, the nature of causation. Hume had two skeptical worries about causation: he could find no sound reason to believe that every event must have a cause and no sound reason to believe that a particular cause necessarily produces its effect. In his positive account, he maintained that we say "C causes E" when events of type C have regularly been followed by events of type E. But this "constant conjunction" of Cs and Es establishes no necessary connection. Perhaps a C could occur without an E; perhaps an E could occur with no cause at all.

In "Kant's Second Analogy," Paul Guyer offers a plausible account of the main lines of Kant's celebrated "reply to Hume" on causation. On Guyer's analysis, Kant starts with two assumptions: we cannot perceive time itself and we can distinguish events or happenings from situations of no change. To use Kant's own examples, we can distinguish the cases of a ship moving downstream from an unchanging house. But all of our perceptions are successive. We perceive the downstream position after the upstream position, but we also perceive, for example, the roof of the house after the front door. How can we know that one position followed another in the case of the ship but that the door and roof of the house are coexistent? Guyer takes Kant to be arguing that we can know that the ship moved and that the house did not change, only by recognizing the presence of a causal force in one case (the current) and the absence of causes in the other. We know that the ship moved downstream by recognizing that—given the current—it *had* to. Hence Kant argues that we can know that an event happens only by recognizing the presence of some causal force (even if we don't have a completely precise notion of the cause) and only by recognizing that causes necessitate their effects. Hence in reply to Hume's skeptical doubts, he argues that any cognizable event must have a cause that necessitates its occurrence.

Lewis White Beck's essay, "Did the Sage of Königsberg Have No Dreams?" is not concerned with the preconditions of Kant's argument for the categories, or with its exact form, but with the plausibility of its conclusion. If Kant is right, that all of our cognition must be permeated by causal relations, then it would seem to follow that we can have no knowledge of dreams, which are notoriously made out of disconnected bits and pieces. Since Kant very probably had dreams, and since he must have seen this potential counter-example (see A 112), Beck wonders how he fitted dreams into a causal framework. His plausible suggestion is that although the content of dreams is bizarre, the occurrence of dreams must be understood as part of the causal order. Perhaps Freud did not fathom the true or complete causes of dreams, but there is no particular reason to believe they are uncaused. Dreams would be no different from any other phenomenon whose causes remain hidden from us: we assume that there is some cause, and we may have a general idea of its nature, even in the absence of more specific knowledge.

At the end of the positive part of the *Critique*, in the chapter on phenomena and noumena, Kant examines the implications of his central epistemological claim that knowledge is a conjoint product of sensory data and the mind's ways of combining those data. If the world as we know it is partly a reflection of our ways of knowing, then what is the world like, independently of our ways of knowing? Kant characterizes the known world as "phenomenal" and the world that is independent of human cognition as "noumenal." What is the relation between the phenomenal and noumenal worlds? In "The Metaphysics of Transcendental Idealism" and in the opening chapters of *Kant's Transcen-*

*dental Idealism*, Sir Peter Strawson and Henry Allison offer radically opposed answers to these questions. With great wit and great force, Strawson argues that Kant's epistemological account is incoherent. Since one of the contributions of the mind to cognition is temporality, Kant must be maintaining—inconsistently—that the noumenal mind creates the phenomenal world "after" it has received noumenal sensory data. In direct contrast, Allison maintains that the phenomenal-noumenal distinction is completely benign. It indicates nothing more than Kant's correct recognition that human knowledge is limited to those things that can be known through our ways of knowing. About things that cannot be known through the human capacity for sensation and thought, we can, of course, offer no speculation. Yet even if Allison's understanding of the phenomenal-noumenal distinction is correct, Strawson's essay revives one of the earliest and most enduring questions about Kant's entire philosophy: are Kant's epistemological claims to be understood as phenomenal or as noumenal?

Although the "Dialectic of Pure Reason" presents the "critique" of pure reason, it also makes important positive claims about reason, the faculty of making inferences. In "Projecting the Order of Nature," Philip Kitcher argues that Kant's account of the contributions of reason to cognition offers important insights into the nature of science. To see Kant's point, consider the then contemporary hypothesis that the motion of the planets was caused by the gravitational force exerted by matter. Newton explained several phenomena, including planetary motion, by reference to another, gravity. But what about gravity itself? Is it just a brute fact about the universe, that masses of matter attract each other with gravitational force, or does this phenomenon have a further explanation? Both options have pros and cons. Assuming that gravity is a brute fact would hinder efforts to develop a further explanation; on the other hand, we have no sound reasons for assuming that some further explanation is possible. In Kitcher's view, Kant's account enables him to reap the benefits of both answers without incurring the costs of either. According to Kant, human reason inevitably demands that we seek deeper explanations, which is why science naturally progresses; yet the demand of reason is just that. It drives research, often well beyond anything that appears to have practical utility, but it must not be understood as describing nature, as positively asserting that nature has a structure that can be fathomed at ever deeper levels.

In "Kant's Compatibilism," Allen Wood examines one of the most important negative results of the "Dialectic," Kant's famous claim that resolving the question of free will and determinism is forever beyond the bounds of human knowledge. In his later ethical works, Kant argued that free will is necessary for moral responsibility. The argument of the "Third Antinomy" is supposed to allow room for that possibility, by proving that we cannot know actions to be causally determined. As we have just seen, by the argument of the Second Analogy, Kant takes himself to have shown that any cognizable phenomenal event must have a cause. Hence the actions in question must be beyond our knowledge, and so noumenal. As Wood notes, standard compatibilists try to maintain that actions can be both caused (usually by the agent's considered desires) and free; by contrast, Kant tries to argue that determinism in the phenomenal world is compatible with noumenal freedom. Kant's resolution of the free will problem has earned few adherents. The principal obstacle has been making sense of noumenal freedom. Borrowing from work in philosophy of religion, Wood argues that we can understand how free noumenal agents could timelessly bring about their actions in the same way that we can understand how a timeless God can play a role in human affairs. In both cases, the suggestion is that God's nature and the nature of free agents timelessly determine their actions, which unfold in the course of time.

Although Wood defends Kant's unpopular contribution to the free will debate, in the final essay in the collection, "Kant's Critique of the Three Theistic Proofs" he sharply criticizes the *Critique*'s highly regarded attack on the possibility of rational defenses of religious faith. Prior to the writings of Hume and Kant, it was fairly standard for philosophers and theologians to propose logical arguments purporting to prove the existence of God. Aquinas offered five different proofs; the proofs of Descartes, Berkeley, and Leibniz were prominent features of their philosophical systems. If current students find it hard to believe that an intelligent person would even try to prove the existence of God, that attitude is a reflection of the influence of Hume's and Kant's searching and courageous attacks on rational theology. (Hume's opinions on religion cost him any chance of a professorship; Kant's lectures and writings on religion led the King of Prussia personally to ban him from any future teaching on the subject.)

Kant's strategy for dealing with purported proofs reflected his mathematical background. He first tried to argue that all the different proofs were actually special cases of the "ontological" argument, which attempts to derive the existence of God from the standard theological concept of God as an all-perfect being; then he attacked the ontological argument itself. Kant's critique of the ontological argument is often summarized in a slogan—"existence is not a predicate." To say that a house "exists" seems very different from saying that it is, for example, "messy." "Messiness" is a property of some houses at some times, but not of all houses at all times; by contrast all real houses—and cabbages and kings—must exist. Alternatively, only an existing thing can have any properties at all, so existence cannot be considered on a par with "other" properties, and "exists" is not a proper predicate. Wood's objection is that although Kant's point seems intuitive, it is very hard to find any argument for it in the text of the "Ideal of Pure Reason."

The essays in this collection are intended to help students read the *Critique of Pure Reason* with a greater understanding of its central themes and arguments, and with some awareness of important lines of criticism of those themes and arguments. They cannot substitute for an engaged, critical reading of the text itself. Since it appeared over two hundred years ago, the *Critique* has inspired influential schools of interpretation that have dominated scholarly discussion for longer or shorter periods of time. But the history of its interpretation is antithetical to the spirit of the work itself. If Kant is right, then slavish adherence to the views of previous interpreters is no way to read his book; the only route to a proper critical appreciation of the deep and difficult ideas in the *Critique of Pure Reason* is to think about them for yourself.

### Notes

1. The system of references to the *Critique of Pure Reason* is explained in the "Bibliography," pp. 283–84. The translations from Kant are my own.

2. References to Kant's work other than *Critique* are explained on p. 283.

3. An "antinomy" arises where there appear to be sound arguments supporting both a proposition and its contradictory.

# Acknowledgments

"Kant's *A Priori* Framework." Parts of this essay are reprinted with permission of the author and the publisher from Philip Kitcher, "A Priori Knowledge," *Philosophical Review* 89 (1980): 3–23, copyright 1980 Cornell University; other parts are reprinted with the permission of the publishers from Philip Kitcher, "How Kant Almost Wrote 'Two Dogmas of Empiricism' (and why he didn't)," that appeared in J. N. Mohanty and Robert W. Shahan (eds.), *Essays on Kant's Critique of Pure Reason*. Norman: University of Oklahoma Press, 1982: 217–49.

"Was Kant a Nativist?" Reprinted with permission of the publisher, Johns Hopkins University Press, from Lorne Falkenstein, "Was Kant a Nativist?" *Journal of the History of Ideas* (1990): 573–97.

"Infinity and Kant's Conception of the 'Possibility of Experience.'" Reprinted with permission of the author and the publisher from Charles Parsons, "Infinity and Kant's Conception of the 'Possibility of Experience,'" *The Philosophical Review* 73 (1964): 183–97, copyright 1964 Cornell University.

"Kant's Cognitive Self." Parts of this essay are reprinted with permission of the author and the publishers from Patricia Kitcher, "Kant on Self-Identity," *Philosophical Review* 91 (1982): 41–72, and from Patricia Kitcher, "Kant's Paralogisms," *Philosophical Review* 91 (1982): 515–47, copyright 1982 Cornell University.

"Kant's Transcendental Deduction as a Regressive Argument." Reprinted with permission of the author and the publisher from Karl Ameriks, "Kant's Transcendental Deduction as a Regressive Argument," *Kant-Studien* 69 (1978): 273–87.

"Did the Sage of Königsberg Have No Dreams?" Reprinted with the kind permission of Mrs. Lewis White Beck.

"Kant's Second Analogy." Material from this essay appeared in Paul

Guyer, *Kant and the Claims of Knowledge*. New York: Cambridge University Press, 1987: 237–66. It appears here by permission of Cambridge University Press and the author. Paul Guyer kindly edited the paper for publication in this volume, including making numerous handwritten amendments to the translations of cited passages.

"The Metaphysics of Transcendental Idealism." Reprinted with permission of the author and the new publishers from P. F. Strawson, *The Bounds of Sense*. Methuen, 1966: 235–73 (now published by Routledge).

"An Introduction to the Problem" and "Transcendental Realism and Transcendental Idealism" from *Kant's Transcendental Idealism*. Reprinted with permission of the publisher from Henry E. Allison, *Kant's Transcendental Idealism*. New Haven, Conn.: Yale University Press, 1983: 3–34.

"Projecting the Order of Nature." Reprinted with permission of the publishers from Philip Kitcher's "Projecting the Order of Nature," from Robert E. Butts (ed.), *Kant's Philosophy of Science*. The University of Western Ontario Series in Philosophy of Science, Dordrecht, Holland: D. Reidel, 1986: 201–35. With kind permission from Kluwer Academic Publishers.

"Kant's Compatibilism." Reprinted with permission of the publisher from Allen W. Wood, "Kant's Compatibilism," which appeared in Allen W. Wood (ed.), *Self and Nature in Kant's Philosophy*. Ithaca, N.Y.: Cornell University Press, 1984: 73–101.

"Kant's Critique of the Three Theistic Proofs," [partial] from *Kant's Rational Theology*. Reprinted with permission of the publisher from Allen W. Wood, *Kant's Rational Theology*. Ithaca, N.Y.: Cornell University Press, 1978: 95–116.

# 1

# Kant's *A Priori* Framework

*Philip Kitcher*

## I

"*A priori*" has been a popular term with philosophers at least since Kant. It is also a central notion in Kant's own philosophy, a notion that must be understood if there is any prospect of grasping his distinctive approach to the problems of epistemology and metaphysics. Yet, despite the frequency with which it has been used in twentieth-century philosophy, there has been little discussion of the notion of the *a priori*. Odder still, despite the obvious importance of the *a priori* in the *Critique of Pure Reason*, few Kant scholars have made serious efforts to offer a precise account of this notion and its relation to other key concepts, such as necessity and universality. A common practice is simply to present Kant's own explanations: judgments are *a priori* if they are "necessary" and "universal" (B 3–4)[1]; *a priori* knowledge is knowledge "absolutely independent of experience" (B 3). Like most of Kant's claims, however, these pronouncements are hardly self-explanatory. Further, although "*a priori*" enters the *Critique* as an epistemological predicate, attaching primarily to items of knowledge, it quickly becomes applied to almost everything in sight: judgments, concepts, intuitions, faculties, and syntheses are all labeled "*a priori*." Obviously, I will not be able to cover the whole territory of the *a priori* in this essay. My primary aim is to clarify Kant's notion of *a priori* knowledge, and to relate it to his distinctive positions on necessity, analyticity, *a priori* concepts—and his important claim about the centrality of synthetic *a priori* propositions to philosophy. At the same time, I hope that the Kantian account of *a priori* knowledge developed here will provide at

1

least one clear sense in which contemporary debates about the apriority of this or that body of knowledge can be framed. At several points, I will explicitly relate Kant's views on this cluster of issues to contemporary positions.


## II


I begin with Kant's oft-quoted explication that *a priori* knowledge is knowledge "absolutely independent of experience" (B 3). Two questions naturally arise. What are we to understand by "experience"? And what is to be made of the idea of independence from experience? Apparently, there are easy answers. Count as a person's experience the stream of her sensory encounters with the world, where this includes both "outer experience," that is, sensory states caused by stimuli external to the body, and "inner experience," that is, those sensory states brought about by internal stimuli. Now we might propose that someone's knowledge is independent of her experience just in case she could have had that knowledge whatever experience she had had. To this obvious suggestion there is an equally obvious objection. The apriorist is not necessarily a believer in innate knowledge: indeed, Kant emphasized the difference between the two types of knowledge. So we cannot accept an analysis which implies that a priori knowledge could have been obtained given minimal experiences. Many philosophers (Kant included) contend both that analytic truths can be known *a priori* and that some analytic truths [i.e., judgments in which the predicate-concept is (covertly) contained in the subject-concept, *CPR*, A6, B10—Ed.] involve concepts that could only be acquired if we were to have particular kinds of experience. If we are to defend their doctrines from immediate rejection, we must allow a minimal role to experience, even in *a priori* knowledge. Experience may be needed to provide some concepts. So we might modify our proposal: knowledge is independent of experience if any experience which would enable us to acquire the concepts involved would enable us to have the knowledge.

It is worth noting explicitly that we are concerned here with the *total* experience of the knower. Suppose that you acquire some knowledge empirically. Later you deduce some consequences of this empirical knowledge. We should reject the suggestion that your knowledge of those consequences is independent of experience because, at the time you perform the deduction, you are engaging in a process of reasoning which is independent of the sensations you are then having. As Kant recognized, your knowledge in cases like this is dependent on your total experience: different total sequences of sensations would not have given you the premises for your deductions (B 2–3).

Let us put together the points which have been made so far. A person's experience at a particular time will be identified with his sensory state at the time. (Such states are best regarded physicalistically in terms of stimulation of sensory receptors, but we should recognize that there are both "outer" and "inner" receptors.) The total sequence of experiences X has had up to time t is X's *life at t*. A life will be said to be *sufficient for X for p* just in case X could have had that life and gained sufficient understanding to believe that p. (I postpone, for the moment, questions about the nature of the possibility involved here.) Our discussion above suggests the use of these notions in the analysis of *a priori* knowledge: X knows *a priori* that p if and only if X knows that p and, given any life sufficient for X for p, X could have had that life and still have known that p. Making temporal references explicit: at time t X knows *a priori* that p just in case, at time t, X knows that p and, given any life sufficient for X for p, X could have had that life at t and still have known, at t, that p. In subsequent discussions I shall usually leave the temporal references implicit.

Unfortunately, the proposed analysis will not do. A clear-headed apriorist should admit that people can have empirical knowledge of propositions which can be known *a priori*. However, on the account I have given, if somebody knows that p and if it is possible for her to know *a priori* that p, then, apparently, given any sufficiently rich life she could know that p, so that she would meet the conditions for *a priori* knowledge that p. Hence it seems that my account will not allow for empirical knowledge of propositions that can be known *a priori*.

We need to amend the analysis. We must differentiate situations in which a person knows something empirically which could have been known *a priori* from situations of actual *a priori* knowledge. The remedy is obvious. What sets apart corresponding situations of the two types is a difference in the ways in which what is known is known. An analysis of *a priori* knowledge must probe the notion of knowledge more deeply than we have done so far.

### III

We do not need a general analysis of knowledge, but we do need the *form* of such an analysis. I shall adopt an approach which extracts what is common to much recent work on knowledge, an approach which may appropriately be called "the psychologistic account of knowledge." The root idea is that the question of whether a person's true belief counts as knowledge depends on whether the presence of that true belief can be explained in an appropriate fashion. The difference between an item of knowledge and mere true belief turns on the factors which produced the belief; thus the issue revolves around the way in which a particular mental state was generated. It is important to emphasize that, at different times, a person may have states of belief with the same content, and these states may be produced by different processes. The claim that a process produces a belief is to be understood as the assertion that the presence of the current state of belief is to be explained through a description of that process. Hence the account is not committed to supposing that the original formation of a belief is relevant to the epistemological status of later states of belief in the same proposition.

The question of what conditions must be met if a belief is to be explained in an appropriate fashion is central to epistemology, but it need not concern us here. My thesis is that the distinction between knowledge and true belief depends on the characteristics of the process which generates the belief, and this thesis is independent of specific proposals about what characteristics are crucial. Introducing a useful term, let us say that some processes *warrant* the beliefs they produce, and that these processes are *warrants* for such beliefs. The general view of knowledge I have adopted can be recast as the thesis that X knows that p just in case X correctly believes that p and X's belief was produced by a process which is a warrant for it. Leaving the task of specifying the conditions on warrants to general epistemology, my aim is to distinguish *a priori* knowledge from *a posteriori* knowledge [i.e., knowledge derived from experience—Ed.]. We discovered above that the distinction requires us to consider the ways in which what is known is known. Hence I propose to reformulate the problem: let us say that X knows *a priori* that p just in case X has a true belief that p and that belief was produced by a process which is an *a priori warrant* for it. Now the crucial notion is that of an *a priori* warrant, and our task becomes that of specifying the conditions which distinguish *a priori* warrants from other warrants.

At this stage, some examples may help us to see how to draw the distinction. Perception is an obvious type of process which philosophers have supposed *not* to engender *a priori* knowledge. Putative *a priori* warrants are more controversial. I shall use Kant's notion of pure intuition as an example. This is not to endorse the claim that processes of pure intuition are *a priori* warrants, but only to see what features of such processes have prompted Kant (and others) to differentiate them from perceptual processes.

On Kant's theory, processes of pure intuition are supposed to yield *a priori* mathematical knowledge. Let us focus on a simple geometrical example. We are supposed to gain *a priori* knowledge of the elementary properties of triangles by using our grasp of the concept of triangle to construct a mental picture of a triangle and by inspecting this picture with the mind's eye. What are the characteristics of this kind of process which make Kant want to say that it produces knowledge which is independent of experience? I believe that Kant's account implies that three conditions should be met. The same type of process must be *available* independently of experience. It must produce *warranted* belief independently of experience. And it must produce *true* belief independently of experience.

Let us consider these conditions in turn. According to the Kantian story, if our life were to enable us to acquire the appropriate concepts (the concept of a triangle and the other geometrical concepts involved), then the appropriate kind of pure intuition would be available to us. We could represent a triangle to ourselves, inspect it,[2] and so reach the same beliefs. But, if the process is to generate *knowledge* independently of experience, Kant must require more of it. Given any sufficiently rich life, if we were to undergo the same type of process and gain the same beliefs, then those beliefs would be warranted by the process. Let us dramatize the point by imagining that experience is unkind. Suppose that we are presented with experiments which are cunningly contrived so as to make it appear that some of our basic geometrical beliefs are false. Kant's theory of geometrical knowledge presupposes that if, in the circumstances envisaged, a process of pure intuition were to produce geometrical belief then it would produce warranted belief, despite the background of misleading experience.

So far I have considered how a Kantian process of pure intuition might produce warranted belief independently of experience. But to generate *knowledge* independently of experience, *a priori* warrants must produce warranted *true* belief in counterfactual situations where experiences are different. This point does not emerge clearly in the Kantian case, because the propositions that are alleged to be known *a priori* are taken to be necessary, so that the question of whether it would be possible to have an *a priori* warrant for a false belief does not arise. Plainly, we could ensure that *a priori* warrants produce warranted *true* belief independently of experience by declaring that *a priori* warrants only warrant necessary truths. But this proposal is unnecessarily strong for a general account of *a priori* knowledge. Our goal is to construe *a priori* knowledge as knowledge that is independent of experience, and this can be achieved, without closing the case against the contingent *a priori*, by supposing that, in a counterfactual situation in which an *a priori* warrant produces belief that p, then p. On this account, *a priori* warrants are ultra-reliable; they never lead us astray.

Summarizing the conditions that have been uncovered, I propose the following analysis of *a priori* knowledge.

(1) X knows *a priori* that p if and only if X knows that p and X's belief that p was produced by a process that is an *a priori* warrant for it.

(2) α is an *a priori* warrant for X's belief that p if and only if α is a process such that, given any life e, sufficient for X for p, then

(a) some process of the same type could produce in X a belief that p

(b) if a process of the same type were to produce in X a belief that p then it would warrant X in believing that p

(c) if a process of the same type were to produce in X a belief that p, then p.

It should be clear that this analysis yields the desired result that, if a person knows *a priori* that p then she could know that p whatever (sufficiently rich) experience she had had. But it goes beyond the proposal of §II in spelling out the idea that the knowledge be obtainable in the same way. Hence we can distinguish cases of empirical knowledge of propositions which could be known *a priori* from cases of actual *a priori* knowledge. It also extends the basic Kantian position, because it does not presume that *a priori* propositions are *ipso facto* necessary.

## IV

In this section, I want to be more explicit about the notion of "types of processes" which I have employed, and about the modal and conditional notions that figure in my analysis. To specify a process which produces a belief is to pick out some terminal segment of the causal ancestry of the belief. I think that, without loss of generality, we can restrict our attention to those segments which consist solely of taste and events internal to the believer. Tracing the causal ancestry of a belief beyond the believer would identify processes which would not be available independently of experience, so that they would violate our conditions on *a priori* warrants.

Given that we need only consider psychological processes, the next question which arises is how we divide processes into types. It may seem that the problem can be sidestepped: can't we simply propose that to defend the apriority of an item of knowledge is to claim that that knowledge was produced by a psychological process and that *that very process* would be available and would produce warranted true belief in counterfactual situations where experience is different? I think it is easy to see how to use this proposal to rewrite (2) in a way which avoids reference to "types of processes." I have not adopted this approach because I think that it shortcuts important questions about what makes a process the same in different counterfactual situations.

Our talk of processes which produce belief was originally introduced to articulate the idea that some items of knowledge are obtained in the same way while others are obtained in different ways. To return to our example, knowing a theorem on the basis of hearing a lecture and knowing the same theorem by following a proof count, intuitively, as different ways of knowing the theorem. Our intuitions about this example, and others, involve a number of different principles of classification, with different principles appearing in different cases. We seem to divide belief-forming processes into types by considering content of beliefs, inferential connections, causal connections, use of perceptual mechanisms, and so forth. I suggest that these principles of classification probably do not give rise to one definite taxonomy, but that by using them singly, or in combination, we obtain a number of different taxonomies which we can and do employ. Moreover, within each taxonomy, we can specify types of processes more or less narrowly. Faced with such variety, what characterization should we pick?

There is probably no privileged way of dividing processes into types. This is not to say that our standard principles of classification will allow anything to count as a type. Somebody who proposed that the process of listening to a lecture (or the terminal settlement of it which consists of psychological states and events) belongs to a type which consists of itself and instances of following a proof would flout *all* our principles of dividing processes into types. Hence, while we may have many admissible notions of types of belief-forming processes, corresponding to different principles of classification, some collections of processes contravene all such principles, and these cannot be admitted as genuine types.

My analysis can be read as issuing a challenge to the apriorist. If someone wishes to claim that a particular belief is an item of *a priori* knowledge then he must specify a segment of the causal ancestry of the belief consisting of states and events internal to the believer, and type-identify conditions which conform to some principle (or set of principles) of classification which are standardly employed in our divisions of belief-forming processes (of which the principles I have indicated above furnish the most obvious examples). If he succeeds in doing this so that the requirements in (2) are met, his claim is sustained, if he cannot, then his claim is defeated.

The final issue which requires discussion in this section is that of explaining the modal [i.e., concerning possibility, actuality, or necessity—Ed.] and conditional notions I have used. There are all kinds of possibility, and claims about what is possible bear an implicit relativization to a set of facts which are held constant. When we say in (2) that, given any sufficiently rich life, X could have had a belief which was the product of a particular type of process, should we conceive of this as merely logical possibility or are there some features of the actual world which are tacitly regarded as fixed? I suggest that we are not just envisaging any logically possible world. We imagine a world in which X has similar mental powers to those he has in the actual world. By hypothesis, X's experience is different. Yet the capacities for thinking, reasoning, and acquiring knowledge which X possesses as a member of *Homo sapiens* are to remain unaffected: we want to say that X, *with the kinds of cognitive capacities distinctive of humans*, could have undergone processes of the appropriate type, even if his experiences had been different.

Humans might have had more faculties for acquiring knowledge than they actually have. For example, we might have had some strange ability to "see" what happens on the other side of the Earth. When we consider the status of a particular type of process as an *a priori* warrant, the existence of worlds in which such extra faculties come into play is entirely irrelevant. Our investigation focuses on the question of whether a particular type of process would be available to a person with the kinds of faculties people actually have, not on whether such processes would be available to creatures whose capacities for acquiring knowledge are augmented or diminished. Conditions (2(b)) and (2(c)) are to be read in similar fashion. Rewriting (2(b)) to make the form of the conditional explicit, we obtain: for any life e sufficient for X for p and for any world in which X has e, in which he believes that p, in which his belief is the product of a process of the appropriate kind, *and in which X has the cognitive capacities distinctive of humans*, X is warranted in believing that p. Similarly, (2(c)) becomes: for any life e sufficient for X for p and for any world in which X has e, in which he believes that p, in which his belief is the product of a process of the appropriate kind, *and in which X has the cognitive capacities distinctive of humans*, p. Finally, the notion of a life's being sufficient for X for p also bears an implicit reference to X's native powers. To say that a particular life enables X to form certain concepts is to maintain that, given the genetic programming with which X is endowed, that life allows for the formation of the concepts.

The account I have offered can be presented more graphically in the following way. Consider a human as a cognitive device, endowed initially with a particular kind of structure. Sensory experience is fed into the device and, as a result, the device forms certain concepts. For any proposition p, the class of experiences which are sufficiently rich for p consists of those experiences which would enable the device, with the kind of structure it actually has, to acquire the concepts to believe that p. To decide whether or not a particular item of knowledge that p is an item of *a priori* knowledge we consider whether the type of process which produced the belief that p is a process which would have been available to the device, with the kind of structure it actually has, if different sufficiently rich experiences had been fed into it, whether, under such circumstances, processes of the type would warrant belief that p, and would produce true belief that p.

**V**

Given the notion of *a priori* knowledge, it is easy to introduce a derivative notion of *a priori* proposition. A proposition is *a priori* just in case human beings could know it *a priori*. Waiving doubts about how we are to understand the type of modality which is appropriate here, we could use this equivalence to unpack many of Kant's remarks. When

Kant contends that a proposition (judgment) is *a priori*, he would be read as maintaining that there is some special type of process which could serve as an *a priori* warrant for our belief in that proposition. Unfortunately, matters are not so simple. As noted, very early in the *Critique*, Kant yokes the concept of apriority to two further notions: "Necessity and strict universality are thus sure criteria of *a priori* knowledge, and are inseparable from one another" (B4). For the purposes of this paper I am going to ignore Kant's concept of universality and the claims he makes which involve it. The connection between necessity and apriority is problematic enough to justify us in focusing on it, independently of the further tie to universality.

One of the most obvious consequences of Kant's linkage of apriority to necessity is that he is led to advance the thesis that a proposition is *a priori* for a number of different reasons. Sometimes he is concerned to argue that the proposition can be known *a priori* and to explain how it can be known *a priori*. On other occasions he wants to show that the proposition is necessary and to explain why it is necessary. Occasionally he engages in both projects at once. I shall now suggest that *some* of the complications of Kant's investigations of the "province of pure reason" stem from his oscillation between epistemological and metaphysical enterprises.

Kant's approach to necessity involves problems of its own. It is helpful to understand Kant's conception(s) by introducing the familiar idiom of possible worlds semantics for modal logic—an idiom which descends, of course, from Leibniz. On this account necessary truths are understood to be propositions true in all possible worlds. Kant has a distinctive approach to necessity because he takes a possible world to be a totality of possible appearances—that is, a totality of appearances which could constitute the experience of a subject. There are two *loci* of vagueness in this formulation. First, different conceptions of the nature of the subject can give rise to distinct conceptions of possible worlds (and, derivatively, to alternative doctrines about necessity and possibility). Throughout the *Critique*, Kant's primary usage holds fixed the cognitive constitution of the human subject (as I did above in explicating *a priori* warrants), so that possible worlds are taken as totalities of appearances for subjects with the types of faculties found among *Homo sapiens*. One of the most obvious occurrences of this usage is Kant's attribution of necessity to certain statements about space and time, where the notion of possible experience is clearly subjected to the conditions of spatiotemporal (Euclidean) experience. There are also, however, indications of "higher" types of necessity, generated by relaxing the constraints on possible worlds so as to allow for the experiences of nonhuman but rational subjects. The second *locus* of vagueness alluded to above lies in the term "experience." Notoriously, Kant sometimes uses "experience" in a very strong sense, so that for something to count as a total possible experience for a subject it would have to involve (in some way) judgments, or even particular kinds of judgments, by the subject. At other times, for example, in the Aesthetic, Kant's conception of experience is much weaker, and a total experience can be taken as a sequence of sensory states (as I did above). I shall not attempt to fix a determinate Kantian notion of possible world (or of necessity or possibility) which can then be used to analyze the central theses of the *Critique*. For the reasons just indicated, it seems to me to be a mistake to try to find *one* notion which will answer to all Kant's claims, and I suggest that the general view that a possible world is a totality of appearances which could constitute the experience of a subject should be filled out in different ways for application to different parts of the *Critique*.

One might think that by recognizing a number of different interpretations of the notion of necessity we could ascribe to Kant some true thesis asserting the equivalence of necessity and apriority. This hope is unfounded. As a number of contemporary philosophers have argued[3], the doctrine that necessity and apriority are equivalent fails in both directions: there are contingent truths which are knowable *a priori* and necessary truths (including knowable necessary truths) which are not knowable *a priori*. The counterexamples are equally applicable to the versions of the equivalence thesis which employ Kantian conceptions of necessity. Hence Kant's claims to the effect that particular propositions are *a priori* are dangerously ambiguous.

Yet even if we were to grant Kant's equivalence between apriority and necessity, we would still have to separate two distinct enterprises which he sets for himself. In justifying the thesis that a proposition is necessary (or *a priori*), the equivalence might prove useful: from a premise asserting the apriority (necessity) of the proposition we could employ the equivalence to reach the conclusion that it is necessary (*a priori*). However, Kant does not simply want to argue that certain favored propositions are necessary (*a priori*). In many cases his principal interest lies in explaining why they are necessary (*a priori*). To grant the equivalence thesis would not *ipso facto* allow for the transmutation of explanations of the necessity of propositions into explanations of

the apriority of those propositions or *vice versa*. Indeed, the account I
have offered of Kant's notions of apriority and necessity enables us to
see what explanations of the necessity and apriority of propositions will
be like and why those explanations will be different. To understand
why a proposition is *a priori*, we shall need a specification of a process
which could warrant belief in it, independently of experience. By contrast, to explain the necessity of a proposition, we shall show why that
proposition holds at any possible world. The general Kantian conception of a possible world points to the way in which the story will go:
we may show either that the proposition owes its truth to some feature
with which our minds inevitably structure appearances or that it states
some condition on the possibility of a particular kind of experience
(the former style of explanation is prominent in the Aesthetic; the latter, in the Analytic). Quite evidently, we may put forward explanations
of the necessity of propositions without offering a specification of processes through which we could arrive at *a priori* knowledge of those
propositions. Thus the task of accounting for the apriority of a proposition is not accomplished simply by showing why that proposition is
necessary.

Although we have already seen how Kant's terminology allows him
to include quite different projects under one rubric, this is only the
first stage in separating Kantian themes. I now want to show how consideration of the *epistemological a priori*—reflection on the conditions which *a priori* warrants must meet—could prompt new
distinctions and new enterprises.

## VI

Kant believes that the fundamental problem of *a priori* knowledge is
the problem of synthetic *a priori* knowledge. His belief reflects the
judgment that analyticity is not the solution to the problem of apriority.
Here he agrees with Quine. My goal is to explain how Kant could come
close to advocating the celebrated Quinean dictum "Any statement can
be held true come what may. . . . Conversely, by the same token, no
statement is immune to revision" and how his partial appreciation of
the point could lead him to an interesting articulation of the problem
of *a priori* knowledge.

Let us begin with an important connection. Standardly, apriority is
linked to unrevisability. If someone knows a proposition *a priori*, then,

it seems, that proposition is immune to revision. It is not hard to begin to explicate the notion of immunity to revision which is involved here. We can say that a proposition is unrevisable for a person at a time just in case there is no possible continuation of that person's experience after that time which would make it reasonable for her to change her attitude to the proposition. The explication makes it apparent why one might think that propositions which a person knows *a priori* are unrevisable for that person. If you have *a priori* knowledge that p, then you have an *a priori* warrant for belief that p. Assuming that the warrant is available independently of time, then, given any continuation of your experience, you would have available to you a warrant which would continue to support belief. Hence it would never be reasonable for you to abandon p in favor of its negation. Whatever trickery your experience may devise for you, you will always be able to undergo a process which will sustain the belief.

Unfortunately, however, this argument adopts an overly simple view of the relevant changes in attitude. We take it for granted that the only changes of attitude which might occur are those in which the person passes from belief in the proposition to belief in its negation (or, perhaps, to suspension of belief). Let us call cases in which a belief that p is replaced by a belief in the negation of p *strong revisions of p.* Let us also suppose, for the sake of simplicity, that in cases where experience could lead us from belief to rational suspension of belief, even more recalcitrant experience could engender rational denial of belief. Even with this simplification, the strong revisions of propositions are not the only changes of attitude which should concern us. There are also cases in which we abandon a proposition by giving up the *concepts* which it involves. In such cases we do not come to think of the proposition which we formerly believed as false, nor do we hesitate between that proposition and its negation. Instead we may grudgingly acknowledge the proposition as true, hastening to qualify our endorsement by pointing out that it is vacuous or that it embodies a wrongheaded conception of things. I shall call cases in which we acquire an attitude like this toward propositions which we formerly believed *weak revisions* of those propositions.

An example may help us recognize the possibility of weak revision. I think it is plausible to think that the way we refer to mermaids is fixed so that it follows that mermaids are female inhabitants of the sea whose heads and upper bodies are structured like those of human females but whose lower extremities consist of scaly tails. Once our attitude to the proposition expressed by "Mermaids are female" was one of straightforward belief. From nautical reports we, or more exactly our ancestors, would have supposed that there are mermaids and that all of them are female. Had we been asked to justify our belief, we would have appealed to our concept of a mermaid, insisting that the manner in which the class of mermaids is determined ensures that all its members will be female. Now we no longer maintain the same attitude toward the proposition. Although we might continue to insist that the concept of a mermaid determines that the proposition is true, we would hasten to add that scientific research has convinced us that the concept is useless, that it is inapplicable, and that it plays no role in what, by our current lights, is the best description and explanation of the world. The proposition has not suffered strong revision. Instead it has undergone weak revision and has been demoted from a role in our cognitive endeavors. If the concept of a mermaid lingers on, it does so only because we sometimes use it in storytelling or in intellectual history.

In distinguishing between strong and weak revisions, I have, of course, appealed to a distinction which Quineans regard as anathema, namely, the distinction between changing one's concepts and changing one's beliefs. Let me note an obvious point. Unlike Quine, Kant does not repudiate the notion of analytic truth. His agreement with Quine is restricted to the view that appeals to analyticity fail to achieve a certain purpose. To understand the nature of this agreement, we shall have to make use of a distinction which Quine ultimately rejects.

I shall now use the distinction between strong and weak revision to generate a derivative distinction between complete and incomplete unrevisability. Let us say that a proposition is *completely unrevisable* for a person if it is impossible that experience should continue in such a way that it would be rational for the person to undergo either a strong or a weak revision with respect to it. A proposition will be *incompletely unrevisable* for a person if it is impossible that experience should continue in such a way that it would be rational for the person to undergo strong revisions with respect to it. Our previous argument from apriority to unrevisability can now be interpreted as an attempt to show that propositions which can be known *a priori* are incompletely unrevisable. If we have an *a priori* warrant for belief that p, then, provided that the warrant is available to us independently of time, we can continue to use it to turn back the suggestions of experience against p. Can we argue, in similar fashion, that apriority should entail complete unrevisability?

Kant's answer is "Yes," and it is this answer which embodies part of his agreement with Quine and which also generates some of the projects of the *Critique*. I suggest that Kant believes that propositions which we know *a priori* should not even be subject to weak revisions, that he has good reasons for maintaining this belief, and that his downplaying of the role of analytic judgments in the *Critique* stems from an (implicit) recognition that the analyticity of a proposition does not entail that that proposition is not vulnerable to weak revision. Up to this point he agrees with Quine. The differences between Kant and Quine consist, first of all, in Kant's allowance for a distinctive source of knowledge based on recognizing conceptual relations, and, more significantly, in his reaction to the failure of analyticity to secure complete unrevisability. Whereas for Quine this failure dooms the project of apriorism, Kant views it as imposing more stringent demands on *a priori* knowledge and sets out resolutely to see whether those demands can be met.

Starting with the first difference, Kant believes that analytic truths can be known by means of processes which disclose relations among our concepts. Let us grant him this idea. Do processes of this type count as *a priori* warrants? I would claim that they can be shown to meet conditions (2(a)) and (2(c)) of the analysis given above. Where trouble arises is with condition (2(b)). Given an experience which enables us to acquire certain concepts which are involved in an analytic proposition, but which calls into doubt the applicability of those concepts, the power of the process of conceptual disclosure to warrant belief in the analytic truth is undermined. Once we appreciate this point, two of the theses I have attributed to Kant will follow. First, the failure of the process to serve as an *a priori* warrant results from the possibility that experience might exhibit to us the futility of certain concepts, so that we should infer that *a priori* propositions must not be vulnerable even to weak revisions. Hence (given the usual assumption about the time independence of the relevant warrants) apriority should entail complete unrevisability. Second, the argument shows directly that analyticity cannot be the key to the problem of *a priori* knowledge. Demonstrating that a proposition is analytic does not suffice to explain why that proposition is *a priori*.

The crucial claim in the argument of the previous paragraph is the thesis that experiences which would call into question the applicability of a concept would deprive of their warranting power processes in which we disclosed the relations of that concept to other concepts. This claim can be defended by canvassing intuitions about particular cases and by appealing to general considerations about the goals of inquiry. Discussion of examples will lead us naturally to the general points.

Do we know that mermaids are female? The question is an awkward one: it seems misleading to say either "Yes" or "No." I suggest that the awkwardness should be taken seriously. We no longer retain belief in the proposition that mermaids are female—at least we no longer believe that proposition in a way which allows for it to count as an item of our knowledge. We are prepared to assert "Mermaids are female" only in a limited range of contexts—when we are telling stories, for example—and this distinguishes us from our predecessors who preceded the Nautical Enlightenment. Were someone to have continued the old attitude of believing wholeheartedly that mermaids are female and of asserting "Mermaids are female" within the wider range of contexts embracing contexts of serious scientific discussion, we would characterize the belief as unwarranted. We should not credit an appeal to the concept of mermaid as warranting belief. Instead we should point out that use of that concept is unreasonable, given our experience, so that the process of disclosing the relations between the concept of mermaid and other concepts fails to warrant belief.

So far my discussion may have suggested that the only way in which experience can undermine concepts is by showing that those concepts are not instantiated. That is far too simple a view of the matter. Our right to use a concept may be called into question by experiences which convince us that the concept carves up reality in an inappropriate way (conversely, some concepts—idealizations in science—do an excellent job of carving up reality but are not instantiated). The intuitive point that experience can deprive one of a right to use a concept—even of a concept which is instantiated—and so undermine one's beliefs is well made by a historical case introduced by Mill. Chemists of the early eighteenth century conceived of acids as substances which contain oxygen, and, given that we are prepared to allow the analysis of concepts as a source of knowledge, it is plausible to suppose that their knowledge of the proposition that (what they called) acids contain oxygen was based on processes through which they disclosed conceptual relations to themselves. With the discovery that a substance which bears numerous resemblances to other acids (the substance which they called muriatic acid and which we call hydrochloric acid) does not contain oxygen, the definition of "acid" was revised. Now if there were people who had continued to employ the old concept, maintaining that acids contain oxygen on the basis of the process of conceptual analysis, we should not suppose that they had retained a distinctive item of knowledge. Rather we should view the experiences involving the discovery of the composition of hydrochloric acid as undermining the old concept of acid and as depriving the process of analyzing the old concept of acid of its power to warrant belief.

The general point about inquiry which these examples suggest is that our goal is not simply to utter truths but to utter truths which employ appropriate concepts. Those who persist in using concepts which experience has shown to be inadequate may continue to assert the truth, but we do not credit them with knowledge of propositions involving the outworn concepts. Thus the process of conceptual analysis, which Kant envisages us as using to acquire knowledge of analytic truths, does not warrant belief if experience reveals to us that concepts which we are analyzing are inappropriate. Those who cling to outworn distinctions are not guilty of the same error as that made by those who adhere to beliefs which have been falsified, but they are equally deficient in aiming at the goals of inquiry and, as a result, equally deficient in having knowledge.

What Kant (and later Quine) recognized is that to suppose analyticity entails apriority is to make *a priori* knowledge come too cheap. In a revealing passage written by Kant's disciple Schultz in response to Eberhard's objections to the emphasis on the *synthetic a priori* which dominates the *Critique*, this point is made with great force. Eberhard had suggested that Kant's favored propositions could be replaced by analytic judgments if one expanded the subject concept. Schultz (whose words can reasonably be understood to express Kant's thoughts) replied as follows:

> Let one put into the concept of the subject just so many attributes that the predicate which one wishes to prove of the subject can be derived from its concept merely by the law of contradiction. The critical philosophy permits him to make this kind of analytic judgment, but raises a question about the concept of the subject itself. It asks: how did you come to include in this concept the different attributes so that it [now analytically] entails synthetic propositions? First prove the objective reality of your concept, i.e. first prove that any one of its attributes really belongs to a

possible object, and when you have done that, then prove that the other
attributes belong to the same thing that the first one belongs to, without
themselves belonging to the first attribute.[4]

That is, we cannot account for the apriority of propositions by simply
finding analytic surrogates for them. There are constraints on our concepts, and an analytic judgment is *a priori* only if it accords with these
constraints. To put it another way, the Kantian enterprise is as concerned with the applicability—"objective validity"—of our concepts as
it is with the truth of our judgments.

I have suggested that Kant and Quine agree that analyticity does not
(would not) solve the problem of *a priori* knowledge—even though
Kant still allows analytic judgments. The more important disagreement
is the second one noted above. The thrust of the final section of "Two
Dogmas of Empiricism" is that there is no *a priori* knowledge.[5] Kant,
convinced that we *do* have some *a priori* knowledge but recognizing
that that knowledge cannot simply be attributed to our ability to analyze our concepts, attempts to show that some concepts and some
judgments are privileged.

## VII

If *a priori* propositions are to be completely unrevisable, then they
must contain special concepts. Appropriately Kant calls these concepts
"*a priori* concepts." What features distinguish *a priori* concepts? For
reasons which will shortly become evident, I shall not try to give a full
answer to this question. Instead I shall indicate two approaches which
Kant seems to have taken in response to it.

Two notions of *a priori* concept play a role in the *Critique*. The first,
which I shall call the "objective validity" construal, identifies *a priori*
concepts as those which must find application in our experience. The
simplest way to explicate this idea is to suggest that the concept expressed by the predicate F is an *a priori* concept just in case there is
some X that is F in any (Kantian) possible world. Many of Kant's remarks in the *Critique* seem to be directed at proving that particular
concepts are necessarily instantiated. Nevertheless, there are two reasons for not adopting so simple a reading of his endeavors to demonstrate that concepts are "objectively valid." In the first place, the issue
of whether a concept has instances is not necessarily relevant to the

question of whether that concept is legitimately employed in attempts to describe and explain the world. We sometimes reject concepts which are instantiated, because they do not lend themselves to a simple theory of the world. Similarly, we sometimes continue to employ concepts which we recognize as not being instantiated: idealizations play an important role in our science. Second, even though a concept is necessarily instantiated and even though we concede that having instantiations suffices to make it correct to employ the concept, that would not solve the problem for which I have supposed the notion of an *a priori* concept to be designed. Weak revision of propositions involving concepts which are necessarily instantiated might still be rational, for it might be possible, given certain kinds of recalcitrant experience, that we should mistakenly, but justifiably, believe that those concepts were not instantiated.

Hence I shall propose a different way of explicating the "objectively valid" construal of *a priori* concepts. Kant would maintain that there are some concepts which it must be rational to employ in the description of any experience sufficient to enable one to acquire those concepts. It is not just that these concepts are inevitably instantiated but that anyone whose experience suffices for the acquisition of the concepts could not be justified in doubting that they are instantiated. If one makes a minimally rational response to one's experience, then one will be able to turn back any challenge that the concept in question is inapplicable.

This proposal is not a completely satisfactory explication even of one Kantian notion of *a priori* concept, for it fails to respond to the first point I made two paragraphs back. I have continued to use the property of having instantiations as a necessary condition for conceptual adequacy, adding as a further constraint on *a priori* concepts that it ₁ot be possible for experience to generate a reasonable doubt that they are instantiated. Evidently, a complete account of the notion of an *a priori* concept would be more complicated, but I suggest that my simple first approximation shows the types of conditions which such concepts would have to meet to serve Kant's turn.

Let me now turn to the second construal of *a priori* concepts which I promised above. Sometimes Kant is interested not in those concepts which have to be recognized as being instantiated by any rational subject who has had a sufficiently rich experience but in those concepts which have to be used by anybody who would count as a subject of experience. *A priori* concepts, in this sense, are those which have to figure in propositions which the subject believes if she is to qualify as having experience at all. Let us call this the "subjectively necessary" interpretation of *a priori* concepts. It is relatively easy to see how this notion of *a priori* concept might be thought to resolve the problem posed by the threat of weak revisions. One who jettisons an *a priori* concept in the light of experience has, on this interpretation, ceased to be a subject of experience. Hence, it might be suggested, repudiating propositions by rejecting the concepts they contain must be irrational if the concepts in question are *a priori* concepts.

I shall not try to decide here whether any of Kant's arguments demonstrate that some concepts are *a priori*, because they are either subjectively necessary or objectively valid. hence I will not try to evaluate whether Kant succeeds in vindicating the possibility of synthetic *a priori* knowledge. My goals in this essay have been only to explicate and reveal the connections among some of his key notions—apriority, necessity, and analyticity, and *a priori* knowledge, *a priori* propositions, and *a priori* concepts. Although Kant might have described such preliminary investigations as "dry and tedious," it is hard to see how one could begin to understand—let alone evaluate—the project of the *Critique* without first gaining some grasp of his central technical notions.

## Notes

1. Throughout this paper I shall follow the standard practice of referring to passages from the *Critique* by citing the pagination of the first and second editions. All quoted translations are from the Norman Kemp Smith translation.
2. [For a criticism of Kant's appeal to pure intuition to validate the possibility of *a priori* knowledge of mathematics, see the Parsons essay in this volume—Ed.]
3. See Saul Kripke, *Naming and Necessity* (Cambridge, Mass.: Harvard University Press, 1980); Keith Donnellan, "The Contingent A Priori and Rigid Designators," *Midwest Studies in Philosophy* 2, 1977, pp. 12–27; and Philip Kitcher, "Apriority and Necessity" (reprinted in P. Moser [ed.], *A Priori Knowledge*, Oxford University Press, 1985).
4. 11. See H. E. Allison, ed., *The Kant-Eberhard Controversy* (Baltimore: Johns Hopkins University Press, 1973), p. 175. There are a number of places in the *Critique* where the same thought is expressed, although perhaps never so forthrightly. See, for example, footnote *a* to A242, A252–4/B308–10.
5. W. V. Quine, *From a Logical Point of View* (Cambridge, Mass.: Harvard, 1953).

# 2

# Was Kant a Nativist?

*Lorne Falkenstein*

It has long been supposed that Kant took space and time to be innately originating forms imposed by the mind on the data given in experience. According to Bertrand Russell, "Kant maintained that in virtue of our mental constitution, we deal with the raw material of sense-impressions by means of certain 'categories' and by arranging it in space and time. Both the categories and the space-time arrangement are supplied by us."[1] Before Russell this opinion was sustained in a very explicit fashion by Hermann von Helmholtz: "[Kant] claimed that, not only the qualities of experience, but also space and time are determined by the nature of our faculty of intuition. . . . [A]ccording to him, space is carried to objects by our eyes."[2] And more recently it has been advanced by, among others, Patricia Kitcher. "Kant had a serious argument that the spatial properties of objects, as we perceive them, derive from our perceptual apparatus and not from the properties of objects affecting sensation."[3]

I will challenge this tradition in this paper. While the evidence that Kant took space and time to be in some sense innate is incontrovertible—he explicitly says that space is "in the subject merely as its formal constitution for being affected by objects," to name just one instance[4]—his critics and commentators have failed to grasp the precise sense of this nativism. In what follows I will describe the proper sense of Kant's nativism and argue that he was not a nativist in any of the senses his commentators and critics have supposed.

The nativism/empiricism dichotomy is a notoriously slippery one (some might even argue a false one). One of the reasons for this is that the conflict between nativists and empiricists, which is really a conflict over the role of experience in cognition, has been confused with an entirely different conflict, that over the role of processing in cognition, which I will call the intuitionism/constructivism conflict. The whole of the history of theories of cognition, particularly in the areas of visual perception and space-cognition, has been vexed by a failure to separate the nativism/empiricism conflict on the one hand from the intuitionism/constructivism conflict on the other. Once they are separated, not only Kant's position but much thought on space and vision from the seventeenth to the nineteenth century can be represented more accurately.

## Nativism and Intuitionism

Consider a simple information processing device, like a calculator. The activity of this device can be represented in terms of three distinct moments: first, information is fed into the system (the keyboard is struck); this causes a certain chain of events to take place in the machine which we can refer to as the processing of the input; and the result is the output of a number represented on a screen or paper. The calculator can be taken as a model for the brain, or the mind, considered as an information processing device, with the senses providing the input and the output consisting of knowledge claims or "propositional attitudes."

On the basis of this model I define as maximally empiricistic any theory which holds the following two propositions: (1) all input comes from sensory experience, and (2) the output of all processes is revisable in the light of subsequent sensory experience. These propositions try to capture the basic empiricist intuition that sensory experience should play as large a role as possible in cognition. Applying this intuition to the three-stage model yields the notions that as much of the input to the cognitive system as possible should come from sensory experience and that sensory experience should continue to play as large a role as possible in determining the nature of the processes performed by the system as well as the nature of the output yielded by those processes. The latter means ruling out, as far as possible, fixed processes—processes which, for a given input, must invariably yield a certain output, regardless of whether this output correctly represents the environment or allows the organism to interact successfully with it. Another way to put (2) is to state that all processes are learned from experience, though what this means is not that the capacity to do this kind of processing is learned, but just that the particular output of a process relative to a given input is learned.

Whereas holding both these propositions makes a theory maximally empiricistic, I define as nativistic any theory which denies either of them. If you deny (1), then you are what I will call an innate-ideas nativist. (Innate ideas are not the only possible sources of extra-sensory input, but I will treat them as such throughout this paper; other alternatives such as telepathy, spirit-seeing, and mystical illumination have no epistemological credibility.) If you deny (2), then you are what I will call an innate-mechanisms nativist.

An extreme case of the denial of (1) and hence of innate-ideas nativism can be found in Descartes's *Notes on a Certain Programme*, where it is claimed that all the input we receive is produced by the mind itself from its own inner resources, stimulation of the sense organs providing merely the occasion for this production.[5] Other, less extreme examples of innate ideas nativism include Plato's doctrine of the reminiscence of forms,[6] Leibniz's notion that our knowledge of universal truths arises from inner principles which are innate,[7] and Reid's doctrine of suggestion.[8] Examples of the opposing position, that all input does come from sensory experience, can be found in the Aristotelian dictum that nothing can be in the intellect which was not first present to the senses[9] as well as in Locke's doctrine of the *tabula rasa*[10] or Hume's principle that all ideas must originate from impressions.[11]

There are no extreme cases of the denial of (2) for obvious reasons, but there are many cases of theorists postulating that this or that cognitive process has a fixed output. This underlines a further point, that conditions (1) and (2) are for a *maximally* empiricistic theory of cognition. It is, however, more common for theorists to take mixed approaches—to be nativist with regard to one kind of cognitive process and empiricist with regard to another. Berkeley, for instance, affirmed both conditions for visual depth perception; but on the question of our cognition of spirits he denied condition (1), postulating that we have access to a special, nonsensory input which he called "intuition" or "notion."[12] It is generally more accurate and useful, therefore, to apply the labels "nativist" and "empiricist" with respect just to specific cognitive processes, such as cognition of visible spatial depth, eye-hand coordination, or language acquisition. In this sense an account of a specific cognitive process is empiricistic if it maintains that (1′) all the input for the process in question comes from sensory experience, and

(2′) the output yielded by the process in question is revisable in the light of subsequent sensory experience.

A test for determining if a given individual accepts or rejects (2′) is to ask whether, according to their theory, a mature subject who has never before received the kinds of input that get processed into the kinds of output in question would, on first being exposed to particular instances of this input, spontaneously be able to produce the correct output. If the answer is "no," then the individual likely takes the output to be produced only through a learned association and not through a natural or "hard-wired" process. The classic example of such a test is Molyneux's query whether a blind person, on first being made to see, would be able correctly to identify visible figures without first making the test of touching them.[13]

A further example may help to cement these points. Suppose we are concerned with the cognition of visible spatial depth. Then an empiricist about visible spatial depth is someone who believes both ($1_{SD}$) all the input required to see spatial depth comes from the senses, and (assuming for the sake of argument that the input to the visual sense is two-dimensional only) that ($2_{SD}$) a person previously confined to a two-dimensional environment and newly brought into a three-dimensional space would not at first recognize spatial depth, even given precisely the same sensory stimuli as a sighted person. I will call ($2_{SD}$) and, by association, (2′) and (2) the Molyneux condition, and ($1_{SD}$), (1′), and (1) the base condition. For a theory of spatial depth perception to be nativist it is sufficient that it deny either the base condition or the Molyneux condition.

The base condition for spatial depth perception was denied by Reid. He took our knowledge of three-dimensional space to be, as he put it, "suggested" by tactile sensations. These sensations are in themselves mere feelings with no objective reference and certainly no resemblance to space or any spatial properties.[14] But the mind is innately so constituted that they lead it to form a conception of figures, positions, and magnitudes in three dimensions—that is, the mind itself injects this input into our experience when it receives certain tactile sensations.[15] Visual sensation does not subvert this result. According to Reid, by vision we sense only colors, and these suggest nothing about figure, position, or magnitude. It is rather the physical pattern of light on the organ—what Reid calls the "material impression"—which does this.[16] Here, it might be thought, there may be room for an appeal to processes performed on this original input to yield a cognition of space;

but the space Reid takes to be suggested by the material impression is a two-dimensional Riemannian surface, not Euclidean three-dimensional space.[17] It is only by associating visual stimuli in this apparent space with the (already innately injected) tactile space that visual depth comes to be cognized.[18] The association is admittedly dependent upon experience, so Reid is not an innate-mechanisms nativist. But the extra-sensory element suggested by tactile experience is ineliminable from Reid's account. He is therefore an innate-ideas nativist with respect to depth perception.

Whereas Reid denied ($1_{SD}$), the base condition, Descartes denied ($2_{SD}$). In his *Dioptrics* Descartes described four methods by which we determine visual depth, two of them—judging distance on the basis of the brightness and distinctness of the visual image and judging distance on the basis of a prior knowledge of the size, position, shape, color, or brightness of the object—perhaps presupposing a learned association[19] (at least, Descartes does not rule this out). But the other two methods explicitly do not involve learning. Descartes describes the act of accommodating the eye to focus on objects at different distances as "ordained by nature to make our soul perceive distance," and he describes the act of turning the two eyes to make them converge on an object as giving us a knowledge of distance "as if by a natural geometry."[20] His point was likely not, as Berkeley was later to caricature it, that we actually see the lines and angles traced by light rays and calculate the distance of the object by triangulation; but it was at least that the mind is innately so constituted that certain muscular sensations accompanying accommodation and convergence *automatically* yield a cognition of the appropriate distance. Thus, for Descartes, a person brought up in an environment where only two-dimensional objects were presented on a screen at a fixed distance from its eyes would, on being placed in a normal environment, be immediately able to cognize distances.

Now, it is a strange thing, but histories of the theory of visual perception are written around the nativism/empiricism dispute.[21] Indeed, many of the players in this history—Helmholtz and Hering, for example—characterized their disagreements in these terms. But running across the nativist and empiricist camps is an entirely different set of distinctions, dealing with the role, not of experience, but of processing in cognition—a set of distinctions which no one, so far as I am aware, has noticed or accorded their due. These distinctions are between intuitionism, sensationism, and constructivism.

If you believe that a certain output is already contained in the input to the cognitive system and does not require any process (other than transmission or attention) to become known, then you are what I will call an intuitionist with regard to that output. Aristotle, for example, gives an intuitionist account of color perception in *De Anima*, II, 7. According to this theory, colors exist in objects, and when a transparent medium between the object and the eye is activated by light, the color imposes its form on the medium, which in turn imposes its form on the eye. This account is intuitionist, as I am now using the term, because the color ultimately cognized by the soul is thought to be already contained in the sensory input, and nothing needs to be done to it by the senses or the soul other than to transmit and attend to it.

Of course, one can be an intuitionist without taking sensations to be the intuited items. Those are also intuitionists who have postulated that the fundamental principles of mathematics or logic or metaphysics or ethics are simply received through some extra-sensory mode of awareness, such as Platonic recollection, the Cartesian light of nature, or Reidian suggestion. Accordingly, I will use the label "sensationist" to refer to the position that a given output of the cognitive system is already given in sensation. The alternative position, that the output, though given in the input, is given in some other kind of input than a sensation, I will call non-sensationist intuitionism. (The question of what constitutes a sensation and of how sensations differ—if they differ—from innate ideas is a detail dealt with differently by different sensationist theories; and as my purpose here is classification and not defense, I will pass over it.)

If, in opposition to both sensationism and non-sensationist intuitionism, you believe that a given output is *not* already contained in the input to the cognitive system but needs to be worked up out of that input by some process such as association, inference, comparison, abstraction, combination, or the like, then you are what I will call a constructivist with regard to that output. Locke, for example, was a constructivist about what he called complex ideas, which he took to be assembled by mental acts of combination, comparison, and abstraction performed upon simple ideas.

Berkeley's *New Theory of Vision* is the classic constructivist work on the cognition of visible spatial depth. But Reid, too, was a constructivist on this question: in his view we have to learn how to associate visual appearances with the innate conceptions of Euclidean three-dimensional space suggested to us by our tactile sensations.[22] (For examples of sensationist positions on visual depth perception one must turn to nineteenth-century critics of Berkeley such as Samuel Bailey and William James.)[23] The cases of Berkeley and Reid point to the importance of not confusing intuitionism, sensationism, or constructivism with either nativism or empiricism. A constructivist *could* also be an innate ideas nativist (as was Reid), and of course a constructivist could also be an innate mechanisms nativist (as was Descartes).

The intuitionist/constructivist and nativist/empiricist camps cut across one another in both ways. Not only is there such a thing as constructivist nativism, there is also empiricist intuitionism. All sensationists, for instance, are empiricists. Because they are sensationists, they by definition accept the base condition, and because they take the output of the cognitive system to be already contained in the input, the Molyneux condition does not apply to them. Aristotle, for example, was no less an empiricist for believing that color sensations are directly drawn out of the input to the senses, without having to be subject to processing.

The surprising thing is that one can even be a non-sensationist intuitionist and an empiricist. This might at first seem to entail an absurdity; after all, non-sensationist intuitionism, as I have characterized it, is the position that a certain output of the cognitive system is already given in an input which is not a sensation. But the base condition is just the condition that all input comes from sensory experience. Is there not a direct contradiction here? Not quite. If it could be shown that having sensory experience might involve more than just having sensations, then non-sensationist intuitionism could be consistent with the base condition. Of course, the existence of an extra-sensational element in all sensory experience must be argued for. As a first step, consider the model of an information processing device introduced at the beginning of the section. I originally described the activity of this device in terms of three moments, reception or input of data, processing of data, and output of finished product; but the first moment cannot be described simply as the reception of data because it makes all the difference to the eventual output in what order the data are received. After all 100 is a different number from 001 even though both contain the same bits of data—two "0's" and one "1." The order in which the device receives these bits of data makes all the difference to the output it eventually produces.

In light of this model I suggest that it is at least possible to consider human sensory experience as a compound of (1) various items or bits of information and (2) an order in which these items are received—the

Nativism/Empiricism; Intuitionism/Constructivism
— Conceptual Relations —

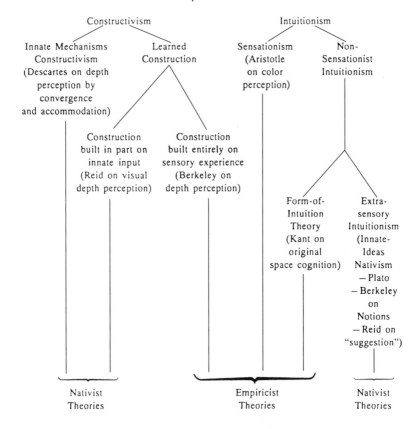

order at least of succession in time and possibly also of disposition in space. If this is so and if we can refer just to (1) as "sensation," then the presence of (2) constitutes the presence of an element over and above sensation in sensory experience. Yet it is far from obvious that this is so. It might be insisted that the spatiotemporal order is either (a) itself given in sensation, or (b) constructed out of sensations (and/ or other innate input), or (c) injected into experience from some extra-sensory source. Indeed, these are the major options traditionally taken on the question of space-cognition—the first by the minor sensationist school of Bailey and James, the second by the dominant constructivist school of Berkeley, Bain, Lötze, Herbart, Helmholtz, Mill, and Wundt, and the third by the nativist school of Reid. But I want to suggest that there is a fourth alternative which has been historically taken on the question of space-cognition. This is the alternative, hitherto ignored by the history of theories of visual perception, that space might be neither a sensation nor a construct nor an innate idea but rather an order in which sensations or sensory stimuli are originally received. This is the alternative which Kant intended to promulgate when he called space a form of intuition.

## The Status of the Forms of Intuition

The previous remarks on theories of space-cognition have shown that there is a deeper and quite different dispute underlying the nativism/empiricism dispute; namely, the sensationism/constructivism dispute. Neither side of this latter dispute reflects Kant's position on space- or time-cognition. The sensationist option can be summarily dismissed. Kant explicitly denied that we have sensations of space and time in the first argument of the Metaphysical Expositions.[24] Nor could he have argued any otherwise. That which corresponds to sensation is the matter of appearance (A20 = B34), so that a space and time given through sensation would be matter and not form.

If we rule out sensation, which it is quite clear we must, then there remain just three cognitive functions which the *Critique* recognizes as possible sources for our cognition of space and time: intuition, synthesis of imagination or what Kant also calls figurative synthesis (B151), and pure intellectual synthesis. There are passages in the Transcendental Deduction where Kant appears to pick imaginative or figurative synthesis as the responsible source. Perhaps the strongest statement of this view is B151–52, where Kant describes imaginative synthesis as being able to "determine sense a priori with respect to its form, in accord with the unity of apperception."

Elsewhere, however, he makes it even clearer that he takes space and time to be given in intuition and not through figurative or any higher mode of intellectual synthesis. The strongest evidence for this reading is that Kant calls space and time forms of *intuition*, not forms of imagination or forms of understanding. Further, he introduces them in the Transcendental Aesthetic, as features of what is given in intuition. He does not introduce them on the Table of Categories or on a special table of the functions of imaginative synthesis. If Kant really believed that space and time are produced by a spontaneous, productive synthesis of imagination, then he ought to have introduced them differently. He also never ought to have said such things as that "the original representation of space is *intuition*" (B40).

Of course, the fact that Kant refers space and time to "intuition" is not sufficient to make him an "intuitionist" in the sense that I have been employing the term. By "intuition" Kant may have meant to refer not to something which is already contained in the input to the cognitive system but to something which is itself constructed by a process— such as figurative synthesis. But this latter reading simply does not square with the text of the *Critique*. Kant is adamant that intuition is *immediate* cognition, and he is adamant that it is not the product of a spontaneous or active process but results from bare receptivity.

> In whatever way and by whatever means a cognition may be related to objects, *intuition* is that whereby it is immediately related to them and that to which all thought is referred as a means. (A19 = B33)
>
> That representation which can be given before all thought is called *intuition*. (B132)
>
> Our cognition springs out of two fundamental sources of the mind, of which the first is [the capacity] to sense representations (the receptivity of impressions), the second the capacity to cognize an object by means of these representations (spontaneity of concepts). (A50 = B74 [Kant immediately goes on to identify what is presented by the first capacity as intuition.])
>
> If we want to call the *receptivity* of our mind ([its capacity] to sense representations so far as it is in some way affected) *sensitivity*, then in contrast the capacity to produce representations, or the *spontaneity* of cognition, is *understanding*. Our nature so brings it about that *intuition* can never be other than *sensory*. (A51 = B75)
>
> All intuitions, as sensory, are based on affections, concepts on functions. I understand by function the unity of the act of ordering different representations under a common one. Concepts are therefore grounded on the spontaneity of thought, as sensory intuitions are on the receptivity to impressions. (A68 = B93)

All but one of these excerpts come from introductory passages in which Kant lays out the basic presuppositions of the arguments which are to follow. Were he, in light of them, to take a constructivist line on space- and time-cognition and hold that spatiotemporal form is created by some process performed upon more primitive given data, then he could not possibly call space and time *intuitions*; they would be products of a synthesis. Nor is constructivism merely inconsistent with Kant's statement that space and time are intuited, for in the latter parts of the Metaphysical Expositions (¶¶3 and 4 for space B, ¶¶4 and 5 for space A and for time) he argues against the contrary alternative, appealing to the essential unity, the mereological structure, and the infinity of space and time in an attempt to prove that, as he puts it at one place, "the original representation of space [and time] is *intuition* . . . and not concept" (B40).

What about passages such as B151–52 where Kant appears to ascribe an essential role to imaginative or figurative synthesis? These passages are not as contrary to Kant's intuitionism as may at first seem. The essential role played by synthesis is that of "combination of the manifold" (B136). It is important to be clear about what this means.

To assemble a jigsaw puzzle is in one sense to combine a manifold in space and time. The many pieces are the manifold and by assembling them you construct a particular set of spatial relations for them. But this is not the only sense of "combination." Consider a child's picture book where the game is to find certain objects cleverly camouflaged in a line drawing—a knife, say, outlined in the bark of a tree, or a train in its leaves. When the child sees the knife or the train there is a sense in which it, too, "combines" the manifold—it takes the various points and lines in the picture and combines them under the concept "knife" or "train" rather than under the concept "tree." Only here the combination of the manifold does not involve actively arranging parts in spatiotemporal relations, as you do when you build a jigsaw puzzle. Instead, the spatiotemporal order of parts is already given in the first glimpse the child has of the line drawing and is preserved unchanged through the process of "combination." The child's task is not to construct the manifold but merely to describe or outline or trace it, but the child is still in a very important sense "combining" the manifold. The child takes the various items presented and brings them to a unity of apperception by thinking or recognizing in this multiplicity an instance of *one* thing—a knife or a train or a tree. This is certainly combination—a combination of many into one—and it is an essential component of cognition. Were the child not to combine in this sense, it would not recognize anything in the manifold and its cognition would be, as Kant puts it at A111, an intuition which, being without thought or knowledge, is for us as good as nothing.[25]

It is this latter sense of "combination," I submit, which is what Kant means by "figurative synthesis." Consider, by way of evidence, B154: "inner sense contains the bare form of intuition" (already!), "but without combination of the manifold in it and consequently without yet containing any *determinate* intuition." Combination does not produce the forms of intuition; it merely outlines the boundaries of a determinate space or time. B137–38 seconds this: "Thus the bare form of outer sensory intuition, space, is not yet any kind of cognition; it only gives the manifold of an a priori intuition to a possible cognition. To cognize something in space . . . I must *draw* it and thereby synthetically bring into being a *determinate* combination of the given manifold." Combination of the manifold and figurative synthesis are essential aspects of Kant's account of space- and time-cognition, but they are processes carried out on input which is already spatiotemporally articulated. Their existence does not make Kant a constructivist. The most we could say is that Kant takes determinate spatial shapes or temporal intervals to be constructed, not that he takes space and time as such to be constructed; but even this says too much. For the sort of process involved in generating a cognition of determinate spaces and times does not involve active sorting or ordering but merely recognizing the unity of boundaries which have been already defined by the way various items are disposed in the intuition.

A qualification is in order, which is that the determinate spaces and times cognized through combination or figurative synthesis may themselves become the input for a higher-level cognitive process. While figurative synthesis merely delineates or describes the manifold, this higher-level process can sort or rearrange the various delineations and descriptions of the manifold. This is what is going on, for instance, in Kant's examples of the house and of the stove-heated room in the Analogies (A190 = B235, A202 = B247–48). While in our subjective experience the parts of a house occur successively and the fire and the heat simultaneously, we think that objectively the parts of the house simultaneously inhere in some substance and the fire precedes the heat in time as its cause. I am far from denying the importance of this higher-level synthesis in Kant's work, but I do want to stress that the objective synthesis described in the Analogies is carried out on a manifold *already* articulated in space and time—the "subjective order" delivered through initial figurative synthesis. While the higher-order, objective manifold may be constructed from parts, like a jigsaw puzzle, figurative synthesis does not construct the primitive manifold, but merely delineates and describes it.

Kant's position makes him an intuitionist, as I have defined intuition-ism. But as noted earlier, his position is also that space and time are not sensations. The only way to reconcile these two claims is to recognize that Kant was a non-sensationist intuitionist on the question of original space- and time-cognition. . . .

For Kant some sort of intuition must deliver a primitive space and time, but what sort? If we reject sensation as the source, where else can we turn to account for an intuition of space and time? One place to turn is to innate ideas. Another, however, is to the notion that space and time are given as the manner in which sensations are disposed or the order in which they are presented in this intuition.

Perhaps the most explicit indication of Kant's adherence to this latter view comes from A20–21 = B35 and A22 = B36. These passages are well known for their statement of what in the literature is referred to as the method of isolation—that were we to take our ordinary human experience and isolate that element in it which is due to sense intuition (or, as Kant also calls it, sensitivity [*Sinnlichkeit*] or empirical intu-ition); and then if we were to isolate everything further in sense intu-ition which arises from sensation, there would still be something left over, namely, space and time as forms of this intuition. Now, there are good reasons for supposing that Kant is not here proposing a workable method for discovering the status of space and time (for one thing, if intuitions are "blind" without concepts, as Kant affirms at A51 = B75, then taking all concepts out of experience would leave us unable to describe what remains). But the isolation passages do at least tell us about the genetic relations Kant conceived space, time, sensation, intu-ition, and concepts to have to one another. They tell us, firstly, that space and time are not originally constructed by synthesis of imagina-tion, if we follow B152 in taking this synthesis to be "an action of under-standing on sensitivity"). They also tell us that we are supposed to be able to remove sensations from this intuition and find that space and time are still left over in it. But this means that the intuition of space and time had to have sensations in it to start with or—which is the same thing—that space and time must have been originally given along with sensations as components of a unitary sense intuition.

There are admittedly places where Kant seems to treat space and time as given in isolation from sensation (for instance, *Prolegomena* §7, Ak. IV: 281). In these places he refers to them as not merely forms of (empirical) intuition but as pure intuitions or formal intuitions, but it is not clear that in these contexts Kant does not intend to refer to a higher-level construct formed by abstracting the spatiotemporal form from empirical intuition and subjecting it to a figurative synthesis yielding an image. On this reading "pure intuition" is a misnomer—we are really dealing with the form abstracted by imagination or understanding *from* empirical intuition, not anything intuited on its own.

Kant has frequently been interpreted as holding that the forms of intuition are not, as I have maintained, manners of disposition or orders of presentation in which sensations are displayed in sense intuition, but rather distinct and separate intuitions in their own right, originating from a unique source. This source is supposed to be the mind itself. Space and time are taken to be innate, preexisting ideas lying a priori in the mind, waiting to be outfitted with sensations. Kemp Smith's whole interpretation of the Transcendental Aesthetic rests on this assumption,[26] but perhaps the major proponent has been Vaihinger. In the section of his *Commentar* devoted to the sentence, "the form of intuition lies ready a priori in the mind" (A20 = B34),[27] Vaihinger rejected the efforts of Riehl, Meyer, Lange, (and, of course, Cohen) to interpret this passage metaphorically and to place a logical rather than a temporal analysis on "lies ready a priori." According to Vaihinger, Kant really meant to say that complete, fully formed representations of infinite space and time exist in the mind prior to all sensory experience; and to cap his argument, Vaihinger cited in excess of fifteen passages from the Aesthetic, the *Prolegomena*, the Analytic, the *On the Progress*, and the *Reflexionen*, which he took to be a clear indication that Kant held this position.

Vaihinger was far from thinking that Kant was right to hold this position or that it was even intelligible. One of the major problems he saw with it was that it turned the correlative apprehension of space and sensation into an impenetrable mystery. Why should I represent one collection of sensations as square, another as triangular; one as oval, another as round? There could be no ground of this in the pure space-intuition because it makes no reference to any sensation, while the sensations themselves are purely qualitative and are only supposed to acquire their order through being placed in space. So why place them "here" rather than "there"? Kant has no answer to give, or so Vaihinger charges.[28]

But it is not at all clear that this problem is legitimately raised against Kant. In an oft-cited passage from his *On a Discovery* of 1790 he rejects the notion that space and time are innate images or containers waiting in the mind to be fitted with sensations: "The *Critique* permits absolutely no implanted or innate *representations*; all whatsoever, whether they belong to intuition or to intellectual concepts, it takes to be *acquired*" (Ak. VIII: 221). In the *Critique* itself Kant denies that sensations originate from a different source than space and that they therefore need to be subsequently assigned to particular locations in space. Assignment is not necessary because when sensations are originally given in sense intuition, they are given as already occurring in a spatial array: "Empirical intuition is . . . not put together out of appearances and space (perception and empty intuition). One is not the correlate of the other in a synthesis; rather they are bound together in one and the same empirical intuition, as matter and form of this intuition" (A429n = B457n).

Vaihinger was not unaware of these passages. His response,[29] one typical for him, was to claim that Kant simply contradicted himself. In his Inaugural Dissertation and in *On a Discovery* Kant is supposed to have propounded a version of innate mechanisms nativism, according to which some "ground" capable of determining a spatiotemporal arrangement of incoming sensations, though not the representations of space and time themselves, is taken to lie a priori in the mind. But in the Transcendental Aesthetic he is supposed to have held an innate-ideas view. Why? Vaihinger's fifteen or more citations, with their bold-face printing of the words "ohne" [without], "vor" [before], "ehe" [earlier than], and "vorher" [before], merely beg the question against Cohen, Riehl, and the others who would read these passages as metaphorical assertions of a purely logical independence, not a genetic distinction. Elsewhere, however, Vaihinger notes that the "spirit" and not just the "wording" of the Transcendental Aesthetic requires that space and time, as forms, be distinct from sensations, as matters, of intuition.[30] Vaihinger simply assumes that *only* a separate genesis can provide for the distinction. Were space and time given in sensory experience, there would supposedly be no ground for distinguishing them from sensations.

Vaihinger's position here is the result of a failure to grasp the difference between the elements of an ordered set and the order in which those elements are placed in the set—a failure which lies at the root of Kemp Smith's approach as well.[31] Both see sensory experience as delivering only sensations, and this leads them to assume that were space and time given in sensory experience, they would have to be sensations. Kant, however, does not see things this way: "[T]hat in which sensations are alone ordered and can be set forth in a certain form, cannot itself in turn be a sensation" (A20 = B34). For Kant sensations, whenever they are exhibited in sensory experience, are always presented in the experience in a certain order. As Kant notes in the passage cited, it would be absurd to take the order of sensations to be itself a sensation; and even a common origin in sensory experience does nothing to diminish this fundamental difference. The fact that sensations are given in an order in sensory intuition does not inhibit our distinguishing what pertains to the sensations from what pertains to their manner of arrangement any more than the fact that the elements of an ordered set are presented to us in their order inhibits us from distinguishing the elements from the order. But if space and time are the orders in which sensations are presented, as Kant argues in the Transcendental Aesthetic, then it follows that space and time, too, must be distinct from sensation—distinct, not because they have a different origin but because they denominate order rather than the ordered elements.

It might be objected that Kant needs to ascribe a distinct, innate origin to space to provide for the necessity and the priority of geometry, but this is not so. There is no contradiction in the possibility of an organism's innate ideas changing over time, so nativism cannot provide any stronger support for Kant's position on the necessity of geometry than can the form of intuition theory. And while nativism does certainly support a position on the priority of our knowledge of geometry, so does taking space to be a form or order in which sensations are presented in intuition. Admittedly, the form of intuition theory does not provide for a cognition of space prior to *some* sensory experience; but according to the form of intuition theory, space is "in" sensory experience only in the sense that it is *given through* having sensations, not in the sense that it is *given in* this or that sensation. Consequently, space can be considered in abstraction from the sensory content intuition contains—we can describe the order in which sensations are fed into the cognitive system without having to remark on what particular sensations happen to be in this order. For this reason our knowledge of space is both "logically prior" to (that is, distinct from) sensation and, in principle, temporally prior to the occurrence of any particular sensation. Thus, propositions describing space, such as the propositions of geometry, can be taken to have validity regardless of what sensations may happen to be presented in space, even though these propositions are synthetic and are ultimately learned only through being given in sensory experience. This even provides for a kind of necessity: geometry is necessary, not in the sense of being immune to falsification by subsequent *intuition* (that is, subsequent experience of the order in which sensations occur), but in the sense that no possible *sensation* or collection of sensations could ever falsify it.

To sum up: supposing that space is originally given in sensory experience as the order or manner of disposition of sensations is not inconsistent with Kant's claim that geometry is a priori. This position is inconsistent with a certain strong reading of what it means for geometry to be necessary, but nativism is no better equipped to provide for this strong sense of necessity, and there are grounds for supposing that Kant intended only a weaker sense. The form of intuition theory preserves Kant's important distinction between space and time on the one hand and sensation on the other. In addition it allows us to absolve Kant of Vaihinger's charge that he contradicts himself in *On a Discovery* and at A429n = B457n, and of the charge that he cannot account for the spatial locations or figures of objects. The form of intuition interpretation, in short, gives a more plausible account of Kant's actual position and intentions than does the innate-ideas interpretation.

### The Sense of Kant's Nativism

The position I have been defending has the surprising consequence that it makes Kant out to be an empiricist on the question of space-cognition, at least by the criteria for empiricism outlined above. For Kant accepts the base condition, that it is sensory experience which delivers the input for the output in question; and since this input already contains space and time prior to any processing, the Molyneux condition does not apply. I call this consequence surprising because Kant claims, in words at least, to be a nativist. I have already noted his claim that the form of intuition "lies a priori in the mind and thereby can be considered apart from all sensation" (A20 = B34). While the adjective "a priori" is easy enough to account for (see above at n. 27), there is still the point about lying "in the mind" to consider. Even more explicit is the continuation of the passage cited earlier from *On a Discovery*.

> The *Critique* permits absolutely no implanted or innate *representations*; all whatsoever, whether they belong to intuition or to intellectual concepts, it takes to be *acquired*. But there is also an original acquisition (as

the teachers of natural right put it), consequently also [an acquisition] of
that which previously did not exist, that is, which did not belong to anything prior to this act [of acquisition]. Such is, as the *Critique* maintains,
*first* the form of things in space and time, *second* the synthetic unity of
the array in concepts. Our cognitive capacity does not take either of these
things from objects, as something given in objects as they are in themselves; rather it brings them into place a priori, out of itself. (Ak. VIII: 221)

This position is familiar from Kant's claim in the B Introduction (B1),
that though all knowledge begins with experience, not all need arise
out of experience—it might be that "even our experiential cognition is
a composite of that which we receive through impressions and that
which our cognitive capacity (merely occasioned by sensory impressions) brings out of itself." However, the claim from *On a Discovery* is
more sophisticated than the Introduction passage, which lends itself to
the reading that space and time are innate images pre-existing in the
mind. *On a Discovery* passage makes clear that space and time are
instead "originally acquired"—acquired, that is, in the way a builder
acquires a house—by working on the given raw materials to create
something which did not exist prior to the act of building. Unfortunately, in offering this qualification Kant appears to be steering his boat
around the Scylla of innate ideas nativism only to have it swallowed by
the Charybdis of innate mechanisms constructivism. For, by putting
the point this way, Kant hints that space and time are originated or
produced by the mind itself out of something which it brings, as he
puts it at the end of the passage cited, "out of itself." The position
appears to be that even if space and time are not themselves innate
ideas, there is at least some mechanism in the mind, in virtue of which
it originates or produces space and time on the occasion of experience;
and this mechanism, at least, is innate. This position is endorsed by the
immediately following sentence in *On a Discovery*: "But there must
certainly be a ground of this in the subject, which makes it possible
that the aforementioned representations appear so and not otherwise,
and can be referred even to objects which have not yet been given, and
this ground at least is *innate*" (Ak. VIII: 221–22).

Kant had pursued this line twenty years prior to *On a Discovery*, in
his Inaugural Dissertation. There he had rejected nativism as a "philosophy of the lazy" which puts a premature end to further research. Instead, he had insisted that each of the concepts of space and time
"without any doubt *has been acquired*, not by abstraction from the

sensing of objects . . ., but from the very action of the mind, an action co-ordinating the mind's sensa according to perpetual laws" (Ak. II: 406).[32]

Just a little further on in the *On a Discovery* passage however, Kant makes an important qualification which entirely repudiates the line taken in the Inaugural Dissertation. The innate ground which determines the appearance of spatiotemporal form is, he tells us, not a mechanism for *producing* spatiotemporal product forms out of sensory experience; it is a ground for *receiving* these forms: "The ground of the possibility of sensory intuition is . . . the mere characteristic *receptivity* of the mind, to acquire a representation according to its subjective constitution when it is affected by something (in sensation). This first formal ground, for example of the possibility of the intuition of space, is alone innate, not the representation of space itself" (Ak. VIII: 222).

The difference here is crucial for understanding Kant's position on the forms of intuition. In the Inaugural Dissertation he made clear that he took spatiotemporal form to be the product of an active process of coordinating or arranging sensations:

> In a representation of sense there is . . . something which can be called the *form*, namely the *specificity* of the sensibles which arises according as the various things which affect the senses are co-ordinated by a certain natural law of the mind. . . . [The form of representation is] only a certain law implanted in the mind by which it co-ordinates for itself the sensa which arise from the presence of the object. For objects do not strike the senses in virtue of their form or specificity. So for the various things in an object which affect the sense to coalesce into some representational whole there is needed an internal principle in the mind by which those various things may be clothed with a certain *specificity* in accordance with stable and innate laws. (Ak. II: 392–93)

The picture depicted in this passage is that which I described earlier as the jigsaw puzzle approach: space and time are constructed by arranging sensations alongside one another, an arrangement carried out in accord with innate principles.

Now it may be surprising, but one never finds, in Kant's post-1780 discussions of the ground of the forms of intuition, any reference to such active sorting or ordering. In *On a Discovery* the ground is "the mere characteristic *receptivity* of the mind, to acquire a representation according to its subjective constitution"; in the *Critique* it is "the formal constitution whereby [the subject] comes to be affected by objects" (B40); in the *Prolegomena* it is "the essential property of our sensitivity, by means of which objects are given to us" (Ak. IV: 287); and perhaps most ominously (for the constructivist view), in *On the Progress* it is simply "the way our senses are affected by objects" (Ak. XX: 269).

The passages from Kant's later works still entail that there is some "ground" of spatiotemporal order existing in the subject prior to all experience. But Kant appears to have retreated from, or at least avoided expressing, the view that the ground consists of a mechanism or a set of principles for the arrangement of incoming sensations. Instead, his position now allows that the ground could figure in a different way. For example, a typewriter receives input when its keys are struck—striking its keys is what brings it to, as it were, "acquire intuitions." But the typewriter's "intuitions" do not exhibit just "matter" (which is different depending on which keys are struck); they also exhibit a certain "form"—the form, namely, of succession in time. Because of the way it is built the typewriter cannot accept simultaneously entered input. When the keys are struck simultaneously it jams (it has an "unintelligible experience"), or it ignores the input. Thus, there is a sense in which the typewriter's constitution determines that the "form of its intuition" will be time alone. But note that this "ground of receptivity" in the typewriter, which determines its "form of intuition," in no way determines the specific temporal locations of the input elements which it receives. That is the prerogative of the typist and not of the machine.

Like the typewriter which is so constituted that it can only receive data successively in time, the human sensory organs carry their own limitations. The eyes, for instance, can receive data simultaneously, but they cannot distinguish data displayed at less than, say, one minute of arc, or include data separated by more than, say, 120 degrees of arc. According to standard theories, the eyes can only distinguish data in two dimensions. But one can grant that the eyes constrain the order in which information is received without granting that they assign the individual locations of the elements in this order. One can grant, for example, that the "constitution" of the eyes dictates that visual space is two-dimensional but hold that the specific locations of the color patches appearing in these two dimensions is determined by the nature of external world objects and that the eyes are purely receptive in this regard.

My point is not that Kant had exactly these sorts of mechanical and physiological cases in mind when he attached the rider about receptivity to his claims in *On a Discovery*, only that you can recognize a subjective ground for the order of intuition without being committed to a jigsaw puzzle account. There are alternatives, not ruled out by Kant, which describe different things a "subjective constitution" might determine. He could be saying no more than that sensations are simply give in a spatiotemporal order and that the subject's constitution dictates certain topological features of the ordering relation—but not the specific locations of the sensations in this order. . . .

These considerations suggest that it is far from obvious that Kant continued to intend a jigsaw puzzle view of space- and time-cognition in his later works. The most conservative account of Kant's position is that he may have taken certain topological features of the spatiotemporal ordering relation, though not the specific locations of elements in this order, to be grounded on the subject's constitution. If so, then Kant is still most accurately classified as an empiricist about space cognition.

There is an element of verbal stipulation to this conclusion. I have simply legislated that the Molyneux condition does not apply in the case of intuitionist theories; and I have referred, in the base condition, to sensory experience as the source of input, rather than just to sensation. The first of these stipulations has an obvious legitimacy—letting the Molyneux condition apply to intuitionist theories would make a nativist not just of Kant but also of, for instance, Condillac. It might be asked, could we not quickly shuffle Kant back into the nativist ranks by tightening up the second stipulation and stating that all the input most come from sensation? We could, but only at the cost of indulging a serious and popular error, which is assuming that the input to the cognitive system can be completely characterized just by the items of data that are fed in. This is an error committed by both sensationists and constructivists who, doubtless because of their obvious common sympathy for sense-datum theories, are in agreement that the original input to experience consists just of sensations. Of all writers on cognition in either the eighteenth or nineteenth centuries, Kant alone appears to have realized that this cannot possibly be the case, that besides the data that are put into the system it makes all the difference in what order the data are put in, and that therefore the order of input, spatial as well as temporal, must be specified along with the input, as an essential further element of the first moment of cognition. As soon as we interpret Kant as a nativist, we slide into thinking of his position as either innate-ideas nativism or innate-mechanisms constructivism and end up losing sight of this unique and profound position.

I have tried to show that Kant takes space and time, as forms of intuition, to be orders in which sensations (or the data that correspond to sensation) are presented in intuition. While I hope I have closed this interpretative issue, the position I have supported opens a host of questions and problems. If space, especially, is a manner of disposition or order of presentation in which matters occur in intuition, then how are we to understand intuition and its relation to understanding? If intuition is physically articulated in space as well as successive in time, does this mean that we must treat it as a physiological event? Or is the order in intuition to be ascribed some other than physical significance? Are the distinct "matters" ordered in space and time in intuition to be thought of as so many distinct consciousnesses which are "combined" in their spatial arrangement in a transcendental unity of apperception? And looking in the other direction, how are we to understand the fact that the spatial locations of sensations are *given* and not constructed? Should we take this as the premise of a sort of mitigated primary quality realism—a realism which does not take the shapes or sizes or directions or dimensions of objects to be directly perceived but which does take their neighborhood structure to reflect the neighborhood structure of stimulus sources in the external world? If this is so, then what are we to say about Kant's position on the unknowability and the non-spatiotemporality of things in themselves?

What ends up being at issue here are some of the most difficult questions of Kant studies: Trendelenburg's charge that Kant has neglected an alternative in failing to consider that space and time might be both orders of things in themselves and forms of intuition, . . . the perennial problem with the existence, nature, and role of affecting objects in Kant, and, of course, the question of the nature of Kant's empirical realism in relation to his transcendental idealism. If what I have said about Kant's position on space- and time-cognition is correct then a new avenue of approach to these questions is opened—an avenue which, I suspect, could show Kant to be much more of a (empirical) realist than has heretofore been supposed.

The main problem with the traditional constructivist and innate-ideas nativist approaches to space- and time-cognition in Kant is not that they invoke processing or innate ideas. As I have shown, Kant's account does appeal to processing (though only for the higher-level

objective representation of space and time) and to our innate constitution (though the role this constitution has to play is not as large as has
often been imagined). These positions are rather to be faulted because
they have obscured the existence of a primitive spatiotemporal order
given in intuition. As a result they have blinded us to the existence of
a unique and profound contribution Kant had to make to the theory of
space-and time-cognition, as well to its deep and disturbing ontological
implications. It is important to recognize what it really means for space
and time to be "forms of intuition" for Kant. Only then can we pierce
through the mist and vapors thrown up by the nativism question and
get a clearer perspective from which to view the questions of realism
and idealism in Kant.

## Notes

1. *An Outline of Philosophy* (London, 1929), 259.
2. "The Facts of Perception," Russell Kahl (ed.), *Selected Writings of Hermann von Helmholtz* (Middletown, Conn., 1971), 373.
3. "Discovering the Forms of Intuition," *The Philosophical Review* 96
(1987), 206. For others see note 26 below.
4. B41. References to Kant's *Critique of Pure Reason* are to the pagination
of the first and second original editions (Leipzig, 1781 and 1787), cited as "A"
and "B" respectively. References to his other works are to the pagination of
the Prussian Academy edition (22 vols.; Berlin, 1900–42), cited as "Ak." All
translations from Kant's German are my own.
5. Charles Adam and Paul Tannery (eds.), *Oeuvres de Descartes* (11 vols.;
Paris, 1974–83), VIIIB, 358–59. John Cottingham, Robert Stoothoff, and Dugald
Murdoch (eds.), *The Philosophical Writings of Descartes* (2 vols.; Cambridge,
1984–85), I, 304. The Adam and Tannery edition of Descartes's writings will
hereafter be cited as "AT," the Cottingham, Stoothoff, and Murdoch edition as
"CSM."
6. *Phaedo* 73a–75e.
7. *New Essays on Human Understanding*, tr. Peter Remnant and Jonathan
Bennett (Cambridge, 1981), 50.
8. Sir William Hamilton (ed.), *The Works of Thomas Reid*, 8th ed. (2 vols.;
Edinburgh, 1880), I, 110–11. (*Inquiry*, ch. 2, sec. vii.)
9. *De Anima* III, 8, 432a5–10.
10. *An Essay Concerning Human Understanding*, Book II, ch. i, §2.
11. *A Treatise of Human Nature*, Book I, Pt. i, §1.
12. *A Treatise Concerning the Principles of Human Knowledge*, Part I, §89.
13. Locke, *Essay*, II, ix, 8.
14. *Works*, I, 140–41 (*Inquiry*, ch. 6, sec. vi).
15. *Works*, I, 121–25 (*Inquiry*, ch. 5, secs. iii–v).

16. *Works*, I, 144–46 (*Inquiry*, ch. 6, sec. viii).

17. *Works*, I, 146–52 (*Inquiry*, ch. 6, secs. viii–ix).

18. *Works*, I, 188–93 (*Inquiry*, ch. 6, sec. xxii).

19. AT, VI, 137–40 (CSM, I, 170–71).

20. AT, VI, 137 (CSM, I, 170).

21. See Nicholas Pastore, *Selective History of the Theories of Visual Perception: 1650–1950* (New York, 1971), which is written around this distinction.

22. *Works*, I, 188–93 (*Inquiry*, ch. 6, sec. xxii).

23. Samuel Bailey, *A review of Berkeley's Theory of vision, designed to show the unsoundness of that celebrated speculation* (London, 1842); William James, *The Principles of Psychology*, vol. II (New York, 1890), ch. XX, esp. 270–82.

24. A23–24 = B37, A30 = B46.

25. See also A253 = B209.

26. Norman Kemp Smith, *A Commentary to Kant's "Critique of Pure Reason"* (2nd ed., London, 1923), 88–94.

27. Hans Vaihinger, *Commentar zu Kants Kritik der reinen Vernunft*, vol. 2 (Stuttgart, 1892), 80–88.

28. Vaihinger, vol. 2, 180.

29. Vaihinger, vol. 2, 85, 94–98.

30. Vaihinger, vol. 2, 84.

31. Kemp Smith, 86–88.

32. The translation is that of G. B. Kerferd in *Kant: Selected Pre-Critical Writings*, trs. G. B. Kerferd and D. E. Walford (Manchester, 1968).

# 3

# Infinity and Kant's Conception of the "Possibility of Experience"

*Charles Parsons*

In this paper I intend to discuss Kant's theory that space is the "form" of our "outer intuition." This theory is intended, among other things, to explain what Kant took to be a fact, namely that we have synthetic *a priori* knowledge of certain basic properties of space and of the objects in space. In particular, Kant thought we knew *a priori* that space is in some respects infinite, for example infinitely divisible.

I shall not challenge Kant's claim that we have such synthetic *a priori* knowledge, but I shall attempt to show that Kant's theory of space must be taken in such a way that it does not explain this putative knowledge. For the intent of the whole of Kant's epistemology is to prove that our synthetic knowledge is limited to objects of "possible experience. Now when we try to give the notion of "possible experience" a concrete intuitive meaning, we shall find that the limits of possible experience must be narrower than what, according to Kant, is the extent of our geometrical knowledge of space.

The alternative to so limiting the possibility of experience is to define it by what, on mathematical grounds, we take to be the form of our intuition. But then the content of mathematics is not determined by any concrete knowledge of the form of intuition and the limits of possible experience associated with it. In this setting, the notion of "form of intuition" loses much of its force, and as an explanation becomes *ad hoc*.

The difficulty seems to me deeper than that which gives rise to the most common objections to Kant's theory of space. These rest on a comparatively accidental feature of Kant's view, namely his belief that we can know *a priori* that space is Euclidean. It is then pointed out that there is no sufficient reason for believing this, and that there are physical reasons for preferring a theory in which space (more strictly, space-time) is not Euclidean. The Kantian might simply concede this point and reply that the form of our outer intuition might indeed not determine the answer to such a question as whether the parallel postulate is true, but it does determine more primitive properties of space, so that these can be known *a priori*. The infinite divisibility in particular is, so far as I know, not denied in any serious application of geometry to physics. The claim that we know properties of this order *a priori* is not absurd even in the contemporary context—and indeed I am not denying it, but only the adequacy of the Kantian explanation of it, if it is the case.

In order to carry our discussion further, we must say something by way of elucidation of the terms which Kant uses, and which we have used to state our problem. Our elucidation will not be completely thorough and satisfactory; to give such elucidation would be a larger and more difficult undertaking than the present paper, and there are probably some irresolvable obscurities. I hope, however, that my elucidation will be sufficient to make my own argument clear.

We shall begin with the notion of "form of intuition." According to Kant, intuitions, like anything "in the mind," are representations. A vital feature of representations is that they have what, after Brentano, is called intentionality. That is, they at least purport to refer to an object; moreover, they have a certain content which they represent as in some way belonging to the object. Kant defines intuition as a species of representation which is distinguished by being in immediate relation to objects, and by being in relation to, purporting to refer to, individual objects (A 19, B33; lectures on logic §1[1]). The implications of the word "immediate" will be considered below. Kant assumes that our faculty of intuition is *sensible*: that is, we have intuitions only as a result of being *affected* by objects. The primary instance of this is *sense perception*—seeing, hearing, and so forth.

Our intuitions have certain characteristics which belong to them by virtue of the nature of our capacity to be affected by objects, rather than by virtue of some characteristics of the specific occasions of affection which give rise to them. These characteristics are said to be the form of our intuition in general. Since spatiotemporality is among them, space and time are spoken of as *forms of intuition*.

This must be understood to mean that the nature of the mind determines that the objects we intuit should be spatial, and indeed intuited as spatial. Outer intuitions represent objects *as* in space. "By means of outer sense, a property of our mind, we represent to ourselves objects as outside us, and all without exception in space" (A 22, B 37). That its objects are in space is perhaps the definition of "outer" intuition, so that space is the form of outer intuition. Since inner intuition is characterized as of "ourselves and our inner state" (A 33, B 49), outer intuition is also distinguished by representing its objects as in some way outside our minds.

It might be remarked that from the fact "we represent to ourselves objects as . . . in space" it does not immediately follow that this is not an illusion. Since Kant characterizes phenomenal objects as "things to be met with in space," what the claim of non-illusoriness amounts to is that phenomenal objects really exist, such that perception puts us into immediate relation to them. That this is so is the claim of the Refutation of Idealism, which in turn (in the second edition at least) rests on the Transcendental Deduction.

Kant also supposed that space has certain mathematical properties which are reflected as properties and relations of the objects in space. It is of course the fact that they describe the *form* of our intuition which makes mathematical propositions *a priori*. Kant, of course, supposed that we know *a priori* that space is Euclidean. This means, in particular, that it is both infinite in extent and infinitely divisible. It is this which is the source of the difficulties which we shall develop.

A final preliminary remark concerns the concept of "possible experience." A main purpose of the *Critique* is to deduce the principles which describe the general nature of the objects given in experience by showing that they describe "necessary conditions of the possibility of experience." It follows, however, that these principles apply only to objects of possible experience. "The conditions of the *possibility of experience* in general are at the same time conditions of the *possibility of the objects of experience*, and . . . for this reason they have objective validity in a synthetic a priori judgment" (A 158, B 197).

If this analysis is to yield its result, the limitation of our knowledge to objects of possible experience must mean more than that the objects should be such as might present themselves in some way or other in a possible experience. For Kant allowed the possibility that the objects of experience should have an existence in themselves, apart from their relation to us in our perception and even apart from the general conditions of this relation. But of this we can know nothing; everything about the object which we can know must be able to show itself in experience and must therefore be limited by the general conditions of possible experience. We shall see that applying this dictum to the infinite properties of space produces difficulties for Kant.

## The "Antinomy" of Intuition

It follows from the fact that the empirical objects of perception are in an infinitely divisible space that they are *indefinitely complex*. For the spatial region which an object occupies can be divided into subregions, which again can be so divided, and so on. This is not to say that the object can be physically separated into parts indefinitely, although Kant does refer to what occupies a subregion of the region occupied by an object as a "part" of the object. Given two disjoint subregions of the region occupied by the object, the "parts" of the object occupying these subregions are distinguishable. One could know a great deal about the state of one "part" while knowing little or nothing about the state of the other.

We shall now develop some apparent implications of the definition of intuition as immediate representation, in such a way as to lead to an absurd conclusion. From the view that space is the form of our outer intuition, it seems to follow that the objects we perceive are represented in intuition as having the structure which objects in space have. Then it seems that they are perceived to be indefinitely complex. Indeed, Kant speaks constantly of a *manifold* of intuition, and says that every intuition contains a manifold.

We shall now take an extreme interpretation of this, and make the following argument. In intuition we have an immediate representation of a spatial extension. Such an extension contains subregions. It follows that we have an immediate representation of these subregions. Consider a particular one, say, one whose surface area is no more than half that of the original one. It follows that if we have an intuition of a region of surface area $x$, we have at the same time an intuition of a region of surface area $\leq \frac{1}{2} x$. By iterating this argument, we can show that we have an intuition of a region of surface area $\leq \frac{x}{2^n}$ for each $n$. In other words, we have *at the same time* intuitions of all the members of an infinite sequence of regions converging on a point. We must suppose that this is something Kant is denying when he says, in the solution to the Second Antinomy, "For although all parts are contained in the intuition of the whole, the *whole division* is not so contained, but consists only in the continuous decomposition" (A 524, B 552). But we do not have an interpretation of what it means for the parts to be "contained in the intuition of the whole."

We shall now make another deliberate misinterpretation of Kant. Kant also says that we can perceive the manifoldness of something given in intuition only by picking out its parts or aspects one by one:

> Every intuition contains in itself a manifold which can be represented as a manifold only in so far as the mind distinguishes the time in the sequence of one impression upon another; for each representation, *in so far as it is contained in a single moment*, can never be anything but absolute unity. [A 99]

Now what is suggested by the last part of this sentence is that what "representing as a manifold" means is apprehending a succession of simple parts one by one at different times. Then by the Threefold Synthesis which it is the purpose of the whole passage (A 97–104) to describe, the mind will impose certain relations on these simple entities so that the system of objects thus related will be a spatial whole. Some such interpretation as this is suggested by a number of statements by Kant to the effect that apprehension of a manifold is a successive act. "We cannot think a line without drawing it in thought" (B 154). It is hard to see what the simple entities might be in cases like this if not the points of the line. But then a "single moment" in the above passage would have to be an instant. Absurdities follow immediately. First, it contradicts Kant's repeated statements that the parts of space are not points but spaces, and that the successive synthesis in the apprehension of a space is a synthesis of these parts. Moreover, it is hard to see how the doctrine could be carried over to a two- or three-dimensional space. Of course the points of such a space can be placed in one-to-one correspondence with the instants of time in a time interval. But it would be fantastic to suppose that in thinking of, say, a square, we run through its points in the order deriving from such a correspondence. Indeed, since there is a one-to-one correspondence between the points of the whole of infinite space and the instants of a finite interval of time, it is hard to see why we should not be able to run through *it* in a finite time, contrary to the position of the First Antinomy. . . .

## Solution of the "Antinomy"

We have considered two interpretations which resemble the antithesis
and the thesis of the Second Antinomy. The first was a naïve reading
of the doctrine that space is a form of sensible intuition, the second a
naïve reading of Kant's view that perception presupposes a synthesis. I
think that neither of them is plausible either in itself or as an interpretation of Kant. Mentioning them ought to make clear that it is not so
obvious what is meant by saying that space is a form of sensible intuition. The measures we take to reconcile the two tendencies expressed
by the two sides of our antinomy will reveal the difficulties I mentioned
at the beginning.

In order to interpret the passage from the synthesis of apprehension,
we have to make a distinction which Kant does not explicitly make and
which has some consequences which I am not sure that Kant would
have accepted.

The most likely interpretation of the passage is that the manifoldness
of an intuition can be apprehended *explicitly* only by going over the
details one by one, in such a way that the times at which the different
details are taken in are distinguished from one another. Although Kant
may not be disputing that we can *in some sense* take in at least a limited
complexity at a glance, it still appears that Kant is claiming something
false. For in such cases as the perception of at least short written words,
it seems that our perception of what the letters are can hardly be made
more explicit by going over them one by one. The same is true of the
divisions of a region of space provided that they are marked and the
number of them is sufficiently small.

This, however, allows us to save something of Kant's point. The
amount of complexity and division which we thus take in is finite and
in fact has an upper limit, even if this limit is indeterminate. We can
take in the letters of a four-letter word at a glance, but not the letters
of a printed page. If we consider a ten-letter word, we might find that
some could, some could not, and others would not be sure whether to
call what they did "taking the word in at a glance."

More generally, we observe that those details or parts of something
which we perceive which we can apprehend are themselves given in
perception, and therefore have the same indefinite complexity which
the whole has. But this complexity is not as explicit to us as what we
might call the "first-order" complexity. If it were in general, the antithesis of the above "antinomy" would follow, that is that *all* the complexity of the object is given to us at once. On Kant's grounds, this would

imply the decidability of any mathematical question about the continuum, and in general it would imply that our senses are infinitely acute. It is not really possible to imagine what the world would be like if this were the case. A number of examples will show that it is not. Many of us can improve our perception of detail by putting on glasses, and it is likely that some (for example, Ted Williams) see better than we do even then. Our ability to perceive details decreases continuously with an increase in distance, from which it follows that it was not unlimited at optimum distance. The problems about submicroscopic entities arise because our senses cannot take in anything which occupies less than a certain amount of space.

It seems that Kant is not asserting that in momentary perception the complexity beyond what we take in explicitly (on his view *all* the complexity) is not given to us at all. Indeed, it is hard to see what this would mean. We could hardly say that the letters of a word which we look at look simple and undifferentiated. We might take the perception to be of an aggregate of "sense data" which are themselves simple, but then it could be only by virtue of external relations that they could be appearances of objects which are themselves complex (for example, the letters). This is simply the thesis of our antinomy.

The complexity which is given in a nonexplicit fashion can be perceived explicitly by taking a closer look directed specifically at some aspect of it. This seems to be what Kant calls, in the section on the synthesis of apprehension, running through the manifold.

We claim to have shown that the distinction between explicit and implicit givenness is necessary in order to save the doctrine of continuous space as a form of outer intuition from a contradiction with the fact of the limited acuteness of our senses, as is presented in the "antinomy" above sketched. In fact, the distinction is that which is made in Gestalt psychology between "figure" and "ground." The data of the senses at any given time are divided into that toward which the attention is primarily directed, called "figure," and that to which it is not, called "ground." In the simplest case of looking at a physical object the latter includes the "background." The figure appears more clearly and definitely. What needs to be noted is that within the spatial boundary of the figure, many aspects of the object appear as ground—subtle differentiations of its color, irregularities of its shape, all but a few of its spatial divisions. There is here, however, no definite line between appearing as ground and not appearing at all.

In the appearance of objects to us we can thus distinguish three levels: primary complexity or figure, which appears explicitly; secondary complexity or ground, which appears in a nonexplicit way which is difficult to describe; and tertiary complexity, which does not appear at all but which might appear in some other perception of the same object.

## Relation to Kant's Actual Views

That Kant was not fully in possession of this distinction can, I think, be shown by analysis of the Threefold Synthesis and the Mathematical Antinomies.

In the Threefold Synthesis Kant argues that an intuition containing a manifold can be represented as manifold only by attending to its different aspects individually at different times (running through) and yet keeping them in mind as aspects of *one* intuition (holding together). This, however, presupposes a *reproduction* of the previous elements of the series and their *recognition* as "the same as what we thought a moment before" (A 103). In terms of the analysis I have given, there seems in the description of the threefold synthesis to be a striking omission: what is given *explicitly* to closer attention must be identified as what was given *implicitly* at an earlier stage of perception.

In the Second Antinomy, Kant speaks in what seems to me a not at all clear way about an object as a "spatial whole given in intuition" in such a way as to insure that a division of it (in the conceptual sense mentioned above) can continue without end. He is not clear as to why he asserts this and yet denies that "it is made up of infinitely many parts," on the grounds that "although all parts are contained in the whole, *the whole division* is not so contained" (A 524, B 552).

If Kant saw the matter clearly in the way we suggest, then he might very well not have made the distinction he makes between the solution of the First Antinomy and the solution of the Second. In the case of the Second, his solution might be taken to mean that if a part is given implicitly, and appears explicitly in a later perception, then this perception is of the same type as the preceding, so that the process can be repeated. There seems, however, to be no reason not to make the symmetrical assumption at least with respect to the infinity of the world in space. For the figure in our perceptual field is surrounded by ground. It is just as natural to assume that for any given direction, some element of the ground immediately in that direction can be made figure by a shift of attention, with a result of the same type as the previous perception, so that the result can always be repeated. This would mean that there would always be something outside any spatial region which we clearly perceived.

There is still a difference, but it is not the one in the text between an infinite regress, where we know at the outset that at every point we shall be able to find some further term, and an indefinite regress, where we can never know that we shall *not* be able to continue, but need not know that we always *can*. The difference is that the regions in the outward progression may be of objective size decreasing fast enough so that they can all be included in one bounded region. I am not quite convinced that this can be true while in the case of the division the objective size of the parts *must* tend to zero. It seems that in either case we might have some liberty in devising the measuring system so that the objective size of the whole does or does not become infinite in the first case, or so that the objective size of the parts does or does not tend to zero in the second.

## Intuition and Infinity

We can now return to the question we raised at the beginning, of the sense in which space and its properties are conditions of the possibility of experience, and in which the objects in space are objects of possible experience. Let us consider the assumption that justifies the continuation at every stage of the regress of the Mathematical Antinomies. This assumption is that whatever appears to us as ground can become figure, in such a way that it will have the same structural properties as the figure of the previous perception. We shall call this the Continuability Principle.

The expression "structural properties" is somewhat vague. By using it we require that the new figure should have a nonnull spatial extension (area) and that the new perception should have primary, secondary, and tertiary complexity. Of course, some of what belonged to the tertiary complexity will now be secondary.

That the objects in arbitrarily small or arbitrarily distant regions of space will be objects of possible perception, and therefore of possible experience, follows from iterated application of the Continuability Principle. The question arises what sort of possibility is in question. I shall argue that it cannot be practical possibility, and that it must be a sort of possibility which implies some circularity in Kant's explanations.

There are a number of circumstances which might prevent us from following out a part of the ground and making it figure. The object might change or be destroyed; *we* might die or be unable to make some necessary motion; we might have reached the limit of the acuteness of our senses.

The problem of change in the object is very complicated. In order to make a transition from ground to figure, it seems there must be some element of stability. For example, one could not look more closely at some part of a surface, and see clearly what one previously saw less clearly, if the surface changed in some wild way. How *much* continuity there has to be, however, depends on what one wants. In particular, I do not believe change gives rise on the macroscopic level to difficulties in principle about identifying subregions of the region occupied by the previous figure, or in identifying regions just outside it.

The limit of the acuteness of our senses seems to me more serious. Something which is too small or too distant cannot be seen as clearly as the things we see in everyday life. For this reason it is doubtful that the Continuability Principle applies in the sense of practical possibility to things which are so small or so distant that they appear as "dots." The range of application can be greatly extended with the aid of optical devices. But even with this latitude, physics would place a certain definite limit on our microscopic perception.[2]

In the case of great distance, we have to bring in the third limitation, that something might happen to *us*. In view of the fact that, according to present-day physics, our speed of motion must be less than that of light, if the object is very distant it will be a very long time before we can get close enough to it to see it much more clearly. But biology (or, perhaps, common sense) sets a definite limit on the amount of time we shall have to get there. If the question is not what one individual can perceive but what the species can perceive, then it seems that the second law of thermodynamics places an upper limit on the longevity of the species.

There is reason to believe, therefore, that (speaking vaguely) every aspect of our perceptual powers is limited in a definite way by natural conditions. We could call a being of which this is true a *thoroughly finite* being. For such a being, there is an $n$ such that he can have no perception of what is within any sphere of radius $1/n$, or outside a certain fixed sphere of radius $n$. I believe that in this statement we can replace "perception" by "empirical knowledge," if we limit empirical knowledge to what can be inferred from observations by induction. For by these means, we could not verify that the laws by which we might extrapolate to very distant or very small regions would not fail at these magnitudes.

Thus it appears that the "possibility of experience" for Kant must extend beyond what is practically possible for the sort of being we have reason to think we are. It would be possible to describe the perceptual powers of a being for whom the Continuability Principle would be true, but who would still be finite, in the sense that he would not need to have infinitely acute senses, or be immortal, or be able to perform infinitely many acts in a finite time, or anything similar. Such a creature (call him *U*) would be more bizarre than appears at first sight; for example, he would have to be able to increase the acuteness of his senses beyond any limit. The difficulty for Kant, however, is not so much one of forming an abstract conception of such a being, but of explaining how it can be that the *form of our sensibility* leads us to represent "appearances" as having the structure and relations which *U*'s experience would reveal them to have. In the case of the Continuability Principle, this does not seem so unnatural, but if it is spelled out it seems unavoidably dogmatic: namely, the structure of ordinary macroscopic perception, in which the figure appears with its internal and external ground, is certainly compatible with the notion that the ground appears as something which "can become figure" in a sense in which this "possibility" is in some sense an aspect of the intuition and not, for example, something which would have to be inferred from general rules. Kant must, however, suppose that "intuition" must represent its objects as having the structure which is revealed in this most favorable situation, even those which are in fact presented only on the margins of our sense experience. As an extrapolation, this is quite natural. But when it is carried to infinity, far beyond the actual limits of our experience, it is not so clear that it is the only possible one. Even if it is, however, it is also not clear why it is to be regarded as a form in which objects must be "given" rather than as an imaginative or intellectual construction. Perhaps Kant came close to saying that it *was* imaginative. The reason he did not regard it as intellectual seems to be that he thought that, apart from something nonconceptual, there was no source of any representation of infinity. That only the form of intuition can allow us to represent indefinite continuation in space seems to me to be the sense of the following dark saying: "If there were no limitlessness in the progression of intuitions, no concept of relations could yield a principle of their infinitude" (A 25).

The upshot of all this is that the "possibility of experience" must be a quite abstract kind of possibility, defined by the form of intuition. It is interesting to consider how it is related to contrary-to-fact possibility. If "object of possible experience" means "object of possible perception," then there must be objects which I *might have* perceived but did not. This is obvious without our earlier argument, if we bring in time and change. Since one cannot be in two places at once, everything about the state of the world *now* which I cannot perceive from my present vantage point must, on our assumption, be something I might have perceived but did not.

There is, however, an important difference between this sort of case and those of very distant and submicroscopic regions of space. Consider these three cases:

(1) I might have seen the Red Sox play yesterday if . . .
(2) I might have seen the explosion (on a planet $10^{10}$ light years away) if . . .
(3) I might have seen (something happening in a certain region of diameter $10^{-100}$ cm.) if . . .

In (1) what might fill the blank would be something which could easily have been the case; for example, if the idea had occurred to me, if I had felt like it, if I had not had to see my tutees, and so forth. What would fill the blank in (2) would be something which could be the case only if my origin and that of the whole human race were quite different from what I take it to be, transposed to a quite different part of the universe. What would fill the blank in (3) would be something which could be the case only if our units of measure, and therefore we ourselves, were of a totally different order of magnitude in relation to such physical quantities as the size of atoms and electrons and the wave length of light. It is not clear that we could even describe the circumstances which, if they obtained, would be such that we could identify some spatial region of diameter $10^{-100}$ cm., let alone find out what is going on in it.

In any case, the possibilities (2) and (3) are of such a sort as Kant would have regarded as idle and unverifiable, for a reason which makes it difficult for him to make any use of contrary-to-fact possibility. That reason is the view expressed in the Postulates of Empirical Thought (A

230–232, B 282–285) that we cannot know that there is more than one possible experience, and that all our empirical knowledge must be brought under the unity of a single experience. For this reason, he asserts that we cannot know that there is anything really possible which is not actual.

It ought to be remarked that the extension of the possibility of perception to infinity depends on the *iterated* application of the Continuability Principle. Even with the assurance that the Continuability Principle is true, we should not obtain the indefinite complexity of objects and the infinity and infinite divisibility of space without this iteration; we should not be able to deduce them without mathematical induction. It appears that, for Kant, mathematical induction is in some way founded on the form of our intuition, but Kant gives no explicit statements to make clear how. I do not see that the case is much better with the modern Kantians in mathematics (for example, Brouwer and Hilbert).

## Conclusion

Kant's theory that space is a form of intuition has two conflicting pulls. On the one hand, it implies that the objects of outer intuition have certain characteristics, in particular that of being in some form of mathematical space. But in order to be an explanation of this fact, and in view of the fact that intuition is representation, nothing ought to be attributed to the form of intuition which is not revealed in the way objects present themselves to us in perception.

The first pull leads Kant to assume an aspect of the form of our intuition, namely the potential infinity of certain kinds of series of perceptions, which is beyond our actual powers of perception. He must hold that we represent objects as being in a space and time having parts which are beyond the experience of a thoroughly finite being, and that this arises from the form of our sensibility. But this cannot be justified phenomenologically. I should like to say that in this situation the term "form of sensibility" has no explanatory force. I am inclined to think that we cannot be justified in saying that our having a concept of the infinite is explained by the fact that the form of our sensibility contains the possibility of indefinite continuation and division.

Thus, if he is to maintain the view that the form of intuition is the *ratio essendi* of the mathematical infinite—in particular the infinite divisibility of space—Kant must take the uncomfortable position of say-ing that mathematical considerations are the *ratio cognoscendi* of the form of intuition, which in turn defines the possibility of experience. The content of mathematics is thus not determined by concrete knowl-edge of the form of intuition and the limits of possible experience asso-ciated with it. In addition to the difficulty about explanation, there are two further limitations of this position. First, it is hard to see how on this basis the notion of form of intuition can be used for critical pur-poses, to determine the boundaries of mathematical evidence. Second, this position has for the argument of the *Critique of Pure Reason* as a whole the implication that at some point the "synthetic" method which it purports to follow, of arguing directly from the nature of expe-rience to the conclusions of transcendental philosophy, must be sup-plemented by the "analytic" method of the *Prolegomena*, of starting with the given content of science and arguing hypothetically to its *a priori* conditions, a method which Kant regarded as acceptable only as an expository device in a semi-popular work. (See *Prolegomena*, §§4–5.)

The situation we have described provides some explanation and jus-tification of Heidegger's claim that Kant took the finiteness of our un-derstanding more seriously than did his predecessors, but even he did not follow this through to the end. One reason he did not is that he also took seriously the fact that mathematics requires that there be some source in our cognitive apparatus for some sort of representation of infinity. And as he said, the possibility of mathematics is proved by the fact that it exists. But he did not fully succeed in reconciling this so often cited support of rationalism with the empiricism implicit in restricting the content of our knowledge to "possible experience."

## Notes

1. I.e., *Critique of Pure Reason*, A19; B33. With a few minor modifications, all quotations will be from Kemp Smith's translation (2d ed., London, 1933).

2. In the case of the most powerful devices, a great deal of physical theory intervenes between our perception and our interpretation of it as of a certain very small object. And it is not clear that this interpretation will be true more than schematically; it may be that, as with a photograph, the fine structure of what we see no longer belongs to the object.

# 4

# Kant's Cognitive Self

*Patricia Kitcher*

## I. Introduction

Kant's work on the self has had little impact on contemporary discussions. The problem with Kant's views about the self is that he had too many of them, because the self had too many roles to play in his system. I hope to reveal and explicate just one important theory of the self that underlies both the "subjective" half of the Transcendental Deduction and his important claims about the limitations on self-knowledge in the Paralogisms chapter. The publication of a German translation of James Beattie's *Essay on the Nature and Immutability of Truth*[1] made available to Kant central passages from Hume's infamous discussion of personal identity. I believe that the theory of the self I ascribe to Kant developed partly in response to Hume's problem. Reading the so-called "Subjective Deduction" as concerned with an account of the self in response to Hume casts new light on a number of otherwise perplexing passages. It also reveals Kant as providing an effective reply to Hume's attack on the idea of personal identity. Since the Subjective Deduction's theory of the self is presupposed in the "Paralogisms of Pure Reason," with this theory in hand, it is also a relatively easy matter to disentangle the otherwise opaque argumentation of the Paralogisms chapter. More importantly, I think that this approach leads to a plausible Kantian theory of the self as a continuing cognitive being that can complement theories that have tried to account for our continuity as moral beings.

My approach faces an obvious objection. Hume's name does not appear in any of the passages in which I will claim Kant is grappling with

Hume's skepticism about the self; indeed, Hume's views about personal identity receive no mention in the *Critique*. Why, then, is it reasonable to look at some of Kant's discussions of self-identity in this light? The principal reason is the one already given: by using this handle we can make sense of many of Kant's remarks about the self and the "transcendental unity of apperception" that are unintelligible on other interpretations. This point requires the rest of the paper for defense. In the meantime I will try to increase the initial plausibility of my approach by offering some historical considerations.

When engaged in substantive discussion of an issue, Kant often fails to mention his opponents by name: Leibniz is not mentioned in the Paralogisms chapter or in the Aesthetic's discussion of space and time; none of Kant's discussions of space or time refers to Newton; Berkeley's name does not appear in the first edition's treatment of dogmatic idealism; the Second Analogy section contains no reference to Hume; and perhaps most surprisingly, in the first edition, Kant's concern about causation is not linked to Hume at all until the "Discipline of Pure Reason," five hundred and fifty pages after his celebrated "reply to Hume" in the Second Analogy. In light of these cases Kant's failure to mention Hume in discussions of the self can hardly be regarded as decisive.

What are the positive reasons for supposing that Hume's views about personal identity enjoyed Kant's attention? I think there is no question that Kant knew about Hume's skepticism concerning personal identity. Besides Beattie's generous citations, Hume's views were described by the psychologist Johann Tetens in his *Philosophical Investigations concerning Human Nature and its Development*,[2] a book Kant knew well. Tetens' discussion suggests that his audience was familiar with Hume's denial of personal identity and with the criticisms of Reid and Beattie. Thus at the time Kant was writing the *Critique*, Hume's views on personal identity were known and regarded as false but as worthy of philosophical refutation.

Beyond the contemporary interest in the project, Kant should have had his own reasons for tackling Hume's skepticism about personal identity. Kant appreciated the insights behind Hume's skeptical conclusions and thought he could learn from them. Moreover, the theory of personal identity is a fairly straightforward consequence of Hume's denial of the causal relation, a topic that certainly interested Kant. Finally, Hume's theory presents an intellectual challenge because it is both obviously false and very difficult to refute. Given these considerations, if

Kant did not feel motivated to take on Hume's skepticism about personal identity, I do not understand the lapse. Before we can consider a possible Kantian reply to Hume, we must look more closely at the challenge Hume poses.

## II. Hume's Problem

Beattie's *Essay on Truth* provided Kant with the following excerpts from Hume's attack on the idea of personal identity:

> The question concerning the substance of the soul is unintelligible. . . . What we call a *mind* is nothing but a heap or collection of different perceptions (or objects) united together by certain relations and supposed, though falsely, to be endowed with perfect simplicity and identity. . . . If anyone, upon serious and unprejudiced reflection, thinks he has a different notion of himself, I must confess I can reason with him no longer. All I can allow him is, that he may be in the right as well as I, and that we are essentially different in this particular. He may perhaps perceive something simple and continued, which he calls *himself;* though I am certain there is no such principle in me. But setting aside some metaphysicians of this kind, I may venture to affirm of the rest of mankind, that they are nothing but a bundle or collection of different perceptions, which succeed each other with inconceivable rapidity, and are in a perpetual flux and movement. . . . There is properly no simplicity in the mind at one time, nor identity in different (times), whatever natural propension we may have to imagine that simplicity and identity. . . . They are successive perceptions only that constitute the mind.[3]

Some aspects of Hume's reflections about the self (or mind) are not mentioned by Beattie: the causal theory of mind (T, 261) and Hume's celebrated dissatisfaction with his account of personal identity (T, 633 ff.). However, these excerpts do contain three central and distinctive theses about the self, two in direct opposition to the Cartesian view. By Hume's lights there is no reason to believe that there is an entity in one that thinks, and so no reason whatsoever to believe that there is a simple thinking self.

Like Kant, Hume accepts Locke's analogy between sensory perception and a faculty of "inner sense" through which we "perceive" the contents of our minds. Although Locke's characterization of our ability to monitor and report mental states is misleading, Hume was not mis-

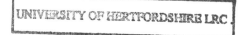

led by it on this point. Whatever he might have expected inner sense to present him with, he realized that his ability to monitor his own states did not enable him to perceive a thinking self. Hume's concession that another "may perhaps perceive something simple and continued, which he calls *himself*" is obviously meant to be ironic. If inner sense does not enable us to perceive a self at all, then it cannot disclose the existence of a simple self. Kant agrees with Hume's reason for rejecting these two pieces of the Cartesian account of the mind. In terms reminiscent of Hume's discussion, Kant points out that inner sense does not reveal a self:

> For the empirical consciousness, which accompanies different representations, is in itself diverse and without relation to the identity of the subject. . . . [If inner sense were the only form of self consciousness], I should have as many-colored and diverse a self as I have representations of which I am conscious to myself.[4] (B 133–34)

This point is repeated in the Paralogisms chapter, twice in the first edition and once in the second (A 350, A 381, B 413).

Hume's third claim about the self presents his positive conception. A mind is a collection of different perceptions (mental states) that are connected by certain relations. Anyone familiar with the basic tenets of Hume's philosophy would know that there are just three candidates for these relations: resemblance, contiguity, and cause and effect (e.g., I, 64). Moreover, he would know that in Hume's eyes the holding of any or all of these relations among the members of a set of mental states would not establish a real or necessary connection among the states. It is this positive view, that mental states are connected by these three relations, that stands behind Hume's claim that there is no real identity in the mind: the mind is nothing but a heap of different perceptions.

Since the precise meanings of "real connection" and "necessary connection" for Hume are matters of scholarly debate, it is also debatable exactly what Hume wants to claim in denying real connection among mental states. It would take me too far from my main topic to try to offer a complete interpretation of Hume's remarks about necessary connection or real connection. To be in a position to consider a relation between Hume's and Kant's views of the self, however, we need to have a clear idea of Hume's position on real connection at least as it pertains to mental states. I take Hume to understand real connection in this context as requiring existential dependence. That is, two objects are really connected only if one would not have existed or would have been different had the other not existed. The major reason to read Hume's remarks about real connection this way in his discussions of personal identity is that, in lamenting his problems with this issue in the Appendix to the *Treatise,* he points out that it is precisely this relation that is lacking among mental states:

> All perceptions are distinct. They are, therefore, distinguishable, and separable, and may be conceived as separately existent, and may exist separately, without any contradiction or absurdity. [T, 634]

> If perceptions are distinct existences, they form a whole only by being connected together. But no connexions among distinct existences are ever discoverable by human understanding. We only *feel* a connexion. [T, 635]

I think these passages virtually force a reading of Hume's denial of real connection among mental states as a denial of the relation of existential dependence among them.

Hence, I think one clear way to understand Hume's positive doctrine, that mental states are related by resemblance and cause and effect, and hence not by any real connection, is to regard him as denying any connection among the existences of the various mental states that are said to constitute one mind. In his view, the existence of one of my mental states is not actually tied to the existence of any others; we say that they are both mine only because we associate them in thought. Although Kant apparently did not have access to some passages I have used to defend this interpretation, I think he knew enough about Hume's views about habit, causation, and existential inference to see this implication of the theory of personal identity. In the *Inquiry,* Hume is quite explicit that it is only experience and habit that stand behind our inferences from causes to effects, because an effect is a distinct event from its cause and no other connection is discernible between distinct events (I, 44, 56). Thus I think that Kant would have read Hume's third point about the self as implying that the different states we ascribe to one mind are completely independent of one another. They are connected only by our minds.

Hume's application of his skepticism about the causal relation to the mind itself would arrest any moderately sympathetic student of his philosophy. Although this doctrine is a straightforward consequence of

Hume's basic position, it is incompatible with the theory of mental activity that is the heart of that position. Consider Hume's most famous skeptical explanation: we say that one event causes another—for example, the application of heat causes the melting of ice—only because events of these types have been constantly conjoined in our experience so that when we see a new instance of heat being applied to ice we are led "by a customary transition" to the "thought" of the melting of the ice (I, 87). Past experience forms in us the habit of thinking of melting ice when we think of heat being applied to ice, and the presence of this habitual connection leads us to claim a causal connection between the two types of events (I, 87). The explanation of causal beliefs in terms of mental habit commits Hume to the view that present mental states are the effects of earlier mental states in the strong sense that these states would not have existed had the earlier states not existed: in the absence of past experience, there would be no habit, and in the absence of the habit, there would be no causal claim. As I have just argued, however, Hume's third point about the self denies exactly this connection among mental states.

Seemingly, knowledge of these passages about personal identity would have afforded Kant a devastating criticism of Hume's account of causation. However, Kant had almost no interest in revealing the shortcomings of Hume's skeptical analyses. His objective was to meet Hume's challenge by justifying the use of a stronger conception of causation than Hume would acknowledge. Familiarity with Hume's reflections on personal identity would not have simplified Kant's task; it would have made it more difficult. The "vindication" of the causal concept in the Second Analogy depends essentially on the legitimacy of talking about the mental states of one person. Moreover, it is difficult to imagine how any concept could be shown to be a legitimate or illegitimate part of a conceptual repertoire without presupposing existential connections among mental states. Hume's skepticism about personal identity would confront Kant with a circle: to establish the legitimacy of a stronger than Humean sense of "causation," he needs to assume the legitimacy of the concept of a single mind; however, the latter concept will be of service only if it includes the idea that some mental states would have been different had other mental states not existed; thus in using the concept of a single mind, he must assume the legitimacy of the idea of existential connection, and an essential part of Hume's attack on causation is the denial of the possibility of discerning connections among actual existents.

How can the circle be broken? Kant employs the idea of existential connection in describing our mental activities in the sections of the Analytic preceding the Second Analogy. Further, the text of the Second Analogy makes no reference to the necessity of imputing non-Humean causal connections to mental states; the thrust of the argument seems to concern the necessity of finding non-Humean causal relations among *external* objects. Hence Kant's strategy must be to justify the idea of an existential connection *among mental states* when it is first used. My thesis is that the real argumentative goal of the Subjective Deduction is to justify the imputing of existential connections among mental states. If Kant's argument succeeds, then the way will be cleared for at least setting up the argument of the Second Analogy, because Kant will have removed the basis for Hume's objection to personal identity and can legitimately appeal to the idea of one mind. Of more relevance to our present purpose, if Kant can defend the idea of existential connection among mental states, then he will have countered Hume's skepticism about personal identity—that what we call a person is nothing but a heap of diverse perceptions.

### III. The Role of the Subjective Deduction

In the preface to the first edition Kant characterizes the Subjective Deduction as being concerned with the properties or faculties of the understanding. He then confesses that this part of the Deduction is both "somewhat hypothetical in character" and inessential to his chief purpose (Axvii). (I will use "Deduction" to refer to the entire *Transcendental* Deduction in both versions, employing "Subjective Deduction" or "Objective Deduction" when I wish to focus on more specific aspects of the Deduction.) Kant's prefatory remarks and various material in the Deduction itself, particularly the first edition version, have led critics to regard the Subjective Deduction as a useless exercise in speculative psychology. A standard view is that Kant took over or hit upon three basic mental faculties to explain the possibility of knowledge, sense, imagination, and understanding, and then added epicycles at will. P. F. Strawson's attack on the thesis that the mind imposes the order of nature on the chaotic given suggests that he regards the Subjective Deduction as worse than mere but coherent speculation.[5] Rather, Kant descends into nonempirical psychology in order to provide some account of how the mind (atemporally) shapes the atemporal raw given to make it fit for human experience.

There is solid textual support for regarding the Subjective Deduction as armchair psychology and as the most detailed account of how the mind imposes its form on noumenal data. My objection to these unflattering portraits is not that they are unwarranted, but that they are seriously incomplete. I think that commentators have fastened on these unfortunate elements because they have seen no legitimate work to be done by a Subjective Deduction, because they have taken the existence of a continuing mind possessed of various states to be an unproblematic initial premise of the entire Deduction. But this widely held interpretative assumption is highly implausible if Kant knew about Hume's attack on personal identity. I think it is also quite implausible in light of Kant's remarks at B 133–34 (cited above) and A 107 (cited below).

Kant needs the principle that different mental states belong to a continuing being for the deduction of the categories; indeed, he needs a stronger principle that this connection of mental states in a self is a necessary feature of our experience. He would have no hope of "deducing" the categories unless he can offer a reply to Hume's denial of all real connection among mental states. Thus I think the worthwhile project of the Subjective Deduction is the fashioning of this reply. Notice that on this interpretation the Subjective Deduction is essential to the overall Deduction, a point Kant explicitly denies. However, I think Kant's own assessment of the Subjective Deduction is a product of confusing the task of providing a highly abstract description of the feature a mind must have, namely, existential connections among its states, with the task of explaining how the mind has that feature, which involves the positing of various processes responsible for establishing the needed connections. This is not a silly conflation. If one wants to argue that X must be the case, then although it is not strictly necessary, it is certainly very useful to provide some account of how X could have come about, particularly if your opponent has denied X's possibility. Kant's problem is that this strategy is inapplicable here, because eighteenth-century psychology provided too few clues about mentality. I think Kant denigrated the first edition Subjective Deduction because he realized that his psychological speculations lacked proof and because he dimly saw that this type of psychological story could not be necessary, without seeing exactly how much of this material presented necessary features of all mental life, and how much presented accidental features of human cognition. In the second edition, the discussion of mental states and processes is remarkably abstract, and there is no apology.

Kant appreciated the force of Hume's point about the difficulty of imputing existential connections among mental states. I think that he also felt he understood why Hume had failed to produce a correct account of personal identity. After noting that we cannot establish the presence of an abiding self through introspection, he points out that this method is incapable of producing the desired result.

> Consciousness of self according to the determinations of our state in inner perception is merely empirical and always changing. No fixed and abiding self can present itself in this flux of inner appearances . . . What has *necessarily* to be represented as numerically identical cannot be thought as such through empirical data. To render such a transcendental presupposition valid, there must be a condition which precedes all experience, and which makes experience itself possible. (A 107)

As a diagnosis of Hume's methodological "error," this analysis is unfair. Although Hume needs to establish existential dependence among mental states, it is unclear why he would have to show that mental states *have* to be existentially connected. Regardless of the aptness of Kant's criticism, his analysis of this "mistake" provides a clear indication of his own proof-strategy. As with other contested principles, Kant will try to establish existential connections among mental states by arguing that they are a necessary condition for the possibility of experience. Kant's ubiquitous interest in a necessary connection or necessary synthesis of mental states has very little to do with speculative psychology. It is a natural Kantian response to the problem Hume laid before him.

## IV. Transcendental Synthesis and Apperception

Hume denied the possibility of discovering certain kinds of relations among mental states. In both editions of the Deduction Kant continually refers to a relation among representations, the relation of synthesis. He offers an explicit definition of this relation at A 77/B 103: "By *synthesis,* in its most general sense, I understand the action of adding various representations together, and of grasping their multiple [contents] in one cognition" (amended translation). For Kant, "representation" signifies both "mental state" and the "content of a mental state." The last clause clearly refers to the contents of different mental states being combined in a further mental state. As Kant realized, token mental states are episodic, occurring at different times, so they themselves cannot literally be put together. I think that Kant expresses himself in this way to press the point that the content of the resultant state does not merely duplicate the contents of the earlier states. Rather the content of the later state, and so the state itself, is produced out of the earlier states and their contents.

In light of this passage we might try to capture Kant's use of "synthesis" as follows: *Mental state $M_1$ and mental state $M_2$ are synthesized if and only if there is some mental state $M_3$ such that, other things being equal, the content of $M_3$, and so $M_3$ itself, would not exist or would be different had $M_1$ and $M_2$ not existed or had different contents.* When this situation obtains we may say that $M_3$ is the "synthetic product" of $M_1$, $M_2$, or both. Thus a more general relation of synthesis could be defined: *$M_1$ and $M_2$ stand in the relation of synthesis if and only if $M_1$ is the synthetic product of $M_2$ or $M_2$ is the synthetic product of $M_1$, or $M_1$ and $M_2$ are synthesized.* The difficulty with this analysis of synthesis is that it is incompatible with Kant's apparent view that the relation of synthesis (or transcendental synthesis) among mental states is a necessary (A 118) and sufficient (B 134) condition for their being states of one and the same thinker self. As just defined, a relation of synthesis among mental states amounts only to a causal dependence of their contents, which is plainly not sufficient for sameness of cognitive self. If Harry screams "Smoke!" then the content of my mental state will be dependent on the content of the state of Harry's that precipitated his scream.

The objection just sketched is familiar from critiques of other nonbodily criteria of personal identity. I think it is generally recognized that this type of deficiency in a nonbodily criterion would have to be remedied by a more precise specification of the relation in question and that such specifications are hard to produce. What is offered instead is the promissory note: "a causal connection *of the kind that typically exists among the mental states of one person."* Similarly, a contemporary defender of Kant's position on coconsciousness would have to rest content with "the right kind of causal connection among the contents of mental states" if no more specific characterization could be offered. Some philosophers dislike this type of place-holder for a yet to be developed theory. In this case, I think the use of place-holder is justified, because I think the promissory note can be redeemed.

Interestingly, the question of whether a Kantian theory of personal identity is ultimately defensible is irrelevant to his dispute with Hume. Even if his philosophical heirs can do better, Kant himself did not adequately define the relation of being states of a continuing thinker. He only sketched a general kind of relation of which this relation might be a species. Nevertheless, the crucial point to realize is that Hume's objection to personal identity is also general. He does not criticize this or that criterion of mental unity. Rather he argues that it is impossible to discover a certain kind of relation among mental states, existential dependence, rightly believing that any plausible criterion must be a relation of this kind. The relation of synthesis is a relation of existential dependence. Thus if Kant can argue that we are justified in imputing this general type of relation to a set of mental states, he will have countered Hume's general objection to the possibility of discovering a relation that unites different mental states into a single mind.

To avoid confusion, I will distinguish between Kant's two senses of "synthesis." I will use "Synthesis" with a capital "S" to stand for the precise relation of contentual causal connection that holds among the mental states of one mind and "synthesis" with a lower case "s" to stand for the more general relation of contentual causal interconnection. The definition of "synthesis" given above may thus be allowed to stand so long as we recognize that the lower case "s" is a crucial part of the definition. Where I have not disambiguated Kant's usage I will use "synthesis*."

Although Kant discusses various "empirical" syntheses*, his real interest is in "transcendental" synthesis*. Kant's discussions of transcendental synthesis* sometimes portray it as a special kind of faculty or operation that imposes necessary features on the given (e.g., A 122–23). The root meaning of this expression is, however, epistemological: to posit a transcendental synthesis* is to claim that a relation of synthesis* among mental states can be known to exist in a special way, viz., by revealing it as a necessary condition for the possibility of experience (A 93–94/B 126). Kant also uses "experience" ambiguously.[6] On one usage, a person is "having experience" if and only if he is making judgments about states of affairs or objects that are regarded as existing independently of his mental states (B 147, B 128). In other places Kant allows experience to involve only the having of mental states, that is, having intuitions and judgments (B 161; see also B 275). It has often been noted that no interesting anti-Cartesian or anti-Humean argument can assume the existence of experience in the first stronger sense. So in considering the necessity of synthesis* for the possibility of experience we should use "experience" in the weaker sense. I will mark this special sense of "experience" by using a capital "E."

Thus Kant's endorsement of a transcendental synthesis* can be understood as support for the claim that a synthesis* among mental states can be shown to be a necessary condition for the possibility of Experience. This unusual doctrine is hardly something Kant can just assume. He must offer some argumentation. And given that he lacks a precise account of the relation of Synthesis, the only doctrine he is in a position to defend is that the generic relation of synthesis among mental states is a necessary condition for the possibility of Experience. This, however, is all he needs for the argument against Hume. If he can establish a doctrine of transcendental synthesis, then he will have met the challenge about the impossibility of imputing existential connections to mental states that stands behind Hume's denial of personal identity.

## V. The Arguments for Transcendental Synthesis

Typically, Kant tries to justify the doctrine of transcendental synthesis by marshaling a variety of arguments, some of which would be better left out. For reasons of space, I will consider only his best argument. It occurs at A 116–18, although its basic lines are repeated, even more cryptically, at B 131–32. Unfortunately, this argument is cast as an argument for the doctrine of transcendental Synthesis:

(1) If a relation of Synthesis did not hold among mental states, then they could not be representational (A 116, B 131–32).
(2) Something that is not representational is impossible as a mental state (A 116, B 131–32).
(3) Therefore Experience—having intuitions and judgments—is possible only if mental states are connected by relations of Synthesis (A 116, B 131–32).

Given that Kant cannot even define the relation of Synthesis it is hard to see how he could offer any support for the crucial initial premise. One could try to use a "right kind of contentual causal connection" formulation and try to find some argumentation linking the representational aspects of mental states to the idea of a set of mental states so characterized. Since I have been unable to locate any passages that might be used in connection with this strategy, I think that the only way to salvage the argument is to read it as Kant's hopeful overstatement of an argument about the more general relation of synthesis. If we substitute "synthesis" for "Synthesis" throughout, the conclusion (3) will present the doctrine of transcendental synthesis. And as already noted, all Kant needs against Hume is an argument for transcendental synthesis.

The keystone of this argument is premise (1). Premise (2) seems uncontroversial, and (3) follows validly from (1) and (2). Kant states this claim quite clearly at A 116:

> We are conscious *a priori* of the complete identity of the self in respect of all representations which can ever belong to our knowledge, as being a necessary condition of the possibility of all representations. *For in me they can represent something only in so far as they belong with all others to one consciousness, and therefore must be at least capable of being so connected* [my emphasis].

But neither the text of A 116–18 nor the corresponding passage in B (B 131–32) provides an answer to the obvious question of why mental states can be representational only if they stand in actual or possible relations of Synthesis or synthesis to other mental states. I think the best way to regard these texts is not as presenting full dress arguments, but as drawing out implications of previous considerations that bear on the issues of synthesis and mental unity, and as anticipating some later points.

Both Kant and Hume acknowledge two kinds of mental states. I will use "sensory state" to refer to states produced in receiving information through the sensory or perceptual system, that is, where Kant would use "intuition" and Hume would use "impression." I will use "judgmental state" to refer to the mental state one is in when making a silent or voiced judgment, and I will use "judgmental state" in place of Kant's "concept" and Hume's "idea." This terminology is not faithful to Hume's understanding of impressions and ideas, since he regarded ideas as being just like impressions, except that the former are fainter. My usage reflects the belief that Hume's terminology embodies a substantive error and that Kant's sharp distinction between having an intuition and employing a concept is roughly correct. To find out why Kant believes that mental states must stand in actual or possible relations of

Synthesis or synthesis, we can look back to his accounts of sensory states and judgmental states.

I will begin with judgmental states. In some ways Kant's position on content and judgmental states is as well known as anything in his philosophy: "thoughts without content [i.e., relation to objects in intuition] are empty" (A 51/B 75). Again at A 69/B 94, "It [the concept of body] is a concept solely in virtue of its comprehending other representations, by means of which it can relate to objects." But what those passages omit is any account of how exactly a judgmental state "comprehends" or "contains" the other representations through which it acquires relation to objects and content. Kant provides this account as he "prepares the reader" for the Deduction.

> If we were not conscious that what we think is the same as what we thought a moment before, all reproduction in the series of representations would be useless. For it would in its present state be a new representation which would not in any way belong to the act whereby it was gradually generated. . . . If, in counting, I forget that the units, which now float before my senses, were added together by me one after another, I should never know that a total is being produced through this successive addition of unit to unit, and so would remain ignorant of the number. (A 103, amended translation)

Kant's point is not that I can use information in a judgment only if I retain it. That claim has already been made in connection with the "second synthesis" (see A 102). Rather the claim is that we can attribute content to a thought only if we recognize that mental state as having been generated by a particular (type of) intuition or series of intuitions. Although Kant never assembles the following considerations into an explicit argument, they are there to be assembled, and they both explain and defend his support for this position. Kant recognized that making the judgment "five things," for example, is fundamentally different from having a visual impression of five things. Once this point is clearly grasped, the question of why it is appropriate to regard a judgmental state as having the content "five" looms as a major problem that any theory of judgment must handle. In this passage Kant points out that content cannot be assigned to the state just by considering the state itself, for if the subject "forgets" that this state was produced by the successive addition of units, he would "remain ignorant of the number"—he would have no idea what content to assign the state.

What Kant offers in this crucial passage is an account of judgmental states remarkably like that defended by contemporary functionalists. Functionalism (in one version at least) is the theory that the identity conditions for mental states are given in terms of their causal connections to stimuli, behavioral responses, and other (internal) states. Unfortunately, Kant appeals only to sensory states, and this typical slighting of behavioral effects is costly. If someone says, "There is a bomb in that flower pot," and makes great efforts to get the pot into a steel container and out of the house, then we have excellent reasons to conclude that he thinks there is a bomb in the flowerpot, regardless of what we believe about his previous sensory stimulations. This counterexample is of no help to Hume, however, for even though content ascription can be effected via behavioral connections as well as through sensory connections, it still requires us to acknowledge a relation of synthesis among mental states—in this case the states that issue in behavior are synthetic products of the judgmental state. Insofar as the debate between Kant and Hume is concerned, we may simply patch up Kant's account by adding "output" connections to behavior. The crucial question is whether we can attribute content to judgmental states without acknowledging connections to *any* other mental states. In addressing this question, we find ourselves in the quintessential position of the transcendental arguer. The only way that we can show that some condition (in this case synthesis) is necessary for the possibility of Experience is try to find putative counterexamples to refute.

The contemporary literature offers two theories of mind that seem to support such counterexamples. Central State Materialists regard the concept of a mental state as the concept of a state that is *typically* produced by certain causes and, in turn, *typically,* produces certain effects. On this view, it would be possible to assign an isolated token physical state content on the basis of the fact that most *other* tokens of that type do stand in particular causal connections. Although Central State Materialism may not be the best theory of mind, it seems to provide a possible account of judgmental states. If Kant's claim is that it is impossible to attribute content to a judgmental state without imputing a relation of synthesis to a set including *that very state,* then this theory of mind presents a fatal objection to Kant's position. Notice, however, that Central State Materialism can assign content to an isolated mental state only by assuming that some judgmental states do stand in relations of synthesis. Thus this account of judgment would not constitute an objection to the weaker claim that no judgmental state can be assigned content unless some judgmental states are regarded as synthetically related to other mental states. I think the texts of A 103, A 116, and B 131 suggest that Kant holds the stronger view. Nevertheless, since the stronger view is vulnerable to counterexample, and since the weaker position is all that is required in an argument against Hume, we should modify Kant's argument so that the conclusion (3) claims only that Experience is possible only if a relation of synthesis exists among some mental states.

The idea of a neural code also offers a possible model for ascribing content without connection. If there is a neural code of thought and if we could ever crack this code, then seemingly future generations would be able, in theory at least, to assign content with no assumptions about synthetic connections. Although this scenario seems plausible, actually it is not, if what is meant is not only that structures could be used to assign content but also that in these circumstances we would make no background assumption that at least most states are connected to other mental states. This proposal fails for a familiar reason. Nothing is intrinsically a representation of anything; alternatively, something can be a representation only if it is part of a representational system.

I think the widely accepted rationale for the claim that representations must belong to a system is that a representation acquires meaning only through its position in representational space: the alternative representations it excludes, the other representations it comprehends, the other representations that comprehend it. In the case of human cognizers, we are considering a representational system (the central nervous system) that is a representational system for itself. It doesn't represent contents to something else, but represents them to itself. Hence this system must have some way of realizing these relations among its various representations, since no external agent is available simply to comprehend the connections. And it is very hard to see how this could occur in the absence of relations of synthesis among the representational states.

A simple example can illustrate why this is so. Consider a machine that has five different "representational" states, whose "representations" exclude each other. This machine is too simple to be regarded as containing representations, but that does not matter for my purpose. Suppose there are no real connections among the "representational" states: when presented with objects, it enters one of its states, but this event has no influence on whether it will enter other states. It will not enter other states, but only because the stimuli for the different states are mutually exclusive. Regardless of its other defects, this machine does not contain representations, because its so-called "representations" do not stand in the relation of exclusion to other representations. It is only by courtesy that this machine is regarded as instantiating *alternative* representations; what we actually confront are five separate machines. We could also explore the necessary relations of representational inclusion and reach the same results, but the argument about exclusion is sufficient. Given that a representation must belong to a representational system, and that when a system is a representational system for itself, the logical relations among its representations must be realized in it, it is not possible to regard a mental state as being representational without making the background assumption that it or most members of its kind stand(s) in the relation of synthesis to other mental states. Hence, like the case of Central State Materialism, although we could assign content to some isolated states by "unlocking" the neural code, we would still have to regard *some* judgmental states as belonging to representational systems.

The arguments I have used against these two potential counterexamples cannot be attributed to Kant. Both examples depend on identifying mental states as particular physical structures, and Kant would have had quite different reasons for rejecting them. (See, for example, A 358.) Thus these arguments should be regarded as contemporary replies to unforeseen objections. Kant's contribution is more that of discoverer than that of defender. First, he sharply distinguishes intuitions and concepts, and his doing so sets up the problem of how to assign content to thoughts. Second, he recognizes the crucial role of sensory inputs in assigning content (A 103). Third, he notes the more general point that a mental state can be assigned content only as part of a system: "For in me they can represent something only in so far as they belong with all others to one consciousness" (A 116). And finally, he recognizes the implication of his theory of intuitions and concepts for the problem of self-identity. At both B 131–32 and, less crisply, at A 116, he (over)draws the moral that a representation is possible only if it can be accompanied by an "I think" (that is, only if it can stand in the relation of Synthesis to other mental states).

What about intuitions? Kant raises two different sorts of considerations that support the claim that members of the other class of mental states must also stand in relations of synthesis. One type of consideration, which is raised after A 116, bypasses the idea that mental states and thus intuitions must be regarded as representational and argues directly for (3) as it applies to intuitions. In four different places in the first edition, Kant reiterates the claim that intuitions are nothing, or almost nothing, unless we can be conscious of them, i.e., make judgments about them (A 117a, A 120, A 122, A 123). Their being consists in being known (A 120). These passages may seem to reflect either crude verificationism or support for a Cartesian view of mental states that Kant's own more subtle reflections should have led him beyond. In fact I think Kant is only trying to make the point that intuitions would not concern us, would not be a subject for philosophical reflection, unless we could talk about them. But if we can talk about them, they must be synthetically connected to judgmental states. If I say, "There is an intuition of red," then for reasons we have already seen, my judgmental state must (on most occasions at least) be regarded as generated by an intuition of red if it is to be assigned the obvious content. And further, that judgmental state must also be synthetically connected to others if it is to be construed as representational. Thus any intuition we can worry about must be construed as standing in the relation of synthesis to other mental states, and Hume's predicament of worrying how to connect his distinct intuitions to each other is impossible (cf. A 122).

In claiming that judgmental states must stand in the relation of synthesis, Kant is merely drawing out the consequences of his theory of concepts and intuitions. I think the same is true for his second point about intuitions, which is made only once, at A 116: "Intuitions are nothing to us, and do not in the least concern us if they cannot be taken up into consciousness, in which they may participate either directly or indirectly." Immediately after this statement Kant makes the claim that representations must belong to a self if they are to represent something. I take Kant's point here to be that we would not take something to be an intuition unless we regard it as actually (or perhaps potentially) "participating in" or "flowing into" a judgment. Just as empty "thoughts" are not really thoughts, blind "intuitions" are not really intuitions, because such states could not fulfill the distinctive epistemological role of providing an object for judgment (A 51/B 75). In contemporary terminology, Kant's point would be that something could not be a sensory state—a bearer of information—unless it is at least a potential contributor of information to judgments. Central State Materialism and neural codes would again provide counterexamples to this claim as an exceptionless generalization. Once again, however, both would leave unscathed the more limited claim that Kant needs, that a state can be regarded as an intuition only if *some* intuitions are regarded as synthetically related to other mental states.

If this reading of Kant's point about intuitions at A 116 is correct, then his views about sensory states and judgmental states would be quite symmetrical, and his basic construal of mental states would be functional. At least in part, thoughts are what they are because of the sensory states that generate them and, at least in part, sensory states are what they are because they lead to thoughts. The crucial first premise of the argument given above would be supported by considerations about both sensory states and judgmental states. Mental states can be representational only if there are relations of synthesis among them, because thoughts can have content only if connected to intuitions and to each other, and intuitions can bear information about objects only if they can be connected to thoughts. As already noted, Kant's argument only establishes the doctrine of transcendental synthesis. That, however, is sufficient for the purpose. Since Hume presents no viable alternative to understanding mental states as components of a mental system, he cannot claim that we have impressions or beliefs while denying all existential connection among them, without falling into either contradiction or unintelligibility—without claiming, in effect, that we have representations that lack the necessary conditions for being representational.

The belief that it is impossible to acknowledge real or existential connection among mental states is the foundation of Hume's claim that there can be no criterion of personal identity. By forcing him to acknowledge such relations, Kant effectively disarms Hume's celebrated attack on the idea of personal identity. Perhaps more importantly, in grappling with Hume's challenge about the basis for regarding different mental states as states of a continuing being, Kant is led to reflect on the necessary conditions for our being cognizers at all: our cognitive states—sensory and judgmental—must stand in relations of contentual causal interconnection. Because he cannot define a more precise relation of "Synthesis," this epistemological criterion of mental unity identity is inadequate as it stands. Nevertheless, Kant successfully argues that something like this relation must play an essential role in any adequate account of the continuity of cognitive beings.

Although I have been concerned with Kant's failure to establish a stronger result about the self, his own concern was to avoid an overly strong interpretation of his claims. In the Paralogisms of Pure Reason, Kant's official project was to criticize the attempts of his Rationalist predecessors to establish exciting conclusions about the self or soul on the basis of their analyses of the necessary conditions of thinking. Since his own arguments in the Subjective Deduction are somewhat similar to those of the "Rational Psychologists,"[7] I believe that this chapter was also intended to offer warnings about the limitations of his own endeavors. In the final section, I will briefly consider Kant's important claims about the kind of knowledge about the self that can never be gleaned through philosophical reflection on the necessary conditions for experience or cognition.

## VI. Kant's Paralogisms

Like all of the arguments canvassed in the Dialectic, the arguments criticized in the Paralogisms chapter are supposed to be inevitable errors into which human reason must fall—and by which it will still be tempted even after the error of its ways has been made clear. Kant presents four sophistical arguments by which the Rationalists hoped to show that the I that thinks is a simple substance, a person, and is better known than external objects. Following Kant's own treatment, my discussion will focus on the First Paralogism, treating the Second and Third only briefly and the Fourth (which was replaced in the Second edition of the *Critique*) not at all.

Kant presents the First Paralogism as follows:

> That, the representation of which is the *absolute subject* of our judgments and cannot therefore be employed as a determination of another thing, is *substance*. [Major premise]

> I, as a thinking being, am the *absolute subject* of all my possible judgments, and this representation of myself cannot be employed as a predicate of any other thing. [Minor premise]

> Therefore I, as a thinking being, (soul) am *substance*. (A 348)

Why is this argument so appealing? I think that Kant regards the major premise as acceptable, because it states a commonly accepted definition of "substance." He mentions this definition several times prior to the Paralogisms chapter, without providing any explanation or defense (B 149, B 288, A 241/ B 300). The fact that this definition also occurs in the writings of Leibniz, also without explanation or defense, suggests that it enjoyed some currency at this time.[8] But what about the minor premise? The crucial interpretative fact about this chapter is that Kant endorses, on some reading, the minor premises (and conclusions) of the first three Paralogisms (A 349, A 350, A 354, A 356, A 363, A 365).

Like Descartes, Kant believes that any mental state must belong to a self, which we can then call (in the case of judgments), the "subject of the judgment." Unlike Descartes, however, Kant conceives of this self not as a simple substance, but only as a system of causally interconnected states. And unlike Descartes, Kant believes in this self because he has reflected on the necessary conditions for the possibility of Experience. Thus, given the background of the Subjective Deduction, we can understand how Kant interprets the first clause of the minor premise and why he supports it: it means that any possible judgment must belong to an I [to me or to another], that is, to a system of interconnected states; he supports this claim on the basis of his own argument in the Subjective Deduction. The second clause is more difficult, because Kant never says why the "I" cannot occur as a predication. I conjecture that he throws in the second clause simply because of its occurrence in the standardly accepted definition of "substance" from which he draws the major premise.

What, then, is the error involved in this reasoning? Kant's analysis of the error of his predecessors—and of the potential misstep of his own readers—is refreshingly straightforward and philosophically important. The goal of the Subjective Deduction was to show that thinking beings must have a highly abstract property if Experience is to be possible: the states of such beings must be synthetically or contentually interconnected. The mistake comes in thinking that this type of analysis provides information about what sort of thing a thinking being is:

> The analysis, then, of the consciousness of myself in thought in general, yields nothing whatsoever towards the knowledge of myself as object. The logical exposition of thought in general has been mistaken for a metaphysical determination of the object. (B 409)

Kant puts this point even more clearly at A 398:

> If anyone propounds to me the question, 'what is the constitution of a thing which thinks?' I have no *a priori* knowledge wherewith to reply. For the answer has to be synthetic—an analytic answer will perhaps explain what is meant by thought, but beyond this cannot yield any knowl-

edge of that upon which this thought depends for its possibility . . .
intuition [would be] required; and owing to the highly general character
of the problem, intuition has been left entirely out of our account. Similarly no one can answer in all its generality the question, 'What must a
thing be, to be movable?'

What Kant has realized is that the kind of analysis he has provided
of the necessary properties of subjects of judgments furnishes no serious clues about what kind of thing the soul might be. Despite his predecessors hopes, such analyses do not offer a royal road to knowledge
about the nature of thinking things. This is an important insight. With
the aid of reflecting on the differences between the "hardware" and
"software" in computers, it has reemerged in recent years as the principle that function does not determine form and now serves as a fundamental assumption behind some philosophical accounts of mentality.
In contemporary terminology, the point is that since many different
kinds of hardware can perform the same function, it is impossible to
infer from the functions specified by the software to the kind of hardware that runs it. Kant seems genuinely surprised and impressed by his
discovery: "Suspicion is thus thrown on the view, which at first seemed
to me so plausible, that we can form judgments about the nature of
the thinking being, and can do so from concepts alone" (A 399).

When we turn to the Second Paralogism, I will suggest that Leibniz
may have accepted the minor premise. As far as I know, however, neither Leibniz nor his followers provides anything like the argument for
attaching mental states to subjects that stands behind the First Paralogism's minor premise. Hence this Paralogism seems to be very much
Kant's own paralogism—or a paralogism to which his audience might
well be vulnerable—because the crucial minor premise derives from
his own work on the self. Moreover I suspect that Kant came to understand the general problem of moving from certain kinds of abstract
functional descriptions to substantive or constitutional descriptions by
reflecting on the kind of analysis of the necessary conditions for
thought and judgmental experience that he himself had defended and
by recognizing the similarities between these analyses and some of the
work of his predecessors. In any case, many of Kant's general warnings
about moving from "conceptual analysis" to substantive claims about
the self, and his claims in the First Paralogism, are better understood
as caveats about his own position than as criticisms of his predecessors.

Oddly, the Third Paralogism covers much the same territory as the

First, although with an added (and distinctively Kantian) twist. Like Hume, Kant construes substantival identity as requiring some permanent element which persists throughout whatever changes occur in the enduring thing (A 361–62). Since permanence is also the hallmark of substances, there would be no difference between characterizing the thinker as permanent and characterizing it as a substance. This is his cryptic presentation of the argument:

> That which is conscious of the numerical identity of itself at different times in so far a *person* [Major premise]. Now the soul is conscious, etc. [Minor premise]. Therefore it is a person. (A 361)

Further, Kant seems to regard the major and minor premises as having exactly the same kind of support as their counterparts in the First Paralogism. The major premise offers a definition of "person" that was used by Leibniz and Christian Wolff, as well as by Locke. In light of Kant's Humean recognition that we are not aware of a self through inner sense, he cannot support the minor premise if it is interpreted to mean that each of us is aware of a permanent self at different times. Once again, however, the argumentation of the Subjective Deduction provides an explanation for the acceptability of this claim (properly understood). In effect, Kant has argued that any given mental state must belong with others to one consciousness. Hence any subject must be cognizant of (if not conscious of) a present mental state as belonging to the same self as previous and future mental states. But such a self is merely a synthetically interconnected system of states and no inference can be made to its permanent, immutable, or substantial character.

What errors are likely to infect this reasoning? Beyond the issues covered in the First Paralogism, the chief error that Kant considers in this discussion is the temptation to combine the doctrine of the ideality of time and the theory of the Subjective Deduction into an argument about the unbroken continuity of thinking beings. Many of Kant's predecessors had taken Descartes's claim that thought is the essential attribute of thinking beings to imply that thinkers *always* think. Locke had argued that this implication is clearly false. This is how the pseudo-proof of continuity might go. Time is merely the form of inner sense. Therefore, for me, moments of time exist only in those moments when I am conscious of a mental state through inner sense. Whenever I am conscious of a mental state, however, I must attribute that state to an

"I." Thus, from my own point of view, I must attribute unbroken continuity and permanence to myself.

To see the weakness in this reasoning, Kant invites us to consider our existence from the point of view of an "outside observer." Whenever this individual attributes a mental state to the person he observes, then he must recognize that that state belongs to a continuing thinker. He will not, however, infer permanence or unbroken continuity for the simple reason that there will be times when he does not, or cannot, attribute a conscious state to the person at all, even while he is observing the person's body (if, for example, the person were sleeping). Hence, this I, this inner subject, will not be a permanent element in the experience of the outside observer. If we construe the conclusion of the Paralogism, "I am a person," as meaning that "I exist at every moment of time," then it is not warranted by the argument just given. If the conclusion merely restates the minor premise claim that I or any subject must be cognizant of the identity of my self [a continuing sequence of contentually interconnected states] at different times, however, then it can be asserted.

The Second Paralogism deviates from the pattern set by the First and Third in several important respects.

> That, the action of which can never be regarded as the concurrence of several things acting, is *simple* [Major premise].
>
> Now the soul, or the thinking "I," is such a being [Minor premise]. Therefore etc. (A 351)

As far as I know, the major premise does not state a widely accepted definition of "simple." Further, Margaret Wilson argues that there are hints of such an argument in Leibniz.[9] Nevertheless, the argument Kant supplies in favor of the minor premise also reflects his own analyses of the necessary conditions of thinking. In a passage strikingly similar to William James's well-known discussion of this topic, Kant casts the argument as follows:

> For suppose it be a composite that thinks: then every part of it would be a part of the thought, and only all of them taken together would contain the whole thought. But this cannot consistently be maintained. For representations (for instance the single words of a verse), distributed among different beings, never make up a whole thought. . . . (A 352)

That is, if eight different individuals each thought one word of the verse, "Earth has not anything to show more fair," then no subject would grasp its meaning.

But again, nothing follows about the actual simplicity of the subject from the fact that a mental state containing a thought must be unified; i.e., its parts must not be understood as separate or disconnected from each other. Or, as Kant puts the point very clearly, this inference is invalid, because

> the unity of the thought, which consists of many representations, is collective, and as far as mere concepts can show, may relate just as well to the collective unity of different substances acting together. (A 353)

All that can be correctly inferred is that a collection of different beings can have a thought only if they constitute a mutually dependent system of beings, so that the whole thought is contained in some [collective or simple] subject.

Just in case the Rationalist tries to resist this criticism, Kant drives home the point in the second edition. It is not merely fallacious to try to adjudicate among possible characterizations of the soul by appealing to abstract analyses of the necessary conditions for thought. It is potentially dangerous to the Rationalist cause. If the Rationalist permits himself to argue for the simplicity (and so immateriality and immortality) of the soul by claiming that he does not understand how a material substance (which must have parts) can realize the unity of thought, then the materialist is free to employ the same strategy to "establish" the opposite conclusion. Since the materialist does not understand how an *immaterial substance* can realize the unity of thought, he may claim that the soul is material! (B 418a)

## VII. Conclusion

In the *Critique of Pure Reason,* Kant tries to give some determinate form to the ancient philosophical injunction to "know thyself." Mere reflection on our capacity for knowledge will never enable us to know ourselves as particular kinds of material or immaterial structures; such knowledge requires sensory evidence. Nevertheless, Kant argues that we can gain important insights into what it is to be a self or person by trying to understand our distinctive capacity for knowledge. To be a cognizer at all requires the ability to represent objects and events, and the ability to represent requires that our various mental states be linked together in a complex interdependent system of states. Hence, despite the skepticism of Hume and some of his contemporary followers, there are sound philosophical reasons for believing that a thinking self enjoys some type of continuity through time. The indefensible doctrines of Rational psychology are the additional claims that this self is a simple, immutable, immaterial, and immortal soul.

## Notes

1. In *Beattie's Works.* Philadelphia: Hopkins and Earle, 1802. The edition I cite below is from the sixth edition of April, 1776, which is virtually identical to the second edition, from which the German translation was made.

2. *Philosophische Versuche über die menschliche Natur und ihre Entwicklung,* Leipzig, 1777.

3. These excerpts appear on pp. 79, 249 of Beattie; the excerpted passages appear on pp. 251, 252, and 253 of L. A. Selby-Bigge's *A Treatise of Human Nature by David Hume* (Oxford: Oxford University Press, 1973). Future reference to the latter will be to this edition and will be indicated in the text by "T" and the page in parentheses. References to Hume's *Inquiry Concerning Human Understanding* will be to the Liberal Arts Press edition, 1955, and will be indicated by "I" and the page in parentheses.

4. All references to the *Critique of Pure Reason* will be to Norman Kemp Smith's translation (New York: St. Martin's Press, 1968). Where indicated, I have amended the translation.

5. See essay 8 in this volume.

6. Essays 1, 6, and 7 also discuss this ambiguity.

7. This group would include Christian Wolff, Descartes, and Leibniz.

8. Leroy E. Loemker, editor, *Gottfried Wilhelm Leibniz Philosophical Papers and Letters* (D. Reidel, 1976), p. 307.

9. "Leibniz and Materialism," *Canadian Journal of Philosophy III,* 4 (June 1974): 495–513.

# 5

# Kant's Transcendental Deduction as a Regressive Argument

## Karl Ameriks

Considerable study has been given in recent years to the question of transcendental arguments in general and to Kant's transcendental deduction in particular. Recent analytical studies of Kant have approached his work with a pronounced interest in the former general issue and with broad theories about the way the first *Critique* as a whole should be interpreted. As a consequence there has been a tendency to pass over the complex details of Kant's own discussion of the structure of transcendental argumentation. Indicative of this situation is the absence of any detailed treatment of the second edition version of the transcendental deduction. In this paper I shall argue that once Kant's revisions in the second edition are given their due, his transcendental deduction of the pure concepts of the understanding can be seen to have a surprisingly clear structure and one which is at variance with contemporary interpretations. My main objective is to give a fair representation of that structure, but in so doing I will argue that it has been misrepresented in a fundamental and common way by Kant's most distinguished recent commentators—Peter Strawson, Jonathan Bennett, and Robert Paul Wolff. Whereas their interpretations see Kant's deduction as aiming to provide a proof of objectivity which will answer scepticism, I will argue that on the contrary it is necessary and profitable to understand the deduction as moving from the assumption that there is empirical knowledge to a proof of the preconditions of that knowledge.

**I**

Transcendental deductions are not familiar entities. It is only natural to exploit whatever examples we have of them in order to cast light on the notorious difficulties of Kant's deduction of the categories. Yet surprisingly little attention has been paid to Kant's explicit designation of the argument of the Transcendental Aesthetic as a transcendental deduction (B 119). In a remarkably systematic paragraph added in the second edition Kant explains what he means by a "transcendental exposition" and how it is that his analysis of space is one. Briefly Kant declares a transcendental account of a particular representation (*B*) to be one which shows how *B* explains the possibility of a kind of synthetic a priori knowledge (*A*). Such an account has two parts:

> (1) For this purpose it is required that such knowledge does really flow from the given concept, (2) that this knowledge is possible only on the assumption of a given mode of explaining the concept (B 40).

This means that the transcendental deduction in the Transcendental Aesthetic in particular must show (1) how the science of geometry "really flows" from the representation of space, and (2) how geometry is possible only if that representation has a particular (in Kant's view, ideal) nature. This suggests that a transcendental deduction of a particular type of knowledge demonstrates its necessary and sufficient conditions. The demonstration of the sufficient conditions would be given in showing how the knowledge "really flows" from a given representation; a demonstration of necessary conditions would come in explaining the nature that a representation essential to that knowledge must have—in this case it comes in Kant's argument that geometry is possible as a science only if the representation of space is an a priori intuition, which is possible only if space is transcendentally ideal.

If an argument of this structure is to be found in Kant's Transcendental Analytic, it seems we should expect an account of the necessary and sufficient conditions of the type of synthetic a priori knowledge formulated in the propositions of the Principles of the Analytic, e.g., that "all alterations take place in conformity with the law of the connection of cause and effect" (B 232). This is quite a strong claim; it is the claim not only that Kant is providing an account of what must be the case if the causal maxim is to be valid but also that he is aiming to provide a sound argument which has that maxim as its conclusion.

Commentators have not shrunk from ascribing such a difficult project to Kant's Analytic, and their interpretations appear to be backed by Kant's famous remark in the *Prolegomena* (paragraphs 4 and 5) that the *Critique* employs a synthetic or progressive and not merely an analytic or regressive method, i.e., that it presents arguments which do not merely assume synthetic a priori knowledge and demonstrate its presuppositions but which have synthetic a priori principles as their conclusions. So it would *seem* that Kant's description of one part of a transcendental exposition as involving a demonstration of how knowledge "really flows" from a representation is equivalent to the claim that a transcendental deduction must include an argument which moves deductively to a synthetic a priori principle from premises merely elucidating a particular kind of representation. However, if this is the case, we should be able to find such a progressive argument in Kant's transcendental deduction of geometrical knowledge. In fact, immediately after explaining the two elements of a transcendental exposition, Kant gives us two paragraphs, the second of which obviously addresses itself to the treatment of necessary conditions of geometrical knowledge ("not otherwise than insofar as the intuition has its seat in the subject only"), and this suggests that the preceding paragraph is the account of sufficient conditions. But it is no such thing; the paragraph merely characterizes geometrical knowledge as synthetic a priori and argues that only if the representation of space is an a priori intuition is this knowledge possible. So instead of the expected progressive argument there is only another regressive explanation of necessary conditions for a type of knowledge.

It should be recalled that at this point in Kant's transcendental exposition all that is ever alleged to have been shown is that geometry involves synthetic a priori propositions and this requires an a priori intuition of space, though it may also be assumed from the "metaphysical exposition" of space that we are in possession of an a priori intuition of it (just as the later "metaphysical deduction" shows we are in possession of pure concepts). It is difficult to believe Kant could have mistaken these points for a progressive argument as characterized so far. What Kant has proven at most is something of the logical form: *A* only if *B*, *B*. (Note that *A*, the characterization of geometry as synthetic a priori, does not entail geometry is true of the world, nor does it involve specific claims about Euclidean geometry.) It would be unjustifiably uncharitable to assume he took this to be an argument establishing the truth of *A*. It is only fair to recommend that Kant's requirement that a transcendental exposition show how knowledge "really flows" from a representation not be construed as having to involve a progressive argument in the sense of a deductive proof with a synthetic a priori principle as its conclusion and the mere having of a representation as its premise. There are other considerations backing this interpretive proposal. Kant speaks elsewhere of the "objective" and "subjective" lines of a transcendental deduction (Axvii), the latter tracing synthetic a priori knowledge back to its "original germs" or "sources" in the human mind (A 97, A 786). It thus may be possible to take the "subjective" (as opposed to the "objective" and regressive) part of a transcendental exposition simply to relate a particular type of a priori knowledge to specific faculties, activities or types of representation of the mind, without providing a deductive argument going from the description of a mere representation to a conclusion which is an objective synthetic a priori principle. To say that knowledge "really flows" from a particular representation one should not have to be able to deduce the knowledge from the nature of the representation.

This interpretation not only makes sense of the first part of the transcendental deduction of the Aesthetic; it can also provide a general lesson for reading Kant's transcendental arguments: what at first may appear to be presented as a (non-trivial) deductive argument demonstrating that mere representations are logically sufficient conditions for knowledge is better understood as an essentially regressive argument. Confirmation for this thesis is to be found in the transcendental exposition of time (B 48). Incomplete as the exposition is, Kant's intentions at least are clearly no more than to "exhibit the possibility" of a body of knowledge—obviously this is to supply necessary, not sufficient, conditions. I will argue that the transcendental deduction of the Analytic bears out this general theory and so demonstrates a formal correspondence with Kant's earlier (regressive) argument for idealism. It will also be shown that, contrary to recent interpretations, the deduction of the categories has a material dependence on Kant's doctrine of transcendental idealism.

## II

The best way to substantiate the theory that there are significant formal correspondences between the Aesthetic and the Analytic would be to find that the proof structure of the deduction of the categories parallels that of the transcendental deduction in the Aesthetic. In its most skeletal form the central argument of the Aesthetic (with respect to space) has this structure: The science of geometry (A) requires synthetic a priori propositions which in turn require pure intuitions (B), and these are possible only if transcendental idealism is true. In this way the Aesthetic gives a transcendental explanation of how a body of knowledge (A) is possible only if a particular representation (B) has a certain nature. The argument of the Analytic would have a parallel structure if it is of the form: empirical knowledge ("experience") is possible only if the "original synthetic unity of apperception" applies to it,[1] which is possible only if pure concepts have validity, and this in turn requires that transcendental idealism be true. Such an argument would be transcendental in that it too would explain that a body of knowledge is possible only if there are representations (pure concepts) of a certain kind. The subjective aspect of the deduction, like that of the Aesthetic, could lie simply in the description of the nature and type of representations involved, e.g., in the demonstration of the appropriateness of their being a priori, and would not include the strong claim that the mere possession of certain representations (not cognitive by definition) entails a body of knowledge.

The interpretation of the Aesthetic given here follows rather directly from Kant's text and is hardly controversial. The proposed interpretation of the Analytic, however, appears at the very least to be directly contrary to the approach of the best known recent analyses (which I will refer to jointly as the "received interpretation," *RI*). The major departure of this interpretation is that it takes the *Critique* to accept empirical knowledge as a premise to be regressively explained rather than as a conclusion to be established. Peter Strawson, Jonathan Bennett, and Robert Paul Wolff have insisted at length that such an argument is undesirable, uninteresting, and not representative of Kant's best intentions.[2] They all represent the transcendental deduction as basically aiming to *establish* objectivity, i.e., to prove that there is an external and at least partially lawful world, a set of items distinct from one's awareness, and to do this from the minimal premise that one is self-conscious. Whereas these interpretations see the transcendental deduction as showing that one can be self-conscious only if there is an objective world of which one is aware, my interpretation takes Kant essentially to be arguing that for us there is objectivity, and hence empirical knowledge, only if the categories are universally valid. I will defend this interpretation with the following three-part argument: First, reasons will be given for rejecting the *RI*, then objections to my alternative interpretation will be countered, and finally an account will be given of the data which have appeared to justify the *RI*.

## III

There are two general reasons for being dissatisfied with versions of the *RI*: their representations of the transcendental deduction do not yield what they promise, a (non-trivial) valid argument, and it is highly unlikely they reflect Kant's intentions. To clarify these charges it is necessary to make explicit the various formulations of the argument held to be at the heart of the transcendental deduction.

According to Strawson, the major argument of the deduction is "to establish that experience necessarily involves knowledge of objects, in the weighty sense" (p. 88), and to do this not from the "disappointing" assumption that "experience is necessarily of an objective and spatio-temporally unitary world" (p. 85). Strawson expresses the deduction as "the thesis that for a series of diverse experiences to belong to a single self-consciousness it is necessary that they should be so connected as to constitute a temporally extended experience of a unified objective world" (p. 97). One could object that this formulation is a distortion of Kant's view since he held it is contingent that consciousness is temporal, but it would hardly do to reject Strawson's interpretation on the basis of this dubious doctrine. More significant is the fact that the formulation indicates how strong a claim the transcendental deduction is being expected to support. Strawson's version is no weaker than the thesis that there cannot be a self-conscious subject without an objective world. So expressed, the argument is certainly saved from triviality but its objective is so bold that, not unsurprisingly, many have been unable to find adequate grounds for it.

The reasons for rejecting Strawson's argument have varied. Though it has been argued by some that such transcendental arguments in general cannot succeed against an obstinate sceptic,[3] I will restrict my critique to objections against Strawson's specific formulation of the transcendental argument. What is claimed to be shown is that the fact of encountering a series of temporally experienced items entails that one has the ability to distinguish "subjective" from "objective" items, i.e., from items "conceived as distinct from particular subjective states of awareness of them" (p. 89). However, as Graham Bird has pointed out, the notion of "items conceived as distinct from *particular* states of awareness of them" is inadequate because items could pass Strawson's test for objectivity and still merely be properties of one's mind.[4] If "particular" means "any one particular," then enduring states of mind turn out to be "objective" (my agent, for example, may be distinct from a particular awareness of it); on the other hand, if "particular" means "all particular," then the looks and sounds of things become "subjective" (for how are we to understand the blueness of a flower, for example, independent of any references to states of consciousness?). Even if there is a way to iron out the wording of Strawson's conclusion, a decisive objection can be made by noting a peculiarity of his route to the conclusion:

> It was agreed at the outset that experience requires both particular intuitions and general concepts. There can be no experience at all which does not involve the recognition of particular items *as* being of such and such a kind. It seems that it must be possible, even in the most fleeting and purely subjective of impressions, to distinguish a component of recognition, or judgment, which is not simply identical with, or wholly absorbed by, the particular item which is recognized, which forms the topic of the judgement.
>
> . . . [T]he recognitional component, necessary to experience, can be present in experience only because of the *possibility* of referring different experiences to one identical subject of them all. Recognition implies the *potential* acknowledgement of the experience into which recognition necessarily enters as being one's own, as sharing with others this relation to the identical self. It is the fact that this potentiality is implicit in recognition which saves the recognitional component in a particular experience from absorption into the item recognized. . . . (pp. 100–101)

As Ross Harrison has observed, there is a crucial shift here in the meaning of "component of recognition."[5] At first the component designates the necessity that there be a general or descriptive and not only a demonstrative element in judgments. It is unclear why this should imply the necessity of a "recognitional component" in the quite different sense of a distinguishable subjective portion of experience. It seems that a sense data experiencer could have all that Strawson's original premise requires, a component of recognition in the first sense, without being in contract with an independently existing world.

Other advocates of the *RI* also fail to construct a significant valid argument out of the materials of the deduction. Bennett's analysis includes no less than four accounts of the transcendental deduction:

(1) The aim of the deduction is ostensibly to disprove the Humean conclusion that "objectivity and causality are at any moment liable to collapse" (pp. 100–101).

(2) This is done by arguing not merely that "concepts can be applied only in a causally ordered realm" (a typical regressive formulation), but "by showing . . . there cannot be experience which is not brought under concepts at all" (p. 102).

(3) "The central argument in the transcendental deduction has to do with the ownership of mental states", i.e., employs the premise that "every representation is someone's" (p. 103). (This "central argument" Bennett claims is in the first three paragraphs of the second edition version. The last ten paragraphs are treated as peripheral; this may explain Bennett's view that the second edition is "only marginally clearer.")

(4) "What Kant . . . repeatedly offers to prove in the transcendental deduction is that all experience must be of a realm of items which are objective in the sense that they can be distinguished from oneself and from one's inner states" (p. 131).

These are radical theses since Bennett expressly uses "experience" in the sense of consciousness not knowledge, though he adds Kant's "modest asserveration" that "all suppositions about experience must concern experience . . . which is accompanied by self-consciousness" (p. 106). The term "supposition" is important; it reflects Bennett's awareness that Kant entertains the logical possibility of representations which, although they are "nothing to" the owner, might be had in a "subhuman" way without implying or giving knowledge of objectivity (pp. 104–105). Bennett thinks Kant properly excludes this possibility because "states which one could not know oneself to be in . . . cannot intelligibly be made a subject for speculation" (p. 105). This claim (properly qualified) fleshes out the third account of the deduction but trivializes others; if only those states which one could know oneself to be in are under consideration, obviously "experience" must be brought under concepts and there will be no "experience" of a collapse of objectivity. Only Bennett's fourth account promises an interesting argument, yet this version is one Bennett himself says is not proven in the deduction. He contends the conclusion that consciousness implies objectivity is established only in the Analytic of Principles, that there are only "illegitimate" attempts to derive it in the Analytic of Concepts (p. 130). (The charge of "illegitimacy" is but a consequence of the *RI*'s insistence that Kant is trying to establish experience is objective and its chagrined discovery that he frequently defines it to be so.) Thus, none of Bennett's versions provide an account of the text of Kant's transcendental deduction itself which yields a non-trivial argument with a good claim to soundness.

Wolff's interpretation is more concerned than the others with seeing the whole *Critique* as built around an argument that "the categories are conditions of the possibility of consciousness itself" (p. 94). Wolff even claims "the deduction will not work unless the categories are viewed as "the necessary conditions of any consciousness whatsoever" (p. 159), a view which at the least conflicts with Kant's intentions, since Kant emphasizes the dependence of the deduction on the specific nature of human consciousness. Wolff is determined to construct out of Kant's text a progressive argument showing knowledge "really flows" from "the mere fact of consciousness" in a deductive way. This commits him not just to the already questioned thesis that there cannot be consciousness without an objective world but also to the claim that consciousness without empirical knowledge is a logical impossibility. (Sometimes, Wolff does say the aim is to establish "the *possibility* of empirical knowledge as a necessary condition of consciousness" (p. 112), and perhaps he means this to be equivalent to the earlier thesis.) Wolff treats Kant's pronouncements to the contrary as "incompatible" with "the central argument" and holds that "Kant finally states in absolutely unambiguous language that we cannot be conscious of an unsynthesized manifold" (p. 158).[6] In fact, Kant's text is not so clear:

> For even though we should have the power of associating perceptions, it would remain entirely undetermined and accidental whether they would themselves be associable; and should they not be associable, there might exist a multitude of perceptions, and indeed an entire sensibility, in which much empirical consciousness would arise in my mind, but in a state of separation, and without belonging to a [one] consciousness of myself. This, however, is impossible. For it is only because I ascribe all perceptions to one consciousness (original apperception) that I can say of all perceptions that I am conscious of them. (A 121–122)

Note that what Kant is calling impossible is not the existence of any consciousness which is not self-conscious and does not imply "appearances which fit into a connected whole of human knowledge." What Kant is denying is the possibility of having a "multitude of perceptions," an "entire sensibility" which is "in my mind" while there is no "one consciousness of myself." This is an acceptable though trivial denial if all it excludes is the sense of saying many states can belong to one consciousness while there is no one subject who has those states. If Kant meant to make a stronger claim (perhaps Wolff is right in thinking Kant did, but then it is significant that the passage occurs only in the first edition), the claim is unfounded. Wolff emphasizes the last sentence of Kant's statement as if it clinches his case, but that sentence is equivalent to saying, if I am conscious of $X$, $Y$, $Z$, then there is one consciousness of $X$, $Y$, $Z$. For this inference to work, $X$, $Y$, $Z$ must be my perceptions, not just any perceptions, and so the inference is just equivalent to the above mentioned trivial denial. As Kant's own considerations in the Paralogisms indicate, it is not evident that the having of a series of perceptions requires that one subject have "all perceptions."

Whatever their differences, the advocates of the *RI* agree in striving to find in Kant's transcendental deduction an argument deducing empirical knowledge from consciousness and its conditions. Since even those who have wanted to find such an argument in Kant have failed to construct a significant valid one, it should be determined whether Kant himself was really concerned with developing such an argument. Though there are some prima facie indications to the contrary, which will be dealt with later, the overwhelming evidence is that Kant did not put forth the transcendental deduction as having the aim the *RI* imputes to it. Kant nowhere states that it is to give the sufficient conditions of empirical knowledge or is a proof that there is an objective world. What Kant says he is doing is providing a deduction of the categories, a proof of *their* objective validity, which, since they are pure concepts, can be done only by showing their a priori applicability to experience, i. e., by showing that they are part of the (necessary) conditions for the possibility of experience (A 93, A 95, B 169), where "experience" is defined as "empirical knowledge" (B 147, B 161, etc.). The question to which Kant addressed his argument is whether appearances universally obey pure synthetic principles. His answer was expressly dependent on the use of the notion of "possible experience." He says there is no direct proof, for example, from the concept of an event or happening to the legitimacy of the causal maxim; the argument of the Analytic must invoke the characteristics that an event needs to be empirically knowable in order for it to establish the maxim (B 765, B 815).

## IV

Kant's own statements about the nature of the transcendental deduction support the earlier account of its structure which was proposed as an alternative to the *RI*. But the claim that the deduction should be treated as having this structure cannot rest on this appeal to authority. It must be shown that it is plausible and significant for an argument to have this form—a matter all proponents of the *RI* have doubted. In response to these doubts, I will clarify the form of the deduction on my interpretation and show that the deduction so construed, as employing the possession of empirical knowledge as a premise, is nonetheless not trivial.

The first task is best achieved by taking care of a natural objection to the interpretation given in section I. There it was proposed that Kant's transcendental deductions are in general best regarded as having a regressive and not progressive form. Yet it was also said that a typical progressive argument would have a synthetic a priori principle as its conclusion. Now if the essence of the transcendental deduction is the argument that empirical knowledge is possible only if the categories are applicable and hence only if some synthetic a priori principles are true, it would appear that the deduction is progressive after all. Furthermore, the argument appears to move deductively to its conclusion from premises non-trivially entailing it, since "experience" is not defined as involving synthetic a priori principles. Despite these considerations it can be shown that the proposed interpretation is a genuine alternative to the *RI* and that there is good reason for calling the deduction regressive. What complicates matters here is the relativity of the terms "progressive" and "regressive." It is not adequate to define the former as involving a demonstration of the sufficient conditions of something and the latter as a demonstration of necessary conditions, because in general one and the same argument demonstrates both necessary and sufficient conditions (if $x$ implies $y$, $x$ is a sufficient condition of $y$ and $y$ a necessary condition of $x$). However, once the epistemological concern of transcendental arguments is taken into account, I believe adequate distinguishing definitions of "progressive" and "regressive" are available: a regressive argument would show $y$ is a necessary condition of knowledge *x*; a progressive argument would show *z* is a sufficient condition of knowledge *x*, where *z* is a type of representation not defined as epistemic. These definitions have the merit of making just the distinction advocates of the *RI* would also recognize. When I argue that the deduction is regressive as just defined, this is to say that it is not progressive in their sense, that is, it is not a radical argument from a premise not assuming the possession of knowledge. This does not put me into conflict with Kant's claim in the *Prolegomena* that the *Critique* has a progressive form, for his criterion of "progressive" refers not to the premise but to the conclusion of the argument. It can be agreed that the deduction is progressive simply in the sense that it proceeds toward the establishment of synthetic a priori principles.

The most common objection to regarding the transcendental deduction as regressive is that this would render it trivial. To paraphrase Strawson, doesn't an argument which uses empirical knowledge as a premise just present the sceptic with conclusions which can have no more strength than its questionable assumptions? The first reply to this question is that not every interesting argument has to be a refutation of extreme scepticism. Secondly, there are different levels of triviality and the transcendental deduction is not formulated as trivially as it might be. On this interpretation Kant's premise is not, as is often assumed, Newtonian and Euclidian science but is the relatively weak assumption of some empirical knowledge. Furthermore, the conclusion of the argument is relatively strong. The argument is not the circular claim that experience (empirical knowledge) requires mere objectivity; it is the claim that such experience requires the universal validity of a number of a priori concepts. So the argument does move from a relatively weak premise to a relatively strong conclusion, and while the argument so contrued perhaps does not have to move as far as the *RI* version of it does, it still makes a substantive claim. What makes this regressive argument vulnerable is not that it argues for so little but that it claims so much. Later I will show that it is only by making considerable metaphysical assumptions that Kant manages to complete the deduction, but whatever possible weaknesses this may indicate in Kant's strategy it at the same time lays to rest the most common objection to that strategy.

## V

At this point it may appear a sheer mystery how the *RI* has received the support it has. It would be improper to suggest that the only basis of the *RI* is the penchant of contemporary philosophers to make out of Kant's philosophy a radical refutation of scepticism. There are two prominent features of the text which strongly suggest there is a progressive argument in the deduction. The first is the emphasis on the fundamental importance of the "transcendental unity of apperception," the thesis that representations must be capable of being my representations and meet the conditions of being elements within the unity of consciousness. This point, more than anything else, has been responsible for the view than Kant meant to deduce the validity of the categories from the "fact of consciousness." Even in the second edition Kant begins the deduction with a discussion of the unity of consciousness and the "many consequences" that follow from it (B 132–133). However, it is not clear that developing the consequences of the "original unity of apperception" is equivalent to drawing out the implications of the mere having of representations. If it were, the deduction would appear to have the progressive structure of an argument for consciousness as a logically sufficient condition of the validity of at least some objective concepts. But Kant immediately distinguishes "original apperception" from "empirical apperception" (B 132) in such a way that only the latter designates the mere having of representations. "Empirical consciousness" as such is not argued to have any implications with respect to the objective validity of concepts. On the other hand, "the transcendental unity of apperception is that unity through which the manifold given in an intuition is united in the concept of the object. It is therefore entitled objective and must be distinguished from the subjective unity of consciousness, which is a determination of inner sense . . ." (B 139). Kant makes it clear that the trascendental unity of apperception is a necessary condition of empirical knowledge; representations which cannot be unified as mine cannot be representations which amount to knowledge (B 137). If it is also the case that the condition that representations agree with the transcendental and not merely the empirical unity of consciousness just means for Kant that they objectively be related, then "original apperception" would be a sufficient condition of empirical knowledge as well, though by definition and not because of any progressive argument. In paragraph 19 of the second edition Kant does say that the "objective unity of given representations" is precisely what "indicates their relation to original apperception" (B 142). "Original" and "objective" unity of apperception are here interchangeable terms for Kant. Hence, one cannot argue that the deduction is progressive simply because it begins with a discussion of the unity of consciousness and its conditions, for there is strong evidence that the unity which concerns Kant is not that given with the "fact of consciousness" but is that involved when there is "objective" consciousness, i.e., experience in his sense.

There is a further important reason for not regarding ordinary consciousness as the starting point of Kant's argument. Such a perspective makes unintelligible the structure of the deduction in the second edition. If the *RI* is right, the demonstration in paragraph 20 that intuitions are subject to the categories should complete the deduction, for if the starting point of the argument is the consideration of just any representations that come before consciousness, any proof that representations are subject to the categories should be conclusive. However, Kant insists the deduction's purpose is "fully attained" only later, in paragraph 26, "by demonstration of the a priori validity of the categories in respect of all objects of our senses" (B 145). This statement expresses Kant's view that the aim of the deduction is the proof not of mere objectivity but of the validity of the categories, and also makes clear that the central issue of their validity is settled only after paragraph 20. Contrary to what is assumed by recent analytic interpretations, the later paragraphs are meant not as a mere spelling out of the subjective circumstances involved in the application of the categories but as a continuation of the basic argument of the deduction.

The "beginning" of the deduction concerns the use of the categories for representations already unified in one intuition. Kant's early discussion repeatedly focuses on "the manifold of representations in *an* intuition" (B 133, 135, 139). In paragraphs 20 and 21 he capitalizes "Einer" [One] to indicate his concern with the unity of one intuition. This point stands out in the German but is somewhat lost in the translation,[7] though it is obvious once attention is given to the footnote to B 144, which states the proof "so far rests on the represented unity of intuition" (cf. B 155n, 160n.), and to the repeated statement of paragraph 20 that the argument concerns "the manifold . . . so far as it is given in a single empirical intuition." Kant's argument to this point is that representations in one intuition are unified by consciousness, that the logical functions of judgment just are the ways consciousness unifies representations, hence these representations must be subject to these functions. The argument depends heavily on the general validity of the "metaphysical deduction" and its claim that "the same function which gives unity to the various representations in a judgement also gives unity to the mere synthesis of various representations in an intuition" (B 104). Here I will focus not on that difficult claim but on Kant's remarkable belief that still more has to be established for the transcendental deduction to be complete.

The concern of the second part of the deduction is indicated in the title of paragraph 26: "Transcendental deduction of the *universal* possible employment in experience of the pure concepts of the understanding." Kant's earlier argument that the categories apply to representations which are unified in *an* intuition leaves open the question whether the categories apply to representations not so united. Kant has argued that the unity of an intuition depends on the "original unity of apperception," but if this in turn is just the objective unity of experience it is natural to inquire whether there are representations which "may present themselves to our senses" not in conformity with the categories. In particular, one might wonder whether it is necessary for the elements of mere perception (prior to their unification in the thought of a singular item, an intuition) to be in agreement with the "logical forms of judgment," whether, as Kant puts it, the "empirical synthesis of apprehension" must conform with the "intellectual synthesis of apperception" (B 162n)—a question which Kant takes not to have been resolved earlier. It is very significant that Kant's answer here is not to directly invoke the conditions of the unity of consciousness but to argue along lines set down by the Aesthetic, which had shown that all *our* representations must be in space or time and that we are a priori certain of the unity of space and time. Kant now argues that since all unity (and hence this unity too) "presupposes a synthesis which does not belong to the senses" (B 160n) but to the understanding and its categories, "everything that is to be represented as determined in space or in time must conform" to the categories (B 161). It is thus the universality and unity of space and time, not the unity of consciousness as such, which is invoked to guarantee the "universal validity" of the categories for us. In this way Kant's deduction in the Analytic depends on the doctrine of idealism in the Aesthetic, for only the thesis that space and time are forms of the mind, dependent on it and a priori knowable, can justify the certainty that they are unities determining all our representations.

These points can shed light on the second feature of Kant's text which might appear to lend support to the *RI*. In paragraph 13 Kant considers the possibility of

> appearances so constituted that the understanding should not find them to be in accord with the conditions of its unity. Everything might be in

such confusion that, for instance, in the series of appearances nothing presented itself which might yield a rule of synthesis and so answer to the concept of cause and effect. (B 123)

Because of this passage the transcendental deduction has often been read as essentially having the purpose of showing against Hume that we can be certain of a lawful and therefore objective world. On this view the deduction's aim is to establish the causal maxim and in this way prove there is something to be distinguished from the arbitrary sequences of one's mental states. However, an alternative interpretation is possible, and there are reasons for believing Kant saw that the transcendental deduction was not designed to establish the causal maxim from scratch. The possibility of a world of chaotic representations which Kant mentions in paragraph 13 can be understood as presenting not the traditional problem of scepticism but rather the problem which the two part structure of the second edition deduction explicitly raises, namely whether the scope of the categories extends to all our representations or just to a subset already considered objective by definition. This interpretation might also explain why in the pivotal paragraph 20 of that deduction Kant reminds the reader to refer back to paragraph 13. While the *RI* takes the notion of representations not subject to the categories as something directly contrary to the central argument of the *Critique,* something the mature Kant supposedly could not have seriously entertained, it is easier (especially in view of the preservation of the section in the second edition) to take it simply to represent the logical possibility, which Kant continued to stress, that our sensibility might have been such that what is given our senses would not be determined as it is by unified pure forms of sensibility.

I will conclude my critique of the *RI* by analyzing those passages in the deduction itself which have supported the belief that Kant's primary concern is to reply to the sceptic and establish the objectivity of experience by proving the causal maxim. In the first edition Kant does argue that "appearances are themselves actually subject to a rule," for otherwise the "reproducibility of appearances," which is itself "necessary to experience" would be impossible (A 100). Kant's conclusion is that "all appearances stand in thorough going community according to necessary laws and therefore in a transcendental affinity," and that without causality perceptions would "be without an object, merely a blind play of representations" (A 112, 114). This suggests that somehow Kant was trying to argue that the necessity of some order among representations is tantamount to the validity of the category of causality. But the "affinity" that Kant argues for is not at all equivalent to the reign of the principle of universal causality. The requirement that the world not be such that cinnabar is "sometimes red, sometimes black, sometimes light," is a requirement that can be met without the law of causality applying to all objective appearances. On the other hand, a world could be so arranged that it universally obeyed strict causal laws and yet was so various that no adequate "affinity" of appearances would be available to human observers. Affinity can be either a stronger or a weaker condition than causality and it really is not essential to Kant's main argument for the objective validity of the categories *in general,* a fact which is evident from Kant's omission of the topic in the second edition. The phenomenon which it was supposed to explain in the first edition, the empirical reproducibility of appearances, is passed over in the second edition as an "only subjective" and secondary feature (B 140).

The second edition also alone gives an appropriate discussion of the "necessary" relation that objects of experience have. The example that the first edition gives of the thesis that "the relation of all knowledge to its object carries with it an element of necessity" (A 104) is the concept of a triangle, which provides a rule for uniting and reproducing representations of it. This suggests that the necessity involved in objective representations is equivalent to the relation of logical necessity between the concept of a thing and its defined constituents (e.g., "three straight lines"). In the second edition Kant rectifies this suggestion by noting that the "necessary unity" of representations which he means to prove signifies not that representations "necessarily belong to one another," but that "they belong to one another in virtue of the necessary unity of apperception in the synthesis of intuition" (B 142). What Kant argues is not that individual representations have a necessary tie with one another but that for representations really to be representations of one item it is necessary that they be thought as combined in an object, and this just is for them to be unified in accordance with the logical form of judgment.

In conclusion, it should be emphasized that I have argued only that a regressive interpretation of the transcendental deduction is supported by evidence of Kant's intentions and by recognition that such an argument need not be trivial, question begging, or tied to the scientific presuppositions of Kant's day. I have not contended that the deduction so construed, as moving from empirical knowledge to the universal validity of the categories, is valid. But as noted before, the progressive interpretation has failed to find a valid argument in the deduction, and if one is to be found it seems only proper to proceed by first testing that proof structure which is best aligned with Kant's own avowed and considered strategy.

## Notes

1. This formulation is an incomplete representation of my interpretation. Later, it will be shown to be an essential part of Kant's argument that the unity of apperception applies universally to all our representations only because of the nature of our forms of sensibility.

2. Peter Strawson, *The Bounds of Sense* (London, 1966); Jonathan Bennett, *Kant's Analytic* (Cambridge, 1966); Robert Paul Wolff, *Kant's Theory of Mental Activity* (Cambridge, Mass., 1963). All quotations without citation in the following section refer to these works.

3. Barry Stroud, *Transcendental Arguments,* Journal of Philosophy, vol. 65, 1968, pp. 241–256. I agree with Stroud's criticism of Strawson, not his interpretation of Kant. Stroud assumes Kant's purpose in the transcendental deduction is that of a refutation of idealism, that Kant means to establish the objective validity of concepts in general.

4. Graham Bird, *Recent Interpretations of Kant's Transcendental Deduction,* Kant-Studien, vol. 65, Sonderheft 1974, pp. 1–4.

5. Ross Harrison, *Strawson on Outer Things,* The Philosophical Quarterly, vol. 20, 1970, pp. 213–221. Cf. Richard Rorty, *Strawson's Objectivity Argument,* Review of Metaphysics, vol. 24, 1970, pp. 207–244.

6. In section V, I argue Kant does not believe any of *our* representations are unsynthesized, for the categories are "universally valid." But unlike Wolff I point out that this belief has an essential dependence on Kant's theory of our forms of sensibility, on the contingency that our senses are as they are.

7. The essential two part structure of the proof is somewhat hidden from English readers because of weaknesses in Smith's otherwise excellent translation. The pivotal sentence in paragraph 21, B 144, should read: "Thus in the above proposition a beginning is made of a deduction of the pure concepts of the understanding; and in this deduction *so far,* since the categories have their source in the understanding alone, independently of sensibility, I have abstracted from the mode in which the manifold for an empirical intuition is given, *in order to* direct attention solely to the unity. . . ."

# 6

# Did the Sage of Königsberg
# Have No Dreams?

*Lewis White Beck*

This question was asked by C. I. Lewis[1] in order to show that Kant demanded too much of his categories. According to Lewis, Kant required his categories to limit experience to what is categorizable and to prevent us from having non-categorizable experiences. Lewis, on the other hand, wanted to leave experience independent of the categories, and to use categories not as a dam against an otherwise uncontrollable flood of experiences but as nets with which to capture some experiences which, for that very reason, will be taken as referring to objects. "A priori principles of categorical interpretation," he writes, "are required to limit *reality;* they are not required to limit *experience.*"[2] Dreams and illusions are experienced, but they are not caught by our normal categorical net; hence they are not taken to be real. But according to Lewis's interpretation of Kant, Kant could not account for even the *awareness* of dreams and illusions, since Kantian categories would keep us from being conscious of them.

My purpose is to find out how Kant would have defended the obvious answer to Lewis's penetrating question.

In §13 of the *Critique of Pure Reason* Kant points out a "difficulty" in justifying the necessary objective validity of concepts which do not arise by abstraction from intuitions.

> The categories of the understanding . . . do not represent conditions under which objects are given in intuition. Objects may, therefore, appear to us without their being under the necessity of being related to the functions of understanding, and understanding, therefore, need not contain

their a priori conditions. . . . Appearances might very well be so constituted that the understanding should not find them to be in accordance
with the principles of its unity. Everything might be in such confusion, for
instance, in the series of appearances that nothing presented itself which
might yield a rule of synthesis and so answer to the conception of cause
and effect.[3]

This famous and puzzling passage has caused "astonishment and
even indignation"[4] among commentators. There are two competing
interpretations. According to the "patchwork theory," when Kant
wrote it he believed that these sentences might be true, and had not
yet found an argument to show that they were not.[5] According to the
other, this possibility was entertained only pedagogically; Kant was asking a question which he imagined his readers would naturally ask and
was preparing them for an argument by which this "difficulty" could
be averted.[6] Both interpretations agree that Kant finally denied the possibility left open in §13, and only differ about whether he had ever
positively affirmed it. If he did really affirm it, at that time he had a
simple answer to Lewis's question; and the more the *Critique* moves
away from it, the more exposed it is to the scorn of the argument from
dreams.

Let us see how Kant removed the "difficulty" of §13, and see if he
still left himself a way to admit that he did have dreams. We must draw
two distinctions which are implicit in the *Critique* but which are never
made explicit.

### Two Meanings of "Experience"

Lewis says that Kant used the word "experience" "as if experience and
the phenomenally real [i.e., the objectively valid] coincide."[7] Sometimes he did so, sometimes not. The opening sentences of the Introductions to both editions use the word "experience" equivocally. In B
we read:

> There can be no doubt that all our knowledge begins with experience.
> For [otherwise] how should our faculty of knowledge . . . work up the
> raw material of sensible impressions into that knowledge of objects which
> is called experience?[8]

In the first sentence, "experience" means "the raw material of sensible
impressions," the manifold of apprehensions or Lockean ideas without

the conceptual and interpretative activities of the mind. In the second sentence "experience" means "knowledge of objects" and does perhaps, in Lewis's expression, "coincide with the phenomenally real." Let us call these two meanings "Lockean experience" and "Kantian experience," or, for short, L-experience and K-experience.

One way of reading the *Critique of Pure Reason* is to see it as an answer to the question: how do we move from L-experience to K-experience? And if this were the whole truth about the *Critique,* Kant would have a simple answer to Lewis's question: we make this move with only partial success. This is, briefly, Lewis's *own* answer.

### Two Meanings of "Intuition"

The *Critique* begins with an inspectional conception of intuition and ends with a functional conception. According to the first, an intuition is a passively received inspectable sensory datum giving consciousness of an individual object independently of all categorization. It is given to consciousness as it were ready-made and labeled. The following examples show this usage:

> In whatever manner and by whatever means a cognition may be related to objects, intuition is that through which it is in immediate relation to them.[9]

> Intuition relates immediately to the object and is single.[10]

> Appearances [ = representations] are the sole objects which can be given to us immediately, and that in them which relates immediately to the object is called intuition.[11]

The inspectional conception of intuition is presupposed in the "difficulty" raised in §13. Given this conception of intuition, it is obvious that there could be intuitions which would not be tractable to categorial rules.

The development of the functional conception of intuition is Kant's way of resolving the "difficult." This development represents the shift from a pre-Copernican to a Copernican conception of the relation of knowledge to object. Kant substitutes for the unknowable relation of representations to ontologically independent objects the rule-governed relation of representations of each other. This brings a new conception of object, and with it a new, a functional conception of intuition.

The new conception of object:

> Insofar as our cognitions are to relate to an object, they must necessarily agree with one another, that is, must possess that unity which constitutes the concept of an object.[12]

> Appearance, in contradistinction to the [mere] representations of apprehension, can be represented as an object distinct from them only if it stands under a rule which distinguishes it from every other apprehension and necessitates one particular mode of connection of the manifold [of apprehension]. The object is that in the appearance which contains the condition of this necessary rule of apprehension.[13]

The object is that the concept of which is a rule for the synthesis of representations which, by conformity to that concept, are descriptive of it or serve as evidence for its existence.

And the new conception of intuition:

> The fact that this affection of sensibility [sc. intuition] is in me does not amount to a relation of such representation to any object.[14]

> Thought is the act which relates given intuition to an object.[15]

Note how radically the second sentence contradicts the inspectional conception. According to this, the pattern was:

$$\text{concept} \rightarrow \text{intuition} \rightarrow \text{object}$$

According to the last quotation, the pattern now is:

$$\text{intuition} \rightarrow \text{concept} \rightarrow \text{object}$$

On the inspectional view, there could be intuitions which relate immediately to objects but do not conform to the categories; representations might not be synthesizable or constructible under the concept of the object and could belong only to L-experience. According to the functional view, representations which do not conform to the concept of the object may be experienced but are not considered intuitions precisely because they fail to conform to the concept of the object.

If this were the whole truth, Kant could easily explain to Lewis how he dreamt. In fact, if this were the whole answer, it would have been so obvious that Lewis would never have raised the question, for Kant would have anticipated Lewis's most original contribution to the theory of categories.

Important as these two distinctions are, they seem nevertheless to be inconsistent with the central line of thought of the *Critique* (which does seem to give Kant difficulties with Lewis's question). This line of thought is the *nervus probandi* of the Transcendental Deduction, which I shall try to compress into four premises and a conclusion.

1. The "I think" must be able to accompany all of my representations of which I am conscious.[16]
2. To think is to judge.[17]
3. To judge is to relate representations to one another according to a rule given by a category.[18]
4. Representations synthetically related to each other according to the rule given by a category as a concept of an object in general are the same as representations related to objects.[19]
5. Therefore, relation to an object must be ascribed to all representations of which we are conscious.[20]

As a result of this argument, Kemp Smith concluded:

Only in and through relation to an object can sense-representations be apprehended. . . . Relation to an object is constituted by the categories, because only thereby is consciousness of any kind possible at all.[21]

From this it follows for Kemp Smith that L-experience is not conscious experience, that animals are not conscious, and, presumably, that dreams are not possible. While Kemp Smith does not always adhere to these shocking conclusions, he describes the position I have just quoted as the "truly Critical position" to which Kant moved when he escaped from the "difficulty" pointed out in §13. What to Kemp Smith appeared "the truly Critical position" appeared to Lewis, however, to be an absurdity which could be exposed by his flippant question.

Through an exhaustive collection of texts Paton showed that Kant did not draw any of these conclusions from the Transcendental Deduction.[22] But while this was historically interesting, it did not show that

Kant *ought not* to have drawn them or how he avoided drawing them. This is what I propose to show.

In one of his private notes Kant added to the first premise another statement which, had it been explicitly stated in the *Critique,* would have made the transcendental deduction less clear. He wrote:

> Consciousness can accompany all representations, *and thus also those of imagination,* which, and the play of which, is itself an object of *inner* sense, and of which it must be possible to become conscious as such an object.[23]

We shall work our way slowly to a justification of this addendum; but first of all we need to see whether the radical Kemp Smith–Lewis conclusions truly follow from the statement of the transcendental deduction in its restricted, classical form. I shall argue that they do not, and thus that Kant could, without inconsistency, have made the addendum in the *Critique* itself.

Kant does not anywhere say that the "I think" must accompany all of my representations; he says merely that it must be able to accompany them. While there is no representation, presumably, which cannot be judgingly related to the rest, it does not follow from Kant's statement that every representation is in fact judged to be related to the rest. A perception that *could not* be accompanied by "I think" "would not belong to any experience, consequently would be without an object, merely a blind play of representations, less even than a dream."[24] While the words "without an object" suggest that K-experience is meant, the last phrase of the sentence shows that L-experience is meant also. I could not even be aware of a representation of which I could not say "I think it," for such a representation would be "nothing to me,"[25] "nothing at all,"[26] "less even than a dream."[27] It would not only not represent an object; "I would not even be able to know that I have [it]."[28]

This modification weakens the claim made in the conclusion, which should now read:

> 5'. Relation to an object must be *ascribable* to every representation of which we are conscious.

This conclusion, however, is rejected by Kant because he holds that some representations have no possible objective reference.[29] The conclusion he wants to draw, and which he does draw in the Refutation of Idealism in B, is:

5″. Relation to an object must be *ascribed* to *some* representations of which we are conscious.

The argument of the Refutation of Idealism is that we do not start with an awareness of subjective representations (L-experience) and subsequently infer that some of them have objective reference. Rather, awareness of the subjective stream of consciousness is cognate with the awareness of the non-self or object.[30] Without the representations of outer sense or spatial intuition we have no conception of an inner nonspatial subjective realm of *mere* representations. I cannot say of one representation that it is merely a modification of *my mind* unless I can say of some other representations that they stand for objects; I cannot be conscious of myself except insofar as I am conscious of what is not-self.

The Refutation of Idealism does not require of any particular outer experience that it be veridical: I can dream of Paris as well as see Paris, and

the difference between truth and dreaming is not ascertained by the nature of the representations which are referred to objects (for they are the same in the two cases) but by their connection according to those rules which determine the coherence of the representations in the concept of an object, and by ascertaining whether they can subsist together in [K-] experience or not.[31]

Outer representations

can very well be the product merely of the imagination (as in dreams and illusions). Such representation is merely the reproduction of previous outer perceptions which . . . are possible only through the reality of outer objects.[32]

Kant is here saying that L-experience is possible only if K-experience is possible; but that there is L-experience (such as dreams and wild sense-data) which is not taken up into K-experience. What is not so taken up nevertheless belongs to the consciousness which must contain veridical representations of objects, and may be seen as modifications of my mind and thus as contributing to knowledge of the self as phenomenon of the inner sense. The subjective or empirical unity of apperception, which is my awareness of myself, is dependent upon the transcendental or objective unity of apperception;[33] but I can synthesize all perceptions "in one consciousness of my state"[34] even when I cannot synthesize all of them into consciousness of one world. Thus we reach the justification of the addendum which, we noted, Kant made to the first premise in his private notes, namely the assertion that the "I think" must be able to accompany *all* my representations, whether they be of outer objects or of objects of inner sense.

You may have noticed that the passages which I have been quoting as making it difficult for Kant to explain how we can be aware of what is not conceptualized have been taken largely from the first edition, and the passages quoted as indicating his answer have been taken largely from the second. It is as if someone read the first edition and asked him, "Herr Professor, do you never dream and never have experiences you cannot relate to objects?" In fact, we can date this apocryphal question. It must have been before the *Prolegomena,* and the first answer he gave in §§18–20 of that work was on the level of argument attained in §13 of the *Critique* but surpassed in the later parts of the *Critique.* For this reason most Kant scholars regard this part of the *Prolegomena* as inconsistent with Kant's mature view and cite in support of this the fact that its teachings are not repeated in the second edition of the *Critique.*[35] But we shall see, I hope, that the passages in the *Prolegomena* can be given a sympathetic interpretation which is consistent with what has been said before.

Kant's distinction between judgments of perception and judgments of experience is analogous to that between L-experience and K-experience.[36] Judgments of perception are "only subjectively valid" and require no category.[37] They obtain "reference to an object" through "superadding" a category which is a rule that "they must agree among themselves" and thus have universal, that is to say, objective, validity. Some judgments of perception, for example, "When the sun shines on the stone it becomes warm," can be converted into judgments of experience, for example, "The sun warms the stone," which make no reference to the contingencies of the matter in which *I* happen to have apprehended the event. But there are other judgments of perception, for example, "The room is warm, sugar sweet, wormwood bitter" which "refer only to feeling, which everyone knows to be merely subjective and can of course never be attributed to the object and can never become objective."[38]

There are at least three reasons to be suspicious of Kant's account of judgments of perception, and to regard it more as a statement of a problem, like the "difficulty" of §13 of the *Critique,* than as a permanent part of the edifice of the critical philosophy.

### Judgment Always Makes a Claim to Objectivity

Kant writes in the *Critique:*

> I have never been able to accept the interpretations which logicians give of judgment in general. It is, they declare, the representation of a relation between two concepts.[39]

This does not adequately distinguish between a mere association of ideas and a judgment. A judgment is indeed a representation of the relation between concepts, but this does not tell us "in what the asserted relation consists." Kant finds that

> a judgment is nothing but the manner in which given cognitions [intuitions and concepts] are brought to the objective unity of apperception. This is what is intended by the copula "is." It is employed to distinguish the objective unity of given representations from the subjective. It indicates their relation to the original apperception, and its necessary unity.[40]

But in a judgment of perception "I merely compare perceptions and connect them in a consciousness of my particular state"; the judgment of perception is "merely a connection of perceptions in my mental state, without reference to the object."[41] Since, according to the teaching of the *Critique,* "reference to object" is reduced to "necessary relation of representations among themselves according to a categorial concept," and this necessary relation is what is intended by the objective claim registered by use of the copula, it follows that a judgment of perception as defined in the *Prolegomena* is not a judgment at all as defined in the *Critique.*

It remains to inquire which of the two accounts of judgment is correct, and I suggest that the view of the *Critique* ought to prevail, not only exegetically but also philosophically.

There is a right way and a wrong way to make a judgment of perception. Even a judgment of perception is under rules. While the judgment, "When I see the sun shining on the stone I feel the stone's becoming warm,"[42] may be true only *of me,* it is not true merely *for me.* It does not say that if *you* see the one *you* will feel the other; but it does say that *you would be right* if you affirmed that when *I* see the one *I* feel the other, and wrong if you denied it. The judgment is subjective in content (it is perhaps about my subjective L-experience) but objective in its claim to your credence.

In such a judgment I am indeed judging about *my* representations as episodes or states in *my* mental history, and not about what objects these representations may represent. But the *Critique* makes room even for this with the generous scope it allows the term "object": "Everything, every representation even, in so far as we are conscious of it, may be entitled object,"[43] and hence may be judged.

### Judgment Always Makes Use of Categorial Concepts

A judgment does not have to mention a categorial concept, but it has to use one. "The cause of the stone's becoming warm is the sun's shining on it" *mentions* the concept of cause; "the sun warms the stone" *uses* it. Kant seems to think that the judgment, "When the sun shines on the stone, it becomes warm," does neither. He is wrong, or at least inconsistent with the teachings of the *Critique* when he thinks this. The knowledge of the objective succession of sun-shining/stone-becoming-warm requires, according to the Second Analogy, the causal principle. More obviously, "sun" and "stone" are names of substances which are borrowed from external objective experience to denote mere representations. Most obviously, if all even tacit reference to objects were excluded from the judgment of perception, the mathematical categories would still apply to the intensive magnitude of the brightness I see when I look at the sun and of the warmth I feel when I touch the stone. The Anticipation of Perception applies even to the data of L-experience.[44]

### Judgments Predicating Secondary Qualities of Objects Can Be Objectively Valid

Kant denies this when he holds "The room is warm" to be a judgment of perception that can never become a judgment of experience because "it refers only to feeling."[45] Kant's position here is more extreme than Locke's, but it is not as consistently held. We must try to work out a consistent view which Kant did hold at least sometimes.

Let us put one of his judgments of perception into a special mode: "This room feels warm (to me)." This judgment does not ascribe a one-place predicate to the room. The warmth, grammatically predicated of the room, exists only in me or in relation to me. The judgment is valid (true) *for me* in the sense that it is claimed to be true *of me.* Yet this judgment is objectively valid, for the equivalent judgment, "The room feels warm to Beck," is a judgment of experience about which others can have evidence and on which they must agree if it is true. What just *I* feel is not part of K-experience; but that I feel what no one else may feel, for example, the uncomfortable warmth of my fever, is a part of K-experience.

If my three criticisms of Kant's views in the *Prolegomena* are sound, we can conclude that judgments of perception are not mere associations of ideas without objective validity. They may be about associations of ideas, but if correct they are correct for everyone. They report about subjective episodes or states of mind, and such judgments are made under the rules of the categories. There is no difficulty in showing them how Kant can be conscious of them. Such judgments do not belong in K-experience about objects like the sun, the stone, sugar, and wormwood—what Kant calls objects of the outer sense supposed to be really existent, and what Prauss calls "objective objects." But they may be objective in the genuine Kantian sense of being made according to categorical rules which exact credence from every knowing subject, even if they are about what Kant calls objects of the inner sense or mere feelings. . . .

A dream is a "subjective object." In a dream I dreamingly-see a three-headed monster. To dreamingly-see it, unlike to-see-it-without-qualification, does not imply that there *is* a three-headed monster. But I say, "Last night I dreamt I saw a three-headed monster," and my judgment about *that* event is as objective as the judgment that I slept in my bed and makes just as valid a claim on your credence. You cannot verify it by inspection, but the occurrence of the dream, unlike the monster in the dream, falls under the Second Postulate of Empirical Thought, fulfilling the criteria of existence. I can verify it by self-observation, and though I get no knowledge of three-headed monsters, I do get knowledge of myself: Inner sense "represents to consciousness even our own self, only as we appear to ourselves, not as we are in ourselves," but in that respect I am in the same epistemological boat as the three-headed monster (if he really exists and I really see him, not dreamingly-see him).

Lewis, it seems to me, would be in agreement with much of what I profess to have found in Kant. "What is not reality of one sort is reality of another," Lewis writes. "What we do not understand in one way, we shall understand in another. The subsumption of the given under the heading 'dream' or 'illusion' is itself a categorial interpretation by which we understand certain experiences."[46] What we do not know as objective objects we can know as subjective objects. Lewis is using the term "categorial interpretation," however, in a much broader sense than Kant would sanction. The difference between seeing Paris and dreaming that one sees Paris is not a categorial difference, but an empirical difference. The "category" *dream* rightly does not appear in Kant's table. The categories Kant is interested in are presupposed in our having and reporting either type of awareness. The categories do not differentiate veridical from non-veridical experience; they make the difference between dumbly facing chaos without even knowing it—"less even than a dream"[47]—and telling a connected story, even if it is false . . .

## Notes

1. *Mind and the World Order* (New York, 1929), p. 221. I discussed other aspects of Lewis's interpretation of Kant in "Lewis's Kantianism" in *Studies in the Philosophy of Kant,* pp. 108–24.
2. Ibid., p. 222. The entire sentence is italicized in the original.
3. *Critique of Pure Reason,* A 89–90 = B 122–23.
4. The quoted words are from H. J. de Vleeschauwer, *La déduction transcendentale dans l'oeuvre de Kant* (1936; New York, 1976), II, 176, who gives a survey of the divergent German-language interpretations.
5. Norman Kemp Smith, *A Commentary on Kant's Critique of Pure Reason* (London, 1923), p. 222.
6. H. J. Paton, *Kant's Metaphysic of Experience* (London, 1936), I, 324–25.
7. Lewis, *Mind and the World Order,* p. 221.
8. *Critique of Pure Reason,* B 1.
9. Ibid., A 19 = B 33.
10. Ibid., A 320 = B 377.
11. Ibid., A 108; not in B. Kant often uses "appearances" where he means "representations," i.e., "appearances" often means "appearances to consciousness" and not "phenomena = objects."
12. *Critique of Pure Reason,* A 104–05; not in B.
13. Ibid., A 191 = B 236.

14. Ibid., A 253 = B 309.
15. Ibid., A 247 = B 304.
16. Ibid., B 130.
17. Ibid., A 79; B 141.
18. Ibid., B 141. "Judgment is nothing but the manner in which given *Erkenntnisse* [intuitions and concepts] are brought to the objective unity of apperception."
19. Ibid., A 191 = B 236, cited and quoted in part above.
20. Ibid., A 108; not in B: "This transcendental unity of apperception forms out of all possible appearances, which can stand alongside one another in one experience, a connection of all these representations according to laws. . . . The original and synthetic unity of the identity of the self is thus at the same time a consciousness of an equally necessary unity in the synthesis of all appearances according to concepts, that is, according to rules . . . which determine an object for their intuition, that is, the concept of something wherein they are necessarily interconnected."
21. Kemp Smith, *Commentary*, p. 222.
22. Paton, *Kant's Metaphysic of Experience*, I, 332 ff.
23. Reflection 6315 (Ak. VIII: 621), italics added. Kant is discussing specifically the imagination "in dreams or in fever." The imagination in these cases are called *Sinnesanschauungen*, intuitions of sense, but "only in the imagination, to which the object outside the representation is not present." That is, imagination may produce intuitions in the inspectional but not in the functional sense.
24. *Critique of Pure Reason*, A 112; similarly A 111, line 33; neither in B.
25. Ibid., A 120; not in B.
26. Ibid.
27. Ibid., A 112; not in B.
28. Letter to Marcus Herz, May 26, 1789 (Ak. XI: 52; Zweig, *Kant's Philosophical Correspondence*, p. 153).
29. In the next two sections of this paper we shall take up this claim.
30. *Critique of Pure Reason*, B, §18; cf. B xl–xli.
31. *Prolegomena*, §13, Remark III (Ak. IV: 290).
32. *Critique of Pure Reason*, B 278.
33. Ibid., A 99–100; B 140.
34. *Prolegomena*, §20 (Ak. IV: 300, line 8; Beck translation, p. 48, line 5). This content of inner experience (L-experience) is called "empirical self-knowledge" and is identified with the subject of empirical psychology (Reflexion 5453). Yet to be even knowledge of the self (expressible in judgments) it must be *categorized* without being *objectified* in the normal sense (viz., ascribed by outer sense to a spatial object); see p. 113 below.
35. Kemp Smith, *Commentary*, pp. 288–89; Paton, *Kant's Metaphysic of Experience*, I, 330–31.
36. Even the genetic psychology of the first paragraph of B is repeated in *Prol.* §18, where Kant says all our judgments are "at first merely judgments of perception . . . and we do not until afterward give them a new reference to an object."

37. *Prolegomena,* §18 (Ak. IV: 298, line 3; Beck p. 45, bottom).
38. Ibid., §19 and note.
39. *Critique of Pure Reason,* B 141.
40. Ibid., B 141–42.
41. *Prolegomena,* §20, para. 1 [Ak. IV: 300].
42. Kant's example is merely "When the sun shines on the stone it becomes warm." But the sense he must want requires the judgment to be in the autobiographical. . . . Accordingly, in the part of the *Critique of Pure Reason* which comes closest to repeating the *Prolegomena* distinction, Kant contrasts, "If I support a body, I feel an impression of weight" with "It, the body, is heavy" (B 142).
43. *Critique of Pure Reason,* A 189 = B 234; cf. A 108, end.
44. *Critique of Pure Reason,* A 166 = B 208.
45. *Prolegomena,* § 19 note [Ak. IV: 299].
46. Lewis, *Mind and the World Order,* p. 225.
47. The representations which may not be accompanied by consciousness (*Critique of Pure Reason,* A 320 = B 376) are like Leibniz's *petites perceptions.* If there were not the understanding, I would not be able to *know* I have even sense data; "consequently for me, *as a knowing being,* they would be absolutely nothing. They could still (*I imagine myself to be an animal*) carry on their play in an orderly fashion, as representations connected according to the empirical laws of association, and thus even have an influence on my feeling and desire, without my being aware of them (assuming even that I am conscious of each individual representation but not of their relation to the unity of representation of their object by means of the synthetic unity of their apperception). This might be so without my knowing the slightest thing thereby, not even what my own condition is." Letter to Marcus Herz, May 26, 1789 (Ak. XI: 52; Zweig, *Correspondence,* pp. 153–54), italics added.

# 7

# Kant's Second Analogy: Objects, Events and Causal Laws

*Paul Guyer*

## 1

The Analogies of Experience are both the historical and philosophical heart of Kant's transcendental theory of experience as that existed prior to 1787—prior, that is, to Kant's addition of his ultimate argument for the objective validity of the categories of the understanding in the form of his Refutation of Idealism. Seen from the perspective of the latter argument, the Analogies are an indispensable but also incomplete part of an epistemological theory of the necessary conditions of time-determination. That is, they try to show us that certain principles are required in order to ground temporal determinations about objects. But they assume that we can and must make such determinations, and it is only in the Refutation of Idealism that Kant attempts to defend this assumption by showing that temporal determinations about objects distinct from our own representations of them are themselves necessary conditions of the temporal determinations of our own representations considered merely as such. Further, although the exposition of the Refutation proceeds as if the success of the Analogies of Experience may be assumed, the success of the Analogies, particularly of the second Analogy's argument for a principle of universal causation, actually presupposes the chief consideration underlying the Refutation of Idealism.

Kant himself does not present the Analogies of Experience in such provisional light. By the time he reaches the Analogies, Kant takes the necessity of knowledge of objects already to have been established (by the Transcendental Deduction which itself, however, cannot stand independently of the Refutation of Idealism).[1] So Kant presents the Analogies of Experience as if the necessity of the application of the categories (of relation) to objects beyond our own representations of them had already been established, and as if what remains to be done is only to determine what principles can be inferred from the further fact—alleged by the Schematism—that this application must be by means of representations given successively in time.

In the first edition of the *Critique,* Kant starts the general discussion of this issue by saying that the "general principle of the analogies is: *All appearances, as far as their existence is concerned, stand a priori under rules of the determination of their relation to one another in one time*" (A 176–7).[2] Given that by "appearance" Kant usually means "empirical object," one might take this statement to mean that some basic machinery for judgments that subjective representations represent independent objects and events is already supposed to be in place prior to the Analogies, and that what the latter are intended to do is only to ground certain *special* judgments about certain special temporal determinations or aspects of objects or events already judged to be objective—for instance, judgments about *how long* given objects have endured or what the *relative order* of two given events is. But such an interpretation of Kant's intentions would be radically mistaken (even on Kant's own conception of the progress of his argument). Kant's reformulation of the general principle of the Analogies for the second edition makes this clear. Here Kant speaks of the necessary connection of *perceptions,* and this suggests that without the principles of the three Analogies there can be no grounded judgments about *objective* entities or events at all. The Analogies are not intended to *supplement* some principles for judgments about objects that have been established prior to them. Rather, they *are* the basic principles for judgments about objects, though formulated with reference to the specifically temporal form of our empirical intuitions and their objects rather than in the more abstract manner of the earlier stages of the *Critique.* Without the Analogies, there can be no justification for our interpretation of our *intuitions* as representing *objects and events in time* at all.

In other words, the Analogies of Experience are the conditions of empirical knowledge itself, "that is, a cognition which determines an object through perceptions" (B 218). What is necessary for empirical knowledge is "the synthetic unity of the manifold [of perception] in one consciousness . . . which constitutes the essential in a cognition of *objects* of the senses, that is, of experience (not merely of intuitions or sensation of the senses)." Why should this be so? Precisely because "in experience," taken now in a sense exactly the opposite of that just used, that is, in mere apprehension or uninterpreted sensation, the mere given, "perceptions are only juxtaposed accidentally, so that no necessity of their connections is revealed by the perceptions themselves, nor can be revealed, since apprehension is only a juxtaposition of the manifold of empirical intuition and yields no representation of the necessity of the connected existence of appearances . . . in space and time" (B 219). What this means is that representations themselves come in a temporal order, and so must the objects they are to represent, but that there is no basis for assuming that the contingent or accidental succession of representations bears *any* relation to the determinate temporal structure of objects or events beyond them. Yet for experience, now again in the strong sense, knowledge of the latter is what is required: "Experience is a cognition of objects through perceptions, consequently a cognition of the relation in the existence of the manifold, not as it is [merely] juxtaposed in time, but as it is objectively in time." And why are the principles defended by the Analogies of Experience needed to ground such cognition? Kant's initial answer to this is as hasty as it is pregnant: "since time itself cannot be perceived, the determination of the existence of objects in time can only take place by means of their connection in time in general, thus only through *a priori* connecting concepts" (B 219).

Precisely what Kant means by saying that "time itself cannot be perceived" and just why "*a priori* connecting concepts" are what is needed to remedy this problem are the questions that must be answered by the detailed examination of the three Analogies of Experience. But before we turn to the particular one of these that will concern us here, the second Analogy, we must prevent a confusion about the perception of time that Kant's own remarks could create. Kant opens the first edition discussion of the Analogies by saying that there are three different "modes" of time—duration, succession, and coexistence—and that there are three corresponding Analogies. It might seem natural to conclude that each one of these three Analogies independently serves to ground determinations in one "mode" of time—that the first will show how we ground objective determinations of duration, the second, objective relations of succession, and the third, objective relations of simultaneity or coexistence. But other statements that Kant makes belie such a supposition. Thus, the opening paragraph of the first edition argument for the first Analogy says that "All appearances are in time. Time can determine the relation in their existence in a *twofold* [my emphasis] way, either as *they succeed one another* or as they *are simultaneous*" (A 182). The next paragraph, retained in both editions, similarly says that "simultaneity and succession are the only relations in time" (A 182/B 226). There is an apparent conflict here, and thus a question about the independence of the three Analogies. In fact, the initial expectation raised by the mention of the three "modes" of time is misleading. Except for one unfortunate line of thought in the first Analogy, *what Kant actually argues is that the basic distinction to be made in placing an objective interpretation on representations, which are always successive, is whether they are to be taken as representing successive or coexistent states of affairs— change or the absence of change—and that to judge either that there is any objective change at all or objective coexistence requires the presupposition of enduring, indeed ultimately permanent objects governed by causal laws of action and interaction.* There are not three different modes of time that can be judged of independently of one another; in a way, it is almost misleading to speak of even *two* different relations of time, as if *they* could be judged of independently (and indeed Kant sometimes suggests that *succession* is the only purely temporal relation; see A 31/B 47). Rather, there is a basic distinction to be made between the alternative temporal possibilities for the objective states of affairs represented by any two successive perceptions—they may succeed one another or not, that is, coexist with one another— and to decide which of these is the case will always require both the presupposition of an enduring object or objects as well as the postulation of laws governing the behavior of such objects.

The interdependence of both the *use* of the principles of the Analogies and the *arguments* in their behalf is a major theme of my whole treatment of the Analogies. But my subject here will be only the second Analogy and *its* dependence on the underlying presupposition of the Refutation of Idealism.

The second Analogy is the single argument intended to replace both the rationalists' misguided confidence that the principle of sufficient reason can be derived from laws of logic alone as well as Hume's skepticism that necessary connections among distinct states of affairs can be known by human understanding at all. The intended conclusion of the second Analogy can most readily be stated by combining the versions of the principle from the two editions of the *Critique.* In the first edition, what is to be proved is that "Everything that happens (begins to be) presupposes something from which it follows *according to a rule*" (A 189). In the second edition, the principle is that "All alterations take place according to the law of cause and effect" (B 232). The second edition's reference to "all alterations" is preferable to the first edition's mention of "Everything that happens (begins to be)" for two reasons. First, the first Analogy already argues that the only *empirically cognizable* sorts of happenings are changes in the states of enduring substances, or alterations: the second edition reflects this prior development, but the first edition does not. Second, the first edition refers only to commencements but not to cessations of states of affairs, whereas a truly universal application of a principle of causation will surely entail the existence of causal explanations of cases of cessations as well as commencement. However, the first edition is superior to the second insofar as it does not simply invoke the unanalyzed concepts of cause and effect, but conveys the content of these concepts: to say that two things are related as cause and effect is to say that one follows from the other according to a rule. Thus, the two statements together suggest that what is to be demonstrated is that all cases of empirically recognizable alterations in substances must *also* be successions of states of those substances according to rules. The second Analogy thus does *not* concern a *different* "mode of time" from the first; it concerns an *additional condition* necessary for the experience of objective change, the condition that empirically recognizable changes must be not only alterations but also rule-governed.

At the end of this essay, we will see that this condition must be stated with care in order to avoid Arthur Schopenhauer's pungent objection that "in fact even the succession of day and night is undoubtedly known to us objectively, but they are certainly not *regarded* as cause and effect of each other."[3] But for now I will make only the preliminary observation that although Kant defines causality in terms of succession according to a rule, *he does not say anything about the precise force of such rules.* That is, though it is natural to identify universal causation with complete *determinism,* it is not actually *part of Kant's argument* that the kind of rule according to which one state can be determined to follow another must be fully deterministic as opposed to, say, merely probabilistic. The possibility that the laws of nature might be statistical rather than fully deterministic would *not* undermine Kant's account of their role in empirical knowledge.[4] Of course, the force of the causal laws employed in time-determination would carry over to the conclusions they ground: that is, if the causal laws used to ground judgments about the temporal order of states of affairs are only highly probable, then our judgments that some states succeed others will themselves be only highly probable rather than completely certain. But nothing Kant ever says commits him to the certainty of empirical time-determinations. If anything, Kant's general position on empirical knowledge assumes the *uncertainty* of all such judgments, and would receive support—though undoubtedly unforeseen support—from a non-deterministic conception of the force of natural laws.

2

We may now consider Kant's actual argument in behalf of his principle of causation. The problem that can only be solved by the employment of laws of cause and effect, according to Kant, is posed by the following circumstance: "The apprehension of the manifold of appearance is always successive. The representation of the parts follow one another. Whether they also follow each other in the object is a further point for reflection, which is not contained in the first" (A 189/B 234). That is, *any* distinct representations, whether they *represent* states of affairs that coexist or states that succeed one another, *themselves* succeed one another. So the fact that the represented *states of affairs* succeed one another in a determinate order—that an alteration is occurring in the objects of perception—cannot be inferred from the successive occurrence of the *representations of* those states of affairs themselves. This is one sense in which time cannot be directly perceived: representations as such *have* a temporal order, but nothing about the temporal order of *what they represent* can be inferred from their own temporal order, just because the temporal order of the representations themselves will be of precisely the same character—successive—whether or not they represent any objective change. Furthermore, individual representations reveal nothing about the relations of their objects to any extended time (relative or absolute): unlike television images of sporting events, they have no digital timers in their corners. But the temporal order of the objective states of affairs cannot be determined by any direct access *to the objects* either, for it is of course *only* by the representations that the objects are given. So representations themselves can determine the order of the states of affairs they represent neither in isolation nor by their own order. Yet we have no other and no more direct access to objects. So the determination of the temporal order of the represented states must be grounded on something other than *either* the order of the representations, even if that is directly apprehended (although it is ultimately crucial to Kant's argument that it is not), *or* the order of the objective states themselves.

This is the moral of Kant's famous contrast between the successive perceptions of the parts of an unchanging house and the successive perceptions of the locations of a moving ship:

> For example, the apprehension of the manifold in the appearance of a house that stands before me is successive. Now the question is whether the manifold of this house in itself is also successive, which certainly no one will concede. . . . That something happens, that is, that something or a state comes to be that previously was not, cannot be empirically perceived except where an appearance precedes that does not contain this state in itself; for a reality that would follow on an empty time, thus an arising not preceded by any state of things, can be apprehended just as little as empty time itself. Every apprehension of an occurrence is therefore a perception that follows another one. Since this is the case in all synthesis of apprehension, as I have shown above in the case of the appearance of a house, the apprehension of an occurrence is not yet thereby distinguished from any other. (A 190–2/B 235–7)

Kant follows this statement of his problem with what is both the most detailed account of his solution that he offers but also the one that has caused the most confusion about his theory:

> Yet I also note that if in the case of an appearance that contains a happening I call the preceding state of perception A and the following one B, then B can only follow A in apprehension, but the perception A cannot follow B but only precede it. For example, I see a ship driven downstream. My perception of its position downstream follows the perception of its position upstream, and it is impossible that in the apprehension of this appearance the ship should first be perceived downstream and only afterwards upstream. The order in the sequence of the perceptions in apprehension is therefore here determined, and the apprehension is bound to it. In the previous example of a house my perceptions could have begun at its rooftop and ended at the ground, but could also have begun below and ended above; likewise I could have apprehended the manifold of empirical intuition from the right or from the left. In the series of these perceptions there was therefore no determinate order that made it necessary when I had to begin in the apprehension in order to

combine the manifold empirically. This rule, however, is always to be found in the perception of that which happens, and it makes the order of the perceptions that follow one another (in the apprehension of this appearance) *necessary.* (A 192–3/B 237–8)

Such a rule is supposed to be a causal law:

> In our case I must therefore derive the *subjective sequence* of apprehension from the *objective sequence* of appearances, for otherwise the former would be entirely undetermined and no appearances would be distinguished from any other. The former alone proves nothing about the connection of the manifold in the object, because it is entirely arbitrary. This connection must therefore consist in the order of the manifold of appearance in accordance with which the apprehension of the one thing (that which happens) follows on that of the other (which precedes) *in accordance with a rule.* Only thereby can I be justified in saying of the appearance itself, and not merely of my apprehension, that a sequence is to be found in it, which is to say that I cannot arrange the apprehension otherwise than in exactly this sequence.

Note Kant's remark that the function of such a rule is that of *justifying me in saying* (or judging) of an empirical object that it contains an objective succession. Here—and almost nowhere else—Kant precisely delineates just what it *means* to call a principle such as that of causation a principle of the possibility of experience. It is not to say that such a principle is one that constitutes an empirical object in any ontological sense, nor that it is one that is somehow a psychological precondition of the occurrence of a representation, even a propositional representation of—a belief about—an object. Rather, to call a principle a condition of the possibility of experience *is to say no more and no less than that it is a principle that must be used in order to justify, verify, or confirm judgments about empirical objects made on the basis of our representations of them*—to whatever degree of confirmation they actually admit.

This is a point of tremendous importance, but not one that can be explored here. Instead, we must try to understand why Kant thinks only causal laws regulating the states of objects can solve the problem that arises from the fact that representations are always successive. The initial statement of the argument added in the second edition offers some help by providing a succinct though abstract statement of the task to be addressed, the premise that creates the problem, and the inference to be drawn. First, the objective is to show how I may ground a judgment that "appearances succeed one another, i.e., that a state of things exists at one time the opposite of which existed in the previous state" (B 233). But, second, it is presupposed that I cannot directly determine that any two represented states actually exist at different times because neither absolute time nor absolute temporal position is directly a part of the content of any single representation, *and* because "I am conscious only that my imagination places one state before and the other after, not that the one state precedes the other in the object; or, in other words, through the mere perception the *objective relation* of the appearances that are succeeding one another remains undetermined" (B 233–4). Finally, Kant draws the inference that for this relation to be known "as determined, the relation between the two states must be thought in such a way that it is thereby necessarily determined which of them must be placed before and which after rather than vice versa." This Kant takes to imply that, since necessity is required, there must be a pure concept of the understanding, and that it must be that of *"the relation of cause and effect"* (B 234). Since we now understand the problem to be addressed, two things remain to be explained. First, we must understand just what follows from the supposition that I am conscious merely that my *imagination* sets the representation of one state before the other. Second, we must explain why Kant assumes that we can infer from the *determinateness* of a sequence to the *necessity* of its occurrence, for it would seem that the utterly contingent commencement of one state of affairs after the cessation of another would be just as *determinate* a succession as a truly necessitated sequence. Further, we must examine Kant's transition from the need for *some* pure concept to the concept of cause and effect.

The case of the house and the ship will start—but only start—us on these problems. First, this discussion suggests that the significance of the claim that I am conscious merely that my imagination sets the representation of one state before the other, but not that one state succeeds the other, is that the mere fact of the successive occurrence of representations of two states of affairs is not sufficient evidence to exclude the simultaneous coexistence of the represented states of affairs themselves. This is because the mere occurrence of such a sequence of representations is not incompatible with the possibility of the occurrence of precisely the opposite sequence of representations—I can see the roof before the ground floor, or the ground floor before the roof— and this possibility is presumably to be explained precisely by the *si-*

*multaneous existence* of the objects of both representations. Thus, the evidence furnished by the mere fact of a succession of representations is compatible with the possibility that there is simply a changing perception of a complex object rather than any change in the object at all.

But, Kant now supposes, if one state of affairs actually succeeds rather than coexists with the other—if there were an actual occurrence—then, *ceteris paribus* (and this is a matter of some significance), such indifference between the possible orders of their perceptions is not possible. If there were an actual event, and if one state of affairs did succeed the other, then the *perception* of the one would not only succeed that of the other, but would *have* to succeed it. "In the case of an appearance that contains a happening . . . B can only follow A in apprehension, but the perception A cannot follow B but only precede it" (A 192/B 237).

At this point, however, we must be precise about just what Kant's argument is. The fact that in the case of an event the *perception* of one state of affairs can only succeed but not precede another is *not* itself what *constitutes* the event we are interested in, a change in the object. Nor is it itself what must in the first instance be explained by a rule. Rather, it would be a *consequence* of the occurrence of an event in what is being perceived, which *could* be used as a *symptom* of the occurrence of the event *if* it were directly given to consciousness.[5] But what Kant's underlying assumption means is precisely that such a modal fact about the sequence of perceptions is *not* given to consciousness by apprehension alone. At best—and we shall soon see that even this is not the whole story—unaided apprehension or "imagination" indicates only that one representation succeeds another, not that it *necessarily* does so. And of course the necessary succession of one representation after another, even if this were what we were primarily interested in, could not be inferred from the succession of one state of affairs after another, for that is what must be discovered. So Kant's idea is that no alternative remains but that the occurrence of an event be inferred by *adding* to the omnipresent succession of mere representations a *rule* from which it may be inferred in the circumstances at hand that one state of affairs could *only* succeed the other. In Kant's clearest words,

> Therefore I always make my subjective synthesis (of apprehension) objective with respect to a rule in accordance with which the appearances in *their* sequence, i.e., as *they* occur, are determined through the preced-

ing state, and only under this presupposition alone is the experience of something that happens even possible (A 195/B 240, emphasis added).

Or, in another of Kant's formulations, his claim is that if *in addition* to merely *having* a succession of representations I *also*

> . . . anticipate that there is in this sequence a relation to the preceding state, from which the representation follows in accordance with a rule, then I represent something as an occurrence, or as something that happens, i.e., I cognize an object that I must place in a particular determinate position in time, which after the preceding state, cannot otherwise be assigned to it (A 198/B 243).

And a rule that dictates that in a given situation one state of affairs must succeed another is just what Kant means by a causal law. Thus, judgments that events occur are possible only if the states of affairs that comprise them are linked by causal laws.

## 3

This argument is quite abstract, and of course Kant's conclusion has engendered a great deal of resistance, even outright scorn. The most efficient way to provide some more detail to Kant's argument will be if we now consider some of the chief objections to it, specifically to his inference to causal laws governing relations *among states of objects.*

We may begin with what is not itself an objection, but an interpretation which quickly produces one. This interpretation is that the argument of the second Analogy proceeds essentially by *analyzing* the *concept* of an event. This of course produces the objection that the question whether such a concept has objective validity is then begged. But more important, it fails to explain the crucial requirement of *causal* laws. Graham Bird's version of this interpretation displays exactly this failure. According to Bird, "The Second Analogy may . . . be understood as an analysis of the concept 'event.' "[6] On this analysis, an event is comprised of "two different characteristics, or states" of a single object,[7] and these two "constituent states of the object" must also be "regarded as irreversible." It is to follow from this that in the case of any given event there is a purely "logical necessity" that the states that comprise that particular event occur in the order in which they do; otherwise, those states would comprise not *that* event but some other

event. The necessity in the event of a ship sailing from a point upstream
to a point downstream, for instance, would be the "logical necessity
that to apprehend a ship's sailing downstream is, necessarily, to apprehend an event in which the ship's position downstream followed its
position upstream. The order of *this* event is a necessary order, not
because it is impossible for ships to sail upstream, but because if the
constituent states had been reversed the event apprehended would
have been a different event."[8] And to introduce a role for causal laws
into this analysis, Bird then argues that if what we mean by the concept
of a particular event is just that one state of affairs must follow another,
"then it presupposes the notion of a reason or ground for the constituent states of an object being in such a determinate order."[9] Thus it
follows that any event has a cause.

Now, some passages, such as Kant's final exposition of his argument,
could be taken to offer an analysis of the concept of an event:

> But if this synthesis is a synthesis of apprehension (of the manifold of
> a given appearance), then the order in the object is determined, or, to
> speak more precisely, there is therein an order of the successive synthesis
> that determines an object, in accordance with which something would
> necessarily have to precede, and, if this is posited, the other would neces-
> sarily move to follow. If, therefore, my perception is to contain the cogni-
> tion of an occurrence, namely that something actually happens, then it
> must be an empirical judgment in which one thinks that the sequence is
> determined, i.e., that it presupposes another appearance . . . which it
> follows necessarily. . . . (A 201/B 246–7)

This could be read to argue that the *presupposition* that a given sequence of representations represents the occurrence of a particular
event entails that the states represented must follow one another in
the order in which they do, and that the rule that is employed is just
the rule that the identity of any particular event requires that the states
comprising it *must* succeed each other the order in which they do in
order to comprise *that* event.

But though this rule is true, indeed trivial, it cannot be the rule that
Kant's argument introduces. For it does not justify the assumption of a
*causal* connection between the states comprising an event, at least by
any argument that Kant himself would have accepted. This may be seen
at once. Kant, of course, follows Hume in conceiving of a causal connection as a universal connection, one "where all the objects resem-

bling the [cause] are plac'd in a like relation of priority and contiguity to those objects, that resemble" the effect.[10] But there is no reason why the *necessary* connection that follows from the identity of a particular event must be a *universally valid* rather than completely *unique* connection. If a particular event is that of a ship sailing downstream, then it follows analytically that its being downstream succeeds its being upstream. And as a matter of fact, we also believe that there are causal laws that explain this sequence. But if my car were to up and fly away, it would follow with equal necessity that the moment in which it started to fly succeeded the last moment in which it behaved as an earthbound car. Yet we would call this event a miracle and suppose that there is no universally valid law which explains it.

Bird does try to justify his introduction of causal laws by the following supplement to his "analysis":

> What we mean by 'event' is . . . a determinate temporal order of two states in the same object. But the idea of a determinate order between two states presupposes that of something which determines it; and this idea of a determinant or reason for such an order is that of a cause. . . . Kant has, therefore, some ground for saying that the concept of a cause is required for our discrimination of a time order in phenomena.[11]

But it is implausible to attribute such an argument to the author of the *Critique of Pure Reason,* for it is no more and no less than the rationalist argument for the principle of sufficient reason by means of the equation of *ratio cognoscendi* and *ratio essendi* the rejection of which was one of the fundamental motivations for Kant's entire theoretical philosophy. To *assume* that what is a sufficient condition for *recognition* is also sufficient to *explain* the existence of what is known is to commit exactly the same error that Leibniz made when he argued that from the principle that "All other truths are reduced to first truths with the aid of definitions or by the analysis of concepts" there immediately follows "the accepted axiom that *there is nothing without a reason, or no effect without a cause*[, for] otherwise there would be truth which could not be proved *a priori,*"[12] or which Wolff displayed in his classical statement that "Nothing is without its sufficient reason, why it is rather than is not, that is, if something is posited then something else is also to be posited from which *it can be understood* why the former is rather than is not."[13] Kant tried to save this equation with some fancy footwork in his early work (see *Nova Delucidatio,* Proposition V,

1:393). But it clearly fell victim to his general distinction between "logical" and "real" relations, first hammered out in the case of "negative quantities" in the seminal work of 1763 that represents Kant's substantive (not just programmatic) break with rationalism:

> I understand very well how a consequence can be posited through a ground since it is found to be contained in it through the analysis of the concepts. Thus necessity is a ground of invariability, composition a ground of divisibility, infinity a ground of omniscience, etc., and this connection of the ground with the consequence I can clearly understand, since the consequence is really identical with a partial concept of the ground. . . . But how something flows from something else but not according to the law of identity, that is something which I would gladly be able to make clear to myself. I call the first kind of ground a logical ground, since its relation to the consequent can be understood logically, namely clearly according to the law of identity; but I call the second kind of ground a real ground. . . . Now as far as this real ground and its relation to the consequent is concerned, I put my question in this simple form: how shall I understand it, that, *since something is, something else is?* . . . [A logical ground] I clearly understand by means of the law of contradiction, and I understand how, if I posit the infinity of God, the predicate of mortality is thereby suspended, namely since it contradicts the former. But how, through the movement of one body, the movement of another can be suspended, that is another question. (*Attempt to Introduce Negative Quantities into Philosophy,* 2:202–3)

By 1763, then, Kant had clearly rejected the idea that what might serve as a ground of knowledge in any analysis necessarily explains what it grounds, and there is no reason to think that he ever turned his back on this result.

If the objection to Bird's interpretation were purely historical, it would not be worth mentioning. But it is, because it also involves a radical misunderstanding of Kant's conception of our epistemic situation in attempting to distinguish between merely subjective and genuinely objective successions. For Bird's account seems to presuppose that we are actually *given* knowledge of events, and can then use our knowledge that there *is* a determinate succession to infer further conclusions, such as that there is a cause for that succession. But this is precisely the opposite of what Kant assumes. Kant's idea is that we are *not* given knowledge of objective successions, but that we must infer *that* from something—namely, nothing less than a law that *explains* why, in the given circumstances, one succession rather than another should obtain. In other words, on Kant's theory causal laws are not *logical consequences* of determinacy but the *epistemological preconditions* of *knowledge* of determinacy.

We can illustrate this in the case of the ship sailing downstream. Bird claims that "The order of *this* event is a necessary order, not because it is impossible for ships to sail upstream, but because if the constituent states had been reversed the event apprehended would have been a different event. It would have been the event of a ship's sailing upstream." Plausible as this sounds, it misses the point of Kant's argument. For Kant's claim is that, given only two successive *observations* of positions of the ship, which in imagination can be set in either of two orders, it can be determined that they represent (e.g.) the ship sailing downstream only if, in the circumstances that are being assumed, it *would* be impossible for that ship to be sailing upstream. Kant's theory is precisely that it is only if we are in possession of causal laws which dictate that in the relevant circumstances—that is, not in general, but in the particular circumstances of wind, tide, setting of the sails, etc., which are assumed to obtain—the ship could *only* sail downstream that we actually have evidence to interpret our representations of it to mean that it *is* sailing downstream. Bird's derivation of the logical necessity *from* the identity of the event begs Kant's question of just *how* we can identify the event.[14]

Connected confusions underlie two more illustrative objections to Kant's argument. According to the first of these, Kant can show that knowledge of *some* determinate relations among states of objects is an epistemological precondition of recognizing events, but not that causal relations are. This is because the recognition of an event requires the assumption that the two relevant states of affairs are *opposite* or *incompatible* states of affairs (cf. B 233: *"dass Erscheinungen aufeinander folgen, d.i. dass ein Zustand der Dinge zu einer Zeit ist, dessen Gegenteil im vorigen Zustand war"*), but that this already answers the question: if the two states are incompatible, then of course they cannot exist at the same time, so there must be an event, namely that constituted by the change from one of the incompatible states to the other. Nothing *in addition* to the presupposition of incompatibility is needed to judge that there is an event.[15]

But there are two problems with such an objection. First, it overlooks the fact that the kind of incompatibility that will typically be involved in an event is not *logical* incompatibility derivable from mere concepts of the states of affairs concerned, but something else—the specific real relation that Kant called *real opposition* in the essay on "negative quantities." And although Kant does not mention the fact in the text of the second Analogy, or do more than allude to it elsewhere in the *Critique* (see e.g., A 265/B 320)—perhaps just because he had already devoted an entire essay to it—*real opposition is engendered by nothing other than causal laws.* Kant's "ground rule" for "real opposition" is that "Real repugnance occurs only in so far as of two things as *positive grounds* one suspends the consequence of the other"; for instance, "let a motive force be a positive ground: then a real opposition can take place only in so far as another motive force in relation to the first suspends its consequence . . ." (2:175–6). A state of affairs that can have this kind of effect on the consequence of another, however, is nothing less than a cause of that suspension of consequence—a state from which, according to a rule, another, in this case the absence of something expected, follows. Kant makes this explicit: "In nature there are many [changes] from the conflict of two efficient causes [*wirkenden Ursachen*], of which one suspends the consequence of the other through real opposition" (2:184). So for at least a large variety of cases, our knowledge that a thing cannot be in two different states at the same time cannot be derived from logical opposition between contradictories, but itself depends upon knowledge of what the causal powers of things are. For instance, our knowledge that something cannot be both hot and cold at the same time, so that our perception of it as both hot and cold must constitute a perception of its change from one of these states to the other, is itself knowledge of what the causal powers of objects are: knowledge that one object cannot cause another to melt but yet a third to gel, or cause us to have two different sorts of sensations at the same time. And if this is so, the need for causal laws is not *obviated* by the way Kant's argument is set up; rather, it is almost immediately *implied* by the way the argument is posed.

Second, even if the incompatibility of two states of affairs could be known independently of any knowledge of causation, it could tell us only that *some* event has taken place but not *which*. That is, if A and B are mutually incompatible states of affairs, then we know that the perception of both A and B must represent some event, but we cannot know on that basis alone whether it represents the change from A to B or that from B to A. In order to make the latter determinate, what is required in addition to the incompatibility of A and B is precisely a law of the form that, e.g., B can only follow A, from which it can then be inferred that the particular event being perceived can only be the alteration from A to B.[16]

This has not been obvious for the simple reason that advocates of the present objection (and almost everyone else) have assumed that the *order* of two incompatible states of affairs *can* be determined by the order of *perception* alone. They assume, that is, that if A and B are incompatible states, then the fact that they constitute, e.g., the change from A to B is directly determined by the fact that the succession of my *perceptions* is a perception of A followed by a perception of B, that is, by the fact that whereas I am now perceiving B I previously perceived A. For if A and B are incompatible and if the one of them that I am now perceiving is B, then the event that I have been perceiving can only be the change from A to B. Thus C. D. Broad wrote, "If I perceive that *x* is now in a certain place and I remember that it was in a different place, I know, without any appeal to causation, that it must have changed its place."[17]

This assumption seems natural enough; why is it wrong? Commenting on Broad's version of the objection, D. P. Dryer hints at an answer. Dryer says that Broad overlooks that his contention, "that in order for someone to know that a certain change has taken place in an object, it is sufficient for him to observe it in a certain state and remember that it was previously in an opposite state," is "analytically true," because "when someone is said to 'remember' that any object which he observes was previously in an opposite state, what is meant is that he knows, from what he recalls having observed, that it was previously in an opposite state," and because this knowledge requires the use of causal laws.[18] This points in the right direction, but what has to be emphasized is Kant's fundamental *and synthetic* claim that in any situation in which we seem to recall being successively conscious of two states of affairs, "imagination can connect these states in two ways" (B 233). That is, *at any moment* in which we reflect on what is apparently a present perception plus a memory of a prior one, *it is not actually given which is the present perception and which is the prior one.* For all that can be given in one moment is a *present impression* of the contents of two (or more) possible perceptions, but not both the present *and the past impression* itself. *Which* is the present impression and which the past is something *which itself* must actually be judged. And what Kant's argument ultimately supposes is that this inference requires precisely a law of the form that one *state of affairs* can only succeed the other, which would then entail, other things being equal, that the *perception* of the one can only succeed the *perception* of the other and thus must be the present as opposed to the past impression.

The premise of this argument (like Kant's theory of real opposition) is not even mentioned in the second Analogy itself, but only in a key passage of the Transcendental Deduction. And the conclusion of it is not drawn until the Refutation of Idealism, indeed not until versions of the latter that Kant wrote only *after* publishing the second edition of the *Critique* in 1787.[19] So, as I suggested at the outset, the second Analogy does not stand by itself, but requires both the Deduction and the Refutation for its completion. However, I will say more about the underlying consideration just revealed, but only after expounding a second objection that fails in part for the same reason.

This objection is the famous charge that Kant's argument "can seem legitimate only if the critical faculty is numbed by the grossness of the *non sequitur*" (the ringing word's are Strawson's,[20] but the substance of his objection goes back at least to Lovejoy[21] and Prichard[22]). Simply put, the charge is that Kant confuses "causal transactions or dependencies relating objects of subjective perception to one another . . . with the causal dependencies of subjective perceptions themselves upon their objects."[23] In somewhat more detail, the argument is this. Kant is supposed to hold that "Lack or possession of order-indifference on the part of our perceptions is . . . our criterion . . . of objective succession or co-existence."[24] So for two objective states of affairs, A and B, and two representations of them, $A_r$ and $B_r$,[25] if $A_r$ and $B_r$ are irreversible or lack order-indifference—had to come in that order rather than in the order $B_r$ then $A_r$—it can be judged that they represent the event A then B, whereas if the representations possess order-indifference, they must be taken to represent the coexistence of A and B and not the event A then B. But for the distinction between irreversibility and order-indifference *of perceptions* to be made, Strawson charges, all that is required is the supposition of causal laws relating the states of affairs (A and B) *to the representations of them* ($A_r$ and $B_r$ respectively). This is because *if* it is known that $A_r$ preceded $B_r$ *and that* $A_r$ was caused by A and $B_r$ by B by the same method of transmission or "mode of causal dependency," where that sameness is defined by the fact that no time-lag is present in the one case that is absent from the other, *then* it can be inferred that as $A_r$ preceded $B_r$ so A preceded B. In Strawson's words, if

(1) . . . A and B are objective states of affairs of which A preceded B in time, this succession constituting a single event (the event of A's being

succeeded by B, (2) [A$_r$] is a perception of A and [B$_r$] of B, (3) there is no relevant difference in the modes of causal dependency of [A$_r$] on A and [B$_r$] on B (a relevant difference being any which affects the time taken by the causal process whereby the object (A or B) produces its effect ([A$_r$] or [B$_r$])) to complete itself), then there follows, with *logical* necessity, the consequence that [A$_r$] precedes [B$_r$]. The substitution for (1), however, of the supposition that A and B are coexistent leaves it a logically open question which, of [A$_r$] and [B$_{r}$], comes first. The necessary order of perceptions in the one case, their order-indifference in the other, reduce, it seems, to just this logical necessity and this logical indifference.[26]

But, he claims, Kant just confuses the necessity that A$_r$ and B$_r$ occur in that order, given the order of A and B and the isomorphic mechanisms of perception, with the necessity that *A and B* occur in that order; and it is only by such a confusion that any causal laws regulating the order of A and B are smuggled into the argument.

But the fallacy is Strawson's, not Kant's. Strawson confuses the means and the end: that is, he takes for granted knowledge of the order of A and B and uses it to infer the irreversibility of A$_r$ and B$_r$, whereas it is precisely the order of the objective states of affairs that *cannot* be made a "supposition" but that must somehow be established on the basis of the—insufficient—evidence furnished by the order of perceptions. And this is not Strawson's only misconstrual of Kant's conception of our epistemic situation. Like the incompatibility theorists, he takes for granted that the order of perceptions *is known* independently of anything else, whereas the underlying premise of the Transcendental Deduction undermines precisely this assumption. Further, Strawson's conception of our situation assumes that causal laws relating perceptions to their objects could be known independently of laws regulating the behavior of the objects themselves, whereas everything points against this assumption as well.

Let us consider these points in turn. Strawson concedes that *if* the irreversibility of the sequence A$_r$ then B$_r$ could be known, then it could legitimately be inferred that this sequence represents the occurrence A then B. And he does not, certainly, misunderstand Kant to say that the *irreversibility* of a sequence of representations can ever be directly given. Rather, what he supposes is that if it is directly known simply what the *sequence* of the representations is and that each representation stands in the same temporal relation to its object, then it can be inferred that the objective states of affairs are indeed ordered as are the representations of them, and so constitute an event. But Kant's argument for causation among the states of objects turns precisely on the rejection of the two premises of such an inference. As far as direct knowledge of the order *of representations* is concerned, Kant's Transcendental Deduction and Refutation of Idealism proceed precisely by rejecting the—admittedly natural—supposition that merely having the representation $A_r$ prior to the representation $B_r$ is sufficient for *knowing* that one has experienced $A_r$ prior to $B_r$. The fundamental premise of the Deduction is that "Every intuition contains a manifold in itself, which however would not be represented as such if the mind did not distinguish the time in the succession of impressions on one another: for as *contained in one moment* no representation can ever be anything other than absolute unity" (A 99). Or, as the Analogy itself says, "imagination can connect . . . two states in two ways" (B 233). What these imply is that in the case in which I in fact have $A_r$ prior to $B_r$, what is present to me *at the time of $B_r$* is nevertheless a *single* representational state, which to be sure has both A-like and B-like content, but which must be *interpreted* to count as a *present* experience of $B_r$ plus a representation of a *prior* subjective state $A_r$ rather than as, say, a *present* representation of both A and B. And Kant's view is that this can be accomplished only by relating the *content* of the present representational state to a sequence of states *in the external world* that dictates that the only way in which I could, at the time of $B_r$, be representing both A-like and B-like content is if I am *then having* $B_r$ and *remembering* having previously experienced $A_r$. That is, so far from the sequence A then B being directly inferable from the sequence $A_r$ then $B_r$, the sequence $A_r$ then $B_r$ itself must be inferred from the sequence A then B. And, of course, since the sequence A then B itself is not directly given, *it* can be inferred only from a law that dictates that, in the given circumstances, B *must* have succeeded A. Here is a law that does indeed link A to B and not just $A_r$ to A and $B_r$ to B; and here is the true sense in which "we must derive the *subjective sequence* of apprehension from the *objective sequence* of appearances" (A 193/B 238).

The second point to be made is this. The Strawson objection claims that the event A then B could be inferred from the sequence $A_r$ then $B_r$ combined with knowledge of how $A_r$ is caused by A and $B_r$ by B, in particular knowledge that they are caused with the *same* time-lag—for instance, the production of $B_r$ has not been delayed by any medium or mechanism such that $B_r$ succeeds $A_r$ even though A succeeds B. But it is difficult to understand how knowledge of the laws relating A to $A_r$ and B to $B_r$ could be acquired without knowledge of the order of A and B. How could it be confirmed that, say, $B_r$ was being produced with a delay not present in the transmission of $A_r$ *unless* it were also known that A actually preceded B? Or how could it be tested that $A_r$ and $B_r$ were actually being produced by isomorphic mechanisms unless it were also assumed that in the test case the objects stood in the same temporal relations as the perceptions? In other words, causal laws governing the mechanisms of perception could not be confirmed independently of determinate knowledge about the order of objective states of affairs—so those sorts of laws could not be acquired independently of laws from which the sequence of the objective states of affairs themselves could be derived. Hence, it is not a fallacy for Kant to introduce the latter as well as the former kind of laws into his argument.

A slightly different way of making the same point may be found in a famous passage from Schopenhauer, which Schopenhauer took to be an objection to Kant but which I take as an illustration of the position that Kant ultimately strived to express. Discussing the contrast between the sequence of perceptions of a moving ship and the changing perceptions of an unchanging house, Schopenhauer wrote:

> I maintain that the two cases are not different at all, that both are events, the knowledge of which is objective, in other words one of changes in real objects that are known as such by the subject. *Both are changes in position of two bodies relatively to each other.* In the first case one of these bodies is the observer's own organism . . . and the other is the house; with respect to the parts of the house, the position of the eye is successively changed. In the second case, the ship alters its position relatively to the river [and the unmoving eye], and so the change is between two bodies. Both are events, the only difference is that in the first case the change starts from the observer's own body. . . . Yet this body is nevertheless an object among objects, consequently is liable to the laws of this objective corporeal world.[27]

The final version of the Refutation of Idealism reveals that this was precisely Kant's own position, and what it suggests apropos the present case is that there is no way in which knowledge of the laws explaining the perceptual effects of changing eye-positions could be obtained independently of laws explaining the behavior of the bodies being looked at. How could it actually be confirmed that it is the changing position of the eye that is causing the succession of perceptions of the house unless it is assumed that the house is not changing? or that it is the changing position of the ship that is causing the succession of perceptions of it unless it is assumed that the eye is still? But if this information about the objects is not given directly on the basis of mere representations, whence can it come except from exactly the sort of laws that Strawson thinks are only fallaciously introduced by Kant?

At this point, of course, the reader may well wonder whence knowledge of these objective causal laws itself is supposed to derive. After all, Kant specifically denies that individual causal laws are known *a priori* (cf. A 196-7/B 241-2, or more generally B 142). Yet on the only model of the acquisition of causal knowledge that Kant could have accepted—Humean inductivism without its skepticism—empirical knowledge of causal laws is surely derived from induction on repeated *experiences*. Does this not make Kant's entire theory incoherent?

My view is that it does not, as long as Kant's theory of judgment—or time-determination—is understood not as a psychological model of the generation of beliefs, but as an epistemological model of the confirmation of beliefs, and as long as it is in addition supposed that in any given case, say a case of testing a hypothesis about a sequence of representations, one and the same sequence of representations is not *both* being derived from a particular causal law about objects *and* being employed as evidence *for* the validity of that causal law. But a full exposition of this defence would not only take us into the difficult terrain of the theory of confirmation; it would also require a detailed study of Kant's alleged "transcendental psychology." So for the moment I offer only this programmatic assertion.

4

This completes my exposition and defence of Kant's argument for his principle of causation. I now want to consider the question earlier set aside about the precise form of the principle that Kant is defending. The crux of Kant's argument is that an event can be determined to have occurred only if there is a rule that entails that one of its constituent states must have succeeded the other. Many take Kant to mean that an event can be posited only where the first state is taken to be the cause of the second. This is not surprising, since Kant often writes in just this way. For instance:

Thus if I perceive that something happens, then the first thing contained in this representation is that something precedes, for it is just in relation to this that the appearance acquires its temporal relation, that namely, of existing after a preceding time in which it did not. But it can only acquire its determinate temporal position in this relation through something being presupposed in the preceding state on which it always follows, i.e., follows in accordance with a rule: which then implies . . . that, if the state that precedes is posited, this determinate occurrence inevitably and necessarily follows. (A 198/B 243–4)

Or:

If, therefore, my perception is to contain the cognition of an occurrence . . . it must be an empirical judgment in which one thinks that the sequence is determined, i.e., that it presupposes another appearance in time which it follows necessarily or in accordance with a rule . . . Thus the relation of appearances . . . in accordance with which the existence of that which succeeds (that which happens) is determined in time necessarily and in accordance with a rule by something that precedes it, thus the relation of cause and effect, is the condition of the objective validity of our empirical judgments. (A 201–2/B 246–7)

But the supposition that in any cognizable event what precedes must be the cause and what succeeds the effect is untenable. As Schopenhauer charged, we think that night follows day without being caused by day. Moreover, as Kant himself observes, we often think that the effect is *simultaneous* with rather than subsequent to its cause.

There is really no problem here, however, for the statements we have just considered are only imprecise statements of the conclusion to which Kant's argument actually leads. More precisely, Kant himself says that what is required to determine that perceptions of two states of affairs represent the occurrence of an event is a rule assigning a temporal position to one of the two states—that judged to be the latter in a sequence—"which, after the preceding state, cannot be otherwise assigned" (A 198/B 243); or, he says, we "cannot ascribe sequence . . . to the object . . . and distinguish it from the subjective sequence of our apprehension except when a rule is the ground that necessitates us to observe this order of perceptions rather than another" (A 196/B 241–2). But to satisfy this general condition, all that is required is a rule from which it can be deduced that, given the two states concerned, the latter of them can only have obtained after the former, or that the former can only have preceded the latter. And this determination could be grounded in at least *two* different ways. Given two states, we could judge that one of them must succeed the other because the earlier one is or contains the cause of the latter—the situation that Kant initially envisions—*or* precisely because the earlier state *lacks* the cause of the later. In the second case, the later state could occur only after the earlier state because its cause, *not* being present in the first state, *itself could only have succeeded that first state. Either* the determination that one state must succeed the other because states of its type are caused by and always follow states of the other type *or* the determination that it can only succeed the other because it must await the *addition* of its cause to a state that lacks it would ground the more general claim that there is a necessary and irreversible order to the two states concerned.

Thus causation is necessary to determine that one state succeeds another, but not necessarily causation of the succeeding state by the preceding one. And this is what solves the problem of simultaneous causation, although Kant himself does not recognize it. The problem of simultaneous causation, raised by Kant after his main argument has been completed, is that in many if not most cases of physical causation the effect does *not* appear to succeed its cause but is simultaneous with it. This seems to be the case where cause and effect are both processes, as in Kant's case of a fire that is warming a room, but also in cases where at least the cause is a discrete event, as in the case in which placing a lead ball on a previously well-plumped pillow appears to cause the immediate existence of a hollow in the pillow (A 202–3/B 247–8). Kant tries to explain this problem away by invoking the possibility of a "vanishing" quantity of time that can make the time-*lag* between cause and effect indiscernibly small without disturbing the time-*order* according to which the cause precedes the effect (A 203/B 249). But this expedient is not necessary, precisely because Kant's general position does *not* require that an event can be determined to occur only when a cause precedes its effect. An event can also be determined to occur, or one state to precede another, if the cause of the succeeding state is simultaneous with *it* but succeeds a prior state of affairs that constitutes the initial state of the event. And this is just the situation that obtains in Kant's examples. For in these cases the events that are determined to occur are *not* a fire burning and then a room being warm or a ball being placed on a pillow and then the pillow being dented, but rather *the room being cold and then warm* (its becoming warm) or *the pillow being smooth and then dented* (its becoming dented). In each of these cases, the stated event can be determined to obtain just because a cause *absent* in the initial condition *intervenes* to produce the succeeding condition, even though its own commencement is simultaneous with that of the latter.

In other words, the cause may have to precede its effect where we have only two terms, one of which must succeed the other; but sometimes we may consider a threefold relation between preceding state, succeeding state, and cause of the latter, in which case the third state of affairs might be simultaneous with the second but successive to the first. And Kant himself allows for precisely this possibility, although he is considering a different point, when he says that "if I lay the ball on the pillow, the dent follows its previously smooth shape; but if (for whatever reason) the pillow has a dent, a leaden ball does not follow it" (A 203/B 248). What this assumes is just that in one case but not in another two states of affairs may be ordered because there is a causal law according to which a third state is the cause of the second and itself succeeds upon the first. Thus, as long as Kant maintains only the general position that two states can be ordered only if there is *some* applicable relation of cause and effect and does not slip into the excessively restricted conclusion that states can be ordered only if the former is the cause of the latter, there is no problem about simultaneous causation.

## Notes

This essay was originally presented on a talk at Harvard University in 1983. It was not previously published in this form, though much of the material was incorporated into my *Kant and the Claim of Knowledge* (Cambridge: Cambridge University Press, 1987), pp. 243–62.

1. See "Kant's Tactics in the Transcendental Deduction," in J. N. Mohanty and Robert W. Shahan, eds., *Essays on Kant's Critique of Pure Reason* (Norman: University of Oklahoma Press, 1982), pp. 157–199, or *Kant and The Claims of Knowledge,* Part II, pp. 73–154.

2. The translations from Kant are my own; those from the *Critique of Pure Reason* have been revised in accordance with the translation by Paul Guyer and Allen W. Wood (Cambridge: Cambridge University Press, 1998). Other citations are located by volume and page number of the *Akademie* editions.

3. Arthur Schopenhauer, *The Fourfold Root of the Principle of Sufficient Reason*, sec. 23, in the translation by E. F. J. Payne (LaSalle, Illinois: Open Court Publishing Co., 1974), p. 127; also referred to in A. C. Ewing, *Kant's Treatment of Causality* (London, 1924). p. 89.

4. Contrary to the unexamined assumption of R. C. S. Walker in *Kant* (London and Boston: Routledge and Kegan Paul, 1978), p. 103.

5. But it is not; therefore, unlike Peter Strawson (see below), I do not actually call irreversibility a criterion of the occurrence of an event.

6. Graham Bird, *Kant's Theory of Knowledge* (London: Routledge and Kegan Paul, 1962), p. 153.

7. That the two states belong to a single object is supposed to follow from the first Analogy, which in fact Bird treats as the first stage of the analysis of the same concept analyzed by the second Analogy.

8. *Kant's Theory of Knowledge,* p. 155.

9. loc. cit.

10. *A Treatise of Human Nature,* Bk. I, Pt. III, sec. xiv (Selby-Bigge, p. 172).

11. *Kant's Theory of Knowledge,* p. 161.

12. "First Truths," in L. E. Loemker, ed., *Leibniz: Philosophical Writings,* 2d ed. (Dordrecht: D. Reidel, 1969), pp. 267–268. Kant himself could not have been familiar with this paper, which was not published during his lifetime.

13. *Ontologia,* sec. 70; my emphasis.

14. Bird does not in fact misconstrue Kant's objective of grounding our distinctions between events and non-events by means of the principle of the second Analogy (see p. 155). He must therefore be sharing the assumption, which will be discussed in the next few pages of this essay, that as long as it is known that some event is happening, the question of which event is happening is automatically settled by the mere fact that one of the two representations involved is a present representation, and the other, not. But this, as we will next see, is not Kant's assumption at all.

15. This interpretation has recently been advanced by William Harper in "Kant's Empirical Realism and the Distinction between Subjective and Objective Succession," in *Kant on Causality, Freedom and Objectivity,* ed. William A. Harper and Rolf Meerbote (Minneapolis: University of Minnesota Press, 1984), pp. 108–137, and James Van Cleve, "Four Recent Interpretations of Kant's Second Analogy," *Kant-Studien* 64 (1973): 71–87.

16. This defense is most clearly put in D. P. Dryer, *Kant's Solution for Verification in Metaphysics* (London: George Allen and Unwin, 1966), p. 436.

17. C. D. Broad, "Kant's First and Second Analogies of Experience," *Proceedings of the Aristotelian Society* (1926), p. 208; quoted in Dryer, p. 437.

18. Dryer, p. 437.

19. See my article "Kant's Intentions in the Refutation of Idealism," *Philosophical Review* 92 (July, 1983): 329–383, or *Kant and the Claim of Knowledge,* Part IV, pp. 279–329.

20. *The Bounds of Sense* (London: Methuen & Co., 1966), p. 28; cf. p. 137.

21. Arthur Lovejoy, "On Kant's Reply to Hume," in Moltke Gram, ed., *Kant: Disputed Questions* (New York: Quadrangle Books, 1967).

22. H. A. Prichard, *Kant's Theory of Knowledge* (Oxford: Oxford University Press, 1909).

23. *The Bounds of Sense,* p. 136.

24. *The Bounds of Sense,* p. 134.

25. I replace Strawson's symbolism with that of Lewis White Beck, in "A *Non Sequitur* of Numbing Grossness?" in Beck, *Essays on Kant and Hume* (New Haven, Conn.: Yale University Press, 1978), pp. 146–153.

26. *The Bounds of Sense,* p. 136.

27. *The Fourfold Root of the Principle of Sufficient Reason,* sec. 23; Payne, pp. 124–125.

# 8

## The Metaphysics of Transcendental Idealism [partial]
### *from* The Bounds of Sense

*P. F. Strawson*

Under this heading are to be grouped together a number of interconnected doctrines [that seemed to Kant to be] the indispensable framework of his thought. . . . He constantly speaks of "our" sensitivity,
of "our" understanding, says that this and that are "in us," that "we
ourselves" are responsible for this or that; and it may seem surprising
that the assured use of these personal pronouns and possessives—
seeming to embrace Kant and his readers and the rest of humanity—
should have any power to diminish the sense of the strangeness of
doctrines which themselves show how very far from the ordinary this
use of these words must be. Yet that Kant's use of these words does
have something of this effect becomes clear, I think, when we expel
them, as I shall try to do, from the statement of the doctrines.

After stating the doctrine, I shall try to answer what seem to me the
main outstanding questions about it. But before we have the questions,
we must have the statement.

### I. The Doctrines

These I shall set out in short numbered sections, with the minimum of
qualification. . . .

1. *The supersensible: things as they are in themselves.* There exists the
sphere of supersensible reality, of things, neither spatial nor temporal,
as they are in themselves.

145

Within this sphere there obtains a certain complex relation (or a class of cases of this relation) which we can speak of, on the model of a causal relation, in terms of "affecting" and "being affected by." Let us call it the A-relation. We may speak of the affecting (active) thing (or things) and the affected (passive) thing (or things) which enter into this relation, without prejudice to the possible partial or complete identity of these terms, without prejudice to the possibility of the relation's being partly or wholly self-reflexive.

There is indeed an at least partial identity between the terms in (or in any case of) the A-relation. For there belongs to the affected thing in any such case a feature called "sensibility" in respect of which that thing is affected. But there also belongs to the same thing a feature called "understanding" in respect of which that thing is active, affecting itself in respect of its sensibility.

There are other affecting elements or features which enter into (or into any case of) the A-relation. But whether these belong to the same thing as the (relevant) sensibility and understanding is unknown. If we call sensibility a form-yielding element (to mark its passivity) and understanding a form-producing element (to mark its activity), we may call the residual factors entering into the A-relation matter-producing elements. The reason for the "form-matter" antithesis in these descriptions will appear in the next section.

2. *Experience.* Experience is the outcome of this complex quasi-causal relation holding in the sphere of things in themselves; and the co-operation of all the elements so far mentioned is essential to its production. The matter-producing element and the form-producing element must both affect the form-yielding element in the generation of experience.

Experience consists of temporally ordered intuitions so conceptualized and connected that: (1) many such intuitions have the character of perceptions of a law-governed world of objects (bodies in space and time) enjoying their own states and relations irrespective of the occurrence of any particular states of awareness of them; and (2) their exists for all such intuitions at least the potentiality of their being ascribed by a self-conscious subject to himself as his own states of awareness.

The *temporal* character of experience in general and the possession by some intuitions of the character of *spatiality* which allows of their being ordered in such a way as to confer upon them the character of perceptions of objects *in space* are both alike due to the passive element in the affected thing (the former to "inner," the latter to "outer" sense). That is why the passive element, or sensibility, may be called a *form*-yielding element.

The conceptual connexions in virtue of which intuitions possess the character of perceptions of a *law-governed world of objects* are due, though in their most general character only, to the active or affecting element in the same thing. This is why the active element (understanding) in that thing may be called a *form*-producing element.

The residual characteristics of experience are due to the residual factors entering into the A-relation (the matter-producing elements).

3. *The physical world nothing apart from perceptions.* What actually exists as the outcome of the quasi-causal A-relation is nothing but experience itself, the temporally ordered series of conceptualized and connected intuitions. Although, given the character of the form-yielding and form-producing elements of the affected (and at least partially self-affecting) term, it is necessary that these should include at least some having the character of perceptions of law-governed objects (bodies in space and time) enjoying their own states and relations irrespective of the occurrence of any particular states of awareness of them, yet bodies in space do not actually exist, enjoying their own states and relations independently of the occurrence of *any* states of awareness of them. Apart from perceptions, they are really nothing at all.

4. *Empirical knowledge.* What emerges from the A-relation, viz. experience, may be said to include empirical knowledge of physical nature and empirical self-consciousness or knowledge of states of oneself. This reflects the fact that experience involves the employment of concepts of the objective, hence a commitment to the distinction between experiences themselves and an experienced physical world.

Nothing that emerges from the A-relation can be said to be knowledge or consciousness of things as they are in themselves.

5. *Appearances of things as they are in themselves.* The contents of empirical self-consciousness, being the temporally ordered outcome of the A-relation, are not knowledge or awareness of anything as it is in itself. Yet they may be said to be *appearances* of that thing to which sensibility and understanding both belong. For the conceptualizing power or power of thought is temporally manifested in all empirical recognition or classification; and this power, though its manifestation in experience must be temporal, is really identical with, or has its

source in, the form-producing feature (understanding) of that non-temporal thing in itself to which the form-yielding feature (sensibility) also belongs.

The physical or spatial world, though in a different sense, may also be called an appearance of things as they are in themselves. In a different sense, for it is not simply, like the temporally ordered series of experiences, a *dependent* existence, the outcome of the A-relation. It only *appears* to exist, is really nothing apart from perceptions. Nevertheless there is further point in speaking of the natural world as an appearance of things as they are in themselves, besides the point that is made by speaking of the contents of consciousness, as such, as appearances of that thing to which both sensibility and understanding belong. And this is the point that matter-producing as well as form-producing and form-yielding factors must enter into the A-relation which holds among things in themselves and of which the outcome is experience. The contents of experience in general may be said to be an appearance of the matter-producing factors under the conditions imposed by the form-yielding and form-producing factors.

6. *Creative awareness (intellectual intuition)*. Nothing which emerges from *any* affecting relation can count as knowledge or awareness of the affecting thing as it is in itself. Therefore there can be no knowledge or awareness of things which exist independently of that knowledge or awareness and of which that knowledge or awareness is consequently an effect. More exactly, there can be no knowledge of such things as they are in themselves, but only as they appear—only of their appearances.

Hence either there is no such thing as knowledge of the supersensibly real as it is in itself or the supersensibly real is created by that very awareness and does not exist independently of it. Insofar as the supersensibly real is thought of as a possible object of such a non-sensible awareness (intellectual intuition), it is entitled "noumenon."

7. *Non-empirical knowledge of appearances*. Empirical knowledge is the outcome of the action both of the matter-producing elements (in the supersensibly real) and of the form-producing element on the form-yielding element. But some knowledge of appearances (of natural objects in space and time) is also attainable which is independent of the action of the matter-producing elements and hence may be called non-empirical knowledge of appearances. For the form-yielding and

form-producing elements together determine the character of experience in certain respects, whatever the contribution of the matter-producing elements may be. What these respects are may be ascertained
(in time, but independently of the actual course of experience) in two
ways: (1) the form-yielding elements can be activated, independently
of the matter-producing elements (in "constructions in pure intuition"), to yield, e.g. geometrical knowledge of space and of bodies in
space; (2) the implications of the understanding's requirement of the
conceptualizability-in-general of the temporal data of experience can
be brought out by critical reflection (as in the Analytic).

8. *Non-empirical knowledge only of appearances.* Non-empirical
knowledge, so arrived at, is no more than what it is described as,
namely knowledge of certain features the presence of which in experience is independent of the actual content of experience, i.e. independent of the particular contributions made by the matter-producing
elements. Such non-empirical knowledge, arrived at in experience
though independently of its actual course, is therefore knowledge of
appearances only. Apart from knowledge of such truths as are certified
by logic alone, there is no other possible source of non-empirical
knowledge, arrived at in experience.

## 2. Some Questions

Many questions arise about these doctrines. What claims does Kant
make on their behalf and how should those claims be evaluated? To
what extent can the doctrines be shown to be mutually inconsistent,
or otherwise incoherent, or to be inconsistent with more acceptable
parts of his theory of knowledge? To what extent can they be explained
as perversions of more intelligible principles? What is the exact significance, not merely in the context of transcendental idealism, but in that
of Kant's theory of human experience as a whole, of the relatively familiar kind of phenomenalistic idealism outlined at paragraph 3 above,
and how, if at all, is it reconcilable with Kant's assertion that his transcendental idealism is an empirical realism? Is there anything at all in
these doctrines which should be preserved, or should it be our task to
show that they can be completely detached from what is of value in
Kant's analysis of the structure of experience and thereupon discarded
without loss?

Some answers to these questions will emerge in the course of the following sections.


### 3. The Claims


In several connected but distinguishable ways the doctrines of transcendental idealism appear to Kant to make vital contributions to the rest of his system. I shall first consider briefly, under four heads, the claims which he makes on behalf of these doctrines; and then proceed, in the following sections, to examine in more detail the doctrines themselves.


1. *The demands of morality.* The briefest possible résumé of his views concerning human knowledge must include at least two points: that we can have some non-empirical knowledge (knowledge which does not rest on the actual course of experience) of objects of possible experience in space and time, and that we can have no other non-empirical knowledge, and hence no knowledge at all of anything else. The negative part of this thesis is important to him not only in a negative way, as discrediting, once for all, the pretensions of transcendent metaphysics. It has a different kind of importance as leaving room for certain morally based convictions, not amounting to knowledge. If the natural world were all there was, Kant holds, human freedom would be an illusion and the ideal of moral justice would be a dream perpetually mocked by the facts. But the sphere denied to knowledge is thereby left open to a morally certified, though uncomprehending, faith that the reality of human freedom is somehow secured in that sphere and moral justice is really there attained.

Clearly the belief in the supersensible reality is essential to this part of Kant's doctrine; and the form of that belief seems to be conditioned by the doctrine in a way with which I shall be concerned in the next section. But there will be found few, I think, to regard the ideal of moral justice as an adequate basis for such a belief, or to view the problem of human freedom as demanding, or allowing of, solution with its help. Moreover, it would be entirely foreign to Kant's thinking to rest the case for the doctrines of transcendental idealism on such considerations. Although he claims it as a merit in those doctrines that they make room for faith in human freedom and moral justice, he does not, and he could not consistently, use this claim as a premise from which to argue to their truth.

2. *The principle of significance; the mathematical antinomies.* In his critique of transcendent metaphysics, the elaboration, in its purely neg-ative aspect, of the doctrine that we can have no non-empirical knowl-edge, and hence no knowledge at all, of anything which is not an object of possible sensible experience, Kant frequently invokes what I have called his principle of significance, the principle that we can make no significant use of concepts in propositions claiming to express knowl-edge unless we have empirical criteria for the application of those con-cepts; and he seems to regard this principle as a consequence of certain of the doctrines of transcendental idealism. We must inquire more closely from just which of these doctrines Kant thinks of the principle as deriving its force.

Let us consider, first, the chapter on the antinomies, in which a free and fruitful use of the principle of significance appears, at first glance, to be directly associated with doctrines of transcendental idealism. If things in space and time were things in themselves, Kant says, a certain disjunction framed in terms of concepts of limited or unlimited wholes would necessarily apply to them. Since they are not things in them-selves, but only appearances, it follows that it is only if we could specify a possible experience which would justify the application of such a concept of a limited, or of an unlimited, whole that such notions would, in this connexion, have any significance. Since we can specify no such possible experience, the concepts are empty of meaning.

Here we must ask what is meant by the denial that things in space and time are things in themselves. It is not, of course, the otiose denial that they are supersensible things, things *not* in space and time. It is, rather, the denial that they have any existence apart from our tempo-rally ordered representations or perceptions. If the use of the principle of significance is here made to rest on any aspect of transcendental idealism, it is made to rest on this phenomenalistic idealism regarding the physical world, a doctrine which can be, and has been, maintained, or entertained, by philosophers quite independently of the belief in a supersensible reality or of the thesis that the temporal series of experi-ences is the outcome of quasi-causal transactions in the sphere of the supersensible. . . . The only plausible alternative interpretation which confronts us is one which grants autonomy to the principle of significance and leaves none but an ironical meaning to the phrase "things as they are in themselves."

Elsewhere, where Kant appears to relate the principle of significance to the doctrines of transcendental idealism, it is mainly in connexion with the categories, or pure concepts of the understanding, in general, that he does so. When he writes of them as merely rules for an understanding which is powerless to make use of them in knowledge unless material for their application is given to it, through sensibility, from elsewhere, it is indeed possible to read this warning in terms of the model of the affecting relation between supersensible terms and hence to connect the warning with the whole structure of the metaphysics of transcendental idealism. It is possible. But it is also quite unnecessary. Even if we choose to preserve, in this warning, the psychological idiom of an active understanding, the source of concepts, and a passive sensibility, yielding intuitions, we can perfectly well do so without thinking of "understanding" and "sensibility" as attributes of anything more unfamiliar than human beings, creatures who have a history (are in time) and a bulk (are in space); so that the principle of significance, even when expressed in the idiom of faculties, appears as something quite independent of the structure of transcendental idealism.

We may conclude that the principle of significance is either effectively independent of the doctrines of transcendental idealism or at most it depends, for Kant—in some cases of its application—only on that relatively familiar phenomenalistic idealism which transcendental idealism appears to include.

3. *Non-empirical knowledge of appearances.* What, now, of the non-empirical knowledge of objects of experience which Kant declares to be available to us and of which he claims to explain the nature and the possibility? It is here, surely, at least from the epistemological, if not from the ethical, point of view that the heart of the system lies, and here that the Copernican Revolution is held to yield its large rewards. This non-empirical knowledge is said by Kant to be of two kinds. On the one hand, it embraces mathematical knowledge in general; on the other, it consists of knowledge of certain principles which constitute both the necessary foundation of natural science and the conditions of the possibility of experience in general. As regards the first, it is only in respect of geometry, the "mathematics of space," that Kant makes any serious effort to show that the fact of mathematical knowledge requires the theory of transcendental idealism for its explanation. We have yet

to examine his theory of geometry; but it may be said in advance that, though we strain to the limit our sympathy with Kant's insight in this field, the reach of that straining falls infinitely short of his conclusions.

There remain those principles of which the proofs are variant forms of the thesis that they embody conditions of the possibility of experience. Let us waive the thought that those principles which Kant actually advances do not have the status which he claims for them, and assume, for the present purpose, that some at least of those proofs are valid. It must be noted, as Kant himself notes, that we do not, strictly speaking, have *knowledge* of the principles in question—even though we take them for granted in our empirical inquiries—until the critical inquiry undertaken in the Transcendental Analytic is successfully carried to its conclusion. These principles need proof[1] and no other kind of proof is possible than this. Until it has been supplied, scepticism, such as Hume's, regarding such principles is legitimate, and even welcome, as providing a stimulus to the critical inquiry by which it is finally dispelled.

Non-empirical knowledge of the principles is obtained, then, only by following the course of argument pursued in the Analytic; and it is there obtained solely by reflection on the implications of what "understanding" requires of a possible experience in time. The requirement of "understanding," at its barest minimum, is that experience should be conceptualized, that it should issue in judgement or recognition; and it is this requirement, traced through the necessary self-reflexiveness of experience ("transcendental apperception") and its necessary objective reference, which leads ultimately to the proof of the principles. But the premise of this course of argument, since it does no more than define that of which the conditions of the possibility are to be investigated, in no way depends for its acceptability on the doctrines of transcendental idealism. If the premise does not, then neither does the proof; and if the proof does not, then neither does our non-empirical knowledge of the principles established by the proof.

In this too short demonstration, it might be objected, certain features of the course of argument actually followed in the Analogies are overlooked. For Kant there remarks that if things in space were things in themselves, if they existed independently of our representations (perceptions), we could have no knowledge of them at all. There would be no such thing as knowledge of objects. Yet our perceptions must yield knowledge of objects if experience is to be possible. Hence the objective reference of our perceptions must consist in nothing but their subjection to rules of connexion, such as are provided for by the principle of causality.[2]

On this we may make two comments. . . . If the conception of the objective is to obtain any employment in experience, experience must indeed contain a ground for it in that connectedness of perceptions which is inseparable from the employment of concepts of the objective. But in order to make this point, it is not necessary to invoke the doctrine that what we ordinarily conceive of as objects existing independently of our perceptions of them are really no such things. Of course, this latter view may be independently held on the ground . . . that if objects in space did really enjoy an existence independent of what we count as perceptions of them, then those perceptions could not constitute awareness or knowledge of those objects as they are in themselves; since those perceptions would be the outcome of an affecting relation and nothing which is the outcome of such a relation can be knowledge of the affecting thing as it is in itself. But then this view, thus independently advanced, plays no essential role in the explanation of the possibility of such non-empirical knowledge of objects of experience as is here in question.

The second comment is an obvious, and a recurrent, one. It is that the aspect of transcendental idealism here most prominent is once more that phenomenalistic idealism which it includes, according to which physical things are nothing apart from our perceptions.

It is worth adding that here, as elsewhere, we may be subject to that disconcerting "change of aspect" on the part of some of the doctrines of transcendental idealism. They may seem to change, before our eyes, into blandly ironical reminders that questions we may be tempted to ask about the nature of things in space and time, *as they are in themselves*—apart from anything we could find out about them empirically, through perception, and the construction and testing of perceptually based theories—are senseless questions, empty of content. It would, indeed, be hard to understand how Kant could hold to the doctrines but for this ambiguity of aspect. But . . . we delude ourselves if we persist in viewing them under their acceptable aspect alone.

Behind all the argument and analysis concerned with our supposed non-empirical knowledge of objects in space and of the natural world in general there lies, we must finally admit, a crude and incoherent model of the mind as it timelessly is in itself, and of things as they timelessly are in themselves, the former, affected by the latter and self-affecting, being responsible for certain features of experience of which the mathematician and the critical philosopher, by special exercises of self-analysis, conducted in time, can obtain knowledge, without reference to the actual course of sensible experience.

4. *The fourth Paralogism (first edition).* There is one more point to be mentioned at which Kant explicitly invokes the doctrines of transcendental idealism. In the first edition's version of the discussion of the fourth paralogism, Kant claims, by their help, to show the way of escape from the predicament of problematic idealism and to dissolve the problem alleged to be posed by the action of body upon mind. How can we be confident of the existence of external objects in space when the only ground for this belief must be an inference from inner perceptions? How can the motions of bodies in space produce effects so utterly different in kind as mental states? Both these questions, Kant says, presuppose what is false, viz. that bodies exist independently of our perceptions. Hence both problems disappear when the falsity of the presupposition is recognized. That it *is* false is a part of the thesis of transcendental idealism.

Once more we must recognize that, as in the case of the problems posed by the mathematical antinomies, Kant's solution rests on an appeal to a part only of the doctrines of transcendental idealism, namely to the phenomenalistic idealism which it includes. Though the passages in question were omitted in the second edition, they were omitted not because Kant thought them mistaken, but because he thought them misunderstood.[3]

What is the outcome of this brief review of the claims made by Kant on behalf of the doctrines of transcendental idealism? In asking this question, I am not concerned with the validity of his arguments or solutions but with their structures; and it must surely strike us that, with certain reservations, the only element in transcendental idealism which has any significant part to play in those structures is the phenomenalistic idealism according to which the physical world is nothing apart from perceptions. The reservations concern, first, the crude model alluded to above, which, however, does not feature prominently in any of the detailed structures of argument in the book; second, more specifically, the argument from geometry, which has yet to be considered; and, third, the supposed demands of the moral consciousness which, Kant thinks, can only, and incomprehensibly, be met in the sphere of the supersensible. Of course, we must not assume that Kant would for a moment have regarded the included phenomenalistic ide-

alism as tenable apart from the rest of the metaphysics of transcendental idealism. It is time to seek further enlightenment by examining in
greater detail some of the particular doctrines which belong to that
metaphysics. I begin with one of the obscurest points of all, a point
which is of the greatest importance to Kant if the demands of the moral
consciousness are, however incomprehensibly, to be satisfied.


## 4. The Thing-in-Itself and Appearances in Inner Sense

I have remarked already on Kant's confident use of the first personal
pronouns and possessives in stating, or alluding to, the doctrines of
transcendental idealism. It is, manifestly, of importance to him to ensure that there is a point of connexion, in the way of identity, between
the supersensible world and the world of human beings, between
things as they are in themselves on the one hand and Kant and his
readers, the ordinary referents of personal pronouns and possessives,
on the other. Without such a point of connexion, in the way of identity,
the claim that freedom is at least possible (though to us incomprehen-
sible) as a property of supersensible beings, would be without relevance to the moral nature or situation of human beings. Without such
a point of connexion, in the way of identity, between that thing which
is, in itself, the seat of space, time and the categories, and the human
student of geometry or of the critical philosophy, it would be impossible to assemble, let alone to work, that crude model of imposed necessities available, through self-analysis or self-inspection, to our non-
empirical knowledge. The mere use of the personal pronouns and possessives does nothing, however, to show where the point of connexion
lies. We have to ask what *we* human beings, Kant's readers, can unambiguously understand by "us" and "we" and "our" when these expressions are so easily and loftily used to convey the doctrines of
transcendental idealism.

The answer is indicated at various points in the book. There is an
incautious statement of it in the Antinomies, at a point where the supposed interests of morality are uppermost in Kant's mind:

> Man, however, who knows all the rest of nature through the senses,
> knows himself also through pure apperception; and this, indeed, in acts
> and inner determinations which he cannot regard as impressions of the
> senses. He is thus to himself, on the one hand phenomenon, and on the

other hand, in respect of certain faculties which cannot be ascribed to sensibility, a purely intelligible object. We entitle these faculties understanding and reason.[4]

The point of contact, in the way of identity, between a man as a natural being and himself as a supersensible being is to be found, then, in the man's consciousness of his own possession and exercise of the power of thought, of the faculties of understanding and reason. There immediately arise, on Kant's own principles, the objections, first, that anything which can be ascribed to a man as a case or instance of such self-consciousness must be something which occurs in time and, second, that it must be consciousness *of* himself as reasoning or recognizing or thinking something, as intellectually engaged at some point, or over some stretch, of time. Any such self-consciousness must, it seems, belong to the history of, and must be consciousness of some episode belonging to the history of, a being which *has* a history and hence is not a supersensible being, not "the subject in which the representation of time has its original ground."[5]

Kant faces these difficulties again and again in more cautious passages in the Aesthetic, in the Deduction, in the Paralogisms. He distinguishes between "original" self-consciousness and empirical self-consciousness. In the former, which is not really knowledge of myself at all, I am conscious of myself not as I appear to myself nor as I am in myself but only that I am. "This representation is a thought, not an intuition."[6] In the latter, which yields the only knowledge of myself available to me, I am conscious of myself only as I appear to myself, not as I am in myself.

Repeated like spells, these pronominal incantations are as inefficacious as spells. In the dictum regarding knowledge of oneself (empirical self-consciousness) the identity which has to be explained—the identity of the empirically self-conscious subject and the real or supersensible subject—is simply assumed without being made a whit more intelligible. If the appearances of *x* to *x* occur in time, they cannot be assigned to the history of the transcendental, supersensible subject, for that being has no history. That is to say, they cannot justifiably be described as appearances *to* myself as I (supersensibly) am in myself, nor—since what they are appearances *to* they are also appearances *of*—as appearances *of* myself as I (supersensibly) am in myself. The reference to myself as I (supersensibly) am in myself drops out as superfluous and unjustified; and with it goes all ground for saying that, in empirical self-consciousness, I appear to myself as other than I really am. If, on the other hand, we are not to put a temporal construction on the verb *to appear,* how are we to understand it? Are we to say that it non-temporally appears to be the case, to the transcendental subject, that it enjoys a series of temporally ordered states? The limits of intelligibility are here traversed, on any standard. And if they were not, we should still be as far as ever from making good the identity which is in question. What has the non-history of the transcendental subject to do with us?

Kant fails to overcome the difficulties concerning identity because they cannot be overcome. There is no refuge but incoherence from the question how the connexion is to be made, in the way of identity, between the natural being, the man, with a mental history of thoughts, perceptions, and feelings and the supersensible being, with no history at all, "in which the representation of time has its original ground." It is, indeed, an old belief that reason is something essentially out of time and yet in us. Doubtless it has its ground in the fact that the propositions of logic and mathematics, certified by reason alone, appear to owe nothing to, and to fear nothing from, the accidents of time. And we grasp these timeless truths. But it is too late, now, in the day to think that who grasps timeless truths must himself be timeless.

## 5. The Thing-in-Itself and Appearances in Outer Sense

From one aspect of incoherence in the theory of transcendental idealism we turn to another. The aim is not solely to exhibit incoherence as such, but to observe, if we can, by what distortions and perversions it arises.

Knowledge through perception of things existing independently of perception, as they are in themselves, is impossible. For the only perceptions which could yield us any knowledge at all of such things must be the outcome of our being affected by those things; and for this reason such knowledge can be knowledge only of those things as they appear—of the appearances of those things—and not of those things as they really are or are in themselves.

The above is a fundamental and unargued complex premise of the *Critique.* To it is added the premise that all our "outer" perceptions are caused by things which exist independently of our perceptions and which affect us to produce those perceptions. From this conjunction of premises there follows the conclusion that outer perceptions yield no knowledge of the things which cause them as those things really are, but only of the appearances of those things.

Let us consider, as far as outer perception is concerned, this contrast between appearance and reality in connexion with the thesis of the causal dependence of perceptions on independently existing things which affect us to produce them.

First, as to the contrast between appearance and reality in general. These concepts are not always set in opposition to each other. For we may, and do, say, sometimes, that things are as they appear. But in the present case they clearly are set in opposition to each other. We perceive the things which, by affecting us, cause our outer perceptions, not as they really are, but only as they appear. What, then, we must ask, are the general conditions of the significant application of the contrast, or opposition, between appearance and reality, and are they satisfied in Kant's application of the contrast to the case of outer perception?

Two concepts which seem inseparable from any significant application of this contrast are the concept of identity of reference and what might be called the concept of the corrected view. When it is said that a thing appears to be thus-and-so, but really is not, it seems to be implied that there are two different standpoints from which it would be natural to make different and incompatible judgements about the *same* thing, and that the judgement naturally made from one of these standpoints would be, in some sense, a *correction* of the judgement naturally made from the other. The standpoints, it seems, must have something in common, so that there is some way, neutral as between them, of securing identity of reference to the thing which is judged. This is as general a statement as I can find of the conditions for the employment of the contrast; and it is easy, without a tedious multiplication of examples, to see how both conditions are normally satisfied. The corrected view may be that of an unusually well-placed or well-informed observer vis-à-vis that of the generality; it may be that of a normal observer vis-à-vis someone suffering from special defects or limitations; it may be that which would result from the removal of some distorting factor in the environment; and so on. In many of the commonplace cases that come readily to mind, the condition of securing identity of reference is satisfied in ways that turn on what might loosely be called the spatio-temporal location of the object judged.

It would be irrelevant to linger on commonplace applications of the contrast. But there is one familiar *philosophical* application of it which seems far from irrelevant; for it turns, precisely, on the fact that our sensible experience is the causal outcome of our being affected by the objects we say we perceive. It seems both intelligible and true to say that the appearances which things present to us are causally dependent upon the character both of the things themselves and of our physiological make-up, that they are the joint effect of both. Common sense and common observation can tell us something about the causal mechanisms involved, and science can tell us a great deal more. We are not logically compelled to draw from these facts the conclusion that things, as they really are, are different from things as they appear to us under normal conditions of perception. But equally we are not logically debarred from doing so, provided the general conditions I set out for the application of the contrast between appearance and reality are observed, provided, that is to say, that the possibility of identity of reference is secured and that some standard is adopted for the corrected view. It is important that the adoption of this standard should be made quite explicit; otherwise people will become confused and suffer irrelevant emotional reactions, the result of the fact that the use of habitual standards for the corrected view continues at the same time as the intermittent and perhaps provocative use of the new ones.

   Though there is no logical compulsion to take such a step, the evident fact is that many philosophers (e.g. Locke and Russell) have felt a strong compulsion of some kind to take it. Objects *as they really are* are credited with the properties ascribed to them in the physical and physiological theories in terms of which the explanation of the causal mechanisms of perception is given; whereas those other features which we normally ascribe to them on the strength of our perceptions are eliminated from the description of objects as they really are. Their apparent possession of these properties is explained as simply the effect of a causal process which can be fully described without mentioning such properties, viz. the action of physical things upon our sensory and nervous equipment. Were that equipment different, the apparent properties of things would be different; but things would not differ in their real constitution.

   In this operation the general conditions for a significant application of the contrast between appearance and reality are satisfied. The standpoint of the corrected view is successfully indicated without prejudice to securing identity of reference. Things, as they really are, are not removed from the spatio-temporal framework of reference. They are simply things as science speaks of them rather than as we perceive them. The corrected view is the view of science; it is a different view, but it is a view of the same things as our ordinary uncorrected view is a view of.

Only there is one thing to be added: namely that, in one sense, it is not a *view* at all. That is to say, one element present in ordinary applications of the contrast between appearance and reality to physical objects is sacrificed in this philosophical application of it. In ordinary applications, the standpoint of the corrected view is very often such that from that standpoint things actually (sensibly) *appear* as they are. In this philosophical application, on the other hand, the standpoint of the corrected view is not one from which things *appear* as they are; it is merely one from which things are spoken of, or thought of, in an abstract style in which they could not sensibly appear at all. Berkeley grew indignant over this; but we may merely note it without indignation. (It should be noted, also, that the antithesis I here make between the ordinary and this philosophical application of the contrast between appearance and reality is a fairly crude one which cannot be pressed in detail and all along the line.)

Now it is quite clear that Kant's intention, in making *his* application of the contrast between appearance and reality, was quite different from that of the scientifically minded philosophers who take the step I have just described. He himself stresses the difference, taking pains to put us on our guard against supposing that their view—which he regards, indeed, as far as it goes, with sympathy—is equivalent to that which he espouses in his doctrine of transcendental ideality.[7] Yet it is impossible to ignore the parallels between their view and his. Kant constantly affirms that the fundamental reason why we are aware of things only as they appear and not as they are in themselves is just that the mode of intuition or awareness which we have is one in which the object *affects* our faculties of awareness so that object and faculty thereby jointly produce the representations, the "sensations" or particular experiences of awareness, which we in fact have. He as constantly equates this fact about our mode of awareness or intuition with the fact which he expresses by saying that our mode of intuition is *sensible* intuition. It is just because these remarks, taken by themselves, are reminiscent of the doctrines of the scientifically minded philosophers that they seem in themselves unextraordinary. It is only when we join these remarks with the doctrine that space and time themselves and everything in them fall on the side of appearances, that the reminiscence seems suddenly irrelevant, that the comparison with the doctrine of the scientifically minded philosopher seems nothing but misleading; for the Locke-like doctrine, based upon the causal scientific account of the effects of objects upon our sensory and nervous equipment, turns on regarding the objects as they are in themselves (and indeed our receptive equipment as well) as spatio-temporal things.

Yet, if it seems that the comparison must be misleading, it seems also that it is inescapable. For when we read that, in speaking of space and time in general, all we are really to understand by this is a capacity or liability of ours to be affected in a certain way by things not in themselves in space and time, we have no clue to the meaning of this remark but the analogy with what a scientifically minded philosopher might mean when he says that in speaking of the colouredness of things, all we are really to understand by this is our own liability to be affected in a certain way by objects not in themselves coloured. All the terms used, the talk of objects affecting the receptive faculties of sensibility, seem to belong to a doctrine—that of the scientifically minded philosopher—which is rejected as wholly inadequate in the application made of those terms. And this rejection seems to leave us, so far, with no clue at all as to how the general requirements of any significant application of the contrast between appearance and reality are to be satisfied. How, given this rejection, is it possible to specify the standpoint of the corrected view and to specify it in such a way that identity of reference to objects as they appear and as they really are is intelligibly secured?

This question, or the first part of it, is not left by Kant entirely unanswered. He does undertake, with reservations, to specify the standpoint of the corrected view. Indeed, such a specification is implicit for him in the *generality* of the reason why we can be aware, in perception, only of objects as they appear and not as they are in themselves. The reason for this is that our perceptions are the outcome of our being *affected* by the object; and this reason would hold good for any mode of perception which depended on the independent existence of the object. ("Our mode of intuition is dependent on the existence of the object and is *therefore* possible only if the subject's faculty of representation is affected by the object."[8]) Hence the corrected view would be the view available to a "non-sensible intuition," an intuition not passive or receptive, but active, spontaneous, original; a mode of awareness in which the faculty of awareness was not affected by the object because it created its own object. Of such a mode of awareness Kant frequently remarks that we are unable to comprehend its possibility:[9] an important reservation. The specification of the standpoint of the corrected view is given in terms which, it is admitted, we cannot really understand; and the task of making it intelligible how identity of reference is secured is, *a fortiori,* impossible of performance.

That Kant fails to satisfy the conditions for a significant application of the contrast between things as they really are and things as they appear—that, indeed, he violates his own principle of significance both in his application of this contrast and in the associated use of the concept of cause—is, perhaps, a point evident enough. We are left with the task of trying to explain, if we can, the striking parallel which we have noted and the even more striking failure of that parallel, the extraordinary transposition of the whole terminology of things affecting faculties which takes that terminology entirely outside the range of its intelligible employment, viz. the spatio-temporal range. Perhaps we cannot do more than recall Kant's early and old attachment to the notion of "the intelligible world" and record that he thought he had found the uniquely correct method of connecting it with, and yet sealing it off from, the world of phenomena, in such a way that the interests of morality, of empirical science, of mathematics, and of a reformed metaphysics were simultaneously satisfied. But perhaps a little more, a little more immediately germane to the topic, can be said.

The extraordinary generality of Kant's thinking is constantly straining against what he himself recognized as the limits of intelligibility. He remarks that we cannot comprehend the possibility of any form of intuition other than the sensible. He is not talking about "the senses," as we might enumeratively, or even generally, understand the term. He means that, as far as our comprehension of possibilities goes, the thought, at its most general, of becoming aware of objectively existing things includes the thought of those things as existing independently of our becoming aware of them and hence the thought of our awareness of them as dependent on a relation between those things and whatever powers of awareness we possess. They must *affect* us in respect of our powers of awareness. This general principle of sensible intuition is independent of any empirical discoveries we may make regarding causal mechanisms of sense-perception. Experience is simply what emerges from the affecting relation, and all the distinctions we draw within experience are drawn within the sphere of what emerges from this relation. Yet sensibility *in general,* the power of awareness *in general,* must have a "true correlate," the thing as it is in itself, regarding which, in experience no question is ever asked, or could be an-

swered if it were.[10] But, again, because all the distinctions we draw, all
the concepts we employ must, if they are to be significantly employed,
find an empirical use, have empirical criteria for their application, the
very concepts employed in the general principle of sensible intuition
must find a surrogate application in experience. So we must have our
own usable concepts of the objective, treating certain appearances as if
they were independently existing things, making our own picture—the
scientific picture—of the causal dependence of subjective impressions
on things and our faculties together.

I have tried to make evident here how the drive towards unlimited
generality of principle encounters the limiting requirement of intelligibility in application and how perverse, in spite of its brilliance, is Kant's
treatment of their impact. For of course the general principle that any
perceptual awareness we may have of independently existing things
is causally dependent on those things affecting whatever powers of
awareness we possess, is acceptable; and the empirical content we give
it is acceptable too. The latter is nothing but the specific form, increas-
ingly filled in as knowledge advances, which, as things are, the general
truth assumes. But Kant perversely and inconsistently pays the general
principle the excessive honour of regarding it as stating a truth on its
own, a truth such that no empirical content which might, in any world,
be given to the principle could possibly be a specific instance or case
of just that truth; so that the truth must have its own, non-empirical
field of application, while we, for our part, must be content with representing it, in experience, with what is really only its shadow.

As to why Kant is tempted by such a perversion, we must refer once
more to his old attachments, and to the interests, as he conceived
them, of ethics, metaphysics, and science.

## 6. Transcendental Idealism and Empirical Realism

The topic of the last section and the topic of this interpenetrate each
other. We are to discuss Kant's claim that his transcendental idealism
is an "empirical realism."

Kant's analysis of experience drives steadily to the conclusion that
the experience of a conceptualizing and potentially self-conscious
being must include awareness of objects conceived of as existing and
enjoying their own states and relations independently of the occurrence of any particular states of awareness of them. For us, these ob-

jects are spatial objects, material bodies in space. So far from its being necessary to make a problematic inference from our inner perceptions to the existence of spatial objects as their causes, the very consciousness of inner perceptions as ours is possible only through an immediate consciousness of the existence of objects in space, distinct from our perceptions of them.

Here, surely, is a dualistic realism of some kind. Kant qualifies the titles. It is only an "empirical" dualism, an "empirical" realism he is propounding. The qualification goes with the denial that bodies in space exist as things in themselves. We may be tempted, at times, to think that there is no more to the qualification and the denial than a re-affirmation of the principle of significance in relation to the material world, an insistence, with no further metaphysical implications, that we should be raising a question without meaning if we inquired into the nature of "the objects of our senses as they are in themselves, that is, out of all relation to the senses."[11] We have seen already how difficult it is to hold to any such interpretation. In the assertions of the Aesthetic, in the arguments of the Deduction and the Analogies, in the solutions of problems offered in the Dialectic, we find repeatedly the refrain that bodies in space, being appearances only, have no existence distinct from our representations or perceptions, that they are but a species of the latter, that, apart from our perceptions, they are nothing at all. . . .

Is the proclaimed dualism of bodies in space and states of consciousness really reconcilable with the phenomenalistic idealism which the transcendental variety seems to include? Before we attempt to answer this question, it is worth noting in slightly more detail how, in the first edition version of the discussion of the fourth paralogism, Kant uses this included phenomenalistic idealism to solve two problems. The passages in question, in summarizing which I shall attempt no refinement of statement, contain strikingly bold affirmations of the included phenomenalistic idealism. If the doctrine were affirmed nowhere else, we might simply disregard these passages on the ground that Kant discarded them in the second edition, in favour of the Refutation of Idealism, with which they are by no means obviously compatible. But the doctrine is affirmed too often elsewhere for us to have any reason to disbelieve Kant's declaration that he discarded the passages because he thought them misinterpreted by his critics, not because he thought them false.

Scepticism concerning the existence of body constitutes the first of

these two problems. The grounds of such scepticism are given in the
following short argument. Only what is in ourselves can be perceived
immediately, i.e. is an object of non-inferential awareness. Therefore
the belief in the existence of bodies, external objects, has no more
justification than it receives as the conclusion of a doubtful inference
from the occurrence of perceptions within us which we take to be the
effects of body as an outer cause.[12] Kant's solution is stated as follows.
Bodies are simply a species of our representations or perceptions, viz.
those which we distinguish as belonging to outer sense, i.e. as being
spatially orderable. Therefore we may admit the existence of matter,
not as inferred but as immediately perceived, without going outside
the contents of consciousness.[13] Of course there are illusions, i.e. representations, apparently of outer sense, which are not connected with
other representations according to appropriate empirical laws. But this
does not mean that we are not immediately aware of bodies. For to say
that we are immediately aware of bodies is simply to say that we have
representations of outer sense which *are* connected according to appropriate empirical laws.[14]

The second and related problem concerns the action of body on
mind. How, it is asked, can matter, which is essentially spatial and extended, produce by its action (which is nothing but movement) such
utterly heterogeneous effects as states of consciousness, representations, thoughts, feelings and perceptions which are not themselves in
space?[15] Kant answers that the question is entirely misconceived. For
bodies are not distinct in kind from representations. They are nothing
but representations of a certain kind. We have manufactured for ourselves a difficulty which does not exist. To say that bodies cause our
representations of bodies can really, at best, be only a misleading way
of saying that "the representations of our sensibility are so interconnected that those which are entitled outer intuitions can be represented according to empirical laws as objects outside us"—a truth
which "is not in any way bound up with the supposed difficulty of
explaining the origin of our representations from quite heterogeneous
efficient causes outside us."[16] Other questions about the action of body
on mind present no greater difficulty. For, once more, bodies are simply one kind of representations or contents of consciousness; and
there is nothing strange about the law-like association of different kinds
of representations, different kinds of contents of consciousness. "As
long as we take inner and outer appearances together as mere repre-

sentations in experience, we find nothing absurd and strange in the association of the two kinds of sense."[17]

How, then, is the doctrine that bodies are but a *species of representations* to be reconciled with the doctrine that we are immediately conscious of the existence of objects in space, *distinct from our perceptions?* There is but one way which can at all plausibly be represented as Kant's way of even seeming to effect this reconciliation. What is needed is a distinction between the import of the question, "Do bodies exist independently of perceptions?" as raised within the conceptual scheme to which we are committed in experience, and the import of that question as raised within the context of the entire critical philosophy. One of the results of the critical philosophy—of that part of it which is concerned with the analysis of experience—is to show that we *must* connect our intuitions with the aid of concepts of objective things, existing independently of our perceptions, which we take those intuitions to be perceptions of. Nothing would count as a possible experience, as a kind of experience which we could make intelligible to ourselves, for which this necessity did not hold. So long as our questions and replies are raised and given within the framework of the scheme of ideas to which we are necessarily committed in experience, the answer to our question must be affirmative—and a trivial enough affirmative at that.

But the critical philosopher, Kant must hold, achieves a certain detachment from the scheme to which, as a being concerned with empirical questions and answers, he is wholeheartedly committed. The detached point of view from which the necessities of that scheme can be appreciated is also a point of view from which our question assumes a quite different import and demands, not an affirmative, but a negative, answer. From this point of view, we have a quite different standard for what really exists from the standard to which we are empirically committed. Judged by this critical standard there really exist only, on the one hand, the transcendental and to us unknown causes of our perceptions or representations and, on the other, the effects of those causes, the representations themselves. The former we do not, the latter we do, "attain in themselves." There is no place in this scheme for bodies as real existents, though there is a place, and that a necessary one, for the operation with that conceptual scheme which includes the *conception* of our awareness of bodies distinct from our experiences of them.

As it is with the question "Do bodies exist independently of perceptions?", so it must be with the question, "Do bodies cause our perceptions of them?" From the point of view of the scheme to which we are
empirically committed, the answer again must be "Yes." We investigate
empirically the physical and physiological mechanisms of this causation. But from the point of view of the critical scheme, the answer must
be that bodies are nothing apart from perceptions and that the real
cause of the latter is the unknown transcendental object.

It is unnecessary for me to repeat the criticisms of this doctrine
which have already been set out in previous sections. The fact that
within the framework of the theory of transcendental idealism a form
of reconciliation is possible between the thesis that we are aware of
bodies in space as objects distinct from our perceptions and the thesis
that bodies in space have no existence apart from our perceptions has
no power to restore to the theory of transcendental idealism the coherence and intelligibility it has been shown to lack. But one or two comments of a different order may be made.

First, it might seem that Kant had, after all, a more substantial reason
than the risk of misinterpretation for omitting from the second edition
those problem-solving exercises which he undertook in the earlier discussion of the fourth paralogism. Was it not disingenuous to represent
the supposed heterogeneity of outer causes and inner effects as constituting even the appearance of a problem when his own thesis commits
him to no smaller a degree of heterogeneity of causes and effects—
transcendental causes, outside space and time, and temporal effects,
representations in time? Again, was it not disingenuous to represent his
solution to the problem posed by sceptical idealism as a real solution to
a real problem when he holds us necessarily committed to a conceptual scheme of which one of the governing principles is that we are
*immediately* aware of bodies in space distinct from our perceptions of
them? Or, if he is not, in this second respect, disingenuous, must he
not hold the awkward view that, if experience is to be possible, we
must be empirically committed to a conceptual scheme which is itself
incoherent?

This last consequence Kant might be ready to accept; and he might
point to his treatment of the mathematical antinomies in support of
his readiness. But I think, in the present connexion at least, he is in a
position to reject this alternative and to rebut both charges of disingen-
uousness. For he is committed, as we have seen, to the overriding
principle that no perceptions dependent, as ours are, on indepen-

dently existing objects as their real causes can possibly yield knowledge of those objects as they really are. He could hold that the arguments of the sceptical idealist and of those who cannot stomach "physical influence" represent a confused apprehension of this truth: an apprehension of it insofar as they both involve rejecting the thought that we could ever *know* the real causes of our perceptions to be independently existing objects in space and time; a confused apprehension insofar as they envisage no other status for bodies in space and time except that of really existing independently of our perceptions. The arguments, on this view, do not merely pose pseudo-problems. They embody, rather, a confounding of the two conceptual schemes, the critical and the empirical. This natural confusion itself constitutes a real problem, which is solved by separating the schemes and acknowledging that each has its own validity.

Next, and more importantly, we must ask how the situation stands regarding "empirical realism" when we discard the doctrines of transcendental idealism. Of course the situation is transformed. The analytical argument to conclusions about the necessary structure of experience must be evaluated on its own merits. If we accept the conclusion that experience necessarily involves awareness of objects conceived of as existing in time independently of any particular states of awareness of them, then we must accept it without reservation. We have no extraneous standard or scheme in terms of which we can give an esoteric sense to the question whether such objects *really* exist, as we must empirically conceive of them as existing, independently of our perceptions. The question can be understood only in the sense of the scheme itself to which we are committed and in that sense it admits of but one commonplace answer. The philosophical achievement consists in showing that the answer is not merely a commonplace, though it is that. It consists in showing the place of this commonplace in any intelligible conception of experience we can form, in showing that it holds such a place even if we take the conception of experience to the last point of abstraction it can reach before disintegrating.

It might be pointed out that if we discard the doctrines of transcendental idealism, we not only discard the incoherences associated with the conception of the supersensible reality—which has to be at once linked with and sealed off from the natural world—but also deprive ourselves of the problem-solving and analytical argument-aiding powers ascribed by Kant to the enclosed phenomenalistic idealism. But to lose these is to lose nothing. We have already noted the ultimate dis-

utility of the doctrine in connexion with the problems of the Antinomies; we have repeatedly seen it to be superfluous to the analytical
argument; and that argument itself deprives the pseudo-problems of
the fourth paralogism of any force unborrowed from principles belonging to the theory of transcendental idealism.

Finally, I must mention the possibility of its being disputed that what
I have called Kant's way of reconciling the denial with the affirmation
of the distinct existence of bodies is really his way of effecting this
reconciliation. It might be urged that when Kant declares bodies to be
in us as a species of representations, he does not mean by this to deny
that, even in terms of the scheme of transcendental idealism, they
really enjoy an existence in space distinct from the existence of our
perceptions of them. He merely means to affirm that their existence in
space is the outcome of the transcendental subject's being affected by
things in themselves. It seems almost too obvious for argument that
this is not his view. None of the problem-solving powers he ascribes to
the thesis that bodies are not things in themselves would even seem
to belong to that thesis on this interpretation. Moreover, the thesis
would generate problems of its own. For example, we should have to
answer the question whether our perceptions of bodies in space were
the direct outcome of our being affected by things in themselves or
were the outcome of our being affected, in our empirical constitution,
by bodies in space. The former answer would require a thesis of preestablished harmony such as Kant explicitly rejects; the latter would
require us to have knowledge of the real causes of our perceptions, a
thesis which he also explicitly rejects.


### 7. Formal Concepts and Significance: Experience and Reality

Among the doctrines which together form the metaphysics of transcendental idealism we have not yet found, nor shall we find, any which
there is a case for preserving as well as explaining. But there are one
or two truths which can perhaps be seen in faint analogy with some of
those doctrines, can be heard, perhaps, as their muted echoes. They
can best be so seen or heard in relation to the themes of the chapter
entitled Phenomena and Noumena.

The structure of the chapter is fairly simple. It begins with an em-
phatic statement of the principle of significance. The employment of
concepts in judgements involves essentially the thought of their possi-

ble application to objects—ultimately to objects not themselves concepts. The general conditions of the applicability of concepts to objects
essentially involve the general conditions of our becoming aware of
objects, i.e. involve our modes of intuition. Our mode of intuition is
sensible and spatio-temporal. We are aware of objects, in experience,
under the conditions of space and time. We cannot detach our concepts from these conditions of their application to objects and hope
at the same time to preserve any significant employment for them in
recording, or advancing, knowledge of objects. It is only in application
to objects of possible experience that concepts have any such use. We
must remember above all that this truth holds for the categories, those
pure concepts of the understanding which secure to the contents of
experience that unity without which the objective reference of experience would be impossible.[18]

For in respect of the categories, Kant goes on, "we are subject to an
illusion which it is difficult to escape."[19] The categories in a sense do
"extend further than sensible intuition, since they think objects in general without regard to the special mode in which they may be given."[20]
Now by the whole structure of the metaphysics of transcendental idealism we are committed to the conception of objects in general, objects
as they are in themselves, independently of our modes of sensible intuition. Hence we are subject to the temptation, to the illusion, of supposing that the categories supply us with the conceptual resources for
arriving, by pure thought, at valid conclusions about objects as they are
in themselves.

The corrective to this illusion is to remind ourselves that we cannot
divorce the significant use of concepts from the conditions of awareness of the objects to which they are applied. But no kind of awareness
involving sensibility, i.e. no kind of awareness which depended on the
faculties being affected by an independently existing object, could possibly be awareness of things as they are in themselves. We can indeed
say to ourselves that there might be a kind of awareness in which sensibility played no part, in which understanding gave itself its own object;
and we can introduce the name of "noumena" for the objects of such
a purely intellectual intuition. But we cannot in the least understand
what we are talking about when we say this. We can form no conception of such a kind of intuition, or of an understanding capable of such
a kind of intuition. The pure concepts of *our* understanding, the categories, remain useless and inoperative unless material for their application is given them from elsewhere, through sensibility, through our

being affected by things as they are in themselves, of which, since we are aware of them only in being affected by them, we continue to know nothing as they are in themselves.

It would be unprofitable to pursue the struggle with Kant's thinking deep into the mysterious terrain here hinted at. We may remember the anxiety which Kant displays, when the interests of morality and religion are uppermost in his mind, to qualify the doctrine that we can have no *knowledge* of supersensible objects through the categories with the contention that we may nevertheless legitimately *think* of such objects in terms of the categories; and we may wonder how this contention is to be reconciled with the doctrine of the present chapter, and of the Note which follows it, that the objects of a non-sensible intuition would not be known through categories at all,[21] that the categories would not be "appropriate to,"[22] or "valid in respect of,"[23] such objects. Kant claims that though we cannot comprehend the possibility of non-sensible intuition, the idea of such an intuition, and of its non-sensible, noumenal objects, is free from contradiction.[24] About this contention we may wonder, too, when we read his critique of Leibniz, an exercise which he conducts, with some brilliance and, as usual, some forcing of points, in that concluding Note. Leibniz was supremely one who committed what Kant regarded as the original sin of dogmatic metaphysics. He undertook to affirm truths about objects in abstraction from the spatio-temporal conditions of sensible intuition which in fact alone give sense to our talk of objects. This attempt to speak of objects of a purely intelligible and wholly non-sensible character had, as Kant points out, the natural enough consequence that much of what Leibniz says is coherent only on the assumption that he is not really talking about objects, as opposed to concepts, but about concepts themselves. Kant once more affirms that for any knowledge of purely intelligible objects—as opposed to concepts—we should require that of which we cannot comprehend the possibility, viz. a non-sensible, purely intellectual intuition. We may wonder whether it is not, instead, something of which we can comprehend the impossibility. Can the words mean anything but that the objects of such an intuition would both have to have, and have not to have, the abstract character which belongs to general concepts or to such abstract individuals as numbers?

It is better to turn from these fruitless calculations to try to catch those faint echoes I spoke of. The categories are said to "extend further than sensible intuition, since they think objects in general without regard to the special mode in which they may be given."[25] We are reminded of many features of the critical apparatus: of the so seriously held duality of faculties; of the metaphysical deduction of the pure categories from the forms of logic; of the further limiting step taken in the Schematism, where the categories acquire empirical use and life through a temporal interpretation. We have seen how much there is in this to invite doubt. But there is also something to be preserved. There are a number of concepts which we might call "formal concepts" and which share certain features at least analogous to some of the features ascribed by Kant to pure categories. They include such concepts as the following: identity, existence, class and class-membership, property, relation, individual, unity, totality.

Perfectly general deductive connexions belonging to formal logic can be asserted as holding in the region of formal concepts: e.g. from any assertion to the effect that a certain individual has a certain property there follows an assertion of the existence of something having that property. Such concepts are also *applied* or *exemplified* in empirical propositions which do not belong to logic. The concept of identity is *applied* in any straightforward statement of identity; the concepts of individual and property are *exemplified* in any statement to the effect that a certain specified individual has a certain property. Of course the application or exemplification of the formal concepts in empirical propositions turns on the existence of *empirical* criteria for the application of other, non-formal, empirical concepts, of, e.g., properties or kinds of individual. But we cannot specify in advance what empirical criteria are permissible in the application or exemplification of the formal concepts in non-logical statements. We cannot impose any limitations in advance on the possible formal analogies which may permit the use or exemplification of the formal concepts in ways antecedently undreamt of by us. There must be conditions, directly or indirectly related to what Kant calls intuition (i.e. awareness of objects not themselves concepts) for any employment or exemplification of the formal concepts in non-logical statements. But those conditions are not limited in advance by the scope of our actual knowledge and experience.

Kant remarks of the categories that their meaning is not restricted by sensible intuition, since "they think objects in general without regard to the special mode in which they may be given." Of the formal concepts we may make the parallel remark that their meaning is not restricted by any empirical criteria we in fact employ in their application or exemplification. Kant accompanies his remark with the warning that we must not therefore suppose that we can significantly employ the categories in assertions about objects without regard to the conditions of sensible awareness of objects. We may issue a parallel warning: formal concepts cannot be significantly employed in making non-logical assertions without the employment of empirical criteria for the application of other concepts, giving body to the particular applications or exemplifications of the formal concepts involved in such assertions. Kant's warning derives its urgency from his belief in things as they are in themselves which, if objects of awareness (as they are in themselves) at all, would be objects of a special kind of intellectual intuition. The bounds of sensibility are not co-extensive with the real. The point of the warning is that we must not think we can cross those bounds and gain knowledge of nonsensible objects with the help of the categories.

At this point the echo grows fainter; but it does not entirely disappear. The bounds of the real, we may say, are indeed not co-extensive with the types of sensible experience we in fact enjoy. We must not suppose that the nature of reality is exhausted by the kinds of knowledge which we have of it. To suppose this would be a kind of restrictive dogmatism as unjustified in its way as the inflated dogmatism which pretends to a knowledge transcending experience. The latter makes an unjustifiable *a priori* claim to expand knowledge beyond experience. The former would make an equally unjustifiable *a priori* claim to restrict reality within the bounds of the kind of experience we in fact have.

Of course, in resisting this kind of restrictive dogmatism, in allowing the concept of objective reality to extend beyond the types of sensible experience which we enjoy, we make no such divorce as Kant made between objective reality as it is in itself, things as they are in themselves, and objective reality as we know it, things as we experience them. In refusing to commit ourselves to the dogmatic position that, though we do not know everything, we know at least every kind of thing there is to know about every kind of thing there really is, we do not have to deny that we know things of some kinds about some kinds of things there really are. What we do, for example, is modestly to recognize that just as it would be folly for the blind to deny that things of which they have experience have a kind of property of which they have no experience, so it would be folly for the sighted to deny the possibility that with a richer equipment of sense organs they too might discover in objects properties of which, as things are, they can form no conception. Again, it is a familiar truth that, in the advance of science, the existence of both new types of property and new types of individual entity is acknowledged. (We sometimes, though not always, express such results in terms of discoveries about the composition and make-up of more commonplace individuals.) It would again evidently be folly to suggest that there can be no further discoveries of this kind just because we can at present form no conception of them. Nor is it only in these two rather specific directions, suggested by ordinary experience and theory-making, that this rejection of restrictive dogmatism is supposed to leave the way open. We have, and can have, no reason to deny *a priori* the possibility of different kinds of revelation of objective reality for which we have no easy analogy like that of a new sense-organ or a new scientific theory. (And of course no reason to affirm it either.) The only thing we can insist on is that any further aspect of reality must stand in some sort of systematic connexion with those aspects we know already.

To admit *this* concept of objective reality as thus limiting the claims of actual sensible experience (and of actual theory based upon it) to be "co-extensive with the real" is, as I have remarked, very different from adopting the Kantian conception of things as they are in themselves. The disanalogy extends to the conception of the role of formal concepts and categories respectively in relation to these different limiting ideas of "the real." Kant appears, as we have seen, to deny that categories would be applicable to the noumenal, to the real as object of a non-sensible intuition. It is quite otherwise with the relation of formal concepts to the modestly conceived substitute for the noumenal. To admit this modest conception is simply to reject the dogmatic denial of the possibility of knowledge of new types of *individual, property,* and *relation,* new applications of the concept of *identity*. It is precisely to see such formal concepts as possibly admitting of new types of employment or exemplification in non-logical propositions.

There remains a point of analogy. Kant's main concern in this chapter is to insist that the necessary admission of a reality transcending sensible experience altogether does not disclose a field for transcendent metaphysics, though the open character of the pure concepts may delude us into the belief that it does. Similarly the admission that the conception of reality is not bounded by the types of sensible experience we actually enjoy discloses no field beyond that of empirically based theory (or purely formal science) for the fruitful employment of formal concepts. The modest concept we substitute for that of the noumenal really has the negative character which Kant claims for the concept of the noumenal. It simply means: those aspects of reality, if any, of which we have not, as things are, any conception.

In the place of Kant's reflections on the nature of "pure understanding," we may find it more realistic, and certainly less perilous, to see the formal concepts as emerging, in all their unlimited generality, as a result of progressive analogy and extension from their basic paradigms in experience. Nevertheless, in the recognition of the unlimited generality of the formal concepts; in the complementary recognition that the concept of reality must be allowed an extension beyond the limits of our actual sensible experience; in the warnings against supposing that both recognitions together open a field for metaphysics; in these we may, if we choose, see some uncontentious and unpretentious parallels to some theses belonging to the metaphysics of transcendental idealism.

It must be added, finally, that Kant's formulation of the principle which underlies the warning, his description of the conditions of making significant assertions about objects, or aspects of reality, is crude and narrow. That description is always framed in terms of the necessity of a mode of *intuition* of the object or aspect, a way in which it is *given* to us. The phrases suggest difficulties about, e.g., "unobservable" entities of science. A partial answer, on Kantian lines, might be that insofar as such entities are conceived as spatio-temporal, they thereby fall within the scope of what Kant refers to as our modes of sensible intuition. This is an issue which Kant scarcely refers to in the *Critique,* and insofar as he does, his words suggest a different answer. On the subject of the "magnetic matter" which we know to "pervade all bodies" he sounds a little like Locke deploring our lack of microscopical eyes: "were our senses more refined, we should come also in experience upon the immediate empirical intuition of it."[26] That is to say, the items in question are taken to be in principle directly observable. Neither type of answer seems particularly satisfactory. The concept of spatial location, for example, seems to have little relation to the entities of depth psychology; and as far as direct observation is concerned, the questions of what is to count as such or whether anything is, seem often somewhat arbitrarily decidable or of little moment.

A fuller answer, then, than any which Kant gives is called for to the question how we should describe that condition of the significant employment of concepts which is loosely expressed by saying that they must be so employed as to have application in a possible experience. I shall not attempt to answer the question. But the main conditions which a fuller description would have to provide for can be indicated. We should begin by noting that there is little difficulty in explaining what we mean by observational criteria for the application of many kinds of established, unproblematic concepts. Then we may remark that in order for a newly introduced or problematic concept (or concept-extension) to have significant employment, it is necessary that it should be possible to state or indicate types of observable situations in which it has application—which is not to say that its *objects* must be observable. It is further necessary that its application in such a situation should have consequences or implications which do not merely duplicate those of other, established, non-problematic concepts. The temptation here is to say "testable consequences or implications"; and that addition, though calling for further elucidation, is no doubt on the right lines insofar as we are concerned with the concepts we call scientific. But perhaps we can also be said to extend our knowledge of the world by learning to see it afresh, to extend or modify our classifications and descriptions, in ways and directions with which natural science has little to do. And then the consequences will relate more to the nature of our experience itself and to the connexions we make in it than to the possibility of confirmatory or disconfirmatory tests which we might undertake.

### 8. Conclusion: The Structure of Experience

Interwoven with, and dependent upon, the other doctrines of transcendental idealism is that strand of theory which seemed to Kant to constitute a revolution in philosophical thinking analogous to the Copernican revolution in astronomy. On behalf of the doctrine that appearances conform to our modes of representation, to the forms of sensibility and understanding, he claimed that it alone explained both the possibility of geometry and of pure mathematics in general and the feasibility of the entire programme, carried out in the Analytic, of establishing the necessary structure of experience.

The latter part of this claim has already been briefly discussed and dismissed. But it may be felt that its dismissal leaves us at least with an unanswered question. How is it, after all, possible to establish that experience must exhibit such-and-such general features? We may reply that this is just an abbreviated way of saying that we can form no coherent or intelligible conception of a type of experience which does not exhibit those features. But the more careful formulation merely leads to further questions. If we cannot, what is the explanation of the fact that we cannot? And by what kind of argument is it shown that any particular feature has this character of being an indispensable element in any coherent conception of experience we can form? What are the tests for this kind of indispensability?

Now if someone should ask *in general* why there should be any limits at all to what could be conceived of as constituting a possible experience, we should think his question absurd. For this would be like asking how it should be possible to say "Experience might be like this . . ." and then go on to put words together in incoherent ways. So any question which asks why there are limits to any coherent conception of experience we can form must be asking why there is *this* or *that* limit. And now we can see that such a question cannot be asking for anything wholly different in kind from what is asked for in the questions about arguments and tests. For it is quite clear that there is no sense in the idea that we might look to facts altogether outside our experience in order to find an explanation of there being this or that limit. (This is why—apart from the fact that his arguments do not rest on it—we can simply dismiss Kant's "model.")

There remains the question concerning the kind of argument, or test, by which certain features are shown to be indispensable in any coherent conception of experience we can form. Here we may remark to begin with that we are concerned with the temporally extended experience of conceptualizing or thinking beings. This conception is filled out, given content, by reference to general features of our actual experience which are exhibited in relations of progressive or mutual dependence. Thus we proceed from the necessity of conceptualization to the self-reflexiveness of experience—to objectivity and the potentiality of self-consciousness—to the distinction between objective time-relations and time-relations between subjective experience—to the idea of a persisting framework within which objective time-relations hold—to the idea of re-identifiable particular objects—to that of causal law or regularity—to that of law-governed objects in space. The governing principle is that any element already admitted as necessary to the general conception must be provided with some basis in experience, must reflect, e.g. some distinction which could actually be drawn within experience. If the governing principle is accepted and some particular feature is admitted as providing a basis of the sort admitted to be generally necessary, then the necessity of that particular feature can be effectively challenged only by making us able to understand the possibility of an alternative. The possibility of effective challenge is minimized by maximizing the *generality* of the statement of conditions and at the same time introducing into that statement a looseness, or vagueness, which is in marked contrast with the strict *universality* of some of Kant's principles. Nevertheless, as has been sufficiently indicated, challenge might effectively be offered at certain points, notably as regards spatiality as we ordinarily understand it, and as regards the singleness of the persisting framework of the objective.

It might be asked: could not the enterprise be carried farther than it is here carried? and: was not Kant in error to separate so sharply the cognitive, or "speculative," from the active, or "practical," side of our natures? Perhaps it could and no doubt he was. My aim has been to show what he achieved and how his arguments and conclusions might be so modified as to be made more acceptable. That he conducted the operation under self-imposed handicaps—though not in itself a matter for congratulation—makes it the more remarkable that he achieved so much.

But surely, it might finally be objected, we have a much wider and less restrictive conception of a possible experience *in general*—even of a temporally extended experience of a conceptualizing being—than is here allowed for. Surely it is absurd to claim that the ideas listed as entering into any coherent conception of experience that we can form really, even though only implicitly, enter into all experience. Surely infants and non-human animals have experience!—This is not denied. But we must think of how we think, of how we must think, of the experience of such creatures. We have no way of doing so except on a simplified analogy with our own. Any specific ascription of experience to animals we may make involves thinking of them as perceiving this or that kind of thing, recognizing this or that individual, pursuing this or that purpose in relation to such things. Any description we can give, any thought we can entertain, of *their* experience must be in terms of concepts derived from ours. We can say, if we like, that such ascriptions must, in these thoughts, bear some confused or attenuated or diminished sense. But we must admit that we cannot say what that sense is. At best we can draw on cooler recollections of confused states of our own; and the inadequacy of this resource becomes clear when we reflect that it is absurd to say that a healthy animal is, in normal circumstances, confused.

180      *P. F. Strawson*

We must, in this matter, be content with knowing ourselves. We lack words to say what it is to be without them.

## Notes

1. Cf. A 737/B 765.
2. Cf. A 190–91/B 235–36.
3. The significance of these passages is discussed more fully in section 6 below.
4. A 546–47/B 574–75.
5. B 422.
6. B 157.
7. A 29–30/B 45, A 45–46/B 62–63.
8. B 72.
9. He says, once, that "as far as we can judge," it could belong only to God, the primordial being (B 72).
10. Cf. A 30/B 45.
11. A 380.
12. A 367–68.
13. A 370–72.
14. A 376.
15. A 386–87, 390.
16. A 387.
17. A 386.
18. B 294–305.
19. B 305.
20. B 309.
21. A 256/B311–12.
22. A 287/B 343.
23. A 286/B 342.
24. A 254/B 310.
25. B 309.
26. A 226/B 273.

# 9

# Kant's Transcendental Idealism, Chapters 1 & 2

*Henry Allison*

## An Introduction to the Problem

The aim of this work is to provide both an interpretation and, where possible, a defense of Kant's transcendental idealism. Since this idealism is inseparable from Kant's views on the nature, conditions, and limits of human knowledge, as well as his critique of other philosophical positions, this project involves a discussion of many of the central topics of the *Critique of Pure Reason*.[1] . . . It differs from other treatments of Kant in the recent literature first in its emphasis on the connection between Kant's idealism and his substantive claims, and second in the philosophical weight that it gives both to this idealism and to these claims. Unlike most writers on Kant, I take much of the *Critique* to be not only "interesting" or to "contain more of value than is sometimes supposed," but to be philosophically defensible. At the very least, I believe that with a bit of help from the sympathetic interpreter it can be defended against many of the familiar criticisms that are repeatedly presented as "devastating."

As a first step in this admittedly ambitious project, I shall briefly characterize what I take to be the standard picture of Kant's idealism (which is the source of the familiar criticisms) and attempt to indicate its adequacy as an account of what Kant actually maintained. I shall then introduce and discuss in a preliminary way the conception of an epistemic condition. My claim is that this conception, although merely implicit in the *Critique,* is the real key to the understanding of transcendental idealism, and with it Kant's philosophical achievement. . . .

## I. The Standard Picture and Its Inadequacy

According to the standard picture, Kant's transcendental idealism is a metaphysical theory that affirms the unknowability of the "real" (things in themselves) and relegates knowledge to the purely subjective realm of representations (appearances). It thus combines a phenomenalistic account of what is actually experienced by the mind, and therefore knowable, with the postulation of an additional set of entities which, in terms of the very theory, are unknowable. In spite of the obvious difficulties that it creates, this postulation is deemed necessary to explain how the mind acquires its representations, or at least the materials for them (their form being "imposed" by the mind itself). The basic assumption is simply that the mind can only acquire these materials as a result of being "affected" by things in themselves. Thus, such things must be assumed to exist, even though the theory denies that we have any right to say anything about them (presumably including the claim that they exist).

Although this picture, which can be traced back to Kant's own contemporaries, has been repeatedly criticized, it is still widely accepted, especially in the Anglo-American philosophical world. To a considerable extent this acceptance is due to the influence of P. F. Strawson, who, echoing the standard picture, defines transcendental idealism as the doctrine that "reality is supersensible and that we can have no knowledge of it."[2] Starting with this understanding of Kant's idealism, Strawson sets as his avowed task the separation of what he terms the "analytic argument" of the *Critique* from the transcendental idealism with which he believes Kant unfortunately and unnecessarily entangled it.[3] In the latter respect he has been followed by numerous commentators who have tried to formulate and defend some vaguely Kantian "transcendental arguments" that are uncontaminated by any idealistic premises.

But Strawson not only rejects transcendental idealism as incoherent and attempts, as it were, to save Kant from himself; he also provides an account of what led Kant to this "disastrous" doctrine. As Strawson sees it, transcendental idealism is the direct consequence of Kant's "perversion" of the "scientifically minded philosopher's" contrast between a realm of physical objects composed of primary qualities and a mental realm consisting of the sensible appearances of these objects (including their secondary qualities). This mental realm, like its Kantian counterpart, is thought to be produced by means of an affection of the mind, in this case by physical objects. Kant allegedly perverts this model by assigning the whole spatiotemporal framework (which according to the original model pertains to the "real," that is to say, to physical objects) to the subjective constitution of the human mind. The resulting doctrine is judged to be incoherent because, among other reasons, it is with reference only to a spatiotemporal framework that one can talk intelligibly about "affection."[5]

Although Strawson himself does not put it in quite this way, the usual manner of making essentially the same point is to claim that Kant is an inconsistent Berkeley. The Berkeleian element consists of Kant's subjectivism, namely, the limitation of knowledge to appearances, with these being understood as "mere representations." The alleged inconsistency stems from Kant's combination of his essentially Berkeleian phenomenalistic idealism with his postulation of an inaccessible realm of things in themselves. This conception of what Kant was up to generates, in turn, the standard criticisms, many of which are reflected in Strawson's account. . . . I will consider merely those which concern the claim that we know only appearances.

Since it equates 'appearance' with 'mere representation', the standard picture takes Kant's claim that we know only appearances to mean that we know only the contents of our minds, that is, ideas in the Berkeleian sense. This reading of Kant is then sometimes used as the basis for a critique of the doctrine of the ideality of space and time, which Kant presents in the Transcendental Aesthetic. Simply put, the claim is that Kant's subjectivistic starting point forces him to choose between the following equally unpalatable alternatives: either (1) he must maintain that things only *seem to us* to be spatial (or temporal), a doctrine which entails that our consciousness of a world of objects extended and located in space is somehow illusory; or (2) he must claim that appearances, that is to say, representations, really are spatial, a doctrine which is absurd because it requires us to regard mental items as extended and as located in space.

Although this line of criticism has echoes in Strawson, it has been developed most fully by H. A. Prichard, who concentrates much of his attack on the alleged incoherence of Kantian "appearance talk." According to Prichard's highly influential critique, Kant's whole conception of appearance is vitiated by a confusion of the claim that we know only *things as they appear to us* with the quite different claim that we know only a particular class of things, namely, *appearances*. He also suggests that Kant's tendency to slide from one of these claims to the other prevented him from confronting the dilemma posed by the abovementioned alternatives. Thus, on his reconstruction, what Kant really wished to claim is that we know things only as they appear to us; but since this, according to Prichard, entails that these things only seem to us to be spatial (the illusion thesis), in order to defend his cherished empirical realism, Kant is forced to shift to the doctrine that we know appearances and that they really are spatial.[6]

The most basic and prevalent objection stemming from the standard picture is that by limiting knowledge to appearance, that is, to the subjective realm of representations, Kant effectively undermines the possibility of any genuine knowledge at all. In short, far from providing an antidote to Humean skepticism, as was his intent, Kant is seen as a Cartesian skeptic *malgré lui* [despite himself]. Some version of this line of objection is advanced by virtually every proponent of the standard picture, including Strawson. Once again, however, the sharpest formulation is provided by Prichard, whose account can be taken as paradigmatic for the standard picture.[7] Prichard construes Kant's distinction between appearances and things in themselves in terms of the classic example of perceptual illusion: the straight stick that appears bent to an observer when it is immersed in water. Given this analogy, he has little difficulty in reducing to absurdity Kant's doctrine that we know only appearances. His analysis proceeds through various stages, but the main point is simply that this claim is taken to mean that we can know things only as they "are for us" or "seem to us" (in virtue of the distortion imposed by our perceptual forms), not as they "really are." Since to know something, according to Prichard, just means to know it as it really is, it follows that for Kant we cannot really know anything at all. Clearly, such a conclusion amounts to a *reductio* of the Kantian theory.

It seems obvious that, if this is how Kant's transcendental idealism is really to be understood, the Strawsonian project of trying to locate in the *Critique* a philosophical core that can be neatly separated from the idealistic trappings is very attractive. Indeed, it presents itself as the only philosophically fruitful way of dealing with Kant's thought. Nevertheless, in spite of the fact that it does seem to have some textual support, one can raise serious doubts about the adequacy of this interpretation, which is so frequently accepted as a matter of course. The root of the problem is that it tends to neglect altogether, or at the very least to minimize, certain distinctions that are central to Kant's whole transcendental enterprise.

Specifically, it fails to distinguish sharply between the empirical and the transcendental versions of two generally acknowledged and closely related distinctions. These are the distinctions between ideality and reality and between appearances and things in themselves. The issues here are complex, and at this point I can only attempt to provide a rough sketch of what these distinctions involve. I believe, however, that even this rough sketch should suffice to demonstrate the inadequacies of the standard picture as an interpretation of Kant's actual teaching.

'Ideality', in the most general sense in which Kant uses the term, signifies mind dependence or being in the mind *(in uns)*; while 'reality' *(Realität)*, in the sense in which it is opposed to 'ideality', signifies independence of mind or being external to the mind *(ausser uns)*. In both the Transcendental Aesthetic and the Transcendental Dialectic, Kant distinguishes between an empirical and a transcendental sense of 'ideality', and, by implication at least, of 'reality'. Taken in its empirical sense, 'ideality' characterizes the private data of an individual mind. This includes ideas in the Cartesian-Lockean sense or, more generally, any mental content in the ordinary sense of 'mental'. 'Reality', construed in the empirical sense, refers to the intersubjectively accessible, spatiotemporally ordered realm of objects of human experience. At the empirical level, then, the ideality-reality distinction is essentially between the subjective and the objective aspects of human experience. When Kant claims that he is an empirical realist and denies that he is an empirical idealist, he is really affirming that our experience is not limited to the private domain of our own representations, but includes an encounter with "empirically real" spatiotemporal objects.

The transcendental version of the distinction is quite another matter. At the transcendental level, which is the level of philosophical reflection upon experience (transcendental reflection), 'ideality' is used to characterize the universal, necessary, and, therefore, a priori conditions of human knowledge. In the Transcendental Aesthetic, Kant affirms the transcendental ideality of space and time on the grounds that they function as a priori conditions of human sensibility, that is, as subjective conditions in terms of which alone the human mind is capable of receiving the data for thought or experience. He terms these conditions "forms of sensibility." Things in space and time (empirical objects) are ideal in the same sense because they cannot be experienced or described independently of these sensible conditions. Correlatively, something is real in the transcendental sense if and only if it can be characterized and referred to independently of any appeal to these same sensible conditions. In the transcendental sense, then, mind independence or being external to the mind *(ausser uns)* means independence of sensibility and its conditions. A transcendentally real object is thus, by definition, a nonsensible object or noumenon.

The transcendental conception of ideality provides the basis for the transcendental conception of appearance and for the transcendental version of the contrast between appearances and things in themselves. Thus, to speak of appearances in the transcendental sense is simply to speak of spatiotemporal entities (phenomena), that is, of things insofar as they are viewed as subject to the conditions of human sensibility. Correlatively, to speak of things in themselves transcendentally is to speak of things insofar as they are independent of these conditions. In several places Kant insists upon the importance of not confusing this distinction with its empirical counterpart. One of the clearest of these is in "On the Progress of Metaphysics," where, in a discussion of the transcendental ideality of space and time, Kant writes:

> Furthermore, it is to be noted that appearance, taken in the transcendental sense, wherein it is said of things that they are appearances (phenomena), means something completely different than when I say, this thing appears to me in some manner or other, which should designate appearance in the physical sense, and which can be called semblance [*Appareeenz*] and illusion [*Schein*]. For although these objects of the senses are mere appearances, since I can only compare them with other sensible objects . . . by the language of experience they are nevertheless thought as things in themselves. Thus, if it is said of such a thing that it has the look [*Anschein*] of an arch, in this context the seeming refers to the subjective aspect of the representation of a thing, which can be a cause for it to be falsely taken in a judgment as objective. And, therefore, the proposition that all sensible representations only yield knowledge of appearances is not at all to be equated with the claim that they contain only the illusion [*Schein*] of objects, as the idealist will have it.

The "language of experience," of which Kant speaks here, includes both ordinary and scientific experience. Both involve a distinction between those properties that a given object actually possesses and those it merely seems to possess for a particular observer under certain empirically specifiable conditions. The object as it "really is" (with its actual properties) is the thing in itself in the physical or empirical sense, while the representation of the object possessed by a particular observer under given conditions is what is meant by the appearance or semblance of the object. The main point here is simply that at the empirical level, or in "the language of experience," 'appearances' and 'things in themselves' designate two distinct classes of entity with two distinct modes of being. The members of the former class are "mental" in the ordinary (Cartesian) sense and the members of the latter are "nonmental" or "physical" in the same sense. At the transcendental level, however, things are quite different. There the distinction between appearances and things in themselves refers primarily to two distinct ways in which things (empirical objects) can be "considered": either in relation to the subjective conditions of human sensibility (space and time), and thus as they "appear," or independently of these conditions, and thus as they are "in themselves." Indeed, as Gerold Prauss has pointed out, when Kant is concerned with articulating the transcendental sense of his distinction, he usually does not use such expressions as *thing in itself, thing itself in itself, object in itself;* rather, he uses locutions, such as *thing* or *object considered as it is in itself.*[10]

It is certainly possible to detect a dim grasp of the distinction between the transcendental and the empirical conceptions of appearance in Prichard's contrast between things as appearing and appearances. Transcendental-level talk about appearances can be described as talk about things as appearing. Similarly, talk about appearances belongs naturally to the "language of experience." The problem here lies in Prichard's contention that Kant slides from one notion to the other. Given the preceding analysis, this is equivalent to the claim that Kant systematically confuses the transcendental and the empirical versions of his basic distinction. This is itself highly implausible, especially in light of Kant's frequent efforts to distinguish between these two senses of 'appearance'. Even apart from this, however, it can easily be shown that Prichard is guilty of the very confusion of which he accuses Kant. We have seen that part of Prichard's basic objection to what he views as Kant's empirical realism is that it involves the absurd notion that appearances (mental contents) are spatial (extended). Kant is thus judged guilty of spatializing sensations, a charge that with much greater propriety can be directed against Hume. But obviously this "absurdity" arises only if Kant's claim about the spatiality of appearances is taken in the empirical sense. If, as Kant clearly wishes us to do, we construe claims about the spatiality of appearances in the transcendental sense, the absurdity disappears; for then spatiality (together with temporality) can be seen as a defining characteristic of things considered as they appear, not as a property mysteriously attributed to sensations.

The objection of Kant's alleged skepticism can be dealt with in a similar fashion. It is clear from his use of the bent stick analogy that Prichard construes the distinction between appearances and things in themselves in the empirical sense. This, in turn, enables him to take Kant to be claiming that we can know only how things seem (appear) to us, which entails the skeptical conclusion. It is by no means certain, however, that this follows if we construe Kant's claim about the limitation of knowledge to appearances in the transcendental rather than in the empirical sense. Understood in this sense, which is the sense in which Kant intended it, it is an epistemological claim about the dependence of human knowledge on certain a priori conditions which reflect the structure of the human cognitive apparatus. These conditions do not determine how objects "seem" to us or "appear" in the empirical sense; rather, they express the universal and necessary conditions in terms of which alone the human mind is capable of recognizing something as an object at all. Thus the doctrine that we can know things only as they appear, not as they are in themselves, can be regarded as equivalent to the claim that human knowledge is governed by such conditions. If, in fact, there are such conditions, and if they function in the ways in which Kant contends, then it hardly makes sense to accuse him of being a skeptic because he denies the possibility of knowledge of things as they are independently of them, that is, of things as they are in themselves.

. . . The problem with this objection is that it fails completely to come to grips with Kant's intent, and thus to see what his transcendental claims actually involve. Instead, these claims are routinely interpreted as empirical or quasi-empirical. Similarly, Kant's talk about the "conditions" of human knowledge is taken in a psychological sense. The inevitable consequence of this is that Kant is seen as a proponent of the very empirical idealism which he took such great pains to repudiate.

## II. The Concept of an Epistemic Condition

The interpretation of transcendental idealism which I hope to develop in this study will, in contrast to the standard picture, emphasize its connection with Kant's claims regarding the conditions of human knowledge: I shall argue that the claim that human knowledge has such conditions is the distinctive, indeed, the revolutionary thesis of Kant's philosophy, and that transcendental idealism is at bottom nothing more than the logical consequence of its acceptance. So far, however, the crucial notion of 'condition' has remained undefined, even unexamined. Any number of things—for example, the brain, the central nervous system, sense organs, and so forth—could legitimately be described as conditions of human knowledge; yet none of these would have very much to do with Kant's central claim or with transcendental idealism. In an effort to clarify and to pinpoint the relevant sense of the term, I propose to introduce the notion of an *epistemic condition.*

Even though this notion is central to Kant's whole transcendental enterprise, the fact that he never explicitly deals with it makes it difficult, if not impossible, to define in any very precise way. For present purposes, then, it must suffice to characterize an epistemic condition simply as one that is necessary for the representation of an object or an objective state of affairs. As such, it could also be called an "objectivating condition"; for it is in virtue of such conditions that our representations relate to objects or, as Kant likes to put it, possess "objective reality." In this respect epistemic conditions are to be distinguished from what Kant terms "logical conditions of thought," for example, the principle of contradiction. The latter serves as a rule of consistent thinking, but not for the representation of objects. Thus it is not an epistemic condition in the sense in which this notion is taken here. Roughly speaking, the distinction between logical and epistemic conditions reflects Kant's own distinction between general and transcendental logic. In fact, the main business of transcendental logic is to establish a set of epistemic conditions, namely, the pure concepts of the understanding.

In addition to the pure concepts of the understanding, which Kant defines as "concepts of an object in general," space and time (the forms of human sensibility) must also be regarded as epistemic conditions. Although together these two types of condition constitute what Kant himself terms "necessary conditions of the possibility of experience," there are two reasons for believing that the broader notion of an epistemic condition better captures the essential thrust of Kant's thought. The first is simply that Kant is not solely, or even primarily, concerned with experiential knowledge. Epistemic conditions must, therefore, also figure in the Kantian account of nonempirical knowledge, that is, of mathematics and metaphysics. . . .

The second and main reason for talking about epistemic conditions, rather than about conditions of the possibility of experience, is that this term makes it easier to grasp the difference between this central Kantian conception and other senses of 'condition' with which it is frequently confused. Such confusions are reflected in many of the stock criticisms of Kant, including those discussed in the previous section, as well as in the standard picture as a whole. Moreover, many of Kant's own criticisms of other philosophical positions can be seen to turn on the claim that they involve confusions of what are here called epistemic conditions with conditions of other sorts. One of these is, of course, the confusion of merely logical with epistemic conditions, which figures largely in Kant's polemic with Leibnizian rationalism. This distinction has already been noted and needs no further comment at this point. For the present, it is important to distinguish epistemic conditions from psychological conditions on the one hand and from ontological conditions on the other.

By a psychological condition I mean some mechanism or aspect of the human cognitive apparatus that is appealed to in order to provide a genetic account of a belief or an empirical explanation of why we perceive things in a certain way. This can be understood to include physiological as well as narrowly psychological factors. Custom or habit, as used by Hume in his account of causality, is a prime example of such a psychological condition. As is well known, Kant was insistent in claiming that, although the appeal to such factors may be necessary to explain the origin of our beliefs and perceptions, or even of our knowledge "in the order of time," it cannot account for its objective validity. In Kant's terms it can answer the *quaestio facti* [question of fact] but not the *quaestio juris* [question of right]. The latter is the proper concern of the *Critique,* and this requires an appeal to epistemic conditions. In fact, Kant's basic charge against Hume is that he confuses these questions and thus, implicitly at least, these two kinds of conditions. The clearest example of this is Kant's claim in the *Prolegomena* that, in his analysis of causality, Hume "mistook a subjective necessity (habit) for an objective necessity arising from insight."[11] Ironically enough, this very same line of criticism is frequently raised against the *Critique* by critics who find in it a dangerous subjectivism.

It is equally important to distinguish epistemic from ontological conditions. By the latter I mean conditions of the possibility of the being of things. Since the being of things is here contrasted with their being known, an ontological condition is, by definition, a condition of the possibility of things as they are in themselves (in the transcendental sense). Newtonian absolute space and time are clear examples of conditions of this sort. Kant describes them as "two eternal and infinite self-subsistent *[für sich bestehende]* non-entities . . . which are there (yet without there being anything real) only in order to contain in themselves all that is real" (A39/B56). In a Second Edition addendum to the Transcendental Aesthetic, Kant indicates the dangerous theological consequences of such a view by pointing out that "as conditions of all existence in general, they must also be conditions of the existence of God" (B71). Even apart from theology, however, Kant believes that this conception of space and time leads to absurdities:

> For if we regard space and time as properties which, if they are to be possible at all, must be found in things in themselves, and if we reflect on the absurdities in which we are then involved, in that two infinite things, which are not substances, nor anything actually inhering in substances, must yet have existence, nay, must be the necessary condition of the existence of all things, and moreover, must continue to exist, even although all existing things be removed,—we cannot blame the good Berkeley for degrading bodies to mere illusion. Nay, even our own existence, in being made thus dependent upon the self-subsistent reality of a non-entity, such as time, would necessarily be changed with it into sheer illusion—an absurdity of which no one has yet been guilty. [B70–71]

Kant's point is that, for all its absurdity, Berkeley's idealism, which he interprets as involving the denial of the reality of material objects ("degrading bodies to mere illusion") makes a certain amount of sense when it is viewed as a response to Newton. This is because once the empirical reality of material objects and persons is seen to depend on the absolute (transcendental) reality of space and time, the absurdities connected with the latter make it plausible to deny the former. But this consequence can easily be avoided if, instead of viewing space and time with Newton as conditions of the possibility of things in themselves, we view them as conditions of the possibility of our knowledge or experience of things. In Kantian terms, instead of being "two eternal and infinite, self-subsistent non-entities," they now become two "sources of knowledge" *[Erkenntnisquellen]* (A38/B55). By analyzing the situation in this way, Kant claims to be able not only to distinguish his idealism

from that of Berkeley but also to provide a critical alternative to both
the Newtonian and the Leibnizian conceptions of space and time.

Consequently, just as Kant's strategy with Hume is to show that the
skeptical consequences of his analysis stem from a confusion of psychological and epistemic conditions, his strategy with Newton is to show
that the untenable consequences of the latter's theory of space and time
are the results of a confusion of epistemic with ontological conditions.
We shall also see that this mode of analysis can be applied to the Kantian
critique of many other thinkers. For the present, however, the key point
to note is the connection between these two distinctions and the consequent confusions. Although the above account may have suggested otherwise, it is not simply the case that there are some philosophers who
just happen to be guilty of one of these confusions and others who just
happen to be guilty of the other. The fact of the matter is rather that,
from a Kantian standpoint, the two kinds of confusion represent two
sides of the same coin, namely, the failure to recognize the role in
human knowledge of a set of distinctively epistemic conditions.

Indeed, one can claim that the fundamental issue raised by the *Critique* is whether it is possible to isolate a set of conditions of the possibility of knowledge of things (in the sense already indicated) that can
be distinguished from conditions of the possibility of the things themselves. Since the former kind of condition would count as a condition
of things as they appear and the latter of things as they are in themselves, an affirmative answer to this question entails the acceptance of
the transcendental distinction, and with it of transcendental idealism.
If, on the other hand, the question is answered in the negative, as it is
by the standard picture, then any purportedly "subjective" conditions
are inevitably construed in psychological terms. The subjectivistic, psychologistic, phenomenalistic reading of Kant, which is characteristic of
the standard picture, is thus a direct consequence of its negative answer to this question. The real problem with the picture, however, is
not that it answers this question in the negative, for Kant's position
may very well turn out to be incoherent or otherwise untenable. It is
rather that, by presupposing a negative answer, it never really addresses itself to the question at all. An explicit focus on this question
should, therefore, at the very least lead to a more accurate interpretation of Kant's intent and of the nature of transcendental idealism. Beyond that, I also hope to be able to indicate that it makes it possible
to regard transcendental idealism as a powerful philosophical position
rather than as a curious anachronism or a mass of confusions.

# Transcendental Realism and
# Transcendental Idealism

The function of this chapter is primarily exegetical. Its goal is to develop more fully the interpretation of transcendental idealism sketched
in the previous chapter. This time, however, the analysis will proceed
in an indirect manner. My strategy is to interpret transcendental idealism by means of the transcendental realism with which Kant on occasion contrasts it. The operative assumption is that transcendental
realism and transcendental idealism can be understood as mutually exclusive and exhaustive metaphilosophical alternatives. I thus begin by
developing an interpretation of transcendental realism. The essential
claims of this interpretation are that all noncritical philosophies can be
regarded as realistic in the transcendental sense and that transcendental realism can be characterized in terms of a commitment to a theocentric model or conception of knowledge. I then use these results to
construct an interpretation of transcendental idealism, with its contrasting commitment to an anthropocentric model. The main contention is that this approach enables us to see clearly the connection
between transcendental idealism and the conception of an epistemic
condition, which, in turn, leads to the recognition of the nonphenome-
nalistic, nonpsychological nature of this idealism.

## I. The Nature of Transcendental Realism

The first difficulty confronting the interpretation for which I wish to
argue is that the significance that I attribute to transcendental realism
seems to be belied by the paucity of references to it in the text. One
would normally expect to find a conception of such alleged importance
analyzed in great detail and subjected to a searching criticism. To be
sure, Kant does claim that "were we to yield to the illusion of transcendental realism, neither nature nor freedom would be possible" (A543/
B571). This certainly suggests that transcendental realism is an illusion
of some significance and that it must be a major concern of the *Critique* to eradicate it. Nevertheless, Kant refers explicitly to transcendental realism in only two other places. Both are in the Transcendental
Dialectic, and in each case Kant contrasts it with transcendental idealism.

The first is in the First Edition version of the Fourth Paralogism. Kant is there concerned to refute empirical idealism, which he contrasts with his own transcendental version. In this context he writes:

> By *transcendental idealism* I mean the doctrine that appearances are to be regarded as being, one and all, representations only, not things in themselves, and that time and space are therefore only sensible forms of our intuition, not determinations given as existing by themselves, nor conditions of objects viewed as things in themselves. To this idealism there is opposed a *transcendental realism* which regards time and space as something given in themselves, independently of our sensibility. The transcendental realist thus interprets outer appearances (their reality taken as granted) as things-in-themselves, which exist independently of us and of our sensibility, and which are therefore outside us—the phrase 'outside us' being interpreted in conformity with pure concepts of understanding. It is, in fact, this transcendental realist who afterwards plays the part of empirical idealist. After wrongly supposing that objects of the senses, if they are to be external, must have an existence by themselves, and independently of the senses, he finds that, judged from this point of view, all our sensuous representations are inadequate to establish their reality. [A369]

Kant is here arguing that transcendental realism leads to empirical idealism, which is the doctrine that the mind can only have immediate access to its own ideas or representations (the "ideal" in the empirical sense). The point is that because the transcendental realist misconstrues the reality of spatial objects ("objects of the senses") he is forced to deny that the mind has any immediate experience of such objects. Transcendental realism is thus presented as the source of the pseudo-problem of the external world and of the typically Cartesian version of skepticism that is associated with it.

The second passage is from the Antinomy of Pure Reason. Kant there defines transcendental idealism as the doctrine that "all objects of any experience possible to us, are nothing but appearances, that is, mere representations, which, in the manner in which they are represented, as extended beings, or as series of alterations, have no independent existence outside our thoughts." In contrast to this, the transcendental realist is said to regard "these mere modifications of our sensibility as self-subsistent things, that is, treats *mere representations* as things in themselves" (A490–91/B518–19).

Both of these passages indicate that the defining characteristic of transcendental realism is its confusion of appearances or "mere representations" with things in themselves. The first passage limits this charge to objects of "outer perception" (empirically external, spatial objects), although it does connect it with the conception of time as well as space as "given in themselves, independently of our sensibility." This emphasis on space and outer experience no doubt reflects Kant's concern at that point with empirical idealism and its connection with transcendental realism.

The second passage, which does not reflect this particular concern, goes somewhat further by presenting transcendental realism as the view that considers *all appearances,* those of inner as well as those of outer sense, as if they were things in themselves. I think that this latter passage expresses Kant's considered view on the subject. It is a central tenet of the *Critique* that inner as well as outer sense presents us with objects as they appear, not as they are in themselves. Transcendental realism thus manifests itself as much in a confused view of the former as of the latter.

This of itself should make it clear that the usual interpretation of transcendental realism as equivalent to the scientific realism of the Cartesians and Newtonians (roughly what Berkeley meant by "materialism") is far too narrow. For while Kant only infrequently makes use of the expression 'transcendental realism', he repeatedly accuses philosophers of a variety of stripes of treating appearances as if they were things in themselves or, equivalently, of granting "absolute" or "transcendental" reality to appearances. Indeed, at one place in the *Critique* he terms this confusion the "common prejudice" (A740/B768), while at another he refers to the "common but fallacious presupposition of the absolute reality of appearances" (A536/B564). Moreover, this general claim is found in even stronger form in other texts. Indeed, he goes so far as to assert that prior to the *Critique* the confusion was unavoidable,[12] and even that "until the critical philosophy all philosophies are not distinguished in their essentials."[13]

Such statements support the contention that the transcendental distinction between appearances and things in themselves or, more properly, between things as they appear and the same things as they are in themselves, functions as the great divide in the Kantian conception of the history of philosophy. Only the "critical philosophy" has succeeded in getting this distinction right. Consequently, despite their many interesting differences, all of the others are at bottom nothing more than variant expressions of the same underlying confusion. Thus, if transcendental realism be understood as the point of view which systematically confuses appearances with things in themselves, it can be assigned the same role in Kant's theoretical philosophy that he assigns to heteronomy in his moral philosophy. In other words, it constitutes the common assumption, prejudice, or confusion which is shared by all philosophers who do not achieve the critical standpoint.

## A. Some Varieties of Transcendental Realism

The best way to test this contention is to see the extent to which it is applicable to various "noncritical" philosophies. It should be noted, however, that in so doing we will explicitly be viewing these philosophies through Kantian spectacles. The question at issue is not whether the charge that these philosophies confuse appearances with things in themselves, and are thus transcendentally realistic, is "fair" according to some independent standard of evaluation. It is rather whether, given Kant's assumptions, it is possible to view these philosophies in such a manner.

We have already seen that Kant maintains that empirical idealism is a form of transcendental realism, which arises from the recognition of the fact that the human mind has no direct access to the putatively "real" things, that is, to physical objects construed as things in themselves in the transcendental sense. This recognition, in turn, leads to the claim of Descartes and his followers that the only objects of which we are, in fact, immediately aware are ideas in the mind. Such idealism, together with its skeptical consequences, is therefore the result of an implicit commitment to transcendental realism. Kant's First Edition version of the Refutation of Idealism turns on this point. As he succinctly puts the matter:

> If we treat outer objects as things in themselves, it is quite impossible to understand how we could arrive at a knowledge of their reality outside us, since we have to rely merely on the representation which is in us. For we cannot be sentient (of what is) outside ourselves, but only (of what is) in us, and the whole of our self-consciousness therefore yields nothing save merely our own determinations. [A378]

At first glance this seems reminiscent of Berkeley's critique of "materialism," and it has frequently been taken in just this way. On such a reading Kant, like Berkeley, succeeds in avoiding skepticism only by identifying the "real" with the immediate objects of consciousness. But such a reading is a gross oversimplification and fails to capture the real thrust of Kant's position. In order to capture this thrust, it is necessary to focus, as Kant does, on the key term "external" or "external to us." The empirical idealist, Kant points out, understands this term in its transcendental sense. In other words, this species of idealist takes the "externality" of the "real" spatiotemporal objects with which science supposedly deals to entail the independence of such objects from the subjective conditions of human knowledge. This would be perfectly acceptable if, in describing these transcendentally external objects, one would refrain from ascribing to them any spatial or temporal predicates. In that case one would be a good transcendental idealist. The problem is that the Cartesian empirical idealist does not do this. Instead, he regards these experientially external objects as belonging to "extended matter." He therefore conflates the transcendental with the empirical senses of "external to us." It is this conflation or category mistake that generates the skepticism connected with this form of idealism. Kant's refutation consists essentially in pointing this out.

An even more obvious example of a transcendentally realistic mode of thought is provided by the Newtonians or "mathematical students of nature." We have already seen that their absolutistic conception of space and time can be viewed as the consequence of a confusion of epistemic with ontological conditions, and that this is equivalent to the confusion of appearances with things in themselves. It is, however, not only Newton but also his great opponent, Leibniz, who can be characterized as a transcendental realist. In fact, Kant explicitly claims that Leibniz "took the appearances for things in themselves" (A260/B320). I propose to reserve a consideration of this perplexing claim, as well as of the Leibnizian version of transcendental realism, for the next section. For the present, I wish to consider only the most obvious candidates to serve as counterexamples to the thesis of this section. These are provided by phenomenalistic positions such as those of Berkeley and Hume. If these thinkers can be said to have confused appearances with things in themselves, then it can be claimed with some justice that the confusion is virtually universal.

I have already suggested that Berkeley's "dogmatic idealism," which Kant equates with "degrading bodies to mere illusion," can be viewed as a direct offshoot of the Newtonian version of transcendental realism. In that respect it stands to Newtonian absolute space and time as empirical idealism stands to Cartesian extended matter. In other words, it

is a form of subjectivism or idealism to which one is driven on the
basis of certain transcendentally realistic assumptions. But Berkeley's
position is more than a mere offshoot of transcendental realism. It is
itself realistic in the transcendental sense. Admittedly, Kant never says
precisely this with regard to the "good Bishop." He does so, however,
with regard to Hume, and his claim is equally applicable to Berkeley.
The crucial passage occurs in the *Critique of Practical Reason,* where
Kant, summarizing some of the essential tenets of the First Critique,
reflects: "I granted that when Hume took the objects of experience as
things in themselves (as is almost always done), he was entirely correct
in declaring the concept of cause to be deceptive and an illusion."[14]

Since Kant was certainly well aware of the fact that Hume characterized the objects of human experience as "impressions," we are inevitably led to ask why Kant should describe such private, subjective objects
as things in themselves. The obvious answer is that Hume treats those
impressions as if they were given to the mind as they are in themselves.
This can be seen as a consequence of his failure to recognize the existence of a priori forms of sensibility through which these impressions
are received (even the private data of inner sense are, for Kant, given
to the mind under the form of time and hence count as appearances).
Since Hume did not recognize any a priori forms of sensibility, he was
not in a position to acknowledge the possibility of any a priori rules of
synthesis through which these impressions are brought to the unity of
consciousness. In the absence of such rules, there is no reason why,
given object (or impression) *A,* something else, object (or impression)
*B,* must likewise be given; this, as Kant sees it, is the source of Hume's
skeptical doubts concerning causality. But, for the present purpose at
least, Berkeleian ideas have precisely the same status as Humean impressions. They too are given to the mind as they are in themselves, a
point that is evidenced by Berkeley's denial of the a priori nature of
the representation of space. Such ideas, therefore, count as things in
themselves in the Kantian sense.

It follows from this that, from a Kantian perspective, both Berkeley
and Hume can be judged guilty of confusing appearances with things in
themselves. Consequently, both may be termed transcendental realists.
The peculiar features of their subjectivism stem from the fact that they
regard appearances (in the empirical sense) as if they were things in
themselves (in the transcendental sense). In this respect their position
can perhaps be contrasted with Cartesian dualism, which regards appearances (in the transcendental sense) as if they were things in them-

selves (in the same sense). The key point, however, is that Berkeley and Hume share with other transcendental realists a failure to recognize the role in human experience of a set of epistemic conditions.

## B. Transcendental Realism and the
## Theocentric Model of Knowledge

I have suggested that transcendental realism can also be understood in terms of an appeal, either implicit or explicit, to a theocentric model of knowledge. By such a model I understand a program or method of epistemological reflection, according to which human knowledge is analyzed and evaluated in terms of its conformity, or lack thereof, to the standard of cognition theoretically achievable by an "absolute" or "infinite intellect." By the latter I understand one that is not encumbered by the limitations of the human intellect, and which, therefore, knows objects "as they are themselves." Such an intellect functions in this model essentially as a regulative idea in the Kantian sense. Thus the appeal to it does not commit one either to the existence of such an intellect or to the assumption that knowledge of this type is actually possessed by the human mind. The point is only that a hypothetical "God's-eye view" of things is used as a standard in terms of which the "objectivity" of human knowledge is analyzed.

This model is the common heritage of the Platonic tradition, but it is particularly evident in the great rationalists of the seventeenth century. One thinks in this connection of Malebranche, who claimed that we "see all things in God," and of Spinoza, who maintained that the goal of human cognition is to view things *sub specie aeternitatis* [under the aspect of eternity].[15] It is also central to Leibniz; in fact, I intend to show that his appeal to this model is the key to the understanding of the specifically Leibnizian version of transcendental realism. Moreover, the empiricists are also committed to this model, although this fact is somewhat obscured by their essentially psychological orientation. This is readily apparent in Berkeley, who was always something of a Platonist, but it is equally true of Locke and Hume. Since the transcendentally realistic dimension of Hume's thought has already been noted, I shall here limit myself to a brief consideration of Locke. Finally, in an effort to suggest the prevalence of this model and to provide a further basis for understanding the nature of Kant's "Copernican revolution," I shall attempt to show how it underlies Kant's own precritical thought.

*Leibniz.* Leibniz's appeal to the theocentric model is quite explicit and
has often been noted in the literature. Following Augustine and Malebranche, he depicts the divine understanding as the realm of eternal
truths, and he claims, in typically picturesque fashion, that it is there
that one finds "the pattern of the ideas and truths which are engraved
in our souls."[16] This is not to say that the human mind for Leibniz is
infinite, or that it is somehow capable of thinking "God's thoughts."
On the contrary, he constantly emphasizes the insurmountable limits
of human knowledge. He explains these limits in terms of the con-
fusedness of our representations, and this is itself seen as a consequence of our finitude. The point, however, is not that human
knowledge is infinite or even adequate; it is rather that it approaches
adequacy as it approaches divine knowledge. Thus, despite the infinite
difference in degree or scope, there is a commensurability or similarity
in kind between human and divine knowledge.

The model is also reflected in Leibniz's key claim that in any true
proposition the predicate is contained in the concept of the subject.
Leibniz's adherence to this principle leads him to regard demonstration as requiring reduction to identity. He thinks that this is quite possible for arithmetical propositions and possible at least in principle for
the axioms of Euclidean geometry. More important, he holds that this
principle is not only applicable to necessary truths or "truths of reason," which are true in all possible worlds, but also to contingent truths
or "truths of fact," which hold only in the actual world. This, as Leibniz
puts it in an early formulation of the principle, is because "it is the
nature of an individual substance or complete being to have a concept
so complete that it is sufficient to make us understand and deduce
from it all the predicates of the subject to which the concept is
attached."[17] Since the complete concept of an individual substance involves an infinity of elements, and since a finite mind is not capable of
infinite analysis, the human intellect can never arrive at such a conception. Consequently, it cannot demonstrate or deduce truths of fact.
Nevertheless, such truths remain deducible in principle, that is, for
God, who is capable of an intuitive grasp of the infinite. Expressed in
Kantian terms, this means that all propositions are ultimately analytic
and that the syntheticity of truths of fact is merely a function of the
limits of analysis, not of the nature of the propositions themselves.

These considerations should better enable us to grasp the main outlines of Kant's critique of Leibniz and to understand the claim that Leib-

niz "took the appearances for things in themselves." Much of Kant's quarrel with Leibniz and his followers focuses on the closely related conceptions of sensibility and appearance. By and large, Kant defines his philosophy vis-à-vis that of Leibniz in terms of their different understanding of these conceptions. He claims that Leibniz and his followers "falsified" both conceptions, and he sees this as the direct result of their misconstrual of the distinction between the "sensible" and the "intelligible." Instead of viewing the difference between these two aspects of human cognition as "transcendental," that is, as a difference of origin, content, and kind, they regard it as merely "logical," that is, as a difference of degree of clarity and distinctness of the representations.[18] All of this is captured by the claim that Leibniz (here being contrasted with Locke), *"intellectualized appearances"* (A271/B327). Now, to "intellectualize appearances" is to abstract from their irreducibly sensible (spatiotemporal) character. But since this character is a defining feature of a Kantian appearance, while independence of it is a defining feature of a thing in itself, it can easily be seen that this charge is equivalent to the charge that Leibniz "took the appearances for things in themselves."

Moreover, in his response to Eberhard, Kant makes it clear that the heart of the difficulty with Leibnizianism is that it fails to recognize that human sensibility has its own a priori forms or conditions (space and time), which serve to determine positively the nature and relations of the objects of human experience. That is why Leibnizians tend to regard sensible (perceptual) knowledge of appearances merely as a confused version of the purely intellectual knowledge of these objects obtained by God. Consequently, all of the sensible components of human experience, including spatiotemporal relations, are deemed reducible (for God) to the purely intellectual (logical) determinations which pertain to things in themselves (monads). This reducibility thesis is the logical consequence of Leibniz's appeal to the theocentric model of knowledge and thus of his transcendental realism. It is also the real point behind Kant's contention that Leibniz and his followers "falsified" or "intellectualized" appearances, or equivalently, "took the appearances for things in themselves." Finally, Kant suggests, in the *Critique* and again in his response to Eberhard, that the same failure also serves to explain the distinctive doctrines and confusions of Leibnizian metaphysics.[19] . . .

*Locke.* Locke's use of the theocentric model is not as obvious but is just as real as Leibniz's. Perhaps the best example of this is his much discussed distinction between nominal and real essence. By the nominal essence of a substance, really of a "sort," Locke understands the complex idea of that sort. This idea is formed by the mind on the basis of the experience of a number of instances, and it constitutes the sense of the term denoting that sort. The real essence, by contrast, is the inner nature or the "real constitution" of a thing. Locke uses the example of gold to illustrate this thesis: "The nominal essence of gold," he tells us, "is that complex idea the word gold stands for, let it be, for instance, a body yellow of a certain weight, malleable, fusible and fixed," whereas the real essence is characterized as "the constitution of the insensible parts of that body, on which those qualities and all other properties of gold depend."[20]

Locke's distinction between the two kinds of essence raises a number of issues, but for our purposes the important point is simply that he correlates it with the distinction between divine and human knowledge. A clear illustration of this is his analysis of the "essence" of man. After briefly categorizing those features that are contained in the complex ideas constituting the nominal essence of man, Locke writes:

> The foundation of all those qualities which are the ingredients of our complex idea, is something quite different: and had we such a knowledge of that constitution of man, from which his faculties of moving, sensation, and reasoning, and other powers flow, and on which his so regular shape depends, as it is possible angels have, and it is certain his Maker has, we should have a quite other idea of his essence than what now is contained in our definition of that species, be it what it will: and our idea of any individual man would be as far different from what it is now, as is his who knows all the springs and wheels and other contrivances within the famous clock at Strasburg, from that which a gazing countryman has of it, who barely sees the motion of the hand, and hears the clock strike, and observes only some of the outward appearances.[21]

Knowledge of real essence is here explicitly equated with the knowledge which our "Maker has," that is, divine knowledge. Human knowledge, by contrast, is limited to "some of the outward appearances of things." Clearly then, human knowledge is judged by the ideal standard of divine knowledge and found wanting. Locke's agnosticism is mitigated considerably, however, by his characteristic insistence that our knowledge of nominal essence and the classifications based thereupon are sufficient for our needs. As he so eloquently expresses himself in the introduction to the *Essay*, "The candle that is set up in us shines bright enough for our purposes."[22] These purposes include, of course, knowledge of God and of our duty; but they also include what Locke calls "the conveniences of life."[23] The point here is that our classification of things into sorts and, more generally, our empirical knowledge, suffices to attain these "conveniences," even though it does not acquaint us with the true nature of things. Locke, therefore, combines his appeal to the theocentric model with an essentially pragmatic account of perceptual knowledge. In this respect his position is not far from that of rationalists such as Descartes and Malebranche.

The primary difference between Locke and the rationalists on this score is that Locke tends to conceive of adequate and, therefore, divine knowledge as basically more of the same; that is to say, he regards divine knowledge as if it were perceptual in nature, albeit involving greatly expanded perceptual powers, such as "microscopical eyes."[24] This contrasts sharply with the usual rationalist version of "adequate" knowledge as infinite reason. Although this may not be the whole story with regard to Locke's theory, it is certainly an important part of it. It also seems to be the part that Kant underscores when, in contrasting Locke with Leibniz, he remarks that Locke "sensualized all concepts of the understanding," and that he viewed sensibility "as an immediate relation to things in themselves" (A271/B327). Thus, in spite of the fact that their views are diametrically opposed, Kant holds that Leibniz and Locke share a common and erroneous assumption: that "genuine" knowledge, whether it be sensible as with Locke or intellectual as with Leibniz, is of things in themselves.

*Kant.* Perhaps the most instructive example of an appeal to the theocentric model of knowledge is provided by Kant himself. Indications of this can be discerned in virtually all of his precritical writings, but for illustrative purposes we can limit our consideration to the early metaphysical essay, "A New Exposition of the First Principles of Metaphysical Knowledge" (1755). This essay reflects a stage in his development in which Kant philosophized very much in a Leibnizian mold. Thus, in support of his claim that the principle of identity is the first principle of all truths, the young Kant writes:

> since all our reasoning is resolved into the discovery of an identity of predicate with subject, considered either as it is in itself or in a combination, as is evident from the ultimate rule of truths, hence we see that God does not require the process of reasoning because, since all things are

crystal clear to his gaze, the act of re-presentation puts before his intelligence which things are identical and which are not, and he has no need of analysis as the darkened night of our intelligence necessarily has.[25]

Kant here expresses as clearly as one could wish his commitment to the theocentric model of knowledge. Being finite, we are forced to have recourse to analysis in order to grasp the identities which the divine intellect sees immediately. Kant's commitment to this model is revealed not only in this formulation of the ideal of knowledge but also in some of the central arguments of the work. Two examples will suffice to make this apparent. The first occurs within Kant's argument for the existence of God as the ground of the possibility and hence of the essence of things. In developing this argument Kant appeals to the example of the essence of a triangle:

> For the essence of a triangle which consists in the conjunction of its three sides is not in itself necessary. What sane person would contend that it is in itself necessary that the three sides should always be conceived as conjoined? This indeed I concede is necessary to a triangle, that if you think a triangle you must necessarily think its three sides, and that is the same as saying "if anything is, it is". But how it comes about that to the thought of the sides, of the enclosing of space, the other ideas follow, namely that it be in a genus which is thinkable (whence every notion of a thinkable thing comes by combining, limiting, or determining), this could not in any wise be conceived unless in God, the source of all reality, there existed everything that is in a real notion.[26]

The second example occurs in connection with the claim that the principle of the coexistence of substances is to be located in the divine intellect. In support of this contention Kant reflects:

> It must be confessed that this relation depends upon a community of cause, namely upon God, as the general principle of existence. And since the mutual reciprocity between these things does not follow from the fact that God has fixed their existence *simpliciter,* unless the same *schema* of the divine intellect which gives them existence has fixed their reciprocities by conceiving their existence as correlated, it is evident that the general intercourse of things is secured by the mere conceiving of the divine idea.[27]

The primary import of both these passages lies in the light which they shed on the elements of continuity and change in Kant's thought.

Both the "precritical" and the "critical" Kant were concerned with the determination of the conditions of possibility, although these conditions are explained in quite different ways. In the first passage the question at issue is the nature of the ground or the condition of the possibility of three straight lines being able to enclose a space. The answer of the young Kant is that the possibility of such a figure is grounded in its conceivability by the divine intellect. By contrast, in his account of mathematical possibility in the *Critique,* Kant argues that the impossibility of two straight lines enclosing a space is based upon the conditions of the constructability of figures in space (A221/B268); and these conditions (which define the Euclidean nature of space) are themselves determined by the nature of human sensibility. The second passage is even more striking in this regard, for Kant poses the very same problem that he later deals with in the Analogies, namely, the ground of the unity of experience. In the *Critique* this unity is explained in terms of the "Principles of Pure Understanding." These principles, as we shall see, function as the conditions of the possibility of the consciousness of a unified time order, and they express the necessary conformity of appearances to the schemata of the pure concepts of the understanding. Here, by contrast, the objects (substances) are held to conform necessarily to the schema of the divine intellect. The appeal to the divine intellect in this early essay thus fulfills much the same function as does the appeal to the human intellect in the *Critique.*

## II. The Transcendental Nature of Kant's Idealism

I have argued in the preceding section that all noncritical philosophies, including that of the young Kant, can be regarded as transcendentally realistic. These philosophies are united in the "common assumption" or "prejudice" that the objects of knowledge are things in themselves. Since this assumption is shared by philosophers with radically different ontologies and epistemologies, such as Spinoza and Berkeley, it cannot be defined in either ontological or epistemological terms. Instead, it must be characterized as a metaphilosophical or methodological assumption concerning the "standpoint" in terms of which human knowledge is to be analyzed and evaluated. In the endeavor to characterize further this standpoint, I have also suggested that it involves a failure to recognize that human knowledge has its own a priori conditions, which in turn leads to a failure to make the transcendental distinction, and that it is necessarily connected with a theocentric model of knowledge.

The remainder of this chapter explores the implications of this result for the interpretation of transcendental idealism. Clearly, the most basic of these implications is that, like its opposite, transcendental idealism must be characterized primarily as a metaphilosophical or methodological "standpoint," rather than a straightforwardly metaphysical doctrine about the nature or ontological status of the objects of human cognition. Moreover, just as transcendental realism is defined negatively in terms of its failure to recognize the role of epistemic conditions in human knowledge and its consequent failure to make the transcendental distinction between things as they appear and the same things as they are in themselves, so transcendental idealism is defined positively in terms of its acceptance of this conception and its insistence upon this distinction. To say this is not to deny that transcendental idealism has important metaphysical consequences. . . . The point is that these consequences follow from the acceptance of the transcendental distinction and must, therefore, be understood in connection with it. A further point deserving emphasis here is that it is only if one assumes that human knowledge has a priori conditions of the kind already noted that it becomes possible to "consider" objects in relation to these conditions. In fact, it is only in light of this assumption that the distinction between two ways of "considering" objects can be viewed as anything other than the familiar contrast between "how things seem to me" (given certain psychological and physiological conditions, and so forth) and "how they really are."

Since the basic thrust of the Kantian position is reflected in his own characterization of transcendental idealism as "formal" or "critical," I shall begin with a brief consideration of how this claim is to be understood. The next step is to examine Kant's account of his "Copernican revolution" in philosophy and the sense in which it can be said to involve a shift from a theocentric to an anthropocentric model of knowledge. Finally, in light of all of this, I hope to establish definitely the fundamental difference between transcendental idealism and a phenomenalism or idealism of a Berkeleian type.

## A. *Transcendental Idealism as Formal Idealism*

In response to the pervasive misunderstanding and criticism of his idealism as it was formulated in the First Edition of the *Critique,* Kant notes in the appendix to the *Prolegomena* that he now wishes transcendental idealism to be termed " 'formal' or, better still, 'critical' idealism." In so doing he hoped to distinguish it from both "the dogmatic idealism of Berkeley and the skeptical idealism of Descartes."[28] Moreover, in a note added in the Second Edition to the previously cited definition of transcendental idealism he remarks, "I have also, elsewhere, sometimes entitled it *formal* idealism, to distinguish it from *material* idealism, that is, from the usual type of idealism which doubts or denies the existence of outer things themselves" (B519).

The predominance of the standard picture strongly suggests that Kant would have been well advised to follow more consistently his own terminological recommendation. Kant's idealism is "formal" in the sense that it is a theory about the nature and the scope of the *conditions* under which objects can be experienced or known by the human mind. This is to be contrasted with the idealisms of the Cartesian or Berkeleian sort, which are first and foremost theories about the *contents* of consciousness (understood in the empirical sense). Again, this idealism is "critical" because it is grounded in a reflection on the conditions and limits of human knowledge, not on the contents of consciousness or the nature of *an sich* [in itself] reality.

Unfortunately, much of this is obscured by Kant's tendency to refer to the objects of human experience not only as "appearances" but also as "mere representations." The latter locution in particular, which is extremely frequent in Kant, is mainly responsible for the standard picture. Nevertheless, even here careful attention to the text suffices to raise serious questions about the correctness of this picture. Consider, for example, the characterization of transcendental idealism to which Kant appended the abovementioned note. We saw earlier that Kant there describes transcendental idealism as the doctrine that "everything intuited in space or time, and therefore all objects of any experience possible to us, are nothing but appearances, that is, mere representations, which, in the manner in which they are represented, as extended beings, or as series of alterations, have no independent existence outside our thoughts." The equation of appearances with "mere representations" in the main clause certainly suggests the standard picture. In the subordinate clause, however, Kant effectively undercuts any such reading by indicating that the characterization of appearances as "mere representations" must be understood to refer to "the manner in which they are represented." The claim, therefore, is not that objects have no independent existence (as one might main-

tain with regard to Berkeleian ideas or the sense data of the phenome-
nalists); it is rather that such existence cannot be attributed to them
"in the manner in which they are represented."

The "manner" in which objects are represented is as spatiotemporal
entities. The claim is thus that this description, together with all that
it entails, can be applied to objects only in virtue of our manner of
representing them, and not to these same objects as they may be in
themselves. Kant states that this result is established in the Transcendental Aesthetic, where he argues that space and time are "forms" or
"conditions" of human sensibility. . . . Behind this argument and, indeed, behind Kant's formal idealism, lies a principle that is implicit in
the *Critique* as a whole, but is nowhere made fully explicit: that whatever is necessary for the representation or experience of something as
an object, that is, whatever is required for the recognition or picking
out of what is "objective" in our experience, must reflect the cognitive
structure of the mind (its manner of representing) rather than the nature of the object as it is in itself. To claim otherwise is to assume that
the mind can somehow have access to an object (through sensible or
intellectual intuition) independently of the very elements that have
been stipulated to be the conditions of the possibility of doing this in
the first place. This involves an obvious contradiction. The transcendental realist avoids this contradiction only because he rejects the assumption that there are any such conditions. In so doing, however, he
begs the very question raised by the *Critique.*

Similar considerations apply to the pure concepts of the understanding, which serve as the intellectual conditions of human knowledge.
Although a detailed analysis of Kant's conception of the understanding
must await the second part of this study, it should be kept in mind
here that all human knowledge is judgmental for Kant (as opposed to
being intuitive) and that the pure concepts are claimed to function as
the ultimate rules or conditions of judgment. Now, insofar as by 'object'
is meant simply the subject of a possible judgment, which is how Kant
sometimes construes the term, these concepts are both necessary and
sufficient to determine what can "count," that is, be represented as an
object. In other words, they define the very meaning of 'object', insofar
as by an object is meant merely something conceptually represented.
On the other hand, insofar as 'object' is taken to mean an object of
possible experience, which, as we shall see, is the "weighty" Kantian
sense of the term, these same concepts are necessary but not sufficient
conditions for the representations of objects or objective states of af-

fairs. They are still necessary conditions because experience involves judgment; but they are not sufficient conditions because they require supplementation by space and time, the forementioned sensible conditions. The main point, however, is that they possess coequal transcendental status with these sensible conditions. Consequently, the transcendental ideality of the objects of possible experience must be understood to involve their conformity to these concepts as well as to the forms of sensibility. Both count as "forms" of experience, and both, therefore, enter into the characterization of Kant's idealism as "formal." Much of this is usually lost sight of because of Kant's tendency to define transcendental idealism almost exclusively in terms of his theory of sensibility, and, therefore, as a doctrine that receives its primary support and proof from the Transcendental Aesthetic. This same tendency is also exhibited in his frequent characterization of appearances as "modifications" or "determinations" of our "faculty of sensibility" or of the "subjective condition of the senses." Nevertheless, there are passages in which Kant does indicate that the transcendental conception of appearance must be understood in terms of the understanding and its a priori concepts, as well as of sensibility and its a priori forms.[29] . . .

## B. Kant's "Copernican Revolution" and the Anthropocentric Model of Knowledge

In a famous passage in the preface to the Second Edition, Kant compares the "changed point of view". . . which he advocates for philosophy with the revolution in astronomy initiated by Copernicus. Not surprisingly, a considerable literature has developed regarding the precise point of the comparison and the appropriateness of the Copernican analogy. The main point at issue is whether Kant has committed what is called the "anthropocentic fallacy" in his reading of Copernicus. Fortunately, we need not concern ourselves with that issue here. The central question is simply how Kant's own philosophical "revolution" is to be understood, and this obviously remains a question even if, as is frequently maintained, the analogy with Copernicus is not particularly apt. Kant describes his revolution in this way:

> Hitherto it has been assumed that all our knowledge must conform to objects. But all attempts to extend our knowledge of objects by establishing something in regard to them *a priori,* by means of concepts, have, on

this assumption, ended in failure. We must therefore make trial whether
we may not have more success in the tasks of metaphysics, if we suppose
that objects must conform to our knowledge. [Bxvi]

Given the preceding analysis, it should be clear that Kant is here
contrasting the "standpoints" of transcendental realism and transcendental idealism. To begin with, the assumption that "all our knowledge
must conform to objects; is readily identifiable as the "common assumption" associated with transcendental realism. Consequently, the
"objects" to which our knowledge presumably conforms must be characterized as things in themselves in the transcendental sense. From
this point of view, then, we can be said to know objects just to the
extent to which our thought conforms to their "real" nature or, equivalently, to God's thought of these same objects. On this model, Kant
tells us, we cannot account for the possibility of a priori knowledge of
objects, because we cannot explain how the mind could "anticipate"
any of the properties of objects so defined, which is required for a
priori knowledge. The problem is that this model assumes that all
knowledge rests ultimately upon a direct acquaintance with its object,
which would, in effect, make all knowledge a posteriori. In the *Prolegomena,* however, Kant goes beyond this to suggest that if the objects
of human knowledge are things in themselves, it is not even possible
to account for a posteriori knowledge.[30] I think it apparent from what
has already been said that this stronger claim represents Kant's considered opinion. In short, his position is that transcendental realism, with
its theocentric model, is incapable of explaining knowledge of any sort.
That is why a philosophical revolution is necessary.

The contrary "supposition," that "objects must conform to our
knowledge". . . expresses the central tenet of transcendental idealism.
It also appeals to an anthropocentric model, the defining characteristic
of which is that the cognitive structure of the human mind is viewed
as the source of certain conditions which must be met by anything that
is to be represented as an object by such a mind. Clearly, this model
presupposes that there are such conditions (epistemic conditions);
this presupposition, in turn, allows us to attach a meaning to the supposed conformity of objects to our knowledge. To say that objects
"conform to our knowledge" is just to say that they conform to the
conditions under which we can alone represent them as objects. Moreover, given this presupposition, there is no difficulty in accounting for
either a priori or a posteriori knowledge of such objects, for it is an

analytic truth that any object represented must conform to the conditions under which it can alone be represented as an object. As already indicated, the key question is whether there are in fact any such conditions and, if so, whether they can be specified.

Since the preface does little more than entertain the possibility that there might be such conditions to which objects must conform, the whole account of the "Copernican hypothesis" must be regarded as a promissory note which will have to be made good in the actual text of the *Critique*. . . . [One] point to be emphasized is that this "changed point of view" brings with it a radically new conception of an object. An object is now to be understood as whatever conforms to our knowledge, and this, as we have seen, means whatever conforms to the mind's conditions (both sensible and intellectual) for the representation of it as an object. Consequently, an object is by its very nature something represented; and in that sense a reference to mind and its cognitive apparatus is built into the definition of the term. This new conception of an object, which is the correlate of the conception of an epistemic condition, is the major outcome of Kant's so-called Copernican revolution.

Finally, it should be noted that one cannot object to this account of the revolutionary nature of Kant's "supposition" on the grounds that other philosophers before him had developed a conception of the object of human knowledge which involves an essential reference to mind. The fact is readily granted; what is denied is simply its relevance to the present point. Everything depends on how this "essential reference to mind" is understood. For Kant, it must be understood in such a way as to allow one to speak of objects as conforming to our knowledge. But the mind-dependent objects of philosophers such as Berkeley and Hume (ideas and impressions) can no more be said to "conform to our knowledge" than can a humanly inaccessible "object" such as a Lockean real essence.

## C. Transcendental Idealism and Phenomenalism

I shall conclude this chapter by returning to the question of the contrast between transcendental idealism and phenomenalism in general and Berkeleian idealism in particular. Jonathan Bennett's fairly standard characterization of the nature of phenomenalism and its distinction from idealism provides a convenient starting point for this discussion. According to Bennett, phenomenalism is essentially a theory about object language statements. It holds that all such statements are translatable into complex statements about sense data (including counterfactual hypotheticals). He further suggests that this is equivalent to the claim that *"objects are logical constructs out of sense data."* Idealism, by contrast, is characterized as the metaphysical view that "objects are *collections* of sense data." He attributes the latter view to Berkeley.[31]

The first and most basic point to be made here is that phenomenalism, as Bennett describes it, is transcendentally realistic in the same sense and for the same reasons as Berkeleian idealism: in spite of its conception of objects as "logical constructs," it treats (implicitly, of course) the sensible data out of which "objects" are supposedly constructed as things in themselves. Consequently, it is no more suitable for explicating transcendental idealism than is Berkeleian idealism. In short, transcendental idealism is neither a theory about the translatability of object language statements into some more precise or primitive sense datum language nor a theory about the ontological type (material object or collection of sense data) of the objects of human experience. Admittedly, the latter interpretation is suggested by much of Kant's language, in particular by his characterization of objects as "mere representations." Nevertheless, we have seen that this manner of expression, which is primarily responsible for the standard picture, must itself be interpreted in light of the conception of the a priori forms or conditions of human knowledge.

We need not, however, stop with these very general considerations. The whole issue can be clarified further by means of a comparison of Berkeley's analysis of statements about unperceived objects in *The Principles of Human Knowledge* with Kant's treatment of the same topic in the Antinomy of Pure Reason. In the *Principles* Berkeley offers two distinct analysis of propositions of the form: $x$ exists, although $x$ is not currently being perceived by myself or by another "created spirit." On one of these analyses, $x$ can be said to exist, if $x$ is being perceived by God.[32] On the other analysis, which is obviously much closer to contemporary phenomenalism, $x$ can be said to exist if statements about $x$ can be translated into hypotheticals of the form: if one were in position or had the proper instruments, and so forth, one would perceive $x$.[33] Both of these analyses are based upon the correlation between existence and perception which is the hallmark of Berkeley's philosophy.

Kant's account of propositions about unperceived entities and events bears a superficial resemblance to Berkeley's second version, and therefore to phenomenalistic accounts. Thus, he allows that we can perfectly well speak of inhabitants on the moon, even though no one has even seen them, but he goes on to note that

> this, however, only means that in the possible advance of experience we may encounter them. For everything is real [*wirklich*] which stands in connection with a perception in accordance with the laws of empirical advance. They are therefore real if they stand in an empirical connection with my actual consciousness, although they are not for that reason real in themselves, that is, outside this advance of experience.

Moreover, he continues:

> To call an appearance a real thing prior to our perceiving it, either means that in the advance of experience we must meet with such a perception, or it means nothing at all. For if we were speaking of a thing in itself, we would indeed say that it exists in itself apart from relation to our senses and possible experience. But we are here speaking only of an appearance in space and time, which are not determinations of things in themselves but only of our sensibility. Accordingly, that which is in space and time is an appearance; it is not anything in itself but consists merely of representations, which, if not given in us—that is to say, in perception—are nowhere to be met with. [A493–94/B522–23]

We can see from this that Kant, like both Berkeley and the contemporary phenomenalist, translates first-order statements about unperceived entities or events into second-order statements about the possible perception thereof. Nevertheless, this superficial resemblance really masks the distinctive feature of the Kantian analysis: the role given to a priori laws or principles. The "laws of empirical advance," or, as he calls them elsewhere, the "laws of the unity of experience" (A494/B522), are nothing other than the Analogies of Experience. . . . [T]he important point is that, on a transcendentally idealistic analysis, the claim that a certain entity or event is to be met with the "advance of experience" turns out to be an elliptical way of affirming some lawful connection or "casual route" between the entity or event in question and present experience. It does not, however, in any sense involve the postulation of a hypothetical mental episode in the history of some consciousness (whether human or divine).

The role of intellectual conditions and, more generally, the epistemic or transcendental thrust of Kant's theory, is brought out particularly clearly in the analysis of 'actuality' . . . in the Postulates of Empirical Thought. Kant there defines the actual as "that which is bound up with the material conditions of experience, that is, with sensation" (A218/ B266). Because of the explicit reference to sensation, this definition of actuality certainly seems to invite a phenomenalistic or even an idealistic (in the Berkeleian sense) reading. Kant's discussion of the postulate, however, suggests a somewhat different story. The claim that something is actual, we are told,

> does not, indeed, demand immediate *perception* (and, therefore, sensation of which we are conscious) of the object whose existence is to be known. What we do, however, require is the connection of the object with some actual perception, in accordance with the analogies of experience, which define all real connection in an experience in general.[A225/ B272]

At first glance, this might still suggest phenomenalism as Bennett defines it. To be sure, it rules out the extreme idealistic requirement that for an empirical object to be actual (real) it must actually be perceived, but it does seem to require the supposition that the object *could* be perceived, which is just the thesis of phenomenalism (with its appeal to counterfactuals). Nevertheless, this is not quite Kant's position. He does hold that whatever is actual must be an object of possible perception, but this is merely a consequence, not a criterion, of actuality. As the passage above indicates, the criteria of actuality are provided by the Analogies of Experience, that is, by a set of a priori principles or intellectual conditions. The full critical position is that whatever can be connected with some given perception in accordance with these principles, or "laws of the empirical connection of appearances," is to be deemed "actual." The appeal to perception or sensation here functions merely as the point of departure, which gives empirical content to the claim of actuality. The claim itself is not about any "subjective experiences."

Kant's illustration of this principle is also highly instructive. It concerns the hypothetical case of the perception of some magnetically attracted iron filings. Such a perception, he notes, would clearly justify the inference to the existence . . . of some material responsible for this attraction. Moreover, it would do so even though our sensory apparatus is not adequate for the perception of this material. Admittedly, he then suggests that if our sense organs were more powerful or more refined we might be able to perceive it. This once more calls to mind the phenomenalist's characteristic appeal to counterfactuals in order to justify the meaningfulness of existence claims. Kant, however, does not appeal to counterfactuals in this manner. Instead, he remarks that "the grossness of our senses does not in any way decide the form of possible experience in general. Our knowledge of the existence of things reaches, then, only in so far as our perception and its advance according to empirical laws can extend" (A226/B273). The key point here is that the meaningfulness of the reference to this magnetic material is not a function of the possibility of sufficiently improving our sensory apparatus so as to enable us to have experiences that we are not presently able to have. It is rather a function of the connectibility of this material with our present experience in accordance with empirical laws and, ultimately, a priori principles or intellectual conditions.

Finally, the same point can be made with respect to the notion of a possible perception. As is already implicit in his "to be is to be perceived" principle, and as is perfectly manifest in his account of the "smallest perceivable thing," Berkeley's account of possible perception is essentially psychological in nature. To be possible means to be actually perceivable. Consequently, anything too small to be perceived, or below the "smallest perceivable thing," can simply be dismissed as impossible.[34] In sharp contrast to this, Kant defines the possibility of perception in terms of the conformity to rules, that is, to a priori principles. Thus he writes:

All that the rule requires is that the advance from appearances be to appearances; for even if these latter yield no actual perceptions (as is the case when for our consciousness they are too weak in degree to become experience), as appearances they nonetheless still belong to possible experience. [A522/B550]

This passage almost seems as if it were written with Berkeley in mind. In any event, it nicely illustrates the radical difference between Kant's transcendental or formal idealism and a phenomenalism or material idealism of the Berkeleian mold. The transcendental concept of appearance is linked here specifically to the notion of a possible experience. The latter notion, however, is defined in terms of conformity to a set of a priori conditions (conditions of the possibility of experience), not in terms of the possibility of a perceptual state. Once again, then,

we see that the appeal to such conditions is the defining characteristic
of transcendental idealism. . . .

## Notes

1. All references to the *Critique of Pure Reason* are to the standard First
and Second Edition pagination and are included in the text following the citation. I usually follow Norman Kemp Smith's translation of the *Critique of Pure
Reason*. Where my departure from Kemp Smith is significant and reflects a
difference in interpretation I call attention to it in the notes. Apart from some
passages from the *Reflexionen* and various versions of the *Vorlesungen*, all
other references to Kant's works are to the standard edition: *Kants gesammelte
Schriften*, ed. Königlich Preussischen Akademie der Wissenschaften (herein-
after cited as *Ak.*). Where possible, I also include a reference to the standard
English version of the work in question.

2. P. F. Strawson, *The Bounds of Sense*, p. 38. [See also essay 8, this
volume—ed.]

3. Ibid., p. 16.

4. For a critical discussion of some of these attempts, see Ralph S. Walker,
*Kant*, especially pp. 14–23.

5. The above is admittedly an oversimplified account of Strawson's position,
based largely upon his introductory account, *The Bounds of Sense*, pp. 38–42.
He also discusses transcendental idealism in several other places in the work,
most notably pp. 235–62, and he distinguishes among various possible interpretations.

6. H. A. Prichard, *Kant's Theory of Knowledge*, pp. 71–100. A rigorous and
sensitive critique of Prichard's Kant-interpretation has been provided by Graham Bird in *Kant's Theory of Knowledge*, especially pp. 1–17. Although I differ
from him on many issues, the strategy of this chapter, and also the overall
direction of my interpretation, owes much to his work. To my mind, he de-
serves credit for being the first English-language Kant commentator of this
generation seriously to challenge the standard picture.

7. Prichard, *Kant's Theory*, especially pp. 78–79.

8. Cf. A28–30/B44–45, A45–46/B62–63, A368–73.

9. *Ak.* XX, 269. Other relevant texts include the *Critique of Pure Reason*,
A45–46/B62–63, and *Prolegomena*, §13, remark II, *Ak.* IV, 289–90.

10. Gerold Prauss, *Kant und das Problem der Dinge an sich* [Kant and the
Problem of the Thing in Itself], pp. 20 ff. Prauss also points out that the short
forms, such as we find in the Transcendental Aesthetic, can generally be seen
as abbreviations of the long forms.

11. *Ak.* IV:258.

12. *Ak.* XX:287.

13. *Ak.* XX:335.

14. *Ak.* V:53.

15. Cf. Spinoza, *Ethics* II, prop. XLIV, Corollary II. Spinoza there claims that

"it is in the nature of reason to perceive things under a certain form of eternity" *(sub quâdam aeternitatis specie)*.

16. G. W. Leibniz, *New Essays on Human Understanding,* trans. Peter Remnant and Jonathan Bennett, book 4, chap. 2, §14, p. 447.

17. G. W. Leibniz, *Discourse on Metaphysics,* trans. G. R. Montgomery, §8, p. 13.

18. Cf. *Critique of Pure Reason,* A43–44/B61–62; *Prolegomena, Ak.* IV:290–91; "On a Discovery," in *The Kant–Eberhard Controversy,* p. 133; and *Ak.* VIII:219.

19. *Critique of Pure Reason,* A271–76/B327–32; "On a Discovery," pp. 156–60; *Ak.* VIII:246–50.

20. John Locke, *An Essay Concerning Human Understanding,* ed. A. C. Fraser, vol. 2, p. 57.

21. See ibid., pp. 57–58.

22. Ibid., vol. 1, p. 30.

23. Ibid., pp. 29, 402.

24. Locke, *An Essay,* vol. 1, p. 403.

25. *Ak.* I:391. English translation, "A New Exposition of the First Principles of Metaphysical Knowledge," by F. E. England in *Kant's Conception of God,* p. 219.

26. *Ak.* I:395–96; "A New Exposition," p. 225.

27. *Ak.* I:413; "A New Exposition," p. 248.

28. *Ak.* IV:375.

29. The passages in which Kant describes transcendental ideality in this way include A129 and Bxxvii–xxix.

30. *Prolegomena,* §14, *Ak.* IV:294.

31. Jonathan Bennett, *Locke, Berkeley, Hume,* pp. 136–37.

32. George Berkeley, *The Principles of Human Knowledge,* §6, in *The Works of George Berkeley, Bishop of Cloyne.*

33. Ibid., §3.

34. Cf. ibid., §132, and *An Essay Towards a New Theory of Vision,* §§79–87, in *Works of George Berkeley.*

# 10

## Projecting the Order of Nature

*Philip Kitcher*

### I

Imagine that you are lucky enough to stand at the end of inquiry. In your hand you hold an imposing volume entitled *Total Science.* You open it. What do you find?

Perhaps this. The work begins with an account of the fundamental constituents of nature and of their essential properties. From the principles that ascribe these properties there proceed rigorous derivations of the laws of nature. These laws express objective natural necessities. Some of them formulate objective causal relationships. Others delineate the essential properties of objective natural kinds. The organization of *Total Science* recapitulates the order of nature. Derivations reflect causal dependencies, categorizations mirror the natural kinds. That organization is recapitulated in its turn in explicit statements about natural necessities, causal relationships, and the delineation of genuine kinds. For, along with more mundane facts about the world, *Total Science* is committed to include those important structural facts which embody the order of nature.

. . . Or perhaps something different. *Total Science* is advertised from the beginning as a manual for anticipating experience. It is full of useful information about general regularities involving familiar characteristics of familiar things. Moreover, these regularities are beautifully and economically organized, for "Such condensing of a multitude of laws into a small number of principles affords enormous relief to the human mind, which might not be able without such an artifice to store up the new wealth it acquires daily."[1] There is no hint of natural necessities, of genuine kinds, or of real causal connections. Some pages even warn the reader that the purpose of *Total Science* is entirely predictive; it does not pretend to address the question "Why?" However, one ingenious younger member of the committee of authors, more liberal than the others, is prepared to relax these strictures: given the right context, any sound argument constructed from the principles of *Total Science* can be offered as an explanation.

My fantasy dramatizes an old controversy about the aims of science and the objectivity of scientific explanation, a controversy that I take to be as significant as the more prominent debates about scientific realism that have occupied philosophers in our century. There is a view of science, as old as Aristotle, according to which scientific knowledge aims to know the reason for the fact. To use Aristotelian terminology, scientists aim to fathom the order of being, an order that is typically opposed to the order of knowing. To fathom the order of being one must identify the genuine kinds of things and their essential properties, and one must trace the dependencies of phenomena on one another, ultimately relating them to the essential properties of fundamental entities, on which all phenomena ultimately depend. The rival conception, perhaps most closely associated with Mach and Duhem, is that there are no joints at which nature can be carved, no objective necessities, no mind-independent causal connections. The task of science is to order the simple kinds of facts of which experience apprises us—call them "Hume facts"—in a way that makes the anticipation of future experience as easy as possible. Convenient organizations have no title to represent "objective dependencies" or "natural necessities"; they signal no deep "structural facts" about nature. All the facts are Hume facts. All the rest is human creation.

Each position has one great merit. Each faces one major difficulty. For, on the one hand, the practice of science seems to testify to the desire for understanding of nature, and the understanding sought seems to be an objective insight, not some subjective feeling of at-homeness with the phenomena. On the other hand, notions of natural necessity, causation, and objective dependency have worried scrupulous epistemologists at least since Hume. Thus the Aristotelian approach honors a straightforward vision of the aims and practice of science at the cost of epistemological opacity, while the Mach-Duhem conception purchases its epistemological purity by renouncing what seem to be widely exemplified scientific virtues.

Logical positivism, and its descendant, logical empiricism, struggled to find a way to have the best of both worlds. The guiding idea was that an objective notion of scientific explanation could be found without the aid of dubious Aristotelian equipment. Causation was to be characterized in terms of explanation. Explanation was to be understood as subsumption under law. Similarly, natural kinds were to be conceived as the extensions of the predicates occurring in lawlike statements, and natural necessities were to be expressed in statements derivable from laws of nature. Finally, laws themselves were to be characterized by their form. So a grand reduction was envisaged which would simultaneously defend the objectivity (and importance) of scientific understanding and honor Hume's epistemological critique of the Aristotelian idioms.

The program failed for all sorts of reasons. Perhaps most poignant was the collapse of a part of the enterprise that Hempel pursued with enormous lucidity, ingenuity, and apparent success. The covering-law model initially promised to characterize scientific explanation without any covert appeal to causal concepts. Recognition of asymmetries in explanation cast a shadow on that promise. The most obvious ways of responding to the asymmetries were to draw on causal concepts in the explication of explanation or to retreat from the thesis of the objectivity of explanation, and these are the lines of response adopted in the most thorough contemporary accounts. So we have returned to my original dilemma.

I claim there is a middle way, charted by Kant in his scattered remarks on the methodology of science. Central to Kant's thinking about science is his conception of inquiry as guided by principles that enjoin us to introduce a certain kind of order into our beliefs. If we are to theorize rationally about nature then we must abide by these organizing principles. Objective understanding is impossible without them and attained through them. Moreover, once the character of these principles is recognized, we find that the concept of objective understanding does not depend on any mind-independent notions of causation, natural necessity, or natural kind. My aim is to show how a welcome middle way leads out of Kant's writings on the philosophy of science.

## II

At the beginning of the Transcendental Dialectic, Kant ponders the question of whether the faculty of reason conforms to objective principles. His initial answer appears to foreshadow the kind of subjectivism that we find in the writings of Mach and Duhem.

> As a matter of fact, multiplicity of rules and unity of principles is a demand of reason for the purpose of bringing the understanding into thoroughgoing accordance with itself, just as the understanding brings the manifold of intuition under concepts and thereby connects the manifold. But such a principle does not prescribe any law for objects, and does not contain any general ground of the possibility of knowing or of determining objects as such; it is merely a subjective law for the orderly management of the possessions of our understanding, that by comparison of its concepts it may reduce them to the smallest possible number; it does not justify us in demanding from the objects such uniformity as will minister to the convenience and extension of our understanding; and we may not, therefore, ascribe to the maxim any objective validity.[2]

Of course, this sober diagnosis of limits to the prescriptive power of reason precedes Kant's detailed critique of the pretensions of rational psychology, rational cosmology, and rational theology. Once the task of exposing an assortment of fallacies is behind him, he is willing to be more positive about the role of reason and of its principles. The Appendix to the Ideal proposes that the principles of pure reason have a legitimate regulative employment. I claim that this section contains the heart of Kant's philosophy of science.

Unfortunately, the theses of the Appendix are obscure—even by Kantian standards—not primarily because of difficulties in parsing the sentences, but because Kant seems perilously close to inconsistency. After some preliminary recapitulations, Kant declares that the ideas of pure reason have "an excellent, and indeed indispensably necessary, regulative employment" (A644/B672). He quickly makes it clear that the task of Reason is to introduce "systematic unity" into our knowledge:

> If we consider in its whole range the knowledge obtained for us by the understanding, we find that what is peculiarly distinctive of reason in its attitude to this body of knowledge, is that it prescribes and seeks to achieve its systematization, that is, to exhibit the connection of its parts in accordance with a single principle. (A645/B673; see also A648/B676; A449/B677–678; A667–668/B695–696)

The pursuit of unity seems to have some important consequences. In the first place, through the activity of reason our knowledge is transformed from a "mere contingent aggregate" to "a system connected according to necessary laws" (A645/B673). Thus, through the pursuit of unity we seem to achieve principles that count as "laws" and that express "necessities." Second, there are cases in which the unification of our knowledge is achieved by using concepts which are not instantiated in nature. Kant cites the concepts of pure chemical substances as examples of the role of idealizations in the unification of nature (A646/B674). Third, Kant develops the contrast between the constitutive use of the ideas of reason and legitimate ("hypothetical") employment by making an epistemological point. We cannot regard a (partial) collection of positive instances as "proving" a universal hypothesis, but, through the regulative use of reason, which aims "to bring unity into the body of our detailed knowledge," we *"approximate"* our hypotheses to universality (A647/B675). Finally, Kant tells us that the search for systematic unity, while yielding only a *"projected* unity," nonetheless furnishes a criterion for the truth of the rules brought forth by the understanding (A647/B675).

To see how puzzling these claims are, we need only begin by looking back at the characterization of Reason as it appears at the beginning of the Dialectic. There, it seems, the enterprise of introducing unity into our knowledge is seen as having no objective force. Kant appears to be saying that it is convenient for us—it eases the burdens of our poor finite minds—if we try to achieve a unified systematization of our beliefs. However, there is no indication that following convenience will do anything so dramatic as elevating some of the universal propositions we believe to laws of nature. Apparently, in the Deductions and in the Analogies, there are arguments for principles about the lawfulness of nature (B165) and for the subordination of all events to causal laws (A195/B240). These discussions contain no hint that some magical "regulative use of reason" is needed to confer lawlike status upon a principle, nor that the magic is performed by following a maxim that has no "objective validity." Moreover, the sanctioning of concepts which lack instances seems to fly in the face of one of Kant's central theses, the claim that exemplification is the touchstone of conceptual legitimacy (A84–86/B116–118). And there are obvious doubts about what might be meant by "approximating the rules to universality" (Aren't the rules employed in our determining of objective time-relations *fully* universal?) or by suggesting that reason is somehow able to provide a criterion of truth for the claims about nature that emerge from the activity of the understanding (Wasn't the task of providing any such criterion of truth achieved in the Analytic?).

The root of our interpretive difficulties is surely Kant's apparent wish to have things both ways: to dismiss the pretensions of Reason and simultaneously to attribute to the search for unity *some* kind of "objective validity" that will credit it with the important effects I have listed. One is inclined to think that the Appendix simply contradicts what Kant has said earlier in the *Critique*. The starkest form of the contradiction lies in the declaration that the maxim of unity has no "objective validity" coupled with the refusal to treat that maxim as a mere piece of subjective advice. A simple way of escaping inconsistency is to forget about the Appendix. Understandably, many commentators on Kant have chosen this route.

Yet, even if we ignore the testimony of the Appendix, other passages in Kant's writings reveal that a simple interpretation of his views about objectivity, necessity, unity, law, and cause is mistaken. Consider the following lines from the introduction to CJ:

> The understanding is, no doubt, in possession a priori of universal laws of nature, without which nature could not be an object of experience, but it needs in addition a certain order of nature in its particular rules, which can only be empirically known and which are, as regards the understanding, contingent. These rules, without which we could not proceed from the universal analogy of a possible experience in general to the particular, must be thought by it as laws (i.e. as necessary), for otherwise they would not constitute an order of nature, although their necessity can never be cognized or comprehended by it. (CJ p. 21)

As I interpret this passage, Kant makes a number of claims. (1) There are laws ("laws of nature in general") that we know a priori. These are the principles enunciated in the Analytic, where Kant explicitly tells us that, through the categories, the pure understanding is able to "prescribe" those laws involved in *"nature in general,"* but that, to learn "special laws" we have to "resort to experience" (B165; see also the immediately preceding discussion). (2) Knowledge of these laws does not suffice for experience. If we are to have experience, then we must also recognize the appearances as ordered, and this presupposes that we can identify particular laws of nature. Given (1), such laws of nature must be apprehended, *and apprehended as laws,* on the basis of experience. (3) Laws of nature are (in some sense) necessary. But, since necessity (and universality—another hallmark of laws) cannot be derived from experience (recall B4), we cannot recognize the necessity of a statement on the basis of experience.

When we put these claims together, it appears that Kant is formulating some unsatisfiable demands. According to a straightforward reading of (2), we must be able to see that certain regularities in nature are (in some sense) necessary. But (1) and (3) block the only avenues to this knowledge—(1) by claiming that the laws in question lie beyond the scope of the understanding to proceed a priori, (3) by denying that the alleged knowledge can be garnered empirically.

In this case, appearances are only slightly deceptive. Kant intends to pose a problem that will be resolved through the introduction of new pieces of critical machinery. Immediately following the passage I have quoted he writes:

> Although, therefore, the understanding can determine nothing a priori in respect of objects, it must, in order to trace out these empirical so-called laws, place at the basis of all reflection upon objects an a priori principle, viz. that a cognizable order of nature is possible in accordance with these laws. The following propositions express some such principle. There is in nature a subordination of genera and species comprehensible by us. Each one approximates to some other according to a common principle, so that a transition form one to another, and so on to a higher genus, may be possible. Though it seems at the outset unavoidable for our understanding to assume different kinds of causality for the specific differences of natural operations, yet these different kinds may stand under a small number of principles, with the investigation of which we have to busy ourselves. (CJ, p. 21)

The propositions enunciated at the end of this passage correspond to the principles of systematic unity that figure in the Appendix to the Ideal. Thus, I suggest, Kant's solution to the puzzle of how we manage to recognize the necessity of laws is that, properly understood, this necessity accrues to lawlike statements in virtue of their incorporation in a system that is constructed by following certain rules. Taken individually, statements that we normally count as laws can only be regarded as empirical and contingent. But, we are required to systematize the body of our beliefs, and, as a consequence of the systematization, some statements (in fact those we count as laws) come to be credited with necessity. In Rescher's succinct summation of the view: "Lawfulness is

the product of the well-founded imputation to empirical generalizations of nomic necessity and hypothetical force."[3]

Plainly, this "solution" requires clarification and development. So
far, I have been concerned only to argue that the themes of the Appendix to the Ideal cannot be conveniently discarded as a murky append-
age, inconsistent with Kant's well-developed epistemology, and
offering no solutions to outstanding problems that that epistemology
must overcome. If I am right, then the early sections of the *Critique*
set the stage for a difficulty with the necessity of laws, a difficulty that
Kant presents in the Introduction to CJ as a problem to be tackled with
the help of an appeal to the regulative use of the ideas of reason.
Hence, the interpretive puzzles we encountered earlier cannot just be
dismissed.

Our task is to articulate three schematic claims to which Kant seems
committed in a way that will bring them into harmony with one another. The claims are as follows:

(A) L is rationally accepted as a law of nature just in case L is a statement playing role RL in an ideal systematization of our beliefs,
constructed by following rules M. Es are rationally regarded as
causally dependent on Cs just in case the Es and Cs comprise
the extensions of concepts that stand in relation RC in the ideal
systematization of our beliefs. K is rationally accepted as a natural kind just in case K is the extension of a concept playing role
RK in the ideal systematization of our beliefs.

(B) There is some sense of necessity in which laws are necessary.
The statements which are accepted as laws are taken to have
this necessity in virtue of their playing role RL in the ideal systematization of our beliefs.

(C) There is some sense of objective validity in which the rules M
that determine the ideal systematization of beliefs lack objective
validity.

(A) embodies Kant's commitment to the mind-dependence of laws—
and I have expanded the thesis to include the mind-dependence of
other epistemologically problematic notions (those of cause and kind).
(B) recapitulates the Kantian idea that laws carry (some kind of) necessity, a burden Kant takes to be essential if they are to discharge their
function in ordering nature. Finally, (C) recalls a point we have found

troublesome before, Kant's explicit denial that the principle of systematic unity in nature is "objectively valid."

There is one obvious feature of my schematic principles that merits comment. Note that (A) does not provide a characterization of what laws *are*. It is an epistemological thesis about the conditions under which we are justified in counting something as a law. At the current stage of our interpretive project, this is the best we can manage. Understanding Kant's characterization(s) of laws (causes, kinds) will require us to come to terms with the notion of "objective validity," a notion apparently attributed to the rules M in (a) and (b) and denied to those rules in (C).

Before attempting to fill in any of the other details, I shall attempt to resolve the tension between (A) and (B) on the one hand, and (C) on the other. The problem of reconciling Kant's seemingly incompatible claims about the status of the principles of systematic unification is, of course, the fundamental interpretive puzzle that has dominated the discussion of this section. I propose that we continue (for the moment) to treat "systematic unification" as a dummy phrase, and consider the following methodological principle:

(D) Let H be a set of sentences stating Hume facts, including all and only the Hume facts that we are justified in accepting. Suppose that S provides the best systematic unification of H. Then we are justified in accepting S.

Despite the presence in (D) of some terms that await analysis, I trust that the intent of (D) is obvious. The principle licenses us in accepting *something* because that something stands in *some* relation to epistemologically unproblematic statements that we are justified in accepting. Now let us ask for the grounds on which (D) rests. One natural answer is to propose:

(E) Nature is systematically unified.

The intuition behind the proposal is that methodological principles about the rational acceptability of theories, hypotheses, explanations, or whatever rest on deep structural facts about the world. So, to take a more readily comprehensible example, we might justify our preference for simple theories by echoing Newton: "Nature is wont to be simple and consonant unto itself." I suggest that Kant's denial that the ideas of pure reason have "objective validity" and his claim that those ideas have a legitimate regulative employment amounts to the thesis that (D) is a methodological principle that we are justified in following but that its justification does not rest on the correctness of (E). Kant would take (E) either to be a cryptic (and misleading) way of formulating (D) or as senseless.

We can achieve a clearer view of the position I have attributed to Kant by contrasting his approach with that of a realist about laws, kinds, and nomic necessities. If realists honor a methodological principle like (D) then their grounds for doing so must be as follows. Our goal in theory construction is to fathom the structure of nature, a structure that exists independently of us and of our theorizing. The preference for unified theoretical accounts of the observable phenomena is defensible only if such accounts accurately describe that independent structure. Hence, the rationality of that preference depends on contingent facts about the world, and there is only a contingent connection between theoretical understanding and unification. Realists believe that our understanding of nature is achieved by exposing the laws, kinds, causal connections, and so forth. *With luck* the search for unified theories will help achieve this understanding, but there is no guarantee that that should be so. A defense of (D) must rest on something like (E).

On the other hand, for those who adopt the Mach-Duhem approach to theories, (D) can only be justified as a subjective maxim for easing the human condition. Methodological principles divide into two types. Those with higher status direct us to prefer certain hypotheses because doing so will help us reach the goal of science, to wit the discovery of all the truths about the world. Since there are no truths about causal dependencies, nomic necessities, or natural kinds, introducing systematizations of Hume facts cannot be defended in this high status way. Preferring one systematization to another cannot reflect the fact that the favored systematization embodies the truths about laws, causes, and kinds. Second-rate methodological principles, like (D), enjoin us to suit our convenience, and they are justified on the purely pragmatic grounds that we find it easier to work with theories that are unified than with those that are not.

I claim that Kant's position lies between these two views. How is it possible to find a middle ground? Let us approach the question by considering a common presupposition of the polar positions. Realists and their Duhemian rivals agree that the goal of science is to discover the truth about nature: *Total Science* ought to contain the truth, the whole truth, and nothing but the truth. For the Realist, the task of understanding nature consists in fathoming special types of truth, trusts about natural kinds and their essential properties, lawlike connections, and causal dependencies. Followers of Mach and Duhem think that there are no such truths to fathom, and they draw the moral that there is no objective notion of science explanation at which inquiry aims. Kant's proposal, as I interpret it, is that there is an objective notion of scientific explanation, irreducible to the idea of setting forth a particular kind of truth, and that the demand for explanation is coequal in importance with the demand for truth.

From this perspective we can understand Kant's efforts, in the Appendix to the Ideal, to distinguish his position both from the view that the regulative principles offer substantive claims about nature (A644–645/B672–673; A666/B694; A668/B696) and from the thesis that they offer only heuristic advice (A651/B679; A653/B681; A661/B689). Particularly interesting are two passages in which Kant commits himself to the view that the search for unity is an objective demand on scientific inquiry. Opposing the notion that "this is merely an economical contrivance whereby reason seeks to save itself all possible trouble," he declares that "reason . . . does not here beg but command" (A653/B681). But on what basis can we attribute a power to command allegiance to a principle like (D)? or, to put the query another way, what would be the consequences of disobeying? Kant answers as follows:

> The law of reason which requires us to seek for this unity, is a necessary law, since without it we should have no reason at all, and without reason no coherent employment of the understanding, and in the absence of this no sufficient criterion of empirical truth. In order, therefore, to secure a criterion of empirical truth we have no option save to presuppose the systematic unity of nature as objectively valid and necessary. (A651/B679 amended translation)

As I understand Kant, he is asserting that the goal of achieving scientific explanations of natural phenomena is necessarily reached by integrating the phenomena into a unified system (there is a necessary connection between explaining and unifying), and this goal is of equal significance with the goal of setting forth the truths about nature *precisely because the latter goal makes no sense apart from the former.*

Here is one way to develop the latter point. Consider any empirical sentence of the form "*Pa*." The claim that "*Pa*" is true is to be understood as asserting that *"Pa"* occurs in *Total Science,* where the latter is constructed by following methodological rules which include the directive to achieve a systematic unification of the phenomena. The true empirical statements are just those that would be accepted by a being with an ideally comprehensive experience who followed the demands of reason, and these demands include a requirement to explain the appearances by unifying them. But the demand may be unsatisfied—or may be satisfied only incompletely—in the theories that we actually construct. Thus our actual theories may fall short of truth because they are couched in terms that would not figure in an ideal systematization of ideal experience. I suggest that this development presents the main outline of Kant's theory of truth and of scientific progress.

It is natural to reply that *"Pa"* is true just in case *"a"* refers to an object and *"P"* refers to a set and the former belongs to the latter. Both my imagined Realist and the followers of Mach and Duhem might suppose that truth consists in a correspondence between signs and elements of the structure of reality that exist independently of human cognition. The difference between these thinkers would consist in acceptance of a broader or narrower collection of elements of the structure of reality: for the Duhemians there are only Hume facts, for the Realists there are facts about kinds and causes as well. Kant's opposition to such positions rests ultimately on his denial that talk of correspondence between representations and an independently structured reality makes sense, and, I suggest, his alternative proposal for a theory of truth is to see truth as obtained in the ideal limit of inquiry. Part of what gives sense to the notion of the "ideal limit of inquiry" is the pursuit of certain goals—systematic unification prominent among them.

We can now return to our Kantian claims (A)–(C) and provide versions which replace the epistemological talk of rational acceptance with talk of truth and its cognates. So, for example, part of the ontological correlate of (A) can be formulated as follows:

(A*)  L is a law of nature just in case L is a statement playing role RL in an ideal systematization of the experience of an ideal subject whose experience was ideally comprehensive (and similar clauses for causal dependency and natural kinds).

Thus we achieve the outline of Kantian theory about law, causes, and natural necessities. As the result of the demands of inquiry, demands that are not separable from the naive suggestion that science aims at the truth, we are prepared to project an order of nature. Laws are statements that play a particular role in the system that would emerge from an ideally extended inquiry. Parallel characterizations apply for kinds and causal dependencies.

# III

Given the picture I have sketched, we can also resolve the tension between the test for conceptual legitimacy formulated early in *Critique,* and the claims about idealizations in the Appendix to the Ideal. Kant's considered view of the legitimacy of concepts is, I think, that exemplification in possible experience is neither necessary nor sufficient for the adequacy of a concept. The full criterion, which can only be formulated with the help of the machinery of the Dialectic, is that concepts are legitimate if they are employed in the systematization of experience achieved by *Total Science.* The exemplification test is simply a crude surrogate, used to raise the issue of legitimizing concepts, and its use does no harm because of the special concepts that Kant wishes to discuss. The Categories are special in that they must be exemplified throughout any possible experience and thus must figure in any systematization of any beliefs we can adopt.

We have removed some of the threatening inconsistencies that I noted above, but we have not yet disentangled Kant's claims about the necessity of empirical laws and his dark utterances about how such laws are "approximated to universality." I shall approach these problems by connecting my interpretation with other Kantian claims about the nature and practice of science.

So far I have discussed Kant's treatment of laws, causes, and natural necessity without considering the passage in which he offers his most celebrated account of these notions. Apparently, part of the famous reply to Hume consists in an attempt to show that we have to make judgments which involve a stronger-than-Humean notion of causation. I shall now try to show that the doctrine I have extracted from the Appendix to the Ideal and CJ completes a project begun in the Second Analogy.

Although the principle of the Second Analogy is the principle of determinism, Kant seems most interested in asserting what Hume denied; namely, that there is an element of objective necessity in causal statements. The focal Humean text is not the *Inquiry,* with its extended worry about the legitimacy of induction, but the critique of causation in the *Treatise,* available to Kant through Beattie's generous citations. The Second Analogy insists on the *necessity of* the causal relation and the *necessity in* the causal relation. Kant claims both

(a)  We have to make judgments of the form "A causes B."
(b)  "A causes B" asserts an objective necessary connection between A and B.

Both claims are at odds with Hume.

The discussion in Book III of the *Treatise* is extremely complex. The official project is to look for the impression on which our idea of causation is based. To see how Hume's critique might have posed a problem to which Kant felt that he had to reply, we need to abstract from the particular Humean theses about conceptual acquisition and identify the underlying epistemological puzzle. Hume's primary concern is to understand how, if at all, we are able to justify causal claims.

The puzzle begins with the recognition that we don't just look and see that a causal relation obtains. In Humean terms, causation isn't a simple idea. Hence judgments in the form "*A causes B*" must have a (nontrivial) analysis, and our epistemological base for asserting these judgments must be the recognition that the conditions described in the *analysans* are fulfilled. Hume's problem is to provide the analysis by completing the schema

"A causes B" is true if and only if . . .

with a description that is *epistemologically unproblematic.* Epistemologically unproblematic descriptions state facts that we can observe to obtain, Hume facts. A paradigm of a Hume fact would be the fact that a middle-sized object has an observable property at a particular time.

Some "analyses" lead us nowhere. Hume rightly rejects the idea of analyzing causal judgments by using the notions of force, power, or energy, which he dismisses as "mere synonyms." The synonymy is fine, but the notions on which the proposed analyses depend raise just the epistemological problems Hume is trying to resolve. Hume's further discussions suggest a number of more apparently acceptable approaches, whose merits and whose Humean pedigrees scholars have debated at length. I shall consider three which will prove helpful in understanding Kant's response.

The most obvious Humean account is the *regularity solution:* A causes B if and only if A-type events are regularly followed by B-type events. This solves the problem of gaining evidence for causal judgments by suggestion that these judgments are justified by observation of instances of succession, from which inductive inference leads us to affirm the conditions in the *analysans.* Causal judgments would thus be as epistemologically unworrying as inductive judgments.

An alternative is the *psychological connection* solution: A cause B if and only if A-type events are regularly followed by B-type events in such a way as to produce a psychological connection between them. On this approach, we could gain evidence for causal judgments by observing regular sequences and monitoring our reactions to them. Again, Hume would have given an analysis that renders the judgments epistemologically unproblematic.[4]

There is a third way to read Hume. Hume failed to solve the problem, but declared that it rested on a false presupposition. We have no rational basis for judgments of the form *"A causes B."* Such judgments do not have truth-conditions that can be stated in an acceptable empiricist vocabulary. They have *assertability* conditions of which we give the following account: we assert *"A causes B"* when we have evidence for "All As are followed by Bs" and when we psychologically connect As with Bs. Causal judgments are made by acquiring evidence for a regularity, and then advancing under the influence of custom.

Verificationists naturally protest that *"A causes B"* is empty noise unless we can specify conditions not simply for its assertability but for its *rational* assertability. But I don't think Hume was a verificationist of this type, and, more to the point, I don't think Kant took him to be one. On Hume's *dissolution* of the problem, our disposition to utter causal statements reflects a general feature of human nature (recall the title of the *Treatise!*), our susceptibility to custom. Hume's point would be that we can't provide any convincing reasons for our causal judgments; we can only indicate the influence of custom upon us. Had we been differently constituted we would not have behaved in this way— and there is nothing rational about our behavior that separates us from hypothetical beings who do not behave in this way.

When we set out Hume's two solutions and his dissolution, it is possible to see how Kant's claims (a) and (b) oppose the Humean treatment. Both the regularity solution and the psychological connection solution are inconsistent with (b), the former because it attributes no necessity to causation, the latter because it attributes a merely subjective necessity. The dissolution is incompatible with (a), in that it suggests that experience is possible for rational beings who do not employ a concept of causation that carries an element of objective necessity.

Because his discussion is extremely general, and because he does not have the resources for making modal distinctions which are routine for us, it is hard to specify the exact sense in which Kant takes causal judgments to carry an element of necessity. Nonetheless, we can fathom the main lines of his approach, and this will suffice to show how the ideas of the last section relate to the achievement of the Second Analogy. A commonplace causal judgment—for example, "The heating of the water caused it to boil"—seems to assert the existence of two events and a causal connection between them. The problem is to understand what modal statement is implied by the conjunct asserting the causal relation.

An obvious suggestion is that any statement asserting a causal relation implies some universal conditional. If the conditional figuring here is the material conditional, then, in essence, we shall achieve Hume's regularity solution, and causal claims will carry no element of necessity. An alternative is to propose that assertions of causal relations imply claims of form

$$N(x)(Fx \supset Gx)$$

Where N is a necessity operator. But Kant cannot suppose that the operator captures the sense of "necessarily" as he uses it throughout the *Critique,* for he explicitly denies the necessity (in this sense) of the regularities corresponding to particular laws of nature (A207/B252). I suggest that he views causal judgments as implying generalizations that *legislate for unactualized possibilities.* In other words, the implied generalizations involve conditionals that are stronger than the material conditional, and, in consequence, these generalizations sustain counterfactuals. The details of this general idea can be articulated in a number of very different ways, and I shall suppose that some development of it underlies the theses about universal rules and necessary connections that permeate the Second Analogy.

We can now explain how the Second Analogy constitutes a reply to Hume. Hume's puzzle began by suggesting that some statements (those stating Hume facts) are epistemologically unproblematic and asking for an analysis of causal judgments that would reveal them also to be epistemologically unproblematic. Kant does not respond by offering the desired analysis. Instead, he claims that the puzzle presupposes—falsely—that we can conceive of beings who discuss Hume facts without making any causal judgments. According to Kant, if we are to make the judgments that Hume takes to be unproblematic, then we must be able to assert statements involving strong conditionals (the allegedly problematic elements that underlie causal judgments). Specifically, if we can make judgments about the objective time-relations among states of affairs, and thus make judgments about objective events, then we have to be able to assert universal statements involving strong conditionals.

Kant's discussion is complicated by the fact that his official principle is the principle of determinism (a principle that Hume had not denied!), but he tries to argue for the conclusion just noted throughout the Second Analogy (A195/B240; A197/B242; A202–203/B246–247). The first version of the argument is as explicit as any. After offering the famous (notorious?) example of watching a ship move downstream, Kant continues:

> In this case, therefore, we must derive the subjective succession of apprehension from the objective succession of appearances. Otherwise the order of apprehension is entirely undetermined and does not distinguish one appearance from another. Since the subjective succession by itself is altogether arbitrary, it does not prove anything as to the manner in which the manifold is connected in the object. The objective succession will therefore consist in that order of the manifold of appearance according to which, in conformity with a rule, the apprehension of that which happens follows upon the apprehension of that which precedes. Thus only can I be justified in asserting, not merely of my apprehension, but of the appearance itself, that a succession is to be met with in it. This is only another way of saying that I cannot arrange the apprehension otherwise than in this very succession.
>
> In conformity with such a rule there must lie in that which precedes an event the condition of a rule according to which this event invariably and necessarily follows. (A193/B238)

I shall not plunge into the details of how the ship example is supposed to work. What seems to me uncontroversial is that Kant argues that we must make judgments involving some kind of necessity—I interpret them as universal judgments involving strong conditionals—if we are to make judgments about objective events. The reply to Hume, then, is that the language Hume sees as epistemologically unproblematic is parasitic on our use of the very notions whose employment is to be justified.

Kant's result is radically nonconstructive. In essence he says: "You Humeans worry about justifying causal judgments, but you take it for granted that you can be justified in talking about events (drawing the distinction between events and states of affairs). I show you that you could not have the latter justification unless you were justified in making the judgments you worry about. The human predicament could not be the Humean predicament." Although this response implies, given Humean premises, that there must be some justification for our claims about causes and counterfactual-sustaining generalizations, Kant does not say explicitly what that justification is. Indeed, his response might even be viewed as making the skeptical challenge worse. Shouldn't we now wonder how we obtain justification for a broader class of claims than those Hume called into question?

I suggest that the Appendix to the Ideal completes the work of the Second Analogy by explaining how we are justified in distinguishing merely accidental regularities from those that are endowed with counterfactual-sustaining force. The distinction is to emerge from our efforts to systematize our beliefs in accordance with the principle of unification. Certain claims come to be regarded as lawlike because they play a particular role in the systematization of belief. This is the constructive rejoinder to Hume's deep concern about the justification for causal judgments, ascriptions of natural necessity, identification of laws of nature, and so forth.

Three points deserve attention. First, we can now understand more clearly why Kant insists in the Appendix that, without the regulative employment of the ideas, there could be no coherent employment of the understanding and no criterion of empirical truth. The thesis of the Second Analogy is that there is no justifying straightforward empirical claims, descriptions of Hume facts, without justification of causal claims. Since the latter are to be justified through the incorporation of statements within a unified system, the justification of ordinary empirical claims depends on our following the principle of systematic unification.

Second, we can now see that it was somewhat misleading to present the principle of systematic unification through the formulation (D), for we can give no sense to the idea that people accept a collection of sentences stating Hume facts without adopting *any* systematization of their beliefs. Rather, the methodological principle must be construed as a directive for choosing among rival systematizations. . . .

Third, it is possible to give a straightforward account of how each of us comes to have the ability to make causal judgments. We do not go through any explicit process of systematizing our beliefs and attempting to maximize the unity of the system. We absorb from our predecessors the order of nature that they have projected, so that, from the beginning of our own discussions of the world of experience, we tacitly operate with claims about causal dependencies and natural kinds that have been generated by the systems of our ancestors. Our justifications are thus parasitic on the history of attempts to construct a systematic unification of human experience.

To summarize: the Second Analogy shows only that there must be some justification for statements involving notions that are problematic from a Humean perspective (nomic necessity, causal dependence, strong conditionals, and so forth) if we are justified in stating Hume facts. This leaves open the question of how we are actually able to achieve justification either for the problematic statements or for those statements, previously taken to be unproblematic, that turn out to presuppose the difficult notions. On my interpretation, this is precisely the topic taken up in the Appendix to the Ideal, and, I claim, consideration of the Second Analogy enables us to see more clearly why Kant makes what initially seem like extravagant claims for the indispensability of the ideas of reason.

## Notes

1. P. Duhem, *The Aim and Structure of Physical Theory,* P. Wiener, trans. (Princeton, N.J.: Princeton University Press, 1954), p. 21.

2. A306/B362–363. I employ the Kemp Smith translation of *The Critique of Pure Reason,* with the usual pagination references to the first (A) edition and the second (B) edition. I employ the Bernard translation of *The Critique of Judgement* (hereafter CJ).

3. Nicholas Rescher, "Lawfulness as Mind-Dependent," in N. Rescher, ed. *Essays in Honor of Carl G. Hempel* (Dordrecht; D. Reidel, 1970), p. 187.

4. In an intriguing section of the Treatise (Book, I, part iii, Section XVI), Hume offers some "rules by which to judge of causes and effects." Given the "psychological connection" interpretation, these can be regarded as principles for adjudicating in cases where our inclinations pull in different directions. Thus Hume would be groping toward the notion of a systematization of our

views about causes, and, in these terms, Kant's position (on the interpretation elaborated here) could be seen as attributing to such rules (such systematization) a greater force than Hume would have allowed. They are transformed from helpful hints for the perplexed into necessary conditions on rational inquiry.

# 11

# Kant's Compatibilism

*Allen W. Wood*

On the issue of free will and determinism, philosophers are usually categorized either as "compatibilists" or as "incompatibilists." Compatibilists hold that our actions may be determined by natural causes and yet also be free in the sense necessary for moral agency and responsibility. Freedom and determinism are compatible. Incompatibilists hold that if our actions are determined to take place by natural causes, then free agency and moral responsibility are illusions. Freedom and determinism are incompatible.

Kant's views on many issues do not fit neatly into the customary pigeonholes, and the free will issue is no exception. He is probably most often regarded as an incompatibilist, and not without justification. Certainly he repudiates Leibniz's compatibilism, which (Kant says) allows us no more than "the freedom of a turnspit (AK.V: 97 [*Critique of Practical Reason*]).[1] Yet Kant himself holds that not only are our actions determined by the causal mechanism of nature but also that they are free. The basic question, he says, is "whether regarding the same effect which is determined by nature, freedom can nevertheless be present or whether freedom is wholly excluded by such an exceptionable rule" (A536/B564). In answering this question in favor of the former alternative, Kant's avowed purpose is "to unite nature and freedom," to "remove the apparent contradiction between the mechanism of nature and freedom," to show that "causality from freedom at least does not contradict nature" (A537/B565; AK.V: 97; A558/B587). But these are precisely the aims of compatibilism. When we consider all Kant's views together, it is tempting to say that he wants to show not only the compatibility of freedom and determinism, but also the compatibility of compatibilism and incompatibilism.

In brief, Kant's theory is that our actions may be simultaneously free and causally determined because we belong to two worlds; this means that our existence can be viewed from two different standpoints. We are, on the one hand, part of nature, of what Kant calls the sensible or phenomenal world. We are objects accessible to empirical observation and natural science. The phenomenal world includes everything as it is subject to our conditions of sense perception and ordered experience. These conditions include space, time, and strict causal connectedness according to necessary laws. From this standpoint, our actions are causally determined. If this were the only standpoint from which we could view ourselves, freedom would be impossible.

Kant, however, holds that nature is only a realm of appearances or things as they fall under the conditions of empirical knowledge. Everything in the phenomenal world, including ourselves, also has an existence in itself, not subject to those conditions. This other realm, that of things in themselves, cannot be known by us, but it can be thought, through our pure understanding, as a noumenal or intelligible world. Because we cannot know our noumenal selves, we cannot know whether they possess the freedom our phenomenal selves lack. Yet because space, time, and causal order are on Kant's theory necessary attributes only of the phenomenal world, there is no way to rule out the possibility that the noumenal self is free. This leaves it open to us to postulate or presuppose noumenal freedom as the metaphysical condition of our moral agency, with which our consciousness of moral obligation acquaints us. Thus when we view ourselves as objects of empirical science, we regard our actions as causally determined and not free. On the other hand, when we assume the role of moral agents, we "transpose ourselves into members of intelligible world," regard our existence as not subject to the empirical conditions of space, time, or natural causality, and think of ourselves as free (AK.IV: 453 [*Groundwork of the Metaphysics of Morals*]).

Kant's compatibilism is of a most unusual sort. The usual intention behind compatibilism is to deny that there really is any deep metaphysical problem about free will, to suppress the free will problem at the least possible metaphysical cost. Most compatibilists try to show how free choices may be comfortably accommodated in the chain of natural causes, so as to present a unified picture of ourselves as both moral agents and objects of scientific observation. Kant's compatibilism, however, is based on the aggressively metaphysical distinction between phenomena and noumena; far from unifying our view of ourselves, it says that freedom and determinism are compatible only because the self as free moral agent belongs to a different world from that of the self as natural object. (Norman Kretzmann has commented to me that this may be likened to saying that a married couple is compatible, but only as long as they live in separate houses.)

I venture to say that Kant's solution to the free will problem strikes nearly everyone who has ever studied it as thoroughly unsuccessful, a metaphysical monstrosity that gives us a far-fetched if not downright incoherent account of our moral agency. At any rate, that is what I used to think. I am still in partial agreement with those critics who find problems in reconciling Kant's account of our free agency with some of the more commonsense features of his own ethical theory. And I share with more orthodox compatibilists the hope that there may exist a simpler and less counterintuitive solution to the free will problem. Still, I am more impressed with the successes of Kant's theory in solving the problem it sets for itself than I am appalled by its shortcomings. As we shall see, the free will problem arises for Kant in a form in some respects idiosyncratic to Kant, and the problem for him is unusually acute. The causal determinism in which Kant believes is very strict, and the conditions for moral responsibility set by Kantian ethics are very strong. Further, Kant's moral psychology blocks the only simple and natural sort of compatibilist solution. What I find quite surprising is that Kant does succeed in reconciling freedom and determinism in the context of his philosophy, and that Kant's compatibilism involves no greater revision of our commonsense view of our agency than it does.

## Kant's Concept of Freedom

Kant distinguishes between 'transcendental' (or 'cosmological') freedom and 'practical' freedom. Transcendental freedom is a purely metaphysical concept, the concept of a certain sort of causality. Transcendental freedom is "the faculty of beginning a state spontaneously or from oneself" (A533/B561). A transcendentally free being is one that causes a state of the world without being subject in its causality to any further causes; that is, a "first cause," or an unconditioned beginner of a causal chain. Practical freedom, on the other hand, is free agency; it is what we ascribe to ourselves when we think of ourselves as morally responsible for what we do.

Regarding practical freedom, Kant distinguishes two concepts: a

"negative" concept and a "positive" one. Practical freedom in the negative sense is "the independence of our will [*Willkür*] from necessitation through impulses of sensibility" (A534/B562). We are free in this
sense if we are capable of resisting our sensuous desires, of acting contrary to their dictates or at least without having them as motives of our
action. Kant apparently believes that nonhuman animals altogether
lack the capacity to resist sensuous impulses, that the action of an animal is always the direct result of some sensuous impulse. When such
an impulse occurs in an animal, it cannot fail to act as the impulse
dictates. It has no faculty of countermanding the impulse or suspend-
ing action on it in order to deliberate and weigh different desires
against each other. Kant calls the animal's will an *arbitrium brutum*
[dull or unreasoned choice], in contrast to the human *arbitrium sen-
sitivum sed liberum* [sensuous but free choice], which is affected by
sensuous impulses but not necessitated by them (A534/B562).

This concept of practical freedom is "negative" because it describes
the free will in terms of the way it does *not* operate. Kant's positive
conception of practical freedom, on the other hand, describes the free
will in terms of what it *can* do. Kant believes that unlike the brutes,
human beings have the power to resist particular sensuous impulses
and the power to deliberate about which ones to satisfy and how best
to satisfy them. In addition, Kant ascribes to us the power to act from
a wholly nonsensuous or a priori motive, to conform our will to a moral
law self-given by our own reason. Freedom in the positive sense is thus
the capacity to act from this nonsensuous motive, "the capacity to will
a priori" (AK.IV: 129). This positive sense of freedom is derived, of
course, from Kant's moral theory. In general, we may be held responsible for our actions only to the extent that we have the capacity to do
what morality commands of us. Kantian morality commands that we act
according to a law we give ourselves a priori. Consequently, practical
freedom consists in the capacity to be motivated by such a law; it is
"the authentic legislation of pure and as such practical reason" (AK.V:
33).

The free will problem arises for Kant because he believes that practical freedom requires transcendental freedom and that there is no room
in the causal mechanism of nature for a transcendentally free being
(A534/B562). All causes in the natural world are sensible or empirical
and all necessitate their effects. Consequently, if our actions were determined by them, then they would be necessitated by something sensuous (so that we would lack practical freedom in the negative sense)

and there would be no room for a nonsensuous motive for our actions (so that we would lack practical freedom in the positive sense). Practical freedom requires that we be able to determine our actions entirely from within ourselves, through our own legislative reason. Natural causes, however, belong to an endless regressive chain in which there is no spontaneous or first cause. We can think of ourselves as practically free, therefore, only by thinking of our actions as subject to a transcendentally free cause lying outside nature.

Because practical freedom, the freedom required for moral responsibility, must involve the capacity to do what morality demands of us, it is obvious that any account of practical freedom must depend on some account of the demands of morality. In Kant's philosophy morality has an especially close association with practical freedom. For Kant, morality is autonomy; it is the conformity of the will to a self-given law of reason. Acting morally, then, is not merely one thing among others that a practically free being can do, but it is the peculiar function of morality to actualize practical freedom.

It has seemed to some of Kant's critics, such as Henry Sidgwick, that an insoluble problem is involved in Kant's doctrine in that only autonomous or moral action actualizes practical freedom.[2] For in that case, apparently only moral or autonomous action is free action, while immoral or heteronomous actions are all unfree. If only actions motivated by pure reason are free, then actions motivated by sensuous desires must be necessitated by the mechanism of nature. Thus it seems that Kant is committed to saying that we are morally responsible only for moral or autonomous actions and that no one can be held responsible for immoral or heteronomous actions.

This problem is illusory, however. If Kant did hold that our immoral or heteronomous actions were determined by natural causes, then he would have to hold that these actions are unfree; that the will that performs them is an *arbitrium brutum*. But Kant's actual view is that since our will is free, our heteronomous actions are performed from sensuous motives without being necessitated by them. Even when we act from sensuous motives, we do so as having the capacity to be moved by the a priori law of reason; we act as practically free beings, and hence are responsible for what we do. If our actions were sensuously necessitated, as by natural determinism, then it would follow that they are all performed from sensuous motives. The converse of this does not hold, however. Not every action performed from sensuous motives must be naturally necessitated. The human will, according to

Kant, is sensuously "affected" but not sensuously "necessitated" (A534/B562). . . .

It is true that when Kant describes practical freedom in the positive sense as "the legislation of pure practical reason," he seems to imply that only autonomous or moral actions are truly free actions. Careful attention to his language shows that for him practical freedom consists in the *capacity* for autonomous action and can exist even when this capacity is not exercised. Thus Kant describes practical freedom in the negative sense as "that property of [the will's] causality by which it *can* be effective independently of foreign causes" (AK.IV: 446, italics added). Again, he says it is "not being *necessitated* to act by any sensuous determining ground," implying that a free being may be motivated by sensuous grounds without being necessitated by them (AK.VI: 226, italics added). Freedom in the positive sense, he says, is "the *power* [*The Doctrine of Virtue*] of pure reason to be of itself practical" (AK.VI: 213–4, italics added). And he defines the free will (*Willkür*) as "the will that *can* be determined by pure reason" (AK.VI: 213, italics altered). Further, "freedom of the will is the *capacity* to determine oneself to actions independently of a subjective cause or sensuous impulses" (AK.XXVIII: Part 2, 129, italics added). We are practically free and morally responsible for our actions whenever we act as having the power or capacity for autonomous action, whether or not that power is exercised or actualized in what we do. Kant's view is that except "in tenderest childhood, or insanity, or in great sadness which is only a species of insanity," we always do possess the power to act autonomously, even if we seldom exercise it (AK.XXVIII: Part 1, 182). Autonomous actions are "freer" than heteronomous ones in the sense that autonomous actions are an exercise of freedom—that is, they actualize the capacity in which practical freedom consists. In heteronomous actions, we fail to exercise our freedom (our power to act autonomously) insofar as we submit ourselves to the motivation of natural impulses. This is wholly different from action of an *arbitrium brutum*, which altogether lacks the power to determine itself independently of the sensuous impulses on which it acts.

Philosophers distinguish two senses of freedom that may be relevant to moral responsibility: the 'liberty of spontaneity' and the 'liberty of indifference'. Loosely speaking, we are free in the sense of spontaneity if we are the cause of our own actions, and free in the sense of indifference if we could have done otherwise than we in fact do. Kant's theory of practical freedom appears to involve both spontaneity and indifference, at least in certain specific or qualified ways. Autonomous action is spontaneous in a very strong sense, because our acts have their determining grounds entirely a priori in our reason, and are wholly independent of all external causes. But even heteronomous action is spontaneous in quite a strong sense. Although heteronomous acts are motivated by sensuous desires, which Kant regards as 'foreign' to our rational will, they are not causally necessitated by such desires. As free agents, we act from sensuous motives only by incorporating them into our maxim, the principle adopted freely by our will. Practical freedom is always spontaneity because it requires transcendental freedom, the capacity to produce an effect without being determined by any prior or external cause.

Kant also ascribes a form of indifference to the human will. He even defines will (*Willkür*) generally as "a power to do or refrain at one's discretion" (AK.VI: 213). Clearly every one of our heteronomous actions could have been other than what it is, since it is performed by a being who has the capacity to act autonomously. Further, because our will is sensuously affected, the possibility always exists that we will fail to exercise our freedom. Hence every one of our autonomous actions also could have been other than what it is.

Kant, however, flatly refuses to define freedom in terms of this indifference. Freedom is the power to choose according to legislative reason. According to Kant, "freedom cannot be located in the fact that the rational subject can make a choice which conflicts with his legislating reason, even if experience proves often enough that this happens (AK.VI: 226). For Kant, freedom consists in a one-way difference, so to speak. That is, freedom consists in the ability to act autonomously even when we do not, but it does not consist in the possibility of acting heteronomously, even if this possibility always does exist for us. If an action is performed from sensuous motives, then it is a free action only if the agent could have acted instead on a priori motives. If a being acts on a priori motives, however, it may be free even if there is no possibility that it could have failed to act as it does. A free will that altogether lacks this indifference is what Kant calls a "holy will," for example, the divine will:

> [The capacity always to act according to reason must certainly be in God, since sensuous impulses are impossible to him.] One might raise the objection that God cannot decide otherwise than he does, and so he does not act freely but out of the necessity of his nature. . . . But in God it is

not due to the necessity of his nature that he can decide only as he does. Rather it is true freedom in God that he decides only what is suitable to his highest understanding. [AK.XXVIII: Part 2, 132]

According to Kant's theory, practical freedom is the power to act from a priori principles. A being may have this power even if there is no possibility of failing to exercise it and hence no possibility of acting other than it does. Such a being is free, and therefore responsible for its inevitably rational acts.

Kant even goes so far as to say that "only freedom with regard to the inner legislation of reason is really a power; the possibility of deviating from legislative reason is a lack of power" (AK.VI: 227). Here again we must avoid the mistake of thinking that for Kant the failure to exercise our power to will autonomously is the same as the failure to have that power, hence the same as the failure to be free. What Kant means is that the possibility of deviating from legislative reason is not a power of any sort but is due instead to a certain sort of weakness or lack of power. This view is quite defensible. Not every possibility is a power. Some possibilities, in fact, are due to a lack of power. The human will has the power to act autonomously and this power is its freedom. If it acts heteronomously, it still has this power, but it has failed to exercise it. Such a failure is not due to a lack of freedom but rather is a failure of execution, a failure to exercise the freedom we have. And this failure is due in turn to a certain weakness or lack of power, leading to a lapse in exercising our freedom. Moral weakness, which makes it possible for our action to deviate from legislative reason, is a lack of power, but it is not a lack of that power in which freedom consists.

Consider a parallel case. An indifferent swimmer may have the power to save himself if he falls into deep water. But he has no power, only a possibility, of drowning in the same eventuality. Although he has the power to swim, he may drown if he does not exercise that power effectively, due (say) to confusion or panic. In the latter case, his possibility of drowning is due to a kind of weakness or lack of power, though not to a lack of the power to swim. The indifference of the human will, on Kant's theory, is rather like the indifference of this swimmer. The swimmer has the power to swim, which he may exercise and save himself, or he may fail to exercise that power and drown, due to a weakness or lack of power leading to a failure of execution. The moral agent has freedom, the power to act autonomously, and may exercise that freedom by conforming one's will to the moral law, or one may fail to exercise it and follow sensuous desires, due to a weakness or lack of power in one's moral character leading to a failure of execution. The possibility of deviating from legislative reason is thus due to a lack of power and not to a lack of freedom.

We may now understand how the free will problem for Kant is different from the free will problem faced by most incompatibilists. Kant does *not* hold in general that freedom is incompatible with causal determination or even necessitation of the free being's actions. As we have just seen, Kant holds that a holy will is free even though its acts are necessitated, because they are necessitated from within by reason rather than by the sensuous impulses that are foreign to our rational nature. In this respect Kant's view is much closer to that of some compatibilists (such as Spinoza and Leibniz) than it is to that of standard, hardline incompatibilists, who see freedom as incompatible with any sort of causation or necessitation.

Kant does not believe, then, that freedom is incompatible with causation generally, but only that it is incompatible with *natural* causation, with the sort of causation found to act on the will within the realm of appearance. He believes this for two overlapping reasons, one of them derived from his moral philosophy and the other from his moral psychology. First, Kant believes that the moral motive, action on which is alone an exercise of freedom, is an a priori motive, and therefore one that cannot be given to us through nature or the causes acting in nature. Second, he holds the complementary belief that the only natural causes that do act on the will are sensuous impulses, motivation by which precludes motivation by reason. In short, the free will problem arises for Kant because he is a thoroughgoing psychological hedonist about all the natural causes that might act on our will. He holds that empirical psychology is excluded in principle from understanding all rational deliberation and all action on the motive of reason. This means that the free will problem would not arise in the same form for someone who is less of a crude Benthamite about the empirical psychology of motivating and allows for the possibility of accounting for rational deliberation and action through natural causes. A standard compatibilist response to the free will problem in its Kantian form seems open to any such person.

## Freedom and Nature

Let us now turn to Kant's attempt to solve his problem, to reconcile freedom with the mechanism of nature given the strictures of his moral philosophy and moral psychology. First we must clarify what Kant does and does not intend to establish. Kant does not pretend to prove that we are free or to provide arguments in favor of any speculative doctrine he believes must be true if freedom and determinism are to be compatible. No such doctrines, he holds, could be either provable or disprovable. What Kant means to show is only that, as far as we can prove, freedom and determinism may be compatible. Kant is fond of forensic analogies. Let us use one here. Kant's role regarding freedom is somewhat like a defense attorney's role regarding his client. Because practical freedom is presupposed by morality, we may assume that freedom is innocent until proven guilty, that the burden of proof lies on those who would undermine our moral consciousness by claiming that we are not free. In confronting the prosecution's evidence against his client, a defense attorney may exploit this fact about the burden of proof by concocting a plausible theory explaining the allegedly incriminating evidence. The attorney need not show that his theory is the correct one, only that it has enough plausibility to introduce a reasonable doubt concerning the prosecution's theory. Likewise, in defending our freedom, Kant concocts a metaphysical theory which, if true, saves our practical freedom despite the fact that our actions are determined by natural causes. Kant does not need to show that this metaphysical theory is correct; indeed, he frankly admits that he cannot. But neither, he claims, can the opponent of freedom refute the theory. Kant rests his defense of freedom on his claim.

The problem Kant faces is formidable. As we have just seen, Kant holds that the human will has freedom, which is the power to resist sensuous impulses and to act from nonsensuous motives. At the same time, Kant also holds that human actions fall under the unexceptionable law of natural causality:

> All the actions of man in appearance are so determined . . . according to the order of nature that if we could investigate all the appearances of his will as to their grounds, then there would not be a single human action we could not predict with certainty and be able to know as necessary from its preceding conditions. [A550/B578]

Kant hopes to save himself from an open contradiction here by distinguishing two standpoints for viewing our actions, each involving a different sort of cause to which the action may be attributed. It is possible, he says, "to regard an event on the one side as a merely natural effect, yet on the other side as an effect of freedom" (A543/B571). As an appearance or phenomenon, the human self plays a natural causal role in the production of its actions, which are events in nature and appearances as well.

> Every efficient cause, however, must have a *character*, i.e. a law of its causality, without which it would not be a cause. And then we as subjects in the world of sense have first an *empirical* character, through which our actions as appearances stand in thoroughgoing connection with other appearances according to constant laws of nature. [A539/B567]

We also have an existence in itself as noumenon or intelligible subject, outside the conditions of sensible nature, unknowable but still thinkable through pure understanding. In this subject we "must make room for an *intelligible character* through which it is the cause of those same actions as appearances, but which is not itself an appearance and stands under no conditions of sensibility" (A539/B567). As effects of our empirical character, our actions are necessitated by natural causes and hence unfree. But as effects of our intelligible character, it is possible that the same actions are produced by a transcendentally free cause, which is not necessitated by anything sensuous and is capable of autonomous or a priori volition.

It is not immediately clear how this theory is supposed to reconcile freedom and determinism, or even how it can be self-consistent. If our actions are indeed causally determined by natural events, then they are apparently necessitated by sensuous impulses acting on our empirical character. From this alone it seems to follow that our actions are unfree. How can anything that might be true about our actions from another standpoint render these same actions free? How can it remove the necessitation of our actions by sensuous causes or restore to us the capacity of acting from a priori motives, which this necessitation appears once and for all to preclude?

Two problems arise here; one concerns the liberty of spontaneity and the other the liberty of indifference. First, practical freedom is the capacity to will autonomously, to act from a priori motives. How is it possible for us to have this capacity if a natural or empirical cause can always be cited for what we do? Second, moral responsibility requires that for any heteronomous action we perform, we must have the capacity to act other than we in fact do. How is this possible if every one of our actions is in principle predictable and knowable as "necessary from its preceding conditions"?

I believe Kant is aware of both problems and attempts to solve them. Let us consider each attempt in turn.

## Empirical Causality and Intelligible Causality

Regarding the problem of spontaneity, I believe that a careful consideration of Kant's texts reveals that according to the theory he is proposing, our free actions are *never* produced by natural causality in the way they would have to be if only natural causality pertained to them. Kant holds that the two sorts of causality do not merely exist side by side but that, at least in the case of human actions, phenomenal causality is grounded in noumenal causality. He asks:

> Is it not possible that although for every effect in appearance a connection with its cause according to natural laws is indeed required, this empirical causality itself, without in the least interrupting its connection with natural causes, can be an effect of a causality which is not empirical but intelligible? [A544/B572]

More specifically, Kant holds that although our actions are causally determined in time by our empirical character and other natural events, this empirical character itself is the effect—or, as he also says, the "sensible schema" (A553/B581)—of the intelligible character, which is freely determined by us outside empirical conditions. Kant says that "reason has causality in regard to appearance; its action can be called free, since it is exactly determined and necessary in its empirical causality (the mode of sense). For the latter is once again determined in the intelligible character (the mode of thought)" (A551/B579).

Empirical causality regarding human actions is an effect of intelligible causality, which (on the theory Kant is proposing) is transcendentally free. Hence empirical causality, on this theory, does not involve the sensuous necessitation of actions, as it appears to do when we ignore its intelligible ground. Practical freedom, says Kant,

> presupposes that . . . an action's cause in appearance is not *so* determining as to preclude a causality lying in our will, a causality which, independently of these natural causes and even contrary to their force and influence, can bring about something determined in the temporal order

according to empirical laws, and thus can begin a series of events wholly
of itself. [A534/B562]

Again, "If appearances were things in themselves, then freedom could
not be saved. For then nature would be the complete and self-sufficient
determining cause of every event" (A537/B565). Kant's theory apparently holds that because appearances are not things in themselves, nature is *not* the complete and self-sufficient cause of events, at least
not of human actions. Rather, the complete and self-sufficient cause of
actions is our free will, located in the intelligible world. Nature, in the
form of sensuous impulses, enters into the production of our actions
only insofar as we freely permit sensuous motives to be substituted for
a priori rational principles in determining our choices. The free causality of the noumenal self, Kant says, "is not merely a concurrence, but
complete in itself, even when sensuous incentives are not for it but
wholly against it" (A555/B583).

It is tempting to describe Kant's theory by saying that for this theory
the natural or empirical causes of actions, their causes in the world of
appearance, are not real causes but only apparent causes; furthermore,
that on this theory everything in the phenomenal world goes on, by a
sort of preestablished harmony, just as if our actions were caused by
antecedent natural events, but in reality their causes lie outside nature
altogether, in a free will hovering above nature in the intelligible world.
I believe, however, that Kant would reject this description as a distortion or caricature of his theory. Kant's principle of empirical causality
says that every event in time is determined by antecedent events according to necessary laws. For Kant every human action does conform
to this principle. This conformity to natural laws entitles the empirical
events upon which our actions necessarily follow to be called the empirical causes of those actions: nothing more is, or could possibly be,
required for them to deserve that title. They are not, therefore, merely
apparent causes, but the real causes of our actions insofar as they fall
under the mechanism of nature. The antecedent events are not "complete" and "self-sufficient" causes, however, because the causality of
human actions can be viewed from another standpoint, that is, as the
effects of freedom.

Although Kant's position here is thoroughly self-consistent, it reveals
something noteworthy and possibly suspicious about his conception
of causality. The concept of cause is bound up with that of causal efficacy, a notion David Hume variously, and aptly, called a cause's

"power," "energy," "force," or "that very circumstance in the cause, by which it is enabled to produce the effect."[3] Regarding this notion philosophers have exhibited two general tendencies. One tendency, which we may call the Aristotelian, is to treat causal efficacy as a property of substances or agents and to regard it as a primitive notion, unanalyzable but built into our basic understanding of how things work. The other, which we may call the Humean tendency, is to treat causal efficacy as a property of events or states of the world and to try to analyze it in terms of some relation between these events allegedly simpler or more accessible to our knowledge than that of causal efficacy itself. The two leading candidates for such an analysis have been the relation of constant conjunction between similar events and the conformity of events to natural laws governing their temporal order.

Kant does not opt unambiguously for either tendency. He wants to treat causality in the sensible world as the conformity of events to laws determining their order in time. Kant's disagreement with Hume about whether these laws are knowably necessary is a disagreement between two philosophers who both follow the Humean tendency regarding natural causality. Kant, however, wants to reserve for himself a more Aristotelian notion of causal efficacy, to be ascribed to free agents as members of the intelligible world. If we agree that Kant's theory at this point is coherent, then it seems to provide a counterexample to the extreme Humean view that we can conceive of causal efficacy *only* as some feature of the temporal order of events. For the theory says that our actions are determined in the temporal order by natural laws, but the causal efficacy responsible for them does not lie in the temporal series at all, but outside it in the intelligible world. If we can imagine this at all, then it suffices to show both that we can conceive of events as lawfully ordered in time without attributing causal efficacy to those events upon which others lawfully follow, and that we have a notion of causal efficacy which has nothing whatever to do with the temporal order of events and the laws governing it. For this reason, stubborn Humeans may reject Kant's theory as unintelligible and his solution to the free will problem along with it. I will not pursue this issue here. But we have seen that if we assume Kant's views about causality are coherent, we must agree that his theory succeeds in showing how natural causality could be compatible with the spontaneity of the human will in its intelligible character.[4]

## Timeless Agency

There remains the problem of indifference, of showing how we can have the capacity to act autonomously even when we do not so act, and even when our heteronomous actions are causally determined to take place. Kant admits that insofar as we conceive ourselves as empirical agents, who cause our actions through the temporal flow of events, we cannot conceive of ourselves as able to do other than we do. Every one of our actions is strictly determined by the temporal series that precedes it, and this series reaches far into the past, before our birth. "Since the past is no longer in my power, every action which I perform is necessary because of determining grounds which are not in my power. This means that *at the point in time when I act* I am never free" (AK.V: 94, italics added). Time, however, is for Kant only a form of sensibility; only as phenomena or appearances are we necessarily in time. As noumena or things in themselves we are subject neither to time nor to the law of causality which goes along with it. As free agents, according to the theory Kant proposes, we are timeless beings.

Kant here presupposes another controversial metaphysical doctrine, that of timeless eternity. The attribute of timelessness, which some theologians ascribe to God alone, Kant's theory must ascribe to every one of us insofar as we are transcendentally free. Some philosophers doubt that we can make sense of the notion of timeless eternity. Some object especially to the idea that a timeless being might be the cause of temporal events, and in particular they object to the idea that it can be thought of as causing events that occur at different times. Clearly, if we cannot form a coherent notion of timeless eternity or a coherent account of a timeless being causing events occurring at different times, then Kant's solution to the problem of freedom is untenable. Once again, however, I will not try to settle this difficult metaphysical issue here. The point I want to investigate is whether, granted that such an account can be coherently formulated, Kant is capable of reconciling natural determinism with the indifference necessary for moral agency.

How is the timelessness of the noumenal self supposed to safeguard our ability to do otherwise than we in fact do? In order to answer this question, we must look more closely at Kant's metaphysical theory of the case, and in particular at the way in which our timeless existence as noumena is supposed to produce our actions, which unfold in the course of time. In the moral subject's noumenal existence, Kant says,

Nothing precedes the determination of his will; every action and, in general, every changing determination of his existence, according to the inner sense, even the entire history of his existence as a sensuous being, is seen in the consciousness of his intelligible existence as only a consequence, not as a determining ground of his causality as a noumenon. From this point of view, a rational being can rightly say of any unlawful action which he has done that he could have left it undone, even if as an appearance it was sufficiently determined in the past and thus far was inescapably necessary. For this action and everything in the past which determined it belong to a single phenomenon of his character, which he himself creates. [AK.V: 97–98]

Kant's theory seems to be the following. Events in time follow a necessary order, as determined by their natural causes. A particular timeless choice of my intelligible character affects the natural world by selecting a certain subset of possible worlds, namely, those including a certain moral history for my empirical character, and determining that the actual world will be drawn from that subset of possibilities. For each such choice there is an almost endless variety of ways in which I might have chosen differently, and endless variety of possible empirical selves and personal moral histories I might have actualized. Of every one of my misdeeds it is true that I would have left it undone had I made a different timeless choice. Hence it is in my power to leave any misdeed undone, despite the fact that in the actual world it follows inescapably from what preceded it in time.

When Kant says of my unlawful action that it and its causal determinants belong to my character, he may intend to claim that my timeless choice affects the course of the phenomenal world merely by affecting the constitution of my empirical character, which is of course an important causal factor in what I do. This would bring Kant's theory into line with the commonsense idea that we are responsible for our actions because we are responsible for our characters. An obstacle to this way of squaring Kant's theory with common sense is that on his theory the phenomenal effects of my timeless choice appear to extend far beyond the constitution of my empirical character. Indeed, my empirical character is itself causally determined by preceding events, and ultimately by events very remote in time from my life and actions. If I am responsible for my character, then my timeless choice must affect the whole course of the world's history, insofar as history includes the actions I in fact perform. Ralph Walker even maintains Kant's theory has the monstrous consequence that I am morally responsible for everything that happens in the course of the actual world, since this world as a whole results from my timeless noumenal choice: "I can be blamed for the First World War, and for the Lisbon earthquake that so appalled Voltaire. Gandhi is no less guilty than Amin of the atrocities of the Ugandan dictator."[5]

In rescuing Kant from these supposed consequences of his theory, it may help to keep in mind that on Kant's theory my intelligible choice is supposed to impinge on the course of the world not by directly selecting a certain history of actions for me. Rather, what my intelligible choice fundamentally decides is my empirical character, the kind of person I will be, or as Kant puts it in the *Religion*, the "fundamental maxim" on which I will act (AK.VI 31 [*Religion within the Bounds of Mere Reason*]). Even if my choice somehow issues in a world containing the First World War, the Lisbon earthquake, and the deeds of Idi Amin, it seems reasonable to hold me morally responsible only for those events which must belong to the actual course of things because I have the empirical character or fundamental maxim that I do. Kant must admit that on his theory this may include events that happen at places and even times remote from my life history in the temporal world. Yet Kant can reply that because in principle we know nothing about how our timeless choices operate on the temporal world, it must be impossible for us to say with confidence which events these may be. It seems open to Kant to suppose that they correspond to those events for which we normally regard ourselves as morally responsible. We must keep in mind that the purpose of Kant's theory is not positively to establish that we are free or morally responsible for our actions and their consequences, but only to suggest one possible way in which the moral responsibility we ascribe to ourselves may be reconciled with the mechanism of nature. We altogether misconstrue the status and function of this theory for Kant if we try to use it to justify or preempt moral common sense concerning such matters as the empirical scope of our moral responsibility.

## Fatalism

But here we must face another objection to Kant's theory not too different from the preceding one. Although Kant does permit us to say of our unlawful actions that we could have left them undone, it may appear that his theory forces on us a certain fatalism about our character and actions at odds both with common sense and with the spirit of Kant's own moral philosophy. As we have already seen, Kant allows that if we had enough knowledge of someone's character and circumstances, "his future conduct could be calculated with as much certainty as a solar or lunar eclipse" (AK.V 99). Suppose, then, that I have enough knowledge about myself to calculate that I will perform a certain unlawful action, for instance, that I will tell a certain malicious lie about an acquaintance against whom I bear an envious grudge. On Kant's theory it is true that I can avoid telling this lie, in the sense that I could have timelessly chosen a different intelligible character from my actual one, resulting in a different empirical character and a different moral history for myself. Yet it appears I already know enough about myself to be certain of my timeless choice regarding this particular action. For I know I will tell the lie and I know this lie is inescapably determined by past events which have already occurred. Hence I know to that extent which possible world I have timelessly chosen to actualize. My future action of telling the lie must therefore seem to me like a past action, or rather like the inevitable future result of a past action, which I can see coming but can no longer prevent. My malicious lie is an action I could have avoided (by choosing a world with a past different from the actual one) but it seems to be an action from which I am now powerless to refrain. As I now view myself, it seems that both my character (as a malicious liar) and my future act of lying are something fated for me. Perhaps I am in some sense to blame for them, but I cannot view myself as now able to alter or to avoid them.

This fatalism is obviously incompatible with the spirit of Kant's moral theory. But one measure of its appeal as an interpretation of Kant's theory of freedom is the fact that it was adopted, not only as an interpretation of Kant, but even as the profound truth of the matter, by Arthur Schopenhauer. Citing Kant's theory of the intelligible and empirical characters, Schopenhauer alleges that it supports his own thesis that everyone's conduct is inescapably determined for good or ill by an innate and unalterable moral nature. According to Schopenhauer, the merit of Kant's theory is that it shows that I am wholly responsible for what I do, despite the fact that it is false to say that I could have done otherwise, except in the sense that in the same circumstances, a different person, with a character different from mine, would have acted differently.[6]

I believe that Schopenhauer's interpretation of Kant is based on some clearly fallacious reasoning from Kant's theory. Insofar as a person's intelligible character is timeless, it apparently must also be immutable. Certainly, however, Kant intends his theory to be compatible with every conceivable state of affairs concerning the constancy or alterability of our empirical character through the course of a lifetime. Presumably this theory is that for every imaginable course of conduct in the phenomenal world, there is a timeless choice of an intelligible character that would yield that course of conduct. Hence there are some such choices whose results in the world of appearance involve changes in empirical character, drastic conversions from evil to good, or sudden degenerations from good to evil. For Kant, whether there are such changes in fact cannot be settled a priori on metaphysical grounds.

Kant also has a reply to the charge that his theory implies we no longer have the power to alter our future conduct. Kant does hold that by knowing enough about our character and situation we can predict with certainty what we will do. Yet it does not follow from this alone that we lack the power to do otherwise. Consider once again my malicious lie. I know how strong my grudge against the victim is, and I know myself well enough to be quite certain that I will persist in my resolve to slander him, that no sense of shame, no pity for my victim, still less any moral scruples, will dissuade me from carrying out my sinister intention. I can predict with absolute certainty that I will tell the malicious lie. But however certain I may be, I am not in the least inclined to think that it is not in my power to refrain from lying when the time comes. On the contrary, although I am certain that I will tell the lie, I am no less convinced that I still can refrain from telling it. It is misleading to express my conviction, as shallower compatibilists sometimes do, by saying that I could refrain from lying *if* I wanted to refrain. For that might suggest that, given my actual wants, I do *not* have the power to refrain. This, however, is exactly what I do *not* believe. Rather, what I believe is that although I know beyond a shadow of a doubt that I *will* tell the lie because I know I want to tell it, nevertheless I still *can* refrain from telling the lie.

Why do I have this belief, despite my certainty about how and why I will act? The belief, I suggest, rests on two other beliefs I have about myself and my future action. First, I believe it depends on me whether I will tell the lie or not. Second, I believe my influence on the situation will become effective regarding the lie only at the time the lie is actually told and not before. These are the reasons I believe that it is now still

in my power whether I will lie or not. If Kant's theory can accommodate these two beliefs about myself, it can also accommodate my belief
that it is still in my power to refrain from telling the malicious lie I
know I am going to tell.

Kant's theory *can* accommodate both beliefs. As we have seen, this
theory does show how my actions all depend on me alone, despite the
fact that they follow causal laws and are predictable according to them.
Kant also holds that my free choice itself becomes effective regarding
a given action only at the time the action is performed. "Every action,"
says Kant, "irrespective of the time relation in which it stands to other
appearances, is the immediate effect of the intelligible character"
(A553/B581). It is an illusion to suppose that my timeless choice of an
intelligible character is located so to speak at the beginning of time, so
that it operates *through* the series of natural causes. Rather, we must
treat our timeless choice as spontaneously determining each individual
act as that act occurs in time, so that in judging it "we presuppose that
we can wholly set aside how [the agent's previous course of life] may
have been constituted, and regard the past series of conditions as not
having happened, but regard this act as wholly unconditioned with respect to the previous state, as if with this act the agent instigated a
series of consequences wholly of itself" (A555/B583).

Kant's theory at this point resembles Boethius's resolution of the
problem of human freedom and divine foreknowledge. Boethius argues that because God is timeless, God's knowledge of what we will
do in the future is not literally foreknowledge. Focusing on the certainty and immediacy of this knowledge, we do best to say that God
knows perfectly what we do *simultaneously* with our future action,
much as I might know an event that is transpiring before my very eyes.
Just as my present knowledge does not predetermine or constrain
what is happening, so God's perfect and immediate knowledge of what
we will do does not compromise our freedom.[7] In a similar manner,
Kant's theory says that our timeless choice does not predetermine our
actions but has its influence immediately on each of them and should
be considered simultaneous with each act as it occurs in the temporal
order. Once again, some philosophers maintain that it is incoherent to
claim that a single timeless choice can be simultaneous with each of a
number of different events occurring at different times. This problem
(which I do not believe is insoluble) is built into the very notion of a
timeless being exerting influence on temporal events.[8] Kant's idea that
our timeless choice is simultaneous with each of our acts raises no *new*

problems not already involved in the notion of timeless agency, and it follows closely one main line of traditional thinking about how timeless agency might operate. Kant's theory, therefore, does not commit him to fatalism about our future actions.

Of course, it is still obvious that this theory does not leave intact our commonsense conception of our free agency. As countless critics of Kant have observed, we surely do think of our moral agency as situated in time. We suppose that our free choices are made in the temporal flow, reacting to the course of events as it unfolds. We believe that we are free "at the point in time when we act," and not timelessly, as Kant's theory requires.

Timeless agency also forces other revisions in our self-conception as moral agents not easily harmonized with Kantian ethics. For example, it makes nonsense of the goal of moral improvement or moral progress, literally understood, a goal to which Kant often attaches considerable importance. On Kant's theory, only our external actions occur in time; our freedom, to which alone true moral worthiness or unworthiness pertains, is timeless, and hence incapable of literally changing for better or worse.

Further, although Kant's theory may allow us to conceive of ourselves as acting on the world at different times, it does not seem that it can consistently allow us to conceive of ourselves as acting *in* time, or producing events *within* and *through* intervals of time. Thus Kant's theory cannot permit us to conceive of ourselves as *trying* or *striving* to produce a certain result over a period of time. Kant's theory need not deprive us of every conception of ourselves as trying or striving, since there may be a notion of trying or striving that is instantaneous and simultaneous with the result striven for. (The old notion of a mental 'volition' simultaneous with every voluntary action might be one ʿuch conception of 'trying'.) But Kant's theory does deprive us of the idea that we may produce a future result by continuously striving to produce it throughout the interval of time which now separates us from it. For instance, there is no place in Kant's theory for the idea that I may resist some passion or inclination of mine tomorrow by struggling with it today, and by striving throughout the day to purify my motives and fortify myself for the crucial hour of decision. The problem is not that I cannot imagine myself having all the thoughts and performing all the actions that I think of as part of this process, for certainly I can. The problem is that I cannot think of them as connected parts of an exercise of agency through time. I can only think of them as results or products of (timeless) agency, and not as the actual exercise of it. In time, there are only *facta* [facts]; yet trying or striving is not a *factum* [fact] but a *facere* [doing]. It is this exercise of agency Kant's theory will not allow me to conceive as a temporal process.

The absence of trying or striving is of course no problem for a timeless God, whose omnipotence and moral perfection presumably obviate the need for trying or striving of any sort. The absence surely is a problem for dedicated Kantian moral agents, however, who must think of themselves as struggling constantly with their unruly inclinations and striving throughout their lives to make the idea of duty the sufficient motive of every action. In some writings after 1793, Kant seems to recognize that his theory cannot accommodate moral striving or moral progress, literally speaking. And he seems to want to employ the notion of our noumenal "disposition" or "attitude" as a sort of timeless analogue or substitute both for moral striving and moral progress. In these passages, Kant seems to be saying that we think of ourselves as striving and morally progressing in time only because we as temporal beings can form no positive notion of timeless eternity: "For then nothing remains for us but to think of an endlessly progressing change in the constant progress toward our final end, through which our *attitude* remains always the same. (But our attitude is not, like this progress, a phenomenon; rather it is something supersensible, and so does not alter in time)" (AK.VIII: 334 [*The End of all Things*]). In the moral life, then, as in Goethe's heaven, *alles Vergängliche ist nur ein Gleichnis*— "Everything transitory is only a parable." Temporal striving and moral progress are the moving images of our eternal moral attitude, which we cannot conceive directly but to which we can relate only through such temporal images or parables. Kant thus hopes to preserve our ordinary experience of moral struggles in time and moral progress through time not as literal truth, but only as the best way we have of representing to ourselves a truth we cannot directly experience or literally comprehend. Nevertheless, Kant must not pretend to deny that his theory requires staggering revisions in our commonsense conception of our agency, even in those features of this theory very dear to Kant himself.

In assessing Kant's compatibilism, it may help to remind ourselves that his theory of timeless agency is put forward only as a means of exploiting the burden of proof in the free will problem, which falls to those who would show that freedom is incompatible with determinism. Kant is not positively committed to his theory of the case as an account of the way our free agency actually works. Indeed, Kant maintains that no such positive account can ever be obtained. Kant does not pretend to know how our free agency is possible, but claims only to show that the impossibility of freedom is forever indemonstrable. If what bothers us about Kant's theory is that it seems too farfetched and metaphysical, then it may help at least a little to realize that once the theory has served Kant as a device for showing that freedom and determinism cannot be proven incompatible, he is just as content to dissociate himself from it and adopt a largely agnostic position on the question how our freedom is possible.[9]

On the other hand, we are justified in expressing some discontent over the fact that the best theory Kant can come up with is one that involves such radical revisions in our conception of free agency. At any rate, this shortcoming makes it difficult to credit the advertisement frequently given for Kantian morality, that it is a moral philosophy faithfully representing the moral life as the ordinary agent experiences and lives it. As with many advertisements, this one calls our attention only to the more palatable and wholesome ingredients in the product, and carefully avoids listing the artificial ingredients with ugly names which, though necessary to keep the product from spoiling, may render it much less appealing.

Before we dismiss Kant's solution, we must take a long, sober look at his problem. The fact is that the free will problem is an old and intractable one. It is bound to be especially so for a strict determinist whose moral philosophy and moral psychology require as a condition of responsibility that I be capable of actions whose motivation lies altogether outside my natural, sensuous being.

Even those who do not face the free will problem in its Kantian form must confront the difficulties raised by more standard incompatibilists. We may doubt that any solution to these difficulties exists that does not force us to abandon common sense in some way, either to alter the moral judgments we make or to revise our commonsense conception of our agency. In the end, solving the free will problem may not be a matter of "saving common sense" (for that may be quite hopeless). Rather the solution may be a matter of saving as much of it as we can, and especially of saving those parts of it which matter most to us. I believe Kant saw the situation in this way, and I suggest we may assume that he decided that the temporality of our agency is the necessary ransom that must be paid to the free will problem if our high vocation as moral agents is to be preserved.

Others, of course, may have different worries and priorities and may wish to negotiate a different settlement. Nonetheless, they should not suppose they can get something for nothing. Moreover, they should evaluate Kant's solution in terms of his own problem. From this standpoint, we may conclude that unless we are prepared to argue for the positive incoherence of certain doctrines which constitute Kant's theory of the case—doctrines about phenomena and noumena, about Humean causality in nature and Aristotelian causality outside it, or about timeless agency and its temporal effects—then we must judge Kant's compatibilism a success in solving the problem it sets itself.

## Notes

1. All translations are my own.
2. Henry Sidgwick, *Methods of Ethics* (New York, 1966), pp. 511–16.
3. David Hume, *Enquiry Concerning Human Understanding* (Oxford, 1979) section 7.
4. I am inclined to say that Kant's refusal to opt exclusively for the Humean concept of cause sheds light on another of the vexed questions of Kantian metaphysics: the causal relation between noumena and phenomena generally. Kant holds that things in themselves cause appearances, or that they appear to us by exercising a causal influence on our sensibility. For two centuries critics have charged Kant with inconsistency or incoherence for holding this doctrine. The critics charge that on Kant's own showing causal relations can obtain only between temporal events, so that it is inconsistent for Kant to regard things in themselves (which are timeless) as causes. It is certainly true that for Kant all empirically knowable causes hold between events in time, since such causes are all Humean. Kant means to allow us through pure understanding to *think* of Aristotelian causes as the noumenal ground of phenomenal objects. The pure category of cause and effect (or ground and consequence) seems to be for him neither exclusively Aristotelian nor exclusively Humean. Here again, Kant is thoroughly self-consistent, although it is easy to see why his critics say he is not and hard to blame them for perceiving something fishy about Kant's doctrine at this point.
5. Ralph Walker, *Kant* (London, 1979), p. 149.
6. Arthur Schopenhauer, *The World as Will and Representation*, tr. E. J. F. Payne (New York, 1958), 1:286–307; *On the Freedom of the Will*, tr. K. Kolenda (New York, 1960), pp. 26–64, 81–83; *On the Basis of Morality*, tr. E. J. F. Payne (Indianapolis, 1965), pp. 109–15.
7. Boethius, *Consolatio philosophiae, Corpus Christianorum* [The Consolation of Philosophy, the Matter of Christianity] (Turnholti, 1957), Lib. 5, Prose 4–Prose 6.
8. The problem is well stated by Anthony Kenny, "Divine Foreknowledge and Human Freedom" in Kenny, ed., *Aquinas* (Garden City, N.Y., 1969). It is

equally well resolved, in my opinion, by Norman Kretzmann and Eleonore Stump, "Eternity," *Journal of Philosophy* 78 (1981), 429–58.

9. It may be argued that the implausibility of Kant's theory makes it unsuitable to his purpose, in the following way. According to the analogy drawn earlier, Kant may be likened to a defense attorney offering a theory of the evidence with a view to creating a reasonable doubt concerning the prosecution's theory. In a courtroom not just any logically possible theory of the evidence will do: the defense attorney's theory must be plausible enough to create a reasonable doubt. Some may believe Kant's theory of noumenal causality and timeless agency is too farfetched to pass this test. Kant's reply to this sort of objection is quite clear, however. In matters of transcendent metaphysics, questions of conjecture or probable opinion never arise: "In this species of investigation, it is in no way allowed to hold *opinions*. Everything which looks like a hypothesis is a forbidden commodity; it should not be put up for sale even for the lowest price, but should be confiscated as soon as it is discovered" (Axiv). This case is unlike the typical court case in that there is no question here of deciding whose theory is the more probable. In matters of metaphysics, any theory which can be neither proven nor disproven with apodictic certainty must count as equally probable. If Kant's theory of the case cannot be strictly disproven, then the contentions of the opponent of freedom cannot be proven. Because the burden of proof is on the opponent of freedom in this case, it follows that the only verdict we can render is to acquit freedom of the charges brought against it.

# 12

# Kant's Critique of the
# Three Theistic Proofs [partial]

## from *Kant's Rational Theology*

*Allen W. Wood*

The best known part of Kant's rational theology is its negative part: the famous refutations of the received arguments for God's existence. Above all, it was this side of Kant which gave the critical philosophy the "world destroying" impact, as Heine dramatically put it, on its own and the succeeding century. But Kant's aim here as elsewhere was to be as systematic and thorough as possible. His critique of speculative theism was not simply a series of attacks on the particular theistic proofs which had been offered by earlier philosophers. Its purpose was to show not only that no such proofs had in fact succeeded but also that no speculative proofs of any kind for God's existence have any prospect of succeeding.

According to Kant, our concept of God, like the other ideas of reason, is necessarily an "empty" or "problematic" one, a concept devoid of sensible content and possible empirical reference. When Kant describes this concept as "problematic" he means to imply that it sets us a problem without a solution, because we can never expect to obtain knowledge of the existence or the properties of any object corresponding to it. At times it seems that Kant means to draw this skeptical conclusion simply from the fact that the ideas of reason are "empty" and necessarily devoid of sensible content. Ideas of reason, he says, are concepts through which objects may be *thought*, but not *known*, as if it followed merely from the fact that no sensible referents for such concepts can be given in our experience that we can never establish the existence or nonexistence of the corresponding objects, or determine the properties belonging to them.[1]

If Kant does mean to argue in this fashion, however, he never tells us explicitly what his argument is. Perhaps his view is that since all the synthetic principles we might use to obtain such knowledge are either derived from experience or recognized as conditions of its possibility, none of them can be trusted in arguments concerned with objects transcending the empirical world. Kant could certainly have found this line of thinking expressed in the writings of Hume. But he could just as surely have found it disputed by a philosopher such as St. Thomas Aquinas, who found nothing wrong with reasoning from empirically derived principles about motion, causality, and perfection to conclusions about a first being who can never be an object of sense experience, or even of univocal description in concepts derived from the senses. Moreover, it is not in the least obvious that Aquinas is mistaken on this point. For why should we be hesitant to draw conclusions which follow naturally from the most certain and comprehensive principles we have, whatever their source?

Theistic arguments, even the most abstract and a priori of them, cannot be dismissed simply by appealing in some vague way to an empiricist epistemology. It is to Kant's credit that he does not take this route when he attempts to establish the impossibility of any theoretical demonstration of God's existence. Instead, he proceeds by dividing all possible theistic proofs into kinds, and arguing in each case that no successful proof of that kind can be given.

## Kant's Strategy

Kant says that there are fundamentally three possible proofs for the existence of a supremely perfect being: (1) the *ontological*, which "abstracts from all experience and argues wholly a priori from mere concepts"; (2) the *cosmological*, which "is grounded empirically only on an indeterminate experience, i.e., on some existence or other"; and (3) the *physicotheological*, which "begins from determinate experience and the constitution of our particular sensible world."[2] For Kant's aim in Sections 3 through 6 of the Ideal of Pure Reason is to show that none of these proofs can succeed. His strategy is first to undermine the ontological proof and then to argue that both the other proofs tacitly presuppose it, so that its failure, by a kind of domino effect, guarantees the failure of all possible speculative proofs for the existence of a supreme being.

To this end, Kant distinguishes in both the cosmological and physicotheological arguments two steps or stages: the first stage argues from some experience to the existence of a being of a certain description, and the second stage argues that any being of that description must be a supremely perfect being. More specifically, the cosmological argument . . . begins with the empirical fact that some contingent thing (myself, or a world in general) exists. It proceeds to argue that since what is contingent must have a cause, a ground, or sufficient reason for its being rather than not being, and since an infinite regress of contingent causes or grounds is untenable, there must exist a necessary being to serve as the first cause or sufficient ground of everything contingent. This completes the first stage of the cosmological argument. The second stage argues that the necessary being demonstrated in the first stage has to be a supremely perfect being. In parallel fashion, the physicotheological argument begins with the order, harmony, and beauty of the natural world, and concludes that they can be explained only by supposing there to be an intelligence from whose wisdom, power, and free volition such purposes proceed. This constitutes the first stage of the argument. The second stage has the task of showing this intelligence to be a supremely perfect being.

Curiously enough, Kant provides no detailed criticism of the first stage of either of these two proofs and seems to grant, at least for the sake of argument, both the inference from some contingent existence to a necessary being and the inference from the orderliness found in nature to a designing intelligence. These concessions, however, can be explained by Kant's overall strategy. It is only the second stage of each proof, in his view, which presupposes the ontological proof. The domino effect in which Kant is interested provides no refutation of the arguments for a necessary being or an intelligent designer of the natural order, but applies only to reason's attempt to identify these beings with a supremely perfect being.

This does not mean that Kant really accepts the first stage of either argument. On the inference from contingent to necessary existence, he enumerates four objections drawn from doctrines already expounded in the *Critique*. None of these objections, however, is clearly decisive, and Kant himself appears to admit that they are too tersely expressed to amount to a definitive refutation.[3] Doubts are also expressed about the analogical reasoning involved in the first stage of the design argument, and Kant suggests that it "perhaps could not withstand the sharpest transcendental critique." Once again, however, his objections are no more than hinted at.[4]

Kant's strategy was formulated with the aim of systematizing his critique of speculative theology as much as possible. But however well it may succeed on this score, it carries with it a couple of serious disadvantages. First, the power of Kant's critique of the cosmological and physicotheological proof is radically dependent on his criticism of the ontological proof. If (as I mean to argue) this criticism should prove to be less than conclusive, then Kant really provides no effective criticism at all of the other two proofs. No doubt Kant was persuaded that the ontological proof is the least persuasive of the three, and the proof whose weaknesses could be most easily shown up. But it just might be that the ontological proof is less vulnerable than the other two in certain ways, and that even if they do depend on it, their shortcomings could be more easily displayed by independent criticisms. A second disadvantage of Kant's strategy is even more serious. By leaving virtually unchallenged the arguments for a necessary being and an intelligent designer of nature, Kant is in effect conceding some very controversial points to the speculative theist. Kant himself always thought that a theology which fell short of establishing the supreme ontological perfection of the divine being would have to be judged a complete failure. The positive side of his own rational theology, both in its metaphysical and its moral aspects, provided him . . . with powerful reasons for thinking this. Nevertheless, it is entirely possible that speculative theologians might disagree with him, and it is hard to deny that if we could demonstrate that there is a necessarily existent cause of the world and intelligent author of its order, this result would have considerable philosophical interest, even if it could not be shown that this being is a supremely perfect being. On both counts, the scope of Kant's "world destroying" criticism of the traditional theistic proofs is sharply limited by his strategy of focusing his attacks on the ontological argument as the "only possible ground of proof" for God's existence.

## The Ontological Proof

*Descartes' Most Baffling Argument*

In his Second Reply to Objections, Descartes sets forth his Fifth Meditation proof for God's existence in the following syllogism:

*Major Premise*
Whatever we clearly understand to pertain to the nature of anything can with truth be affirmed of that thing.
*Minor Premise*
But it pertains to the nature of God that he exists.
*Conclusion*
Therefore, it can with truth be affirmed of God that he exists.[5]

The major premise of this syllogism is based on Descartes' criterion for certainty, that a proposition is known by us with perfect certainty when we "intuit" or "clearly and distinctly apprehend" its truth.[6] It is also based on his view that the mind has innately present to it the ideas of what he calls "pure and simple essences" or "true and immutable natures."[7] These the intellect is capable of apprehending clearly and distinctly by a direct intuition, and they furnish it a priori with a stock of certain knowledge. Probably the best examples of such natures are furnished by mathematics. By inspecting the nature of a triangle, for example, the mind is able to perceive a priori and with complete certainty that it belongs necessarily to this figure to have its largest side opposite its largest angle, to have its interior angles equal to two right angles, and other such properties. Whatever attribute is clearly perceived to pertain to a true and immutable nature is thereby certainly known to belong to it.

But Descartes also holds that we have in our stock of ideas one which represents a being possessing every perfection. The minor premise of Descartes' syllogism is based on the intellectual inspection of the true and immutable nature of this supreme perfection, and the resultant perception that to exist belongs among the perfections pertaining to it. Descartes holds, indeed, that existence is a perfection belonging to *any* nature which does not involve a contradiction. He holds this because he believes, with Hume, that "to conceive a thing, and to conceive it as existing, are nothing different from one another."[8] If I form a mental image of a winged horse, for example, I picture it as it would look if it existed. If I conceive of a triangular body, I endow it in my thought with all the properties it would have if it were an actual thing. Of course, when I think of such things I do not necessarily believe that they exist, nor does it follow from the fact that I conceive them as existing that they really are actual things. This, according to Descartes, is because the sort of existence which belongs to them in thought is only "possible existence." That is, when I think of a triangular body as existing, I naturally think of it as having the sort of existence belonging to a thing whose being is contingent on the being and the causal efficacy of other things. If the triangular body I am thinking of were actually to exist, it would have to be produced by some cause external to itself, and its continued existence would be beholden to various causes and circumstances which sustain it. This contingency of existence is, on Descartes' view, built into the nature of all bodies and finite minds and pertains to our very thought of these things. Hence possible or contingent existence is one of the perfections which we clearly and distinctly apprehend when we conceive of any finite things.

The matter is different, however, when we turn our attention to the nature of a supremely perfect being. For we note that such a being, having every power, cannot be prevented from existing by any being, nor have its existence beholden to anything outside itself. It follows from God's omnipotence, according to Descartes, that "he can exist by his own power" and from this fact "we therefore conclude that he truly exists and has existed from eternity; for we know by the light of nature that what can exist by its own power always exists."[9] To the true and immutable nature of God, therefore, there pertains a higher and more perfect kind of existence than that pertaining to the nature of finite things. Whereas it belongs to the latter to have merely possible or contingent existence, it belongs to the nature of God to have necessary existence.

> For I do not doubt that whoever attends diligently to this diversity between the idea of God and that of everything else will perceive that although these other things are understood as existing, it still does not follow from this that they exist, but only that they can exist, because we do not understand that their necessary being is conjoined with their properties; yet because we understand that actual existence is necessarily and always conjoined with the remaining attributes of God, it does indeed follow that God exists.[10]

The ontological argument as Kant considers it is largely divested of its Cartesian niceties. It seems to amount simply to the claim that God exists because the proposition that God exists is an analytic proposition. "The argument," says Kant, "is this: An *ens realissimum* is something which contains all realities in itself. But existence is also a reality. Hence the *ens realissimum* must necessarily exist. Thus if someone were to assert that God does not exist, he would be negating in the predicate something which is included in the subject, and this would be a contradiction."[11]

In Kant's terminology, . . . a proposition is analytic when the predicate is included or "contained" in the concept of the subject.[12] Every concept for Kant is made up of certain "marks" or "characteristics," consisting in various realities or their negations. The concept of body, for example, contains the characteristics of spatial extension, impenetrability, and shape. Hence when we assert the proposition "All bodies are extended," we are predicating of the subject something which is already contained in its own concept. Hence our proposition is analytic, and its denial involves a contradiction. Such a proposition, according to Kant, may be known to be true a priori, because nothing but an inventory of the subject concept is required for this knowledge. Certain other determinations, however, (e.g., weight and color) fall outside the content of the concept of body. Hence the propositions "All bodies are heavy" and "This body is colored" are synthetic. If they are true, the predicate must "belong to" or "be connected with" the subject concept, without being "contained in" it. And our judgment that such propositions are true, a judgment which "synthesizes" or "puts together" the subject concept and the predicate falling outside it, requires for its justification something else besides this concept. In the case of empirical judgments, this "something else" is our experience of the object. In the case of a priori synthetic judgments, according to Kant, the only available justification is an appeal to the conditions of any possible experience.

The ontological argument, as Kant seems to understand it, begins with the concept of God, a supremely perfect being, . . . a concept containing in it absolutely every reality and nothing at all in the way of imperfection or negation. Consequently, every judgment of the form "God is $F$" is analytic, and hence true a priori, granted only that $F$ be a predicate consisting entirely of realities and involving no negations. But according to the argument, "being" or "existence" is a predicate of this sort. For to say that a thing *exists* or *is* is surely to say something unqualifiedly positive about it. Consequently, the proposition "God exists" is analytic, and thus true a priori.

## Existence and Predication

The main thrust of Kant's attack on this argument seems to be the claim that all existential propositions must be synthetic. This criticism is well known, but Kant's own expression of it involves some difficult terminology and an unfamiliar logical setting. The principal error in the ontological proof, he contends, is its confusion of a "logical" predicate with a "real" predicate or "determination": "Anything we like," he says, "may serve as a logical predicate. . . . But a determination is a predicate which adds to the concept of the subject and increases it. Hence it must not be contained in it."[13]

For Kant, . . . to "determine" the concept of a thing is to add to our stock of information about the thing by predicating something of it in accordance with some rational procedure. Anything whatever may serve as a "logical predicate," or occupy the predicate position in a sentence. But not everything may serve as a "real predicate" or "determination," as a predicate which, when "added" to a concept in a subject-predicate proposition, "determines" it, or gives us some new information about what belongs to it. But, according to Kant, no new information of this kind is provided when we say that a thing *is* or *exists.* "Being," he says, "is obviously no real predicate, that is, it is not the concept of anything which could be added to the concept of a thing."[14]

The relevance of these claims to the ontological argument, however, may not be immediately evident. For the argument, especially as Kant represents it, never claims that the predicate "exists" "determines" our concept of God in the sense of giving us new information about him, or "adding" something to our concept which was not already contained in it. On the contrary, the whole point of the ontological proof is to argue that "exists" is not a predicate which needs to be "added to" the concept of God, because it is precisely the contention of the proof that the proposition "God exists" is analytically true. The proof begins with the concept of a supremely perfect being which, as Kant himself concedes, is already thoroughly determined a priori by its own content; and it draws the necessary existence of God out of this concept as one of the realities contained in it.

Kant's way of putting his criticism, in fact, even makes it seem as though he is claiming just the opposite of what he wants to prove. For if existence is not something which can be *added to* the concept of a thing, the only alternative, given Kant's conception of the structure of a proposition, is that it be something which is *contained in* its concept. But in that case, it would follow that *every* existential proposition is analytic. This, of course, is just the opposite of the view for which Kant is supposed to be arguing. And it is, besides, a view which is so obviously false that not even a proponent of the ontological argument will have a moment's hesitation in rejecting it.

Yet such an interpretation of Kant's words must be mistaken, however natural it may be. When Kant denies that "exists" can be "added to" the concept of a thing, he clearly does not mean to commit himself to the view that all existential propositions are analytic, nor does he mean to deny (what everyone admits without dispute) that sometimes when we say things of the form "*X* exists" we are providing some new information about *X*. Kant's point can be appreciated, I think, if we approach his remarks from a different direction. He is proceeding on the supposition that the content of any concept must be drawn from the same stock of realities and negations which are available to us in the further determination of concepts. The contents of a concept, on his view, provide us with certain identifying marks which enable us to pick out an object for further determination. The concept "body," for instance, identifies a given particular as an extended, impenetrable thing with some shape or other; and, using this concept, we can go on to say of this particular that it is colored, heavy, and so on. Any such identifying mark, however, in Kant's view, must be a property which might (in another context) serve to add to our stock of information about what belongs to a concept. Hence if the (logical) predicate "exists" cannot serve to determine the concept of which it is predicated, then there can be no concept in which it figures as a content or identifying mark. And if this is the case, then no proposition of the form "*X* exists" can be analytic.

According to Kant, "being" or "existence" is not a determination, or real predicate. Hence it cannot serve as an identifying mark which might go to make up the content of some concept. Rather, it is "merely the positing of a thing or of certain determinations, as existing in themselves. When we say 'God is' or 'There is a God,' we attach no new predicate to the concept of God, but only posit the subject in itself with all its predicates." Existence, therefore, is not a reality or perfection. "The actual," according to Kant, "contains no more than the merely possible. A hundred actual dollars do not contain the least bit more than a hundred possible dollars. . . . But there is more in my financial position in the case of a hundred actual dollars than in the case of the mere concept of them."[15]

Kant's criticism thus depends on drawing a distinction between two sorts of synthetic propositions: (1) Those which "determine" the subject concept or "add to" it, by predicating some reality (or negation) of it, and (2) those which "posit" the concept or the determinations thought in it. In the former case, the determinations or "real predicates" which are applied to a thing may (in another context) serve as the contents of a subject concept. And, considering now only those which are made up of realities, we know a priori that any and all of them must belong to the thoroughly determined concept of a supremely perfect being. If "is" or "exists" were a real predicate of this kind, then it could not be denied that the proposition "God exists" is analytic. But, Kant maintains, when we assert that something exists, we do not ascribe any reality to it; we do not determine its concept by anything which could (in another context) go to make up the identifying marks constituting the content of a subject concept. Since existence is not a reality, we are not required to think it in the concept of a supremely perfect being, and hence need not conclude that the existence of such a being is asserted by an analytic proposition. When we assert that something exists, we do not "add to" the subject concept, but only "posit" this concept or the determinations contained in it.

More recent philosophers have spoken not of "positing" but of declaring a concept "instantiated" or asserting that it "applies to something." Their point, however, seems to be the same as Kant's, and Kant is rightly credited with the same criticism of the ontological proof. Like Kant, they maintain that asserting that a thing exists is entirely different from ascribing any property to it. And they also mean to conclude from this that existence cannot be legitimately included in the concept of a thing. It cannot be one of the identifying marks of a thing, or part of the meaning of the word or description that signifies it, that its concept is instantiated, or that this word or description succeeds in referring or applying to something. From this conclusion, however, it follows as a matter of logic that no propositions asserting existence can be analytic ones.

Like most partisans of this view, Kant regards its truth as something obvious, something "every rational person admits."[16] Yet it cannot have been so obvious to Descartes and other proponents of the ontological argument. For surely Descartes knew that to say "God exists" is to say that the concept of God is instantiated, that the word "God" or the description "most real being" succeeds in referring or applying to something. Hence he must have believed, contrary to the Kantian view, that the necessary instantiation of a concept could be included among its contents. What argument does Kant give him for abandoning this belief?

Kant's only real argument (the only one I can find at any rate) is presented in the following passage:

> No matter which and how many predicates I think in a thing (and even if I think it as completely determined), I still do not add the least bit to it when I posit that this thing *is*. For otherwise it would not be just the same thing I thought in my concept which exists, and I could not say that it is precisely the object of my concept which exists. If I think in a thing every reality but one, the missing reality is not added when I say that this defective thing exists. On the contrary, it exists encumbered with precisely the same defect I thought in it, since otherwise what exists would be something other than what I thought.[17]

Kant's argument may, I think, be fairly paraphrased as follows: Let us give the name "almost perfect being" to any entity which has every perfection but one. And let us suppose that we have before us the concept of such a being, only we do not know *which* reality is the missing one in the case of that particular almost perfect being. Now Kant's contention is that we are led into absurdities if we assume that "existence" is the reality we are seeking. For suppose it is. In that case, if the almost perfect being we are thinking of existed, it would have the missing reality, and therefore would not be almost perfect, but wholly perfect. But this contradicts the assumption that we are thinking of an *almost* perfect being, and hence is absurd. Existence, therefore, cannot be the reality we are looking for. But no restrictions whatever were placed on the reality missing from our almost perfect being. Consequently, if existence cannot be the missing reality, this can only be because existence is not a reality at all. And this is what Kant desired to prove.

. . . I find it astonishing that this argument has stood up for so long, and that so many philosophers who are otherwise clearheaded and critical have found it convincing. We can see at once that it *cannot* be correct if we run through it again, this time supposing "omnipotence" (or any other undisputed real predicate) to be the reality missing from our almost perfect being. In that case too we would have to admit that if the almost perfect being were omnipotent, it would have the missing reality, and hence be wholly perfect, contrary to our original supposition. Thus if Kant's argument succeeded in showing that existence is not a real predicate, it would also succeed in showing that nothing could be one.

It seems to me that the supposed absurdity, in both cases, results from an ambiguity in "almost perfect being" or "being having every reality but one." Such expressions can mean either: (1) a being which has all realities but one, and does not necessarily have this one reality; or (2) a being which has all realities but one, and necessarily lacks this one reality. If it means (1) there is no absurdity at all in supposing that it has the missing reality (be that reality existence, omnipotence, or what you will). At most there would be a verbal contradiction, as when a shepherd says that the lost sheep has been found. On the other hand, if "almost perfect being" means (2), then there is an absurdity all right, but this absurdity has nothing to do with what we suppose the missing reality to be. It comes instead from our speculating what would be the case if the almost perfect being had a reality which by hypothesis it necessarily lacks. However we read the argument it does absolutely nothing to show that existence is not a reality, perfection, or real predicate, or that propositions of the form "*X* exists" cannot be analytic.

Kant does succeed in setting forth a view about existence and predication which, if it is correct, does rid us once and for all of the concept of logically necessary existence, and with it the ontological argument. But he provides us with no good reasons for thinking his view to be the correct one. Kant's view has been, and still is, widely accepted and is even (owing to its adoption by Gottlob Frege and Bertrand Russell) incorporated into the standard systems of formal logic, via the existence quantifier. Yet no one as far as I can tell has ever presented a really persuasive argument for it.

Partisans of the Kantian view often cite G. E. Moore's "tame tigers" example as providing evidence in its favor.[18] According to Moore, the sentence "Tame tigers growl" is ambiguous between "All tame tigers growl," "Most tame tigers growl," and "Some tame tigers growl." But, he alleges, there is no such ambiguity in the sentence "Tame tigers exist": it must mean "Some tame tigers exist" or "There are tame tigers." Moore thinks that such sentences as "All tame tigers exist" and "Most tame tigers exist" have no meaning at all, or at least no clear one.[19] An even more significant difference, in Moore's view, between "exists" and real properties (such as "growl" and "scratch") is brought out by comparing the (internal) negations of the sentences "Some tame tigers growl" and "Some tame tigers exist." According to Moore, "Some tame tigers do not growl" has a perfectly clear meaning; "Some tame tigers do not exist," however, has no meaning at all, or at least not a clear one. Moore admits that we can "give" this sentence a meaning, by including fictional or imaginary tame tigers within our universe of discourse. But, he contends, if we do this, we have "changed the meaning of 'exist' " in the two sentences.[20] Presumably what he has in mind here is that "Some tame tigers exist" can be taken as equivalent to "There are tame tigers," but the (internal) negation of the former sentence cannot be taken to be equivalent to the negation of the latter.

It is not clear to me that in these examples Moore has noted any significant differences between "exists" and other properties, or at least any which are relevant to the ontological proof. If, by including fictional or imaginary tigers in our universe of discourse, we can give a sense to "Some tame tigers do not exist," then by the same device we can surely give a sense to "All tame tigers exist" and "Most tame tigers exist." Moreover, it is misleading of Moore to imply that when we do employ such a universe of discourse, we are changing the meaning of the word "exist" or indeed doing anything at all that has any special connection with the property of existence. We could just as well extend our universe of discourse in the same way for sentences like "Some tame tigers growl" and other sentences not involving the predicate of existence. Just how natural this would be depends on the context. If I say "Some cowboy heroes had white horses" it seems natural, in view of the cultural context of my remark, to include fictional cowboy heroes as well as real ones within the scope of the subject term. In other cases, this would be much less natural. It is true, as Moore observes, that such an understanding is positively *required* by "Some cowboy heroes existed, and some didn't." And this fact may perhaps indicate a significant difference between *exists* and other predicates. But it is not at all obvious that this difference does anything to show that existence cannot be included in the concept of a thing, or that all existential propositions must be synthetic. Perhaps the Kantian thesis is rendered more plausible by the fact that there are idioms like "There are tame tigers" as paraphrases for "Some tame tigers exist." For there is no natural idiom of this sort to paraphrase "Some tame tigers growl"; and the idiom itself—lacking as it does the same straightforward subject-predicate form, might lend support to the idea that when we say "*X* exists" we are saying something whose deeper logical form (as opposed to its surface grammatical form) is not that of a subject-predicate assertion. But the existence of such idioms surely constitutes no real argument for Kant's view.

The considerations which philosophers have advanced in favor of the Kantian position on existence and predication all strike me as extremely weak. As far as I can see, the principal reason why some philosophers have accepted this position is that once we do accept it, we have some plausible-sounding reason to give for rejecting the ontological proof, and therefore just possibly some means of freeing ourselves from the horrible nagging suspicion that this proof might be sound. And there can be no doubt that this has to be a strong recommendation for the Kantian position as far as many philosophers are concerned. But it can hardly be expected to make much impression on a convinced Cartesian.

*Another Means of Escape*

Not everyone who has rejected the ontological proof has found it necessary to adopt the Kantian view about existence and predication. Descartes' contemporary Caterus, for example, seems to have held both that existence is a perfection and that necessary existence is contained in the concept of a supremely perfect being, or is implied by its very name. Yet he found Descartes' *Meditations V* proof unconvincing:

> Even if it is granted that the very name of a being of highest perfection implies its existence, it still does not follow that this existence itself is something actual *in rerum natura* [in the world of nature], but only that the concept of existence is inseparably conjoined with the concept of a highest being. From this you cannot infer that the existence of God is something actual, unless you suppose that such a highest being actually exists. For then it will possess all perfections along with the one of real existence.[21]

In this passage, Caterus admits that the proposition "God exists" is analytic (to put the admission in Kantian terminology). Yet he denies that we are entitled to conclude from this that God actually exists, unless we already suppose that he does. It appears to be Caterus' view that nothing can be truly predicated of a subject (even by means of an analytic proposition or an outright tautology) unless the subject exists. Such a view might well follow from the idea, which we have seen in Kant, that in a subject-predicate proposition the subject term is used to pick out something or other, and the predicate term is used to say something about the thing picked out. In order to say something true using such a proposition, both terms must succeed in doing their jobs. Of course, the proposition is false if the predicate does not belong to or apply to the subject picked out. But on this view, the proposition would also fail to be true if the subject term failed to refer to anything. A proponent of this view need not hold that in the latter event the proposition would be false. He might hold this, or he might deny any truth value at all to it. (In Caterus' Objections, I can find no indication of his view on this point.)

One possible disadvantage of Caterus' position is that it requires us to deny truth to such propositions as "A unicorn has one horn" and "Six-headed lions are six-headed," to analytic propositions whose subject terms happen not to refer to anything actual. The view might be rescued from this difficulty by permitting the reference of subject terms to include imaginary or fictional entities, and possessors of other non-real modes of being. Caterus does not seem to permit this, however, and as we shall see presently, his criticism of the ontological argument would lose some of its force if he were to take a softer line on this point. When we consider propositions like "A unicorn has one horn," therefore, the Kantian way of escape form the ontological argument seems preferable to Caterus' way. For it saves the truth of analytic propositions about nonexistent things. On the other hand, as Caterus points out, we can form the concept "existent lion" and from it arrive at the analytic proposition "An existent lion exists," but we are not tempted to regard this as an a priori proof for the existence of lions. Caterus' view seems to explain better than Kant's why this should be so. For Kant must deal with the matter by altogether denying the legitimacy of concepts like "existent lion," and in the absence of a really convincing argument for his view about existence and predication, this seems somewhat arbitrary. Each way of escape from the ontological argument therefore has its advantages, and also its problems.

These two ways of escaping from the ontological argument are quite independent. Either may be adopted without the other, or both may be adopted at once. There is, in fact, good evidence that Kant himself endorsed Caterus' criticism of the ontological argument as well as the "Kantian" one. Probably the most explicit statement of this criticism is to be found in Kant's *Nova dilucidatio* [New Elucidation] essay of 1755. At that time, Kant had evidently not yet completely worked out his more radical criticism of the ontological proof, based on his view about existence and predication, and so drew his criticism of it from considerations very much along the same lines as Caterus':

> I know, of course, that appeal is made [by some philosophers] to the notion of God itself, who postulate that existence is determined in this

notion. But it is easy to see that this may be done with truth only ideally, and not really. You form for yourself the notion of a being in which there is a totality of reality. And it must be admitted that according to this concept existence must belong to this being. The argument, therefore, proceeds thus: if in some being all realities without degree are united, that being exists; if they are conceived as united, existence follows, but only existence in idea. Hence the proposition may be formed thus: In forming for ourselves the notion of that which we call God, we have so determined it that existence is included in it. If then this preconceived notion be true, God exists. Only this much may be said in behalf of those who assent to the Cartesian argument.[22]

In this passage, Kant appears to concede that existence is a reality and hence that it may be found among the contents of the concept of a supremely perfect being. His objection, like Caterus', is to the inference from this to the conclusion that a supremely perfect being exists in reality. All we are entitled to infer, he says, is that such a being exists . . . "in idea."

H. J. Paton notes that in the *Critique* Kant often suggests that even analytic judgments are assumed to be about *objects*, and not merely about concepts, and Paton views this as an instance of Kant's unwavering belief that the truth of a proposition is always its correspondence with an object.[23] Such a view, of course, suggests that the subject term of even an analytic proposition must succeed in referring to an object if that proposition is to be counted as true. Kant even seems to be criticizing the ontological argument from this standpoint in one passage. If, he says, the proposition "this or that thing exists" is taken to be analytic, then "The assertion of the thing's existence adds nothing to the thought of the thing. But then either the thought which is in you is the thing itself, or else you have presupposed an existence as belonging to possibility, and then on the basis of the assertion you have inferred that existence from its inner possibility—which is nothing but a wretched tautology."[24] Kant's line in this passage seems to be that if any proposition of the form "*X* exists" is taken to be analytic *and true*, then the existence of some referent or other for its subject concept has already been presupposed. Either this referent must be regarded as the thought of this concept existing in someone's mind (a highly unnatural way to understand such a proposition, and clearly not what the proponent of the ontological argument means by it), or else it must be presupposed that some object corresponding to the subject concept actually exists in order that this reference may be secured. In the latter case, of course, the ontological argument would be flatly question-begging.

Kant's adherence to the view that every true predication requires the actual existence of some referent of the subject term also helps to make sense of some other things he says in this section of the *Critique*. Immediately after he states his views that "being" is not a real predicate, but only "the positing of a thing or of certain determinations," he proceeds to expound this view as follows: "The proposition: *God is omnipotent* contains two concepts, which have their objects: *God* and *omnipotence*. The little word *is* is not still another predicate over and above this, but only that which the predicate posits *in relation* to the subject."[25] It is tempting (and I believe in the end correct) to dismiss these remarks about the copulative "is" as irrelevant to the ontological argument, which after all has to do not with the use of the verb "to be" in which it serves to connect the subject with other predicates, but the use in which it (allegedly) serves as a full-fledged predicate all by itself. But what the passage indicates is that for Kant the copulative "is," like the "is" which simply asserts existence of its subject, has the function of "positing" something in the real world as standing over against our concepts. For Kant, the "exists" in "God exists" adds no predicate to the subject, but only "posits" an object corresponding to the subject concept. Likewise, the copula in "God is omnipotent" "posits" the real property of omnipotence in its relation to the subject of the proposition. To "posit" something, here as before, must mean to assert the extramental existence of an object corresponding to our concept of it. The copulative "is," therefore, must assert the actual existence of a property (e.g., omnipotence), standing in the categorical relation of inherence to the subsisting subject (God). But of course an actual property cannot inhere in a subject unless the subject also actually exists. Existing omnipotence can only inhere in an existing omnipotent thing. Hence Kant's view about the "positing" function of the copulative "is" seems to commit him to Caterus' view that every true predication presupposes the actual existence of that to which the subject term refers. . . .

## Notes

1. *Critique of Pure Reason*, B. xxviii, A 336/B 393, A 348f, A 609/B 637, A 646/B 619f.

2. *Critique of Pure Reason*, A 590/B 619f.

3. *Critique of Pure Reason*, A 609/B 637.

4. *Critique of Pure Reason*, A 626/B 654.

5. René Descartes, *Philosophical Works*, ed. Haldane and Ross (New York, 1955), 2:45; cf. 2:57.

6. *Philosophical Works*, 1:157f; 1:7.

7. *Philosophical Works*, 1:157f; 1:15. The terms "intuition" and "pure and simple essence" are characteristic of Descartes' first essay on the subject, the *Rules for the Direction of the Mind*. The terms "clear and distinct apprehension" and "true and immutable nature" are characteristic of the *Meditations* and other later works.

8. Hume, *Treatise on Human Nature*, ed. Selby-Bigge (Oxford, 1967), p. 66.

9. *Philosophical Works*, 2:21.

10. *Philosophical Works*, 2:20.

11. AK., 28, 2, 2, p. 1027; *Lectures on Philosophical Theology*, p. 58.

12. *Critique of Pure Reason*, A 610/B 638.

13. *Critique of Pure Reason*, A 599/B 626.

14. *Critique of Pure Reason*, A 599/B 626; AK., 28, 2, 2, p. 1027; *Lectures on Philosophical Theology*, p. 59.

15. *Critique of Pure Reason*, A 598ff/B 626ff.

16. *Critique of Pure Reason*, A 598/B 626.

17. *Critique of Pure Reason*, A 600/B 628.

18. G. E. Moore, "Is 'Existence' a Predicate?" in *The Ontological Argument*, ed. A. Plantinga (Garden City, N.Y., 1965), pp. 71ff.

19. Moore, ibid., pp. 74–75.

20. Moore, ibid., pp. 75–76.

21. Descartes, *Philosophical Works*, 2:7.

22. AK., 1:394f: pp. 223f.

23. H. J. Paton, *Kant's Metaphysic of Experience* (London, 1936) 1:214, fn. 3.

24. *Critique of Pure Reason*, A 597/B 625.

25. *Critique of Pure Reason*, A 598/B 626.

# Annotated Bibliography

## I. Kant's Works

*General Remarks*

The standard edition of Kant's works (1) was begun in 1902 and is finally nearing completion. This massive scholarly undertaking provides a common frame of reference for Kant scholars and students. In this anthology, I have standardized references to all volumes in this work—except the *Critique of Pure Reason* (see below)—by "Ak." (for *Akademie*), the volume number in Roman numerals, and the page reference following a colon—e.g., Ak. IV: 97. Some scholars refer to this work by "AA" or "GS" along with the volume and page reference. Even for English speakers, this edition offers an important resource, because most English translations list the Ak. page reference in the margins. Hence, if a scholar refers to Ak. IV: 470, for example, students may go to an English translation of the *Metaphysical Foundations of Natural Science* and check that passage (where Kant offers an important general claim about the necessity of a mathematical basis for proper science).

For English speakers, the study of Kant has been greatly enhanced in the last decade by a decision of Cambridge University Press to produce a series of translations of Kant's published and major unpublished writings. All translations are based on the Ak. edition and provide page references to it. The existing and soon to appear volumes that are most relevant to the study of the *Critique of Pure Reason* are listed below (4 a–d).

Norman Kemp Smith's translation (2) of the *Critique of Pure Reason* has been widely used for nearly sixty years. Except when they offer their own translations, all of the authors in this anthology use Kemp Smith. The *Critique* appeared in two somewhat different editions, the first in 1781, the second in 1787. Kemp Smith introduced the now universally accepted practice of referring to the first edition by "A" and its original edition pagination and to the second edition by "B" and its original edition pagination. (The Ak. edition also provides the pagination of the original editions in the margins of volume III, which contains the second edition, and volume IV, which contains the first.) When a passage is cited, as, e.g., A 51/B 75, that means that it is common to both editions; a first edition passage that was cut from the later edition would be just, e.g., A 99; a passage unique to the second edition would be cited as, e.g., B 132. Although Kemp Smith's translation has been dominant for many years, a new translation by Werner Pluhar appeared in 1996 (3) and a new translation by Paul Guyer and Allen Wood is about to appear in the Cambridge University Press series (4b).

*Works*

1. Kant, Immanuel. *Kants gesammelte Schriften, Akademie Ausgabe.* Edited by the *Königlichen Preussischen Akademie der Wissenschaften.* 29 vols. Berlin and Leipzig: Walter de Gruyter and predecessors, 1902–.
2. Kemp Smith, Norman. *Immanuel Kant's Critique of Pure Reason.* New York: St. Martin's, 1968.
3. Pluhar, Werner, ed. and trans. *Critique of Pure Reason: Unified Edition.* Introduction by Patricia Kitcher. Indianapolis: Hackett, 1996.
4. *The Cambridge Edition of the Works of Immanuel Kant.* Paul Guyer and Allen W. Wood, general editors. New York: Cambridge University Press.
   a. *Theoretical Philosophy 1755–1770,* trans. and ed. David Walford (in collaboration with Ralf Meerbote), 1992. This volume includes several of Kant's "precritical" (before the *Critique*) writings that are most often cited in trying to understand the development of the ideas in the *Critique*, including the *New Elucidation of the First Principles of Metaphysical Cognition* (1755), *Dreams of a Spirit-seer Elucidated by Dreams of Metaphysics* (1766), *Concerning the Ultimate Grounds of the Differentiation of Directions in Space* (1768), and *On the Form and Principles of the Sensible and the Intelligible Worlds* (1770; usually referred to as the "Inaugural Dissertation").

b. *The Critique of Pure Reason*, trans. and ed. Paul Guyer and Allen W. Woods, to be published in 1998.

c. *Lectures on Logic*, trans. and ed. J. Michael Young (1992). Unable to do the work himself, Kant asked Benjamin Jäsche to compile a book about logic from his marginal notes in the logic text he used. This volume also includes several different sets of student notes from the lectures Kant gave on logic over a period of forty years. It provides important insight into Kant's conception of logic, which differs markedly from contemporary views.

d. *Lectures on Metaphysics*, trans. and ed. Karl Ameriks and Steve Naragon (1997). As he did with logic, Kant gave many lectures on metaphysics over the course of his long teaching career. This volume includes eight sets of student lecture notes.

*Individual Works (Other Than the* Critique)

Allison, Henry E. *The Kant-Eberhard Controversy*. Baltimore: Johns Hopkins University Press, 1973. Eberhard was a Leibnizian who fiercely attacked Kant's system. Kant's reply—provided by his disciple Schulze—offers insights into his understanding of the nature of analytic judgment, the status of the forms of intuition, and other important topics.

Beck, Lewis White, trans. *Prolegomena to Any Future Metaphysics*. Indianapolis: Bobbs-Merrill, 1950. The *Prolegomena* was intended as a "popular" version of the *Critique*. Other than the book itself, it is the text cited most frequently in trying to interpret the *Critique*.

Ellington, James, trans. *Metaphysical Foundations of Natural Science*. Indianapolis: Bobbs-Merrill, 1970. In this book, Kant relates some of his general claims about the *a priori* conditions for the possibility of scientific knowledge to the Newtonian science of his day.

Gregor, Mary, trans. *Anthropology from a Pragmatic Point of View*. The Hague: Martinus Nijhoff, 1974. Kant's anthropology provides many insights into his understanding of the cognitive faculties that figure prominently in the *Critique*'s explanation of the possibility of cognition.

Hatfield, Gary, trans. *Prolegomena to Any Future Metaphysics*. New York: Cambridge University Press, 1997. See the discussion of Beck's translation above.

Pluhar, Werner, trans. *Critique of Judgment*. Indianapolis: Hackett, 1987. Particularly in its "first introduction," the "third critique" of-

fers important further discussions of the faculty of judgment (especially "reflective" judgment) that plays an important role in the first
critique's account of science.

Zweig, Arnulf, trans. and ed. *Kant: Philosophical Correspondence*. Chicago: University of Chicago Press, 1967. Like many scholars of this
period, Kant carried on a lively and important correspondence. This
selection includes many of Kant's most frequently cited letters.

## II. Secondary Sources

*Books*

Allison, Henry. *Kant's Transcendental Idealism*. New Haven, Conn.:
Yale University Press, 1983. This widely influential book covers many
important topics in the *Critique*. Its opening chapters are included
in the anthology (selection 9).

Ameriks, Karl. *Kant's Theory of the Mind*. Oxford: The Clarendon Press,
1982. Ameriks provides a historically informed and philosophically
sophisticated analysis of Kant's understanding of the metaphysical
status of the mind.

Beiser, Frederick. *The Fate of Reason*. Cambridge, Mass.: Harvard University Press, 1987. Beiser gives a clear and readable account of the
contemporary reaction to the *Critique* and its influence on the subsequent development of German philosophy.

Bennett, Jonathan. *Kant's Analytic*. Cambridge: Cambridge University
Press, 1966. Bennett offers contemporary readings and defenses of
some of Kant's central claims about the necessary conditions for objective knowledge.

Broad, C. D. *Kant: An Introduction*. New York: Cambridge University
Press, 1978. This volume contains Broad's lectures on Kant. Although
not primarily a Kant scholar, Broad gave clear and insightful accounts
of central issues and texts.

Brook, Andrew. *Kant and the Mind*. New York: Cambridge University
Press, 1994. Brook relates Kant's cognitive psychology to contemporary work in cognitive science.

Falkenstein, Lorne. *Kant's Intuitionism*. Toronto: University of Toronto
Press, 1995. A clear, scholarly commentary on the Transcendental
Aesthetic that offers a new interpretation of Kant's theory of the
forms of intuition.

Friedman, Michael. *Kant and the Exact Sciences.* Cambridge, Mass.: Harvard University Press, 1992. A scholarly treatment of Kant's understanding of contemporary developments in mathematics and physics and their relation to various central themes in the *Critique.*

Guyer, Paul. *Kant and the Claims of Knowledge.* New York: Cambridge University Press, 1987. Along with Allison's book listed above, this book offers one of the most influential contemporary readings of the *Critique.* Guyer provides an index of passages discussed that is especially useful for students wishing to gain insight to a particular text.

Guyer, Paul, ed. *The Cambridge Companion to Kant.* New York: Cambridge University Press, 1992. This collection of readable essays provides students with a basic, but current, understanding of some of the most important topics in Kant's philosophy.

Kitcher, Patricia. *Kant's Transcendental Psychology.* New York: Oxford University Press, 1990. In this book, I argue that Kant's cognitive psychology should not be dismissed as an exercise in armchair science, but considered an important precursor to contemporary attempts to understand the necessary conditions for cognition.

Longuenesse, Beatrice. *Kant and the Power of Judgment.* Princeton, N.J.: Princeton University Press, 1997. Longuenesse offers an interesting analysis of one of the most central—and least discussed—aspects of Kant's theory of knowledge, his account of judgment.

Melnick, Arthur. *Kant's Analogies of Experience.* Chicago: University of Chicago Press, 1973. Melnick provides a systematic discussion of a central part of the *Critique,* the Analogies, including Kant's famous "reply to Hume" on causation in the second analogy.

Neiman, Susan. *The Unity of Reason.* New York: Oxford University Press, 1994. Like judgment, the topic of Kant's understanding of reason has rarely been discussed systematically—despite its obvious importance to the *Critique of Pure Reason.* Neiman reads Kant as offering an account of the creative faculty of reason, which links the *Critique* both to Kant's own ethical writings and to his German idealist successors.

Strawson, Peter. *The Bounds of Sense.* London: Methuen, 1966. Partially reprinted as selection 8, this classic text influenced a generation's way of reading Kant. Like Bennett's book above, *The Bounds of Sense* seeks to make Kant's work relevant to contemporary issues concerning knowledge and skepticism.

Walker, Ralph. *Kant.* London: Routledge and Kegan Paul, 1978. This book offers a comprehensive and readable account of Kant's philosophy as a whole.

*Articles*

Ameriks, Karl. "Recent Works on Kant's Theoretical Philosophy." *American Philosophical Quarterly* 19 (1978): 1–24. Besides providing clear accounts of recent interpretations, this paper also has a useful bibliography.

Ameriks, Karl. "Understanding Apperception Today." In *Kant and Contemporary Epistemology*, ed. P. Parrini. Dordrecht: Kluwer, 1994, 331–37. Apperception is one of the most central and difficult topics of the *Critique* and this article offers a clear discussion of various recent approaches to understanding the notion.

Beck, Lewis White. "Can Kant's Synthetic Judgments Be Made Analytic?" In *Kant*, ed. R. P. Wolf. New York: Doubleday, 1967, 3–22. Many contemporary scholars have been tempted to argue that, although Kant claimed that his central propositions were synthetic, he really meant that they were analytic. Beck argues that this reading is historically untenable.

Henrich, Dieter. "The Proof-Structure of Kant's Transcendental Deduction." *Review of Metaphysics* 22 (1969): 640–59. This widely influential article tries to capture the structure of the proof of the categories in the second edition.

Henrich, Dieter. "Kant's Notion of a Deduction and the Methodological Background of the First *Critique*." In *Kant's Transcendental Deductions*, ed. E. Förster. Stanford, Calif.: Stanford University Press, 1989, 29–46. Just before beginning the transcendental deduction, Kant makes an analogy between his project and legal deductions. In this important essay, Henrich sheds new light on this 200-year-old clue to Kant's method of proof.

Hopkins, James. "Visual Geometry." *Philosophical Review* 82 (1973): 3–34. Hopkins argues that although Kant's theory that Euclidean geometry captures the nature of space is clearly wrong, he may be correct that it accurately describes human perception.

Kitcher, Patricia. "Discovering the Forms of Intuition." *Philosophical Review* 96 (1987): 205–48. In this article, I argue that Kant's theory of the spatial form of intuition was grounded in the scientific controversies of his day.

Sellars, Wilfrid. ". . . This I or he or it (the thing) which thinks." In his

*Essays in Philosophy and its History*. Boston: D. Reidel, 1974, 63–90. In this highly influential article, Sellars offers a systematic treatment of Kant's puzzling doctrine of the thinking self.

van Cleve, James. "Four Recent Interpretations of Kant's Second Analogy." *Kant-Studien* 64 (1973): 71–87. Kant's "reply to Hume" in the Second Analogy is often considered the centerpiece of the *Critique*. This article analyzes different ways of understanding Kant's argument.

# Index

a priori, viii, 1–20, 34, 38, 45, 47, 58,
  79, 87, 98, 119, 206, 246, 249, 271
Adam, C., 43n5
affection, 146–147, 152, 154, 158,
  161–162, 170, 182–183
affinity, 100–101
agnosticism, 202
Allison, H., xiv–xv, 20n4
alteration, 121, 122, 133, 194, 207
Ameriks, K., xii–xiii, 82–102
analyticity, viii, 1, 12, 14, 58, 200,
  271–279
animals, 107, 179, 242
anthropocentric model, 193–211
antinomy, xvii(n3), 48–50, 155
appearances
  and actions, 249–250
  and inner/outer sense, 156–161,
    166–167
  and intuition/understanding, 29,
    35, 104, 105, 118, 123–125, 128,
    147–148, 205, 235
  and nonempirical knowledge, 152
  possible, 10, 99–100
  and representations, 114n11, 182–
    188, 194–195, 207
  and things in themselves, 197, 201
apprehension, 49–51, 104, 119, 123–
  124, 126, 128, 224, 235, 269, 270
Aquinas, St. T., xvi, 266
A-relation, 146–148
arguments
  progressive, 87, 95–97, 102

regressive, 84–102
transcendental, 85–102, 182
Aristotle, 23, 26, 43n9, 220–221, 252,
  262
assertability conditions, 233
  see also verificationism
association of ideas, 113
attitudes, propositional, 12–13, 22
Augustine, St., 200
autonomy, 243–253
awareness, 147–174

Bailey, S., 27, 28, 44n23
Bain, A., 28
Beattie, J., 59–61, 84n1, 232
Beck, L. W., xiv, 103–116, 143n25
beliefs, 4–9, 13, 190, 226
Bennett, J., 43n7, 85, 89, 92–93,
  102n2, 211–212, 217n16
Bentham, J., 247
Berkeley, G., xvi, 23, 25–28, 43n7,
  44n23, 60, 161, 183, 191–192,
  195–199, 205–217
Bernard, J. H., 237
Bird, G., 90, 102n4, 127–131,
  142n6;7;14
bodies, 149, 155, 165–170, 189, 191
Boethius, A. M. S., 258, 262n7
Brentano, F. C., 46
Broad, C. D., 133, 142n17
Brouwer, L. E. J., 57

capacities, 8–9, 244
categories, xii–xiii, 21, 102n6;7, 103,

112–114, 115n34, 152, 156, 171–
175, 205, 224, 231
deduction of, 66, 85–102, 189
Caterus, 278–281
causation
concept of, 92, 112, 198, 226, 247
first cause, 241, 243
of mental states, xiii–xiv, 7, 61–77,
190, 244, 249, 250
noumenal, 146, 154, 159, 162, 164,
168
simultaneous, 140–141
of world states, 7, 100–101, 104,
117–143, 219–238, 242–243, 249,
250, 252, 258, 266
*see also Critique of Pure Reason,*
Analogies
chaos, 65, 100, 104, 114
character, 254–258
childhood, 244
cogito, 75, 78, 79, 82, 107, 110
cognition, xi–xv, 30, 32, 67, 78, 105,
210
Cohen, H., 34–35
community, 100, 204
compatibilism, xvi, 239–264
concepts, 1–20, 33, 37, 71, 76, 86, 97,
106, 111, 132, 167–177, 222–223,
231, 280
construction of, 45–58, 205
*see also* categories
Condillac, E. B. de, 41
conditions
epistemic, 181, 188–193, 199
non-epistemic, 190–192
consciousness, 76, 81, 92–93, 97–98,
108, 110, 115n20, 116n47, 148,
156, 165–166, 205, 213–214, 254
constructivism, 22–32, 38–42
contiguity, 62
contradiction, 269–270
Copernicus, N., *see* revolution, Copernican
Cottingham, John, 43n5
counterfactuals, 5, 7, 214–215, 235
creativity, 148
*Critique of Pure Reason*

Aesthetic, x, 11–12, 29, 34–36, 60,
86–89, 99, 157, 165, 183, 185,
191, 208–209, 216
Analogies, xvi, 32, 60, 64–65, 117–
143, 153, 165, 213, 231–232, 235,
237
Analytic, 12, 34–35, 65, 88, 93–94,
149, 153, 177, 224
Antinomies, xi, xvi, 49–53, 151, 156,
168, 170, 194
Categories, Table of, 29
Deductions, xii, 47, 51, 59, 65–67,
72, 78–79, 81, 85–102, 118, 134–
136, 157, 165, 173
Dialectic, viii, xv–xvi, 78, 165, 185,
193, 221–223, 231
Discipline, 60
Expositions, 29, 30
Ideal, xvii, 222, 224, 229, 231, 235,
237, 266
Introductions, viii–ix, 38, 104
Paralogisms, xii, 59, 62, 78–83, 155,
157, 165, 168, 170, 194
Postulates, 56, 113, 214
Principles, 86, 205
Refutation, 47, 60, 102n3, 109, 117–
118, 120, 134, 137, 165, 196
Schematism, 118, 173
custom, 233

de Vleeschauwer, H. J., 114
deduction, *see Critique of Pure Reason,* Deductions
definition, ix, 202
Descartes, René, x, xii, xvi, 23–27,
43n5, 62, 69, 76, 79, 84n7, 184–
185, 195–197, 203, 207, 268–270,
274–275, 280, 282n5;7;21
designators, rigid, 20n3
desires, 242
determinations, *see* marks
determinism, 121, 235, 239–241,
248–254
divisibility, xi, 46, 57
dogmatism, 55, 174
Donnellan, K., 20n3
dreams, xiv, 103–116

Dryer, D. P., 133, 142n16
Duhem, P., 220, 222, 228–230, 237n1

Eberhard, J. A., 17, 201
Einer [special capitalization of "einer"], 98
empiricism, x, 21, 22, 27, 29, 41, 199
enlightenment, vii
epistemology, 1, 4, 10, 45, 69, 76, 131, 188, 226, 230, 232, 235, 266
essence, 202, 211
ethics, vii, xvi, 164
event, 84, 129, 131, 134–135, 138, 142n5;14
evil, 257
Ewing, A. C., 142n3
examples
    acids, 16–17
    arch, 186
    attorney, 248
    body, concept of, 273
    bomb, 73
    calculator, 22, 27
    car, flying, 129
    chemicals, 223
    cinnebar, 101
    colors, 162
    couple, married, 241
    creatures, two-dimensional, 24
    dollars, actual vs. possible, 273
    drawings, 31, 32
    eclipse, 256
    earth, seeing other side of, 8
    fever, 113
    filings, iron, 214–215
    gold, 202
    hardware/software, 80
    heroes, cowboy, 277
    horse, winged, 269
    house, perception of, xiii–xiv, 32, 38, 123, 125, 137–138
    ice, melting, 64
    images, television, 122
    lie, 256–258
    lion, existent, 279
    machine, five-state, 74–75
    man, essence of, 202

matter, magnetic, 176
mermaids, 13–16
Molyneux, 24
monster, three-headed, 113
moon, inhabitants on, 213
parables, 260
Paris, dreaming of, 109, 114
perception, microscopical, 51, 54, 56, 176, 203
perceptions, petites, 116n47
photograph, 58
pillow, lead ball on, 140–141
puzzle, jigsaw, 31–32, 39, 41
resolution, visual, 40
room, hcatcd, 32, 113, 140–141
room, sugar, wormwood, 110–113
ship, xiii–xiv, 123, 125, 128, 129, 131, 137, 235
square, 49
stick, bent, 184
stone, sun-warmed, 110–112, 116n42
succession, night/day, 121, 139
swimmer, drowning, 236
tigers, tame, 276–277
triangle, 5, 101, 204–205, 269–270
turnspit, freedom of, 239
typewriter, 40
unicorn, 279
verse, words in, 82–83
water, boiling, 234
word, letters in, 50
World War I, 255
existence not a predicate, xvii, 271–278
experience
    of dreams and illusions, 103, 109, 115n20
    independent of, ix, 5, 12, 174
    inner and outer, 2, 146–147
    as objective consciousness, 98, 154
    possibility of, viii, xi, 10, 47, 55–57, 66–70, 74, 78–79, 94, 124, 153, 177–179, 190, 209, 213
    as relation to noumena, 146–149, *see also* A-relation
    sensory, 21–22, 27–28, 32–38, 119, 155, 266

sufficiently rich, 9
total, 3, 11
explanation, 219–221
externality, 196–197

faculties, vii–viii, 1, 8, 65, 104
Falkenstein, Lorne, x, 21–44
fatalism, 256
figure/ground, 51, 54, 55
finitude, 54, 200, 270
force, 232, 252
foreknowledge, 258
form, 29, 39, 45–47, 146, 148
freedom, xvi, 150, 193, 239–253
Frege, G., 276
Freud, S., xiv
functionalism, 73, 80, 105

Galileo, xi
generality, 164, 179
genetics, 9
geometry, xi, 5, 36–37, 45–46, 86–89,
    96, 149, 153, 155, 177, 200
God, viii, 180n9, 191, 199–204, 212,
    245–246, 253, 258–260, 265–281
Goethe, J. W. von, 260
gravity, xv
grossness, numbing, 134
Guyer, P., xiii, 117–144

habit, 63–64
Hamilton, Sir W., 43n8
harmony, preestablished, 251
Harper, W., 142n15
Harrison, R., 91, 102n5
heap, xii, 61–62, 65
hedonism, 247
Heidegger, M., 58
Heine, H., 265
Helmholtz, H. von, 21, 25, 28, 43n2
Hempel, C. G., 221
Herbart, J. F., 28
Hering, K. E. K., 25
Herz, M., 115n28
heteronomy, 196, 243–253
Hilbert, D., 57
holy will, 245–247

human beings, 8–10, 56, 156, 202
Hume, D., xii–xvi, 23, 59–77, 84, 84n3,
    92, 100, 120, 128–129, 138,
    142n10, 153, 184, 187, 190, 197–
    199, 220, 227, 230–233, 235, 237,
    251–252, 262, 266, 269

idealism, transcendental, 42–43, 88,
    99, 145–180 *passim*, 181–218
    *passim*
ideas, 26, 33, 36, 71, 104, 200, 202,
    222–223, 237, 265, 269
identity, personal, 59–84, 158–160
illusion, 103, 166, 171, 183–184, 186,
    191, 193, 197–198, 258
imagination, 33, 55, 65, 108–109,
    115n23, 125, 133, 136
immateriality, 83–84
immortality, viii, 55, 83–84
impressions, 30, 71, 104, 198
impulse, 242
induction, 55, 57, 138, 232
infants, 179
infinity, 34, 48, 55–58, 191, 200, 203
insanity, 244
inspectionalism, 105
intellect, 55, 199
introspection, 67, 156
intuition, 118, 146, 147, 148, 167, 171,
    172, 175, 176, 194, 208, 222, 269
    faculty of, x–xi, 5, 21–43, 45–58,
        71–72, 76, 103, 105–106, 161–
        163, 173
    manifold/synthesis in, 97, 101,
        102n7, 136
    particular(s), 1, 69, 87, 89, 98,
        115n23, 119, 157
intuitionism, 22, 25–27, 30, 31, 33, 41
irreversibility, 134–135
isolation, method of, 33

James, William, 27–28, 44n23, 82
judgement(s), 1–2, 10, 17, 69–79, 91,
    111, 115n18;36, 118, 122, 124,
    127, 138–139, 153, 170, 208
    logical functions of, 98–99
    subjective, 112

Kahl, R., 43n2
Kemp Smith, N., 20n1, 34, 35, 44n26,
    107–108, 114, 216n1, 237n2
Kenny, A., 262
Kerferd, G. B., 44n32
K-experience, 105, 108–110, 113
kinds, 219–221, 226–228, 230, 237
Kitcher, Patricia, xii, 21, 59–84
Kitcher, Philip, viii–ix, xv, 1–20,
    219–238
knowledge, viii, xiv, 1–20, 31, 55, 57,
    86, 104, 118, 121, 147–152, 156,
    181, 183, 188, 191, 152, 200, 203,
    266
Kolenda, K., 262
Kretzmann, N., 241, 263
Kripke, S., 20n3

Lange, F. A., 34, 35
law, 55, 100, 115n20, 120, 121–122,
    127, 130, 137, 146, 166, 219–221,
    222, 223, 225–226, 227, 228, 229,
    230–231, 235, 240, 242, 243, 249,
    250, 252
  covering, 221
legislation, 243, 246
Leibniz, G. W., x, xvi, 10, 23, 60, 78,
    80–82, 84f, 116n47, 129, 172,
    190, 192, 197, 199–201, 239, 247
Lewis, C. I., 103–116
L-experience, 105–112, 115n34
life, sufficient, 3, 5
Locke, John, 23, 26, 81, 104, 112, 160,
    162, 176, 185, 199, 201, 201–203,
    203, 211
Loemker, L. E., 84n9
logic, 10, 149, 158, 173, 189–201, 212,
    272–273, 276–277
Lötze, R. H., 28
Lovejoy, A., 134, 142n21

Mach, E., 220, 222, 228–229, 230
Malebranche, N., 199–203
manifold, 31–32, 48, 50, 93, 97–98,
    102n7, 104, 119, 123–124, 128,
    136, 222, 235
mark, 272–273

materialism, 195–196
  central state, 73, 76
mathematics, x–xi, xvi, 5, 45, 47, 51,
    57–58, 152, 158, 163, 177, 189,
    200, 205, 269
matter, 29, 40, 146, 148
mechanism, 40
Meerbote, R., 142n15
memory, 133, 136
mereology, 48–49
metaphysics, viii, 1, 164, 175, 176,
    182, 189
Meyer, 34, 35
Mill, J. S., 16, 28
mind, 5, 34, 37–39, 46–47, 61–66, 69,
    99, 104, 109, 154, 155, 182, 183,
    185, 194, 202, 208, 210, 211, 226
Mohanty, J. N., 141n1
Molyneux, W., 24, 27, 37, 41
monads, 201
Montgomery, G. R., 217n17
Moore, G. E., 276
morality, 59, 150, 156, 172, 240
Murdoch, D., 43n5

nativism, ix–x, 21–41, 269
nature, 193, 219–231, 239, 243, 248–
    251, 267
necessity, ix, 1, 10–11, 67, 101, 125–
    131, 190–191, 219, 223–249, 267,
    270, 274–276
Newton, Sir I., xv, 60, 96, 191–192,
    195, 197, 227
noumena, xiv–xvi, 66, 145–148, 150–
    152, 156–158, 163, 168–175,
    182–187, 191, 197–199, 205, 240,
    250, 251, 255, 262

objectivity, 92, 93, 221, 224
objects, 21, 37–39, 42, 45, 61, 65, 72,
    79, 84, 90, 97, 101–109, 112–113,
    117–119, 124, 127, 146, 154, 159,
    161, 165, 166, 171–178, 183, 194,
    205, 208, 210–212, 222, 280
  weighty, 208
objects, subjective, 114
omnipotence, 275, 281

ontological proof, 266–281
opposition, real, 132, 134

Parsons, C., xi, 45–58
Pastore, N., 44
patchwork theory, 104
Paton, H. J. , 107, 114n6, 280, 282n23
Payne, E. F. J., 142n3, 262
perception(s), xi–xiv, 4–5, 22, 35, 50–
    57, 58n2, 61–67, 71, 81–82, 93–
    94, 99–100, 109–113, 118–120,
    123–139 , 147–159, 162, 165, 166,
    167, 168, 170, 190, 195, 203,
    212–215
perception, subjective, 134
perfection, 266–278
phenomena, xiv–xv, 156–157, 163,
    186, 240, 254, 262
phenomenalism, 182, 192, 197,
    211–216
Plato, 23, 26, 43n6, 199
positivism, logical, 220–221
possibility, 8, 56–57
power, 8, 252
Prauss, G., 113, 187, 216
Prichard, H. A., 134, 142n22, 183–184,
    187, 216n6
principle, 222, 225
    continuability, 53–57
    of significance, 151–152, 165, 170
    of sufficient reason, 120, 129, 142,
    267
processes, x–ix, 5, 7, 12
pronouns, 145, 156–158
proofs, existence of God, xvi, 265–267
properties, 66, 175, 220
propositions, ix, 6, 9–10, 13, 15, 18,
    200, 271, 272
psychologism, 192
psychology, 51, 65–67, 78, 84, 138,
    222

quaestio juris/facti, 190
qualities
    primary, 42, 183
    secondary, 112–114, 183
Quine, W. V. O., 12–18, 20n5

rationalism, 77, 78, 83, 120, 129–130,
    190, 199, 203, 246
realism, 42, 149, 164–165, 169, 185,
    228, 230
    transcendental, 186, 193–210
reality, xi, 16, 103–105, 114, 145, 159–
    161, 170, 174, 175, 182, 185, 189,
    195, 204, 270
reason, xv, 2, 8, 10, 78, 157–158, 200,
    203, 222–224, 229, 242–244, 247,
    250
receptivity, x, 30, 39, 40
recognition, 52, 91, 129, 157
reference, 108–109, 159–160, 149,
    185, 225
regularities, 219–235
Reid, T., 23–28, 43n8, 60
Reimann, G. F. B., *see* space, Reiman-
    nian
relation, 15, 56, 175
religion, vii, 172
Remnant, P., 43n7, 217n16
representation, x, 29, 30, 34, 35, 37,
    38, 46, 52, 58, 62, 63, 67, 71, 72,
    74, 76, 87, 89, 100, 101, 109, 107,
    109, 112, 114n11, 118, 119, 122,
    139, 151, 161, 166, 182, 183, 187,
    189, 194, 204, 200, 207
Rescher, N., 237n3
responsibility, xvi, 241
revolution, Copernican, 105, 152, 177,
    199, 206, 209–211
Riehl, W. H., 34, 35
Rorty, Richard, 102n5
rules, xi, 105, 111, 121, 124, 126, 127,
    235, 222, 224, 227, 237–238n4
Russell, Betrand, 21, 160, 276

scepticism, 60, 63–65, 85, 90, 96–97,
    100, 138, 153, 165–166, 184, 188,
    192, 194, 196–197, 235, 265
schemas, 204–205, 250
Schopenhauer, A., 121, 137, 139,
    142n3, 256–257, 262
Schultz [ = Schulze], J. G., 17
science, vii–viii, xv, 16, 152, 161, 163–
    164, 177, 219–222, 228, 231, 240

Selby-Bigge, L. A., 84n3
self, 59–84, 110
self-consciousness, 89, 90, 94, 147,
    157, 164, 178, 196
semblance, 186, 187
sensationism, 25–27, 29, 41
sensations, xv, 2, 3, 21, 28, 33, 35, 36,
    41, 119, 187
sense
    inner, 32, 62, 81, 97, 108, 113, 146,
    156
    outer 146–147, 158
senses, 65, 98, 99, 119, 156, 163, 165
sensibility, viii, xi, 55, 57, 93–94,
    102n1, 146, 147, 148, 162, 166,
    171, 171, 174, 175, 186, 194, 198,
    200, 201, 203, 249
sensitivity, 30, 33, 145
Shahan, R. W., 141n1
Sidgwick, H., 243, 262
simplicity, 82, 83, 84
sleep, 82
souls, 61, 80, 200
space, 35, 36, 39, 45–58, 165, 167,
    168, 170, 184, 187, 195, 204–205,
    208, 209, 240, 271
    Euclidean, xi, 10, 25, 26, 46, 47
    Riemannian, 25
    and time, 10, 21, 29–35, 38, 39, 41,
    42, 119, 145
    *see also* time, space-time, represen-
    tation
space, 86
space-time, 99, 146, 147, 148, 149,
    150, 151, 152, 154, 156, 159, 160,
    169, 171, 176, 183, 185, 186, 188,
    189, 191, 197, 201, 213
    entities, 208
species, 202
specificity, 39
Spinoza, B., 199, 205, 216n15, 247
spontaneity, x, 30, 241, 244, 249–250
state, sensory, 71, 73, 77
statements, revisability of, 12
states, 84
    mental, 64–79, 81, 91, 92, 100, 113,
    129, 155
    sensory, 3, 11

stimuli, sensory, 2
    *see also* sensation
striving, 259–260
Stoothoff, R., 43n5
Strawson, Sir P., xiv–xv, 85, 89, 90–91,
    102n, 134, 135, 138, 142n5, 145–
    180, 182, 184, 216n2;5
Stroud, B., 102n3
Stump, E., 263
subjectivism, 183, 190, 192, 198
subjects, 10, 11, 80, 87
substance, 78, 79, 83, 121
synthesis, xi–xii, 1, 29–32, 35–36, 49,
    58, 67–77, 100–101, 104, 106,
    110, 126, 128, 198
systematization, 222–223

tabula rasa, 23
Tannery, P., xvi, 43n5, 191
taste, sense of, 7
Tetens, J., 60
theocentric model, 193, 199–205
theology, xvi, 191, 222, 265
thought, xv, 8, 30, 31, 72, 76, 79, 82,
    83, 106, 157, 163, 166, 194, 207,
    265, 280
time, 173, 178, 190, 191, 195, 205,
    208, 209, 240, 250–251, 253–255,
    257, 258, 259
    form of inner sense, 81
    objectivity of temporal representa-
    tions, 117–137, 146, 148, 157–158
    point in time, 3, 10, 13
    spatiotemporal ground, 40
    spatiotemporal world, 90
time, instant, 49
Trendelenburg, 42
truth(s), 14, 129, 200, 229–230

understanding, vi, 30, 65, 99, 102n7,
    103–104, 117, 120, 145–146, 148,
    153, 157, 171, 176, 222, 225, 229,
    240, 252
unification, 223, 227–230, 235
unity
    of apperception, xii, 29, 42, 60, 67,
    97, 99, 101, 102n1, 110, 115, 118,
    198

of our knowledge of nature, 222–
    224, 229, 237
universality, 1, 10, 99, 179, 223–235

Vaihinger, H., 34, 37
validity, 89, 94, 98, 101, 102, 102n3;6,
    103–104, 110, 113, 117, 127, 139,
    190, 222–223, 226–227
Van Cleve, J., 142n15
verificationism, 76, 233

Walford, D. E., 44n32
Walker, R. S., 142n4, 216n4, 254–255,
    262

warrants, 4–15
Wiener, P., 237n1
will, 242–245
    free, viii, xvi, 239, 242, 267
Wilson, M., 82
Wolff, C., 81, 84n7, 129
Wolff, R. P., 85, 89, 93–94, 102n2
Wood, A. W., xv–xvi, 141n2, 239–289
world(s), 8, 10, 19, 89, 94, 100, 110,
    147, 183, 200, 227, 241, 254, 259–
    260, 266–267
Wundt, W., 28

# About the Authors

**Henry E. Allison** taught for many years at the University of California, San Diego, prior to taking a position at Boston University. He is the author of two books, *Kant's Transcendental Idealism* and *Kant's Theory of Freedom*, and a collection of essays on Kant, *Idealism and Freedom*.

**Karl Ameriks** teaches at Notre Dame. Besides *Kant's Theory of the Mind*, he has written many articles on Kant and on his successors Fichte and Hegel.

**Lewis White Beck** was Burbank Professor of Philosophy at the University of Rochester. His writings on Kant and related subjects spanned a period of over forty-five years.

**Lorne Falkenstein** teaches at the University of Western Ontario. He has just published the first full-length commentary on the Transcendental Aesthetic in English, *Kant's Intuitionism*.

**Paul Guyer** is Florence R. C. Murray Professor in the Humanities at the University of Pennsylvania. In addition to co-editing the new *Cambridge Edition of the Works of Immanuel Kant*, he is the author of *Kant and the Claims of Taste*, *Kant and the Claims of Knowledge*, and *Kant and the Experience of Freedom*.

**Patricia Kitcher** is the chair of the Department of Philosophy at the University of California, San Diego. She has written on topics in Kant and in the philosophy of psychology.

**Philip Kitcher** is Presidential Professor at the University of California, San Diego. Among other titles, he is the author of *Abusing Science: The Case against Creationism* and *The Lives to Come: The Genetic Revolution and Human Possibilities*.

**Charles Parsons** teaches at Harvard University. Besides his work on Kant, he has written many influential essays in the philosophy of mathematics.

**P. F. Strawson** was Wayneflete Professor of Philosophy at the University of Oxford prior to his retirement. Beyond his influence on Kant scholarship, he has written seminal articles on philosophy of logic, language, and action.

**Allen W. Wood** teaches at Yale. He is co-editing the *Cambridge Edition of the Works of Immanuel Kant*. Besides his contributions to Kant scholarship, he has done important work on the philosophies of Hegel and Marx.